THE STORY OF THE MINACK CHRONICLES

The Minack Chronicles

Also by Derek Tangye

DEREK TANGYE

The Story of the Minack Chronicles

Comprising

Time Was Mine
A Gull on the Roof
A Cat in the Window

Sketches by Jean Tangye

WARNER BOOKS

A *Warner* Book

This omnibus edition first published in Great Britain in 1994
by Michael Joseph Ltd
Published in 1996 by Warner Books
Reprinted 1996

A CIP catalogue record for this book
is available from the British Library.

ISBN 0 7515 1088 2

Printed and bound in Great Britain by Clays Ltd, St Ives plc

Warner Books
A Division of
Little, Brown and Company (UK)
Brettenham House
Lancaster Place
London WC2E 7EN

Contents

Time Was Mine

Time Was Mine was the reason why I met Jeannie. Had it not been for *Time Was Mine*, I would not have written *A Gull on the Roof*, *A Cat at the Window* or any of the other Minack Chronicles. Nor would Jeannie have written *Meet Me at the Savoy*, or her trilogy of hotel novels, *Hotel Regina*, *Home is the Hotel* and *Bertioni's Hotel*.

I was in the front hall of the Savoy Hotel soon after *Time Was Mine* was published. It was the period when bombs were falling on London. I was standing there when a friend said, 'See that very pretty girl over there? She is Jean Nicol, and she is in charge of Savoy publicity. You must meet her. She could arrange to have *Time Was Mine* placed prominently on the bookstall.'

Thus I met Jeannie.

'Will you put my book on the bookstall?' I rushed out.

And she did.

A week later I saw her again.

'I loved your book,' she said.

I was relieved.

Time Was Mine, telling of my journey round the world, had been condemned by the vicar from the pulpit of my family's local church, much to the amusement of my father and mother to whom I dedicated the book, and both of whom were in the congregation; and shortly after we were married and were living at Mortlake overlooking the Thames, a neighbour said to another neighbour, 'I *do* hope Mrs Tangye hasn't read Mr Tangye's book'.

But Jeannie had read the book and told me she loved it.

'Well,' I had replied, 'will you have dinner with me?'

The Minack Chronicles story had begun.

Chapter One

GOODBYE TO THE BEGINNING

THIRTY MINUTES TO GO. I had a hollow feeling inside, reminding me of tearful partings ending happy holidays. I needed a drink. My father had disappeared to buy the platform tickets so it was Mother who accompanied me to the bar. I remember she had a light sherry and I, not wanting her to hear my order, asked the red-haired barmaid in a whisper for a double brandy. I drank it as I would water, and the effect was delightful. I walked off to the platform with a hazy confidence that made chatter easy; what a pity that in the old days of the school train I couldn't go to the bar, in place of stuffing myself with cream buns in a farewell tea.

Fifteen minutes to go. The platform bustled with Americans searching for their seats, and porters wheeling cabin trunks plastered with coloured labels. My father had found my compartment and was standing by the door with Janet Johnson; Jan provokingly attractive in a black velvet coat with cuffs and collar edged with white ermine, and a single gardenia in her black hair. And there too were Clifford Evans, Clement Fuller and Brian Chapman; laughing they were as if a bride and bridegroom off on their honeymoon were the cause of their presence, not me by myself. Then Nigel, my brother, and Ann Todd arrived; Ann with a small Cossack hat perched on her head, and looking so lovely that the group in the next compartment halted their goodbyes to stare.

Five minutes to go. Colin, my eldest brother, came hurrying up the platform. We talked of 'remembering to write.' Then Mother mentioned my keys. She wanted me to have two sets each with a key of my two suitcases. So as we talked, she tied with string my four keys into two bunches. 'You can lose one set now, dear,' she said, 'because you'll have the other.' But that evening in my cabin I discovered she had tied the same two keys on each bunch.

Two minutes to go. Porters were shouting: 'Take your seats, please!' I shook hands. Someone said: 'I wonder what will have happened . . .' Then Nigel making us all laugh, asked: 'A little domestic matter . . . what is it I pay Mrs Moon each week?' I kissed Mother. Colin pushed three £1 notes into my hand. My father said: 'Give my love to the South Sea maidens.' The whistle blew.

I couldn't see them for long. There's a curve on that Waterloo platform. My father was the last one, standing alone waving his black Homburg hat. Then he too was gone. The train gathered speed, past the blocks of grey warehouses, past the backyards of the soot-covered Vauxhall slums. Faster, faster. I chucked the stub of my cigarette on the track, watching the sparks for a second dance between the sleepers before we left them behind. Then I pulled up the window and sat down. The journey had begun.

2

It had begun in my mind nine years before, when, aged seventeen, I was wondering what to do with my life while others were wondering what to do with me. My Harrow schooling wasn't meeting with the success that warranted its expense. Term reports were littered with 'Could do better if he tried' – 'Doesn't seem to concentrate,' and my housemaster would bi-weekly tell me I wasn't pulling my weight in the house.

The criticisms were largely justifiable. For my part I could find no sense in learning ten verses of the Bible every Sunday evening; nor in translating Latin Unseen when my interest lay in modern languages; nor in being examined about a Shakespeare play as if it were a grammar book. The masters, in my youthful opinion, were fools to bother about such things. They bothered, of course, because the line dividing the brain from a dunce in a public school is the Oxford and Cambridge Certificate. In fact, on the second occasion I failed in this test my housemaster described me as being 'Simply useless to society, old man.'

It was amid this depressing state of affairs that the family and I debated my future. It was my own ambition to become a writer, not for any love of words, but because I believed a writer had a more exciting time than most people; and it was with this in view that I had secretly paid £7 for a course in journalism – which I studied underneath the bedclothes of my school-bed aided by a torch when lights were out. Neither I nor the Principal thought much of the results; and on reaching the fifth lesson he advised me to concentrate on my school examinations and leave journalism to a later day. Then it was that the idea was born of making my way round the world. What I needed, I thought, was experience, and a year in the world ought to provide me with enough of it to start me on the road to journalistic success. It was, of course, an old idea; and like the thousands of young men who had had the same idea before me, it didn't materialize. Such an adventure cannot be made on air; and money wasn't plentiful. Besides, despite my protests of 'You don't understand!' my family didn't think me responsible enough to be let loose in the world. The idea had to be shelved, but it was not forgotten; there would come a time, I felt certain, when my ambition would be realized.

Thus on leaving Harrow I became an office boy in one of those mammoth organizations whose employees are nursed by a staff manager and a corps of assistants. In my case, the staff manager was a fat man with pince-nez who waggled a finger at me and assured me that I had only to show zest in my work to be promoted to a traineeship, a managership in embryo. The first six months therefore witnessed a ferocious enthusiasm on my part. I read books on economics. I studied the *Financial Times*. I arrived thirty minutes before the others in my department so as to sort out the morning mail. I worked overtime in the evening. I enrolled in a commercial course at a correspondence school. And at the end of this period my salary was raised 1s. 3d. The rise coincided with a damping of zeal. Bills of Lading began to lose their glamour. Standing in the eight-thirty with the same blank faces no longer amusing. Running errands a bore. And, besides, two things had happened.

The first was my entrance into débutante society. The old Harrovian tie was a magic wand that brought me dumb girls and champagne hangovers. Five days a week I would clamber into bed at dawn and four hours later wish the world would end. Through the day the wish remained – until I hurried from the office to the cocktail party where I was likely to find the strongest sidecars.

The second was a book I'd read called *Through Literature to Life*, by Ernest Raymond. This somewhat balanced my youthful exuberance among the débutantes. It was a book that if I had been given to read when I was fourteen would have stopped me wasting my time at school. Ernest Raymond said in it what my schoolmasters didn't say. He told me what to read from the point of view of pleasure, of enrichment of the mind. He transformed Shakespeare, the Bible, Shelley, Byron, from the category of dreary lesson subjects into books of wisdom and beauty. I heard for the first time of Flaubert, de Keyserling, and Proust. He awoke in me an awareness of the beat of life. I wished only that I had read before these words of his on education:

'There is only one stable theory of education. It is this; that if I were a headmaster and had to choose my assistants, whether they were to teach mathematics or Latin, chemistry or cricket, I would favour those who had a fine proselytizing enthusiasm for literature and art, even though their manners were atrocious and their methods abominable; because it is chiefly in the things of art that the fire of imagination is lit; and hence the master will possess imagination, penetration and sympathy, and he will light up in his pupils their smouldering humour, their essential humanity, their inalienable hunger for beauty, and their inborn desire to create beauty for themselves; which things it is the final business of education to educe.'

3

Both Ernest Raymond and the débutantes had a bad effect on my business career. Both bared the dreariness of sitting at an office desk however important one might become. The one making plain that women and rigid office hours didn't mix; the other firing me with the excitement of living. Once again I decided journalism should be my career; and in my spare time I wrote articles on a variety of subjects which editors regularly returned. This didn't dishearten me because I never really expected to have one published. I had such an inferiority complex that I looked at a journalist with the same scared eyes as an office boy looks at the chairman of the company. So when the miracle occurred and five hundred words on the subject of an archery competition was published in the *News Chronicle*, I felt like the dustman who won the first prize in the Irish Sweep.

That same week I visited a phrenologist who murmured three times, 'You must not barter!' and who went on to say that my bumps displayed a preference for advertising and literary work. So when the day afterwards I was told by the fat man with pince-nez that I had been promoted to selling soap from house to house in Wigan, I sensed fate had warned me to do otherwise and I refused his offer. Moreover, a few days later I sent in my notice, and the fact that I did so was because I have a very exceptional father and mother. It was their belief that a young man shouldn't have to grind along in a career in which he had no interest. Better be in a job one enjoyed than a success in a job one hated. With no prospects on the horizon they let me give up a steady pay packet in return for an allowance of £2 a week and gamble that I would find a place in the career I wanted.

The next five months were uneventful. I wrote more articles which rebounded with regularity. Débutante parties continued. A job seemed as far off as ever. My principal occupation was operating a race-horse system in which Mother and I believed lay a fortune. It involved betting varying sums on six horses a day. The time required each morning to discover which were the horses varied between two and three hours; and the afternoons were spent standing at street corners waiting for the latest editions. The partnership was not successful. At the end of three months we were lucky to find our capital was as we began; and we decided to call it a day.

In the sixth month I had an interview with Max Aitken and from it was given a month's trial on the *Daily Express* in Manchester. The suddenness of the opportunity startled me. The most I'd expected from the interview was an introduction to a provincial editor, so when I found myself at a typewriter in the reporters' room of a national daily I felt like a fourth-form boy sitting among his prefects. Office days being still fresh in my memory, I was also ready for friction with my fellow-workers; I expected them to cold-shoulder me because of my inexperience; I imagined that they would enjoy showing their superiority over a new-comer; and, in fact, that the month would be one of the most unpleasant besides being one of the most important of my life. Of course I was wrong. From the moment I met Brian Chapman, the editor, who, in place of an orthodox interview, told me a funny story about a Liverpool civic dignitary whose head went through the roof of an aeroplane in a storm, I knew it was going to be all right. Further proof came when next day on the first story I was ever sent out to cover, the reporter who was my guide took me to the local pub for an hour before he showed any interest in the news we'd been told to collect. So when the month was over and Brian Chapman took me on the staff, there was no one so happy that day as I.

The work was as exciting as I expected. I interviewed politicians, bishops, and actresses. I hunted the city at night for burglars and outbreaks of fires. I questioned mothers of lost daughters and husbands of lost wives. Many of the things I did were not pleasant; yet such was the fever of news-gathering that all my sense of decency was smothered and I was unconscious of my callousness. There was the evening I was sent off to interview an old couple whose son, a missionary, was believed to have been murdered by Chinese bandits. Taking a leaf from the book

of a confidence trickster I talked on every kind of subject
before I disclosed I was a newspaper reporter; and by that
time I was sitting in their kitchen having a cup of tea.
Having come so far I racked my brains for a novel angle to
my story. Suddenly I had a bright idea. We should kneel
down and pray for the son's safety. The old man brought
out his Bible and the three of us knelt in prayer – simply
because I had seen in my mind the morrow's headlines
describing the event. Another evening sticks in my
memory. Cold rain was driving through the cobbled streets
of Blackburn. The mill girls, shawls round their heads,
were hurrying home to their grey-stoned cottages. I buttoned the collar of my raincoat as I got out of the car to
knock at the door of one. A woman opened it; her face
was lined, her skin yellowish, and I noticed the puffs under
her eyes before I noticed the eyes themselves; to a stranger
in the north she looked middle-aged, but I do not think
she was more than thirty. Behind her were four ragamuffin
children who were standing shyly watching the strange
man at the door. I did not know how to begin. This was
the first time that I had broken the news of death. Yet it
was my job to tell this woman that her husband, a lorry
driver, had been killed in an accident. I took her into a
room away from the children. I remember how I expected
her immediate reaction would be a flood of tears and how
I was surprised at the calm way she behaved. It emboldened
me to ask her for a picture of her husband and she took
one from where it was standing on the mantelpiece. As she
handed it to me, her control snapped and she collapsed
sobbing on the floor. I left her there and ran out to get the
help of a neighbour. But as I did so I remember I was
thinking not of the woman, but of the story I had, and the
picture I held in my hand.

4

London on a Sunday newspaper followed Manchester. Then a year in the film industry and back again on a Sunday newspaper. I was writing articles for magazines as well, some of which were accepted; a particular one was read by an editor of the *Daily Mirror* who was looking for a columnist. The subject dealt with my likes and dislikes and pleased the editor in question: at any rate, he sent for me, invited me to join his staff and offered a salary twice as much as I'd hoped for. The consequences were remarkable. I was transformed overnight from a hack journalist who was lucky to see his name in print into a 'celebrity' whose articles each morning were headlined: 'This brilliant young writer' – 'He writes another stirring article today' – 'Derek Tangye Denounces Hypocrisy', etc. It was highly amusing, and the more extravagant the praises, the more the family and I laughed. When in addition my photograph came careering down the streets of London on the tops of buses, my father gave a celebration party. No fame so strange nor so sudden had ever come to the family before.

That was the humorous side. The serious side was that the kind of column I wrote, laughed at by the intelligentsia for its admitted lack of virility, was in fact an important influence in many people's lives. Godfrey Winn, of course, began the style. He dotted his page with homely truths and the Christian names of stage figures, peers, and peeresses until he became a sort of Sir Galahad and Father Confessor in one; to his readers he appeared to have the glamour of a film star and the patience of a parson; at any rate, five hundred of them used to write to him every day. All those letters he answered personally, besides seeing a score or so of his readers every afternoon in his office; it meant that in a single week he did more practical good than most journalists do in a lifetime. For my part I was amazed at the power that was mine. There was a fund, for instance, from which I drew money to help hard-luck stories that I believed to be genuine; the fund was solely supported by the generosity of readers, and whenever it became low, I had only to appeal in my page, and the postal orders would come rolling in. Then there were the secrets I was expected to share and the advice to give. A girl came to me one morning with the confession she had been stealing from the petty-cash desk of her shop. What was she to do? Another, that she had run away from home because she was going to have a baby. There was the young man whose girl wife had been taken to a lunatic asylum and he wanted to know what future there was for his two-year-old child. There was the middle-aged woman who could not make up her mind whether to tell her husband that the doctor had warned her she had only twelve months to live. There were scores of cases like these, and it was my privilege to try to unravel their problems or at least show my sympathy. But many a time, when I sat in my chair listening to the outpourings of some unfortunate person, I thought how silly it was that I should be the counsellor. After all, I only held the position because of the whim of an editor; one word from him and down from the pedestal I'd fall.

Eventually the word came; and as it is the reason why I'm writing this book I'll tell you what happened. One fine morning my chief called me into his office and informed me that he was most satisfied with my work and wished to lengthen my contract. A few days later it was further decided that I should visit, each weekend at the newspaper's expense, the capitals of Europe, starting off with Paris the coming weekend. That was on a Thursday. On Friday I had come into the office, with my suitcase and my seat booked on the afternoon plane, when my chief had another idea. I was politely informed that he had changed his mind, the policy of the paper had been altered overnight, and my column wasn't wanted any more.

The news, to say the least, was a shock. The ways of Fleet Street are always unexpected, but even so I wasn't prepared for anything quite so abrupt. The blow, however, was immediately softened by the presentation of a large sum of money – produced in the spirit of generosity towards discarded employees that only Fleet Street knows. It eased the situation, but it didn't remove me from the tight corner I found myself facing. I walked out of the office in a daze, and made my way to the Falstaff, where I ordered a large brandy.

While I sipped it I wondered what I should do. I had to act fast, as I was more likely to land a good job before the news leaked out than afterwards. On the other hand, where was there a vacancy for my type of column? Jobs like mine were few and far between. I didn't relish the thought of being pointed out as the young man who skyrocketed to fame, and then fell back to where he began; and yet, if this should happen, it would not be without justification. I was typical of other young men whose success was a pretence, achieved by luck, and not as the result of experience. The kind whose monetary rewards have tempted them to believe so much in their own importance that they have basked in their success until their spirit of adventure had been numbed, and they have been tied hand and foot to the routine of their comfortable lives. I knew that I would become the same as these; that, supposing my chief hadn't fired me, I would have gone on writing my column and handing out advice, until my own spirit was undermined and I fizzled out like a damp squib.

As I was thinking this, it dawned on me that never

before had I possessed enough capital to finance a long journey abroad, and that it was nine years since first I had the idea of going round the world. In that time I'd known both failure and a measure of success, and I'd learnt that, though I enjoyed the pleasures that money could bring, I could in certain circumstances be just as happy as if I were broke. I'd realized, too, that ever since my schooldays my chief ambition had been to live vividly – not to be afraid of making mistakes, only afraid of having to regret things I hadn't the courage to do; and if by doing so I made a fool of myself, I was prepared to take heed of the fact. I wanted to achieve peace of mind, but how, I hadn't discovered, though I believed that this might be done, if, when I was old, I could look back on the years and say: 'I have lived.' The world was there for me to see. I was a good deal more fitted to journey into it than when I was a schoolboy. I was now a moderate craftsman in a profession which it was possible to practise wherever pen and paper were to hand. I was without a job and had no ties; and therefore had nothing to lose by going. I had money, but not much; the lack of it would give added spice to the journey, and make it necessary for me to use my wits. And whatever happened, when it was all over, I would still have my memories. 'I'll go,' I said to myself, and paying for my drink I went up the stairs to the street.

That, therefore, was how it came about that I was sitting in the Southampton boat train as it tore through the green fields of Surrey and Hampshire towards the *Aquitania* and New York.

I had told my chief my plan, and with his blessing I had written an article on what I was going to do. I said I was going away for a year to see the world. I wasn't going to take the journey too seriously, my main object being to enjoy myself; so that if I made mistakes or any illusions were broken I would try to see the funny side. I said I was going to wander as I pleased. If I liked a place I might stay a month; if I didn't, I'd move on. I had no fixed plans. Time was mine to do what I liked with.

Chapter Two

NEW YORK SAYS 'NUTS'!

FOUR HUNDRED and fifty pounds was what I had for my travels. Of this sum, £50 had already been spent on the fare to America and a £100 in Traveller's Cheques was tucked in my wallet. The balance I had entrusted to my father who was to forward me parts of it in answer to each SOS. The sum seemed scarcely enough to pay for a year's travelling, but my intentions were to earn more by writing; for this purpose New York seemed a good starting-point.

Like most people, I nursed certain ideas about New York. I pictured it as the most go-ahead and most hospitable city in the world – and more so than any other city in America. So many of my friends and acquaintances had returned from it, glorifying the generosity and initiative of its citizens above those of their own country, that I was sure I merely had to blow my trumpet loud enough for the contracts and invitations to come rolling in. In this belief I was encouraged by, among others, a publicity friend of mine who insisted on sending ahead of me, to editors of newspapers and magazines, a remarkable pamphlet describing my career in the language of a film producer announcing a new star. Not content with that, he was to gild the lily by cabling the day before my arrival: 'Watch out for Derek Tangye *Aquitania* tomorrow.' He seemed certain that the editors, as a result, would be scrambling over each other in competition to hire me as a guest columnist; that hotels would offer me free rooms, restaurants free meals, and theatres free seats. I would, in fact, 'put one over' on New York.

It was in this mood of expectation that I awoke in my state-room one Tuesday morning as the *Aquitania* neared New York. The state-room, so I'd been told, was as essential to me as books to a library. Americans measured success by the money spent, and if an influential passenger or a reporter discovered I had a poky little inside cabin, they would have nothing further to do with me. I therefore spent in five days what normally would have lasted five weeks.

Unhappily there were no influential passengers. The decks were as bare of celebrities as Brighton pier on a winter's night. I was not unduly upset; because, after all, the reporters were the more important; and I'd planned that as soon as they'd asked for me, I'd invite them to the state-room and load them with drinks as if I were a millionaire.

First, however, I wanted to see the skyline I'd heard so much about. We were due to dock at ten, so I was up at seven, dressed in a summer suit in anticipation of the sunshine a New Yorker, the night before, had warned me would greet our arrival. Up on deck I went, fieldglasses in hand (and even a notebook to record my impressions), only to get as big a surprise as if I'd found snow on a tropical island. No skyline was to be seen. There was a foggy drizzle like on a November day in London; and we were nosing our way towards the Empire State building to the accompaniment of fog-horns.

I consoled myself with the thought I could now spend more time with the Press. I returned to my state-room, brushed my hair, filled my cigarette case with Lucky

Strikes, and stuck a red carnation in my buttonhole. I then wondered whether I should stay downstairs or whether to sit up in the bar. Both were obvious places to find me – so I went to the bar.

On the way up I saw the reporters, who had come aboard by tug, bunched together popping questions at a grey-haired man in horn-rimmed spectacles. I wished they would hurry up. I had the same nervousness as an actor waiting for his entrance on the first night of a play. I chose a stool in the bar near to the door and, sipping a whisky, eyed the passage leading to it. Some minutes went by, and I had another whisky. Someone said we were passing the Statue of Liberty, and I got up and had a look at the green old lady. We left her behind and drew nearer the dock. Perhaps they've gone to my state-room, I thought. On the way down I saw them on the stairs, cigarettes drooping in their mouths, hats on the back of their heads. They took no notice. They looked as if they'd completed their work for the day and were gossiping among themselves. I began to have a little doubt in my mind.

The steward was in my state-room, and I asked if anyone had been inquiring for me. 'No, sir,' he answered brightly, as if he were easing my fears that the police might be after me. I went back to the bar. I had two more whiskies, and chatted to the barman as if I were on top of the world. Someone said: 'They're swinging us into the dock.' I went out on to the deck and hung over the rail. Probably they'll see me on shore, I thought. And as I was thinking this, a passenger at my side laughed like a hyena. 'Did you see those reporters with their flashlights and cameras?' he spluttered. 'They were surrounding a little man who was the only celebrity they could find on the ship . . . the great grandson of Lord Tennyson!'

2

I'd come prepared for a whirl of entertaining; to see the
Rainbow Roof and dance into the dawn in Harlem; not to
have one minute of the day to myself; to have a perfect
stranger place his car at my disposal; to have more invitations than I could possibly accept; and, in fact, all those
things I'd heard happen to foreigners arriving in New
York.

I sent out twelve letters of introduction, and sat in my
room waiting for the telephone bell to ring in answer.
Though I'd flopped like a washed-up actress with the
Press, it wasn't possible my introductions could fail me.
Ever since the Boston tea-party it had been the fashion of
the English to bury their faces in their hands with shame
when comparing American to English hospitality. Here I
was on certain ground. Yet the telephone was silent.

On the second morning the bell rang like an alarm
clock, and I shot out of bed to answer it. A nasal voice
drawled that he represented a news agency: 'We want to
have the pleasure of taking your photograph. We missed
you on the boat. Can we come now?' I was overjoyed that
after all I hadn't slipped into New York entirely unnoticed,
and I invited the gentleman to come round at once. For
half an hour I posed; sitting, smiling, looking severe,
standing. Then the photographer went away. Next day he
returned with the prints, and after I'd admired them – he
handed me a bill for five dollars. A well-known racket, I
learnt later, of preying on the vanity of newly arrived
foreigners.

On the third day, four more people took notice of me.
The first was Russell Swann, the conjuror, who sent me a
bottle of whisky; the second was Randy Burke, a delightful
personality who earns his living inveigling other hotels'

customers into the Waldorf Astoria; the third was John Walters, an English journalist, who, on the fifteen occasions I subsequently lunched in his company, never once let me pay my share; and the fourth was an English friend of my family's, married to an American, who made me an honorary member of his clubs.

This attention improved my morale; but there were still eight other people whom I expected to take notice of me, and the fourth day passed without any of them doing so. It seemed I was playing the part popularly conceived to be that of the American arriving in London. I spent the day alone, sweating in the humid heat of my room, and the evening, wandering among the crowds of Broadway, Seventh Avenue, and Forty-Second Street.

On this fourth evening I was gloomily strolling back like an out-of-work undertaker to my hotel, when outside the entrance I saw a girl bending over a white Persian cat she had on a lead. As I drew near she stood up; and in the light of a street lamp, I saw she had fair hair falling to her shoulders, and a black dress without any frills, and no stockings on her slim legs. Her figure was like one of those in a film magazine, and her face had an arresting sadness with grey-blue eyes, and a lovely, generous mouth.

I went on for a few yards, then stopped, and came back. By the grace of God, as I drew level, the cat made a playful leap at my trousers, and all I had to do was to stoop quickly down, and seize the little beggar by the rump of its neck; and she was brought by the lead to within a yard of me. 'What's it's name?' I asked sweetly, like an old woman asking the name of the Peke of another old woman. 'Dopey,' came the reply in a sharp, New Yorker's accent. 'And now you're going to bed,' she added; to the cat, not to me. She took it from my hands, and showing neither the green nor the yellow light, she walked into the hotel and left me outside.

I waited scarcely a minute before I followed her. I was the fox-hound within sight of the fox, and neither she, shyness, nor an earthquake, would swerve me from my quarry. She was sitting a few yards from the doorway with Dopey at her feet. In the light of the lounge she was more lovely than ever, hardly a touch of make-up on her face, and her hair in need of a comb, tumbling about her shoulders. A devil within me made me walk up unhesitatingly to her; firm and confident was I as I made the steps, but when I reached her I felt like the politician who dried up in his maiden speech in the House; I found myself standing there, muttering the horrid noises of a mute. No wonder she gave me no encouragement.

I didn't give up. I went over to the bar and gulped down a Bacardi; then with my nerves steady again, I went back into the lounge, and found Dopey had been handed to a page-boy, and the girl was walking across to the lift. This was the moment, now or never. I stepped quickly across the lounge, and stood between her and the lift-boy. 'Won't you have a drink with me?' I said; and before she knew whether she was standing on her head or her heels, I had my hand firmly on her arm, and was leading her to the bar.

That was how we met, Sarah and I.

3

Whether that was a good thing is open to question. I'd come to New York full of good intentions to write for my living and to record my reactions to New York life with the exactitude of a Pepys. After meeting Sarah, I did neither. My memory of the two months I was there is a jumble of red checked table-cloths in tiny restaurants off Seventh Avenue, sipping mint juleps in 'Twenty-One,' dancing to 'Always and Always' in the Stork Club, waking up at noon, and in the heat of the day exploring such diverse statues of New York as the Bowery, Rockefeller Centre, Battery Park, and Riverside Drive. There was the evening we went to the Palais de Danse on Broadway where five years before, when she was seventeen, she danced for ten cents a time. She was flat broke at the time, having spent the savings with which she'd left her home in New Orleans to find fame on the stage. But in the second week at the Palais she was walking down Forty-Third Street after the afternoon session, when a man stopped her. 'You're in luck, kid,' he cracked, 'Earl Carroll just saw you go by. He wants a word with you.' She went back with the man to where Earl Carroll was standing by the stage door of his theatre. 'Say,' he said, 'when the best pair of legs in New York walk by my theatre and they don't come in, I send after them, see?' Ten minutes later she had a job, and fifty dollars a week. There was the Sunday afternoon we swelted in Coney Island. The steamer from the Battery, jammed with negroes in straw hats, their women in bright red blouses, saucy girls hatless and bare-legged, men with cigars in striped linen trousers, fleshy women with moustaches. The shore black for five miles, with two million people swarming the sands like flies on bad meat. The barkers on Surf Avenue yelling into the microphones: 'See the four-legged man, ten cents!' 'Never before – the woman with the body of the bear!' Canned music. Burlesque shows; worn women in brassières and slips. Screams of scenic railways. Peanut vendors: 'Take a large packet of delicious roasted peanuts, five cents!' Pineapple drinks. Jitterbug dance-halls. And all the rest that made the place a pandemonium. There was the day we saw Harlem from the top of a bus (ten years older than a London one) and watched negroes playing 'crap' on the pavements. The day we took a train to Long Island, and I found the same sandy dune country of the Belgian coast. The evening we saw the first performance of 'Alexander's Ragtime Band' at the Radio City Music Hall, and out had to go my cigarette as smoking isn't allowed in American cinemas. And there was the evening we shot up to the roof of the Empire State Building, and from its dizzy height saw the fairyland of lights below us, and the neon signs blushing the skyscrapers into a purple darkness.

She was at the time playing the *ingénue* lead in a play in a Forty-Third Street theatre and, because she was in the minor ranks of the well knowns, I found myself getting the attention by being with her that I was unable to get by myself. John Chapman, for instance, in the *Daily News*, wrote a column about me, describing me as 'slender and eager' and beginning with the crack: '"I want to get away from it all – away from the cheap sophistication of the West End," Mr Tangye wrote in effect to his readers when he left. So he gets away from it all by landing at Twenty-One, the Stork, and El Morocco – and likes New York so well he fears he may get no further.'

And a few days later Louis Sobol, in his humorous column in the *Journal American*, wrote about the young British columnist who 'already has the problems of the world sitting on his back like lead weights, so he is taking a trip round the world and he will then write a book in which he explains how different people have told him what our purpose is for being in this world. The young British columnist does not expect to make much money from the book and the Queen says: "Heavens, I should say not. He would do much better just writing a book with lords and ladies in it and how they fall in love or, perhaps, he could make one of those British mysteries out of it."'

These paragraphs of nonsense tickled my vanity, but

they brought work no nearer to me than the North Pole. But it did mean I met a few of these columnists, who become the more important, the more dirt they dig up. Chapman and Sobol are Puritans compared with their colleagues, and their columns are the more readable as a result; the others have the bounce, egoism, and conceit of Nazi *Gauleiters*, and swagger from restaurant to restaurant as if they'd earned the homage of the world. To one such little god I gave, at different times, five stories, each of which was good enough to lead his column; besides providing him with three letters of introductions to prominent newspaper men in London in view of his impending visit there. Hardly a word of thanks I got for my trouble, and his only effort to entertain me was a dollar dinner at a restaurant where he didn't have to pay.

They're as jealous as cats of each other, and pour forth mud on their rivals like women at a hen party. Since Walter Winchell is king of them all, it's like searching for a needle in a haystack to find a good word said in his favour. The night I met him it was so hot that in the Stork Club it was like dancing in an oven, so Sarah and I were sitting on stools at the bar. Ted Husing, the radio commentator, came up and suggested my meeting him; and we went over to the table in the corner of the room where he holds court every evening. He is a spare man, with thinning grey hair, a pinched face, and eyes that never keep still. He began his career as a 'hoofer' on the halls, wrote theatrical gossip in his spare time, and gradually climbed to being the Number One gossip writer of the world by making his news-dirt as witty in its way as an Oscar Wilde play. As I sat down at his table I gave a sop to his vanity by saying he was well known in England. He snapped back: 'By newspaper men, you mean?' I replied: 'Of course, but by the public as well.'

To my astonishment, without a trace of a smile, he

roared to a few people at a neighbouring table: 'Did you hear that? I've got a big name in England. They like me there.' Then turning to me he said: 'It was *Wake Up and Live* that did it. God, what a wow that film was. Zannuck cleaned up on it.' I didn't ask why he hadn't followed it up with another. I didn't have a chance. He kept up a monologue of his achievements, and if in a pause I chipped in with a remark, he gave no appearance of listening. As I was launched in a sentence, he'd yell for a telephone to be brought to his table; or a telegraph form on which he'd scribble with the zest of a maniac. He was the epitome of the popular conception of an American newspaper man; and, let me add, he earns £18,000 for being one, and a further £30,000 for a weekly broadcast.

He is under contract to the great Randolph Hearst; and to young Bill Hearst, the son and heir, Randy Burke got me an introduction. He is a pleasant, well-mannered young man, whose office overlooks such a noisy section of Broadway that it's necessary to shout even in ordinary conversation. My idea was to persuade him to take me on as a guest reporter for a month; but in a quiet voice, quiet even if the office had been in the depths of the country, he explained that as his papers conducted a persistent anti-English policy, he couldn't in the circumstances employ me. That being so, I wanted to tell him the following story about his father.

Five years ago he was on a visit to England, and among his entourage was Miss Marion Davies, the film star. At the time he was in the palmy days of his life, when his fortune was estimated at £28,000,000. Since then, he's been what Hollywood calls 'on the toboggan'; newspaper after newspaper has been sold; his collections put up for auction; his salary cut from £100,000 to £20,000 a year; and most of his other manifold interests disposed of. He still inhabits his castle of San Simeon on the Californian coast, but it is on the scale of a Surbiton household compared with a few years back.

On his arrival in London, my editor sent me off to interview him. He was staying in a suite at Claridge's, and on going along there, I found him sprawling his bulk in a small arm-chair like the panda at the Zoo in a toy one. Miss Davies was there, too, and for an hour and a half I talked to the two of them; Miss Davies on her part describing the Billingsley painted Swansea china she had bought for St Donat's castle, and Mr Hearst, on his part, the chaotic mess in which he'd found Europe.

The interview over, I left the suite and walked down the hotel corridor to the lift. I hadn't gone ten yards, when I heard the pit-a-pat of footsteps behind me and the charming voice of Miss Davies: 'Hey, Mr Tangye, one minute.' I stopped, and found her beaming expansively at me. 'I wonder,' she said, 'if you could write a bit about me. The old man,' this with a jerk of her thumb over her shoulder, 'has been getting all the publicity this trip.'

I promised to do my best, and on returning to the office I wrote two stories, one about Miss Davies, one about Mr Hearst. Not unnaturally Mr Hearst's story was the more interesting, and the following day it was headlined in the centre page, while Miss Davies's story was omitted. I thought no more about it, but that same evening my editor received a telegram: 'Deny ever having seen your reporter. (Signed) William Randolph Hearst.' Ever since I've wondered what he meant.

4

If I'd been wise, seeing that I wasn't going to land a job, I would have left my Forty-Fourth Street hotel, taken an El down town, and found an apartment house off Seventh

Avenue. Instead I preferred to play the part of a pseudo young man about town, and in doing so naturally spent too much money. The hotel room came to £2 10s. a week, and another £7 10s. disappeared on food and gaiety; this wasn't much compared with what I was doing, but I had to remember I was going round the world and had eleven months ahead of me. All New York restaurants have a bar where you can sit without paying a cover charge, though it doesn't stop you having the use of the dance-floor; so Sarah and I, by doing this, didn't have to spend more than ten or twelve shillings of an evening.

To begin with I felt ill at ease with her. I couldn't accustom myself to the accent and the slickness of her phrases. My ears were out of tune with language like: 'I've stood him up for a week,' or 'I'm giving him the brush-off,' or 'He has all the gall in the world,' or 'You'd better hock that watch.' It made me uncomfortable. She didn't, however, suffer from the bossiness which is the chief characteristic of American women. My own idea of an attractive woman is one who, besides physical beauty, has serenity, provocative innocence, and subtle changes of mood that mystify me; but American women, for the most part, are as bare of these qualities as the Serpentine of ice in midsummer. They have the brittle, forceful, competent manner of successful women business executives. They have screamed so long for equal rights with men that they have forgotten there was ever any reason to be proud of being women. Femininity is a forgotten art; they parade the world with the harsh, metallic spirit of careerists, disguised in slim bodies and lovely clothes. Homes and lovers are secondary in importance to the market they can make for themselves in frivolous society of the community centres, university clubs, and other women organizations which litter every American town. They rush at life like racing cars out for speed records, leaving no time for the lights and shades of living.

Nor could I accustom myself to the ease with which they get drunk. 'Drunkenness to an American girl,' said a French born night-club proprietor, 'isn't bad manners or vulgar. She looks at it in the same light as smoking too many cigarettes.' This seemed indeed to be true. I never went to a restaurant in New York, San Francisco or Hollywood, high class or low, which by midnight didn't have among its customers several women (any age from seventeen to seventy) who were as drunk as their male escorts. If they had been just merrily tight, one perhaps wouldn't have minded, but they drank so hard that that stage never lasted for long; they were soon noisy and bawdy, and rolling about the dance floor like music hall drunks. Maybe you're thinking I am exaggerating. I assure you I'm not. In my first week in Hollywood I saw three glamorous film stars, whose names are on everyone's lips, being carried out of La Conga, Clover Club, and the Brown Derby, in such a state that they couldn't have known whether they were in Hollywood, Bournemouth or Pago Pago. Still odder was the number of girls in their teens whom I saw in the same state. Can you imagine seeing an English débutante in her 'coming out' year flopping about the Mayfair like a Saturday night drunk, as you can see an American débutante in the Stork Club in New York or in the Mark Hopkins in San Francisco? When I voiced my disapproval to an American, he replied: 'Oh heck, you English are so darned reserved. The kids are only showing *joie de vivre*!'

5

I did succeed in flirting with work. I got £5 for an article on Barbara Hutton, and another £5 for one on the Duke of Windsor. With my usual optimism, for these two thousand word efforts, I'd expected three times as much; but once again I'd overestimated American standards. Unless the article is syndicated or you have a big name, you're paid less than in England. And as far as the working journalists are concerned, their pay is twenty-five per cent lower than reporters of corresponding standard in London; that, of course, is always excepting the top-flight men who earn astronomical figures.

Two other articles I wrote were eventually published in England. One concerned the Consumer's Union, an organization which protects the man in the street from being duped by advertisements. For 12s. 6d. a year an American can receive a Buying Guide issued by the Union which gives the truth about every product in the market. Take for example toothpaste. All the brands are classified under three headings; 'Best Buys,' 'Also Acceptable,' and 'Not Acceptable.' Only two brands are listed under 'Best Buys,' another two under 'Also Acceptable' and the rest under 'Not Acceptable'; among the latter are most of the best-known ones. One brand which advertises on every other hoarding in England is said to be 'excessively acid. There is some indication that this toothpaste may have harmful solvent action on the tooth enamel.' Another 'will not whiten teeth as claimed. Price excessive.' All kinds of goods are classified in the same way: coffee, tea, silk stockings, beauty creams, face powders, canned foods, cold cures, motor-cars, cameras, radios, etc. Research into the products are carried out mostly by university professors so as to ensure impartiality. Their accuracy must be 100 per cent or the Union would be deluged with libel suits; as it is, in the eight years of its existence, it hasn't had one. Despite this success, newspapers won't have anything to do with it; they see the possibility of their biggest advertisers being run out of business, and rather than that they'd prefer to have the man in the street spending his money on dud articles.

The second article I wrote described a visit to Sing Sing prison. It's a five cent, half-hour train journey from Times Square. I was ushered into the deputy warden's office just in time to hear the end of a telephone conversation concerning some fellow's reception into the death-house. While he talked, I went over to the window, and looked at the prison buildings sloping down the hill until they were stopped by a high wall, the other side of which was the main New York – Chicago railroad. Spaced at hundred yard distances, I could see three watch towers on the wall, each round like a lighthouse; and against their railings there lolled warders, rifles in their hands. Then further away was the vast width of the Hudson River, seldom empty during the day of the little steamers that puff the two hours' journey from Battery Park so that tourists, with field-glasses, can gloat on the prison from afar. I turned back to the warden. He'd finished his call. 'That fellow I was talking about,' he said, 'they had him up for two killings. He was freed on the first, but they've got him on the second. He's due in the death-house tomorrow, where he'll stay till he goes to the chair.'

I sat in the chair myself . . . the officer who was taking me round, thinking it a funny joke to push me in it. Somehow I'd expected the death-room to be modern de-signed like the inside of a modern cinema; chromium plated, plush seats for the witnesses. Instead, I found it low ceilinged, with dirty yellow wood panelling, and three wooden benches of the same colour in one corner; and the chair, in the centre of the room, was a derelict object of rusty steel and dark leather straps. It was like a scene in a Frankenstein film, and I was glad to get out of it.

Star prisoner on the occasion of my visit was Richard Whitney, ex-president of the New York Stock Exchange, who is serving five years for fraud. His cell was one of a block of five hundred. It was about ten feet by five and had a bed, a wardrobe, washing basin and WC. One end was a small grilled window, the other was a barred door, opening on to the landing where the warders walked up and down, day and night. He had no special privileges (he had wireless headphones of course like the rest), and his job in the prison was to teach visual education to fellow prisoners who were too simple-minded to learn any other way. In the cell next to him was a negro who was serving a life sentence for cutting his sweetheart's throat.

The men wore grey flannel trousers and white shirts; and as it was the lunch hour when I made my tour, many were lounging in the sun. As we passed they would touch their caps, saying 'Good afternoon, warden.' He was at pains to explode the idea that the prisoners live a life of ease and luxury. They work eight hours a day. They are not allowed to have food sent in from outside, though they can have a ration of cigarettes. They can have five visits a month from relatives, each lasting an hour, and they can have a letter a day. Certainly, it is more enlightened than any of our British prisons, but in the few hours that I was there, I didn't see any evidence of the wild stories of easy living I'd read so much about.

6

The day following my visit to Sing Sing, there was a line in the Broadway column of the *New York Daily News*, saying: 'Derek Tangye, round the world reporter, can't tear himself away from New York on account of a gal in *Silent Music*.' I had, however, already made up my mind to leave; and I had bought a bus ticket for San Francisco, costing only £8 for the three-thousand-mile journey. If I went through non-stop it would take five days, but I was able, if I so wanted, to stop over at any place on the way. The bus left its terminus in Forty-Second Street one Friday evening at eight o'clock. I remember it was raining so heavily that, though my hotel was only a few hundred yards away, I had to take a taxi to escape being drenched. It reminded me of that gloomy, wet night I'd arrived in Manchester, six years before, to begin my career in journalism, and I had the same depressed and lonely feeling as I had then. Sarah could not be there to see me go, as she had to be at her theatre; but when we had said goodbye she gave me a letter which she made me promise not to open before midnight, when I would be many miles away.

Midnight came. We were careering along at fifty miles an hour across New York State. Jersey City, Clinton, Belvidere had come and gone. I was huddled in the back corner seat, the fabric of the bus on one side of me, a gross German on the other. The lights were out, and I had to read her letter by the light of the moon that jerked its rays through the window.

Please don't be angry with me [I read]. I'm giving you this instead of a cigarette lighter or some other silly thing you'd have no use for. Every bit helps and I'm sure you can use it. Besides, it's very easy to carry and won't take up any room like a book. If you send it back to me – I'll elope with the first man I can find.

Out of the envelope, on to the coat warming my knees, dropped a ten-dollar bill.

Chapter Three

HIGH ROAD TO 'FRISCO

THROUGHOUT THE NIGHT, I was jerked from side to side in the back seat of the bus. Every place was occupied. Beside me was the gross German engineer on his way to California. His fat face would fall first on my shoulder, then on the shoulder of the man the other side of him. In the seat in front of me was a mouse-like little woman who slept peacefully, until I brushed her head while putting on my coat. She awoke with a start, swung round with fists clenched, and demanded: 'Did you hit me?' Every two hours the bus stopped. The lights were switched on, and we had ten minutes to take a walk. At five-thirty in the morning we pulled up at a café somewhere in the Alleghany mountains. A gramophone was blaring dance music from a window. The driver drawled: 'You have thirty minutes here, folks. Early morning breakfast.' Fried eggs and coffee cost 1s. 6d.; then back we scrambled into our seats, the women with faces lined and greasy, the men collarless with stubble on their chins. Off we careered to Warren and Erie.

I gave up hope of sleeping. If I rested my head on the ledge beside me, vibration jarred it like a pneumatic drill. We charged along, as the morning grew hotter, at fifty miles per hour through wooded valleys, past white-washed villages left behind in a cloud of dust. I wondered what would happen if we crashed. One safety door was at the back, the main door was by the driver's seat. The windows were too small for anyone to squeeze through. A nigger strummed a guitar, humming 'Dinah'. The German opened conversation: 'Just come back vom Hamburg. Does England vant var?' Fifteen minutes for lunch. A shilling for corned beef hash. The drivers changed. 'So long, folks,' said the parting one. 'Howdee,' said the new one.

Here was Cleveland. Euclid was the name of the main thoroughfare; on either side of it were sumptuous houses with lawns sloping hedgeless to the sidewalk; and on the fresh green grass were wooden placards, with the words 'Funeral Home.' All over the States, funeral homes are thriving, go ahead businesses, but never did I see so many as on that afternoon in Cleveland.

Something was wrong with the wheel of the bus. Out we clambered, and my two suit-cases were shoved in another. Then on to Toledo. The road lay beside Lake Erie. The curl of a steamer's smoke on the horizon. The lake, grey like a dull day on the English Channel despite the blazing sunshine. A cloud of flies flew in through a window; up jumped a little man, ten days' growth of black beard on his chin, with the ears of a mule and the eyes of Mussolini, who swiped at them like a maniac. The same little man, when we got to Chicago, said to me: 'Whatcha think of sharing a room, cheapa yer know!' We entered Chicago eleven o'clock Saturday night. For an hour before we halted at the bus station, we passed factories ablaze with lights, mile upon mile of them. Black porters in red caps queued up to take our luggage. The German was going on. He had thirty minutes to wait, and then into another bus. No one could have induced me to do the same. I went to the first hotel I could find, had a bath and slept twelve hours. The next morning a gale was blowing old newspapers down the streets. Chicago didn't seem very inviting. The sidewalks were deserted and my hotel empty. A bus was leaving for Omaha at one-thirty and I decided to take it. This time I knew the ropes; I was smart enough to get a seat in the fourth row, where the springing is smooth enough to read a book. The seat tipped backwards and, having hired a pillow for ninepence, I was just as comfortable as sitting in a train. It was the same routine as from New York to Chicago. Ten-minute stops every two hours. Mile upon mile of flat, dusty country. My fellow travellers changed at each stopping-place. First was a traveller in ladies' underwear. He was a thin man with a few fair bristles as a moustache. He had the harsh accent of Ohio, and he spoke with a vehemence that suggested that any argument he was engaged in would be very one-sided. His subject, strange then to my ears but which afterwards I heard spoken of quite often, was revolution in America. 'I get around in my job,' he said, 'I go places and hear things. Take my word for it if there's a war in Europe there'll be revolution here. Here's how it'll happen. You've heard of the Nazi Bund which Mayor La Guardia frequently attacks? They represent the German minority here, and everyone knows they're hand in glove with Hitler. If the fire flares up over there and there's talk of us coming in they'll flood key points of this country with arms. Already they've got arsenals all over the place. Get the idea? It won't matter to them who gets the rifles. Let the Communists do the rest of the dirty work. Hitler'll be satisfied if the civil war that breaks out keeps America from helping the democracies. You wait, that's what'll happen.' He got out at Sterling, Illinois, before I could hear any more.

Darkness was falling, but at intervals summer lightning painted the plains a silver white. The bus was air conditioned, but the night too was cold. I put on my overcoat and buttoned it round my neck. Ten minutes at Ogden, a hamburger sandwich and a cup of coffee, and we settled down for the drive through the night. I couldn't get to sleep, a drainage inspector prevented me. He was a massive man with a small, thin voice; he had a red tie and double chin; and his body overflowed irritatingly into my seat. 'Say, is that so?' he piped good-naturedly when he learnt I was English. 'I've got an uncle living today in Greenock.' (All Americans, incidentally, have an uncle or aunt living in England, Scotland, Norway, Italy or Germany.) It transpired that this gentleman was an employee of the WPA, otherwise known as the Works Progress Administration, the corner stone of the New Deal. It is the biggest industry in the world, employing around 3,000,000 people and paying out £1,000,000 a day in wages. It is Roosevelt's pet panacea for unemployment. His enemies attack it on the grounds that the country cannot afford to support the system indefinitely, that he is using it solely as a vote-catching machine, and that it is being run on lines that are wasteful, inefficient, and corrupt. That is the propaganda they're pouring out to the Little Man of America. The drainage inspector, however, seemed to be unmoved by it. 'They say the country can't afford the WPA,' he said, 'well, let them tax the wealthier classes a bit more. Do you know the average income of persons with £200 and more is taxed less by half than any country in Europe? Mind you, I don't think the WPA is run efficiently – yet. But everyone is in such a hurry. It is only six years since the first WPA worker got his first wage. The Standard Oil wasn't built up in that time – and the WPA is bigger still. I'll tell you one thing. There are a heck sight too many employees of the WPA who are feathering their own nest. Out and out corruption. But that's because we haven't got a class of people like I believe you have – I mean the civil servant.' He paused. Then added: 'Anyhow, what's the alternative? None of the guys who want to run against Roosevelt have a better plan. Even if they said they had you wouldn't believe them. Compared with Roosevelt they're all either ignorant hicks or political crooks.'

Spasmodically I slept through that night. At six we were rumbling into Omaha, chief cattle town of the Middle West, but no one was about; in the half hour we were there I had a wash and a shave. Then we were off for Cheyenne. We weren't tearing along as we did in the Alleghany Mountains, Nebraska had a strict speed limit, and we crawled along at twenty miles per hour. Level to us was the main line to Los Angeles and San Francisco. First there thundered past the 'City of Los Angeles'; then, later in the afternoon, the yellow painted 'City of San Francisco'. Soon after, rain began to fall in torrents. In half an hour the road was a foot deep in water. We were passing Kearney, a village of wooden houses, and as we splashed into the open road a man stopped us with a red flag, warning the driver the road was giving way. 'Thanks, highwayman,' drawled the driver. We moved on slowly. On the railway track, little motor-driven trucks sped along the line, jammed with workmen. After every downpour they inspect the track in this way. As the weather cleared, we set off again at our twenty miles per hour through the Wild West grassland to Cheyenne. I'd intended to drive through the night to Salt Lake City, but in North Platte a red-haired, tipsy old woman got in. For four hours, amid hiccups, she maintained a monologue on the history of her family. Her grandfather was a parson, her father a sailor, her husband a bricklayer, and her son was serving a sentence in Kansas City gaol. 'Not that the polooka deserves it,' she croaked. She was to be tolerated while she sat at the back of the bus, but shortly before Cheyenne she saw a vacant seat behind mine. Over she came, and with her, a smell that suggested she hadn't washed for some months. She began stroking the back of my head. 'Turn round, handsome,' she said. 'All right, sweetheart,' I answered, 'but keep your hands to yourself.' I was thankful when we pulled up at the Cheyenne bus station half an hour later.

The first thing I saw, as I stood on the pavement, wondering where the hotel might be, were three figures clattering past me on horseback. A street lamp lit them up, and I saw the spurs on their long boots, and their high cupped saddles. For the first time in my life I'd seen cowboys. I went into a bar, and found men hunched round the tables throwing dice, in yellow, red, blue shirts, wide cowboy hats, and khaki riding breeches. Each wore an ornamented belt, and one mean-faced little man, lolling against the bar, was waving his belt in the air. 'Yellow rat,' he cried boastfully, 'you have to go far south to get that!' He, like most of the others, was drunk. I accidentally knocked into one. 'Get out of my road,' he murmured. I started conversation with another. 'Sounds like an Englishman,' he said, 'well, well, you're the first one I've ever met . . . Howdee!' He caught my hand in an iron grip. Then he added slyly, with a wink to his comrades: 'But don't think we're ever going over there again to pull your chestnuts out of the fire.' Everyone, including myself, roared with laughter. 'If you get yourselves into trouble,' he went on, 'that's your affair, not Uncle Sam's. We came over to save you last time and what did we get? Nothing except a lot of money you've never paid us.' We talked in this vein for a while, and when we were becoming a little heated, I bade him farewell and went off to the hotel. Next morning I was in the bus again at eight. We passed mile-long cattle trucks, travelling even slower than we were. We saw 'hoboes' perched on the top, and they waved at us as we went by. Nowadays they're allowed to 'jump' goods trains without fear of being ordered off by the railways' police. We were leaving the plains and climbing into the boulder country of the Rocky Mountains. Several times we passed herds of wild horses. We saw them silhouetted against the skyline, standing head to head, flapping their tails; or galloping away from us through the dry pampas grass.

My neighbour was a broad, dark-haired man of thirty, dressed in a dirty grey shirt and creased corduroy trousers. Every so often he burst out in a bass voice into one of Verdi's arias. 'I'm going to be a great singer,' he explained in a slow Middle Western drawl, 'for ten years I've been studying. I'll study for another five and then'll make my début on the concert platform.' He had indeed a fine voice; he had also a whisky bottle in his pocket. He took gulps at it every ten minutes, and towards evening it was nearly empty. By this time he was encouraging the rest of the passengers to sing, but not very successfully, as his own voice was loud and by now out of tune. Suddenly the bus stopped. The driver left his seat, and made his way up the aisle to where my friend was sitting alongside me: 'Gimme that bottle,' he snapped. 'Can't you read?' He pointed to a notice: 'No alcohol in this bus.' My friend spluttered apologetically, made one or two more efforts to rouse the vocal enthusiasm of the rest of us, and then subsided into a drunken slumber.

It was too dark to see the scenery of the Rockies. There was no moon. I could only tell that we must be pretty high as for two or three hours the bus had been in second gear. At last it went into top; and the driver casually over his shoulder said: 'Continental Divide, folks.' Henceforth the rains and the rivers drained into the Pacific. For three more hours we coasted downhill towards the Utah Desert through Evanston, Morgan, Ogden. I dozed awhile, and when I awoke we were driving through the broad avenues of Salt Lake City. It was midnight and the streets were empty.

Salt Lake City is, as you know, the headquarters of the Mormons. I myself didn't know any more about the religion except that I believed they practised polygamy. And when I awoke next morning, the first thing I did was to look out of the hotel window and see how many chimneys the house had on the other side of the street. I had the idea that you could tell the number of wives a Mormon possessed by the number of chimneys in his house, each chimney denoting the private room of a wife. I was fifty years out of date. I saw neither a house with an unusual number of chimneys nor did I meet a Mormon with more than one wife. Polygamy ceased in the 1880s when the United States passed a law forbidding it, and the president of the Mormon Church, John Taylor, received a revelation from the Lord ordering him to obey the law. The Mormons, I therefore found, were ordinary people. I found, too, that they were a practical people. In addition to the ritual of their faith, they face earthly problems such as unemployment. The Elders have put into practice a scheme in Salt Lake City which has cured unemployment as far as members of the Mormon Church are concerned. No Mormon is allowed to accept Unemployment Relief; instead they are guaranteed work. They are allotted jobs according to their capabilities and their desires; and if certain of them aren't physically strong, it's seen they aren't given heavy work to do. The Elders believe that what can be done among a population of 100,000 can be done elsewhere on a far greater scale.

The inhabitants of Salt Lake City are by no means all Mormons; and the most successful paper, the *Salt Lake*

Tribune, is a Catholic-owned organization. Half the day I was in the city I spent at the service of this paper. I accepted the offer of the news editor to write a column on my impressions; and I praised the wide streets, commented upon the many pretty girls, and remarked how willing everyone was to help a stranger. The article stretched down a column of the page with a grinning picture of myself at the top, so I presumed what I wrote was satisfactory. But I scratched my head and wondered – the only sign of hospitality or reward I saw during my stay of thirty-six hours was one Virginian cigarette.

I left at eleven in the morning and was in Reno twelve hours later. It was a monotonous journey of five hundred miles across the alkali desert of Utah and the sage-bush country of Nevada. The bus's air-conditioning apparatus had broken down.

It was stiflingly hot; it wasn't any use opening the window as dust blew in like a snowstorm. At Elko, a strange fellow got in whom I'd seen twice before on the trip. Each time he'd got out at a small hamlet, once about an hour's ride outside Omaha, and another time at Laramie near Cheyenne. He had a grey drooping moustache, a pinched face of reddish complexion, and the watery eyes of a heavy drinker. Though his back was hunched and round, he was still tall, so that in his young days, fifty years ago maybe, he must have been a fine-looking man. At one of the halts he was sitting next to me in the café, so I mentioned I'd seen him before. 'Yes,' he answered, 'I've been two weeks on this journey from New York, hopping on and off. I get bus-sick, you know. My heart begins to beat in jerks. It doesn't get normal till I get my feet on firm ground. I've to take my luck where I get off.' We got back in the bus together and he sat down beside me, pulling out his pipe. We were riding through the Tuscarora

Range; for miles it would be flat, then we'd see an isolated hill, sticking up out of the plain like a man's fist.

'Indian country this,' said my companion, 'out over there in the bush is a big reserve. If a white man wishes to trade with them, he must ask the Chief first, treating him with the respect of his position.' He knocked the bowl of his pipe on the heel of his shoe. 'I was married to an Indian girl once,' he said suddenly in his slow drawl. 'It was a long time ago. Texas was my home state and I worked on a ranch of Captain Ogilvie. He and the Indians got on fine, which was strange, as there were always shootings and goings-on in the ranches around. I did a bit of trading with them on my own account, liquor for furs, and so on. And that was how I came across "Star in the Night," that was the translation of her native name. Pretty, isn't it?' I nodded. Darkness was falling and the driver had switched on the headlights, beaming the road white before us. 'She'd just turned sixteen,' he went on, 'and no one so lovely have I ever seen again in my life. Black eyes like the night, and a body with the litheness of a gazelle. I, a lad of twenty, fell head over heels in love with her. I saw to it that I traded pretty frequently in her village. The Chief saw, too, my reason. Mind you, I hadn't touched her. If I slept with her, I'd have had an arrow in my back within twelve hours. I had to have her legally, according to white man's law, if I were to have her at all. Finally I asked permission of the Chief to marry her. My pals said I was crazy, but I didn't care. I'd decided I couldn't live without the girl. So I went to the Chief, a fat old devil he was, and do you know what he said? In his vernacular, of course: "You can have the girl . . . but give me first six bottles of whisky"!' My friend rocked with laughter at the memory of the occasion. He threw back his head and roared. 'What about the girl?' I asked, when he'd quietened down. 'Oh, she,' he replied, in a tone of voice as if signifying the unimportance of my question, 'she married me, but she couldn't stick it ... After a year she went back to the village.'

Reno wasn't far away. We climbed into hills and down again, round hairpin bends to the valley that lies at the foot of the Sierra Nevadas. For a mile we ran along a boulevard which surprised me with its respectability. Solid three-storey houses like those of Kensington. But then we crossed a level-crossing and encountered the real Reno; stretching across the street above us were these words in lights: 'The Biggest Little City in the World.'

There doesn't seem to be any point in this announcement. Maybe it's because every house in four streets is either a night-club or a gambling-house; and in another part of the town there's licensed prostitution. As one official put it to me: 'You can't do anything wrong here, we make it legal.' The gambling-houses have no doors to their entrances. They're open day and night; and the Bank Club, the chief one, has its entrance paved with silver dollars. The players are a motley collection. You find sleek, Schiaparelli dressed women sitting side by side with 'desert rats,' the uncouth, mining prospectors of the mountains. They play roulette, faro, poker, blackjack, chemin de fer and keno; you'll find the stakes are anything from 6d. to £1000.

Women predominate among the intending divorcees, husbands apparently can't spare the time off for the six weeks' residential qualification; so you see them in droves, gloomily playing the tables or being gigoloed in the night-clubs. While waiting for the divorce, they describe themselves as 'taking the cure,' and having got it, they talk of 'winning my diploma.' Mostly they stay the six weeks on a dude ranch which is the same as an ordinary ranch without its discomforts. The cabins are steam-heated, with electric light, and the food is cooked by French chefs. Handsome cowboys are there, too – usually impoverished New Yorkers dressed to look the part. The cost of staying at one of these places is between £25 and £70 a week. The cost of a divorce slides up and down according to the complications of the alimony settlement. From £50 to £5000. Two hundred and fifty lawyers practise in an area of one square mile: today they're worried because Reno divorces are on the decrease while marriages are on the up; last year there were three thousand divorces compared to eight thousand marriages – and a marriage costs only £1 for the licence.

Jack Cartwright, the publicity manager of Reno, told me that on no account should I leave town without seeing 'The Crib' – the home of licensed prostitutes. The local police have it nicely ordered. The women are registered at the police station where they're told the regulations: not to talk to men beyond a certain street, to submit to a weekly examination, and to ply their trade only in 'The Crib' where they pay the police 2s. an hour for the use of a hut. The police also provide them with whistles in case the visitors are unwelcome. I paid them a visit; to enter 'The Crib' I passed through a gate where I was scrutinized by a police officer. Commenting to me upon his work he said: 'Prostitution in the States is either a gangster or political racket. We prefer to have it on a sensible basis.' Forty-odd huts were built in a horseshoe shape round an open space. Peering through the windows and the doors were a score or more Jezebels, old and revolting. They lured me with their cries of: 'Come on, darling.' I talked to a couple for two or three minutes, and when they saw I wasn't a customer, they lost patience. 'Why don't you go up town where you belong?' one of them snapped. Excusing myself I said: 'I don't belong up town. I'm broke.' Hiss came the reply: 'Scram, then . . . or I'll blow my whistle and the cop'll bag you!'

I was indeed broke. I'd left New York with £3 in cash, and I left Reno with 3s. I wouldn't have had that, if Jack Cartwright hadn't invited me to stay one of the two nights I was there. San Francisco, where a Letter of Credit was awaiting me, was twelve hours away, and I had meals to pay for. The road wound up the pineforested mountains of the Sierra Nevadas, passing lakes cupped in the valleys, and log cabins designed to look from the outside like those of the Wild West days, and in the inside the best the twentieth century can offer. We were half-way to the top when the bus stopped. Here was the state line dividing Nevada from California. We waited five minutes, then a black-shirted policeman in a peaked cap popped his head inside. He had a quick look round to see if any one of us was an escaping criminal, and then departed. We were only a dozen, and none looked a potential criminal except a wizened little Chinaman in the seat in front of mine. He had been sitting impassively with his hands on his knees all the way from Reno, and he continued to do so until we were nearing Sacramento. Then, apparently, the change of temperature from the cold of the mountains to the heat of the valley upset him; for he was violently sick. I pulled down the window beside me, trusting the wind would blow the stench away; even so I needed a gasmask. An English woman, employed as a dress designer in New York, was in the seat behind. She had travelled five days non-stop from New York, and her resistance was low. One whiff of the Chinaman was enough for her. She also was sick.

At Sacramento, thank heavens, we changed buses; and off we went on the last lap. Once again the country for mile upon mile was as flat as a pancake, but this time instead of the desert and the sage bush, as far as the eye could see, was golden corn. At Sacramento it was stickily hot, but the nearer we drew to the coast the colder it became; and when we were within an hour of the journey's end I had my overcoat on, buttoned up to the neck. It grew darker, too, and though it was only six when we reached the tramway lines of Oakland, it was a race of minutes whether night was to fall before we touched the Bay Bridge.

The night won, and all I could see, after we'd passed through the toll-gate, was the spatter of lights through the holes of the girders; high and low they were, against the background of San Francisco. What magic in that name! Somewhere in those hills of stars were the places that for so long had stirred romance and adventure in my heart . . . Barbary Coast, the Embarcadero, Chinatown, Fisherman's Wharf. And away from them, on the right of me, half-way to the Golden Gate that was part of the darkness, was the island of Alcatraz, only a handful of lights as the signpost of its whereabouts. I sat there, fascinated, staring into the night, oblivious of my companions who were collecting their baggage.

The bus pulled up at the terminus in Market Street, soon after we'd left the bridge. As always, negro porters scrambled to take our baggage. I took no notice of their persistence, and, giving up the last slip of my ticket to the driver, I began to lug my two suitcases to an hotel a hundred yards down the street. A cold wind cut my face and bare hands, like March in England, not September in California; and I was glad to reach the warmth of the hotel. I staggered to the reception counter and booked a room. But as I signed my name, I saw out of the corner of my eye that the hotel porter had taken charge of my suitcases. He would not hand them over to me, and up in the lift he went, and along with me to my room. He put them side by side in a corner . . . and then waited. He stood like a rock. He wasn't going to let an Englishman get away without a tip. But he was wrong. There was nothing else I could do. I hadn't a cent. I went into the bathroom and locked myself in.

Chapter Four

CALIFORNIA, HERE I AM!

I'D SPENT PRECISELY £100 since the day, ten weeks before, I'd set foot in New York. It was necessary to economize. I decided to allow myself £25 for the following month, and to stay in San Francisco. For four days I tramped up and down the hills that are so steep that the tramcars are run on cables; and finally I found an apartment at the corner of Sacramento and Stockton Streets on the edge of Chinatown. The rent was 30s. a week, for which I had a sitting-room, bedroom, kitchen, and bathroom. It meant I had a little under £5 a week for food and pleasure, which wouldn't go far if I found myself paying for a round of drinks with a single whisky at 1s. 9d. and a beer at 1s.; and if I mixed with the people with whom I wanted to mix this was certain to happen. One of these people was Gertrude Lawrence who was playing in *Susan and God* at the Curran Theatre. This was pleasant for me, as it meant that on arrival in 'Frisco, I did at least know one person; but it also presented the problem of expense – one evening might see the end of £2 or more. I kept away from the theatre for a few days and wondered what I should do. Obviously this money problem was going to become more and more acute, especially when I landed in Hollywood. It was the old story of 'keeping up an appearance'. Look prosperous and you'll get around. Appear as if money is scarce and you'll find yourself alone. The inhabitants of California, I was told, particularly followed this dictum. I had, however, a long way to go, and I'd no wish to squander my funds. Suddenly I hit upon an idea. I would tell Gertie, and anybody else when it became necessary, that I had lost £200 of my travelling expenses in three nights' wild gambling in Reno; that I was obliged, by what I'd said in my article, to stay away for a year; and that if I were to do so I had henceforth to exercise the strictest economy. The story was an instant success. People thought it gloriously funny. And for the rest of my travels I brought it out whenever I was threatened with expense beyond my means.

2

Gertie was a phenomenal success in San Francisco. She played five weeks longer than she was scheduled, faced queues of fans every night after the performance, and had her activities splashed daily in the newspapers. No actress for fifty years had received such a welcome in the city. Gertie was quite unmoved. She went serenely on, greeting everyone with the warmth that made them go home the first time they'd met her and say: 'Gertie told me this . . .'; while she herself forgot their names and everything else about them. She'd wear her lovely clothes, waltzing out of her dressing-room looking incredibly smart, planting a kiss on Eddie Cooke, the seventy-year-old manager of the show, and lilting: 'Cooky, darling . . . only six dollars in the bargain basement!' – and the next evening wear something fifty times as expensive. There'd be a party every night and she would sing for us – but never 'Someday I'll find you' because: 'I've sung it out of tune often enough.' Authors would come with ideas of new shows and she would give them all her attention; delighted especially with one of Johnny Green's whose 'Body and Soul' she first sang (she had bought a half-share in the royalties for £50) because she explained: 'Darling, the curtain goes up and there I am on a bicycle with my bottom to the audience!' She'd talk of Noel Coward: 'I have never known him any better from the day I first met him to this.' She'd appear vague and charming, but she'd catch you out if you contradicted something you'd said twenty minutes before. She'd go to bed at three, but be up rehearsing a new play at ten. She'd find the maximum of pleasure in the minimum of amusement. One evening she and I were taken on a tour of Chinatown by the Chief of Police. We ate chop suey with chop sticks, walked down dark alleyways and up rickety staircases; and pretended all the time we were risking the dangers that haven't existed in the district for fifteen years. A British warship happened to be on a courtesy visit to 'Frisco, and towards two in the morning we saw three able seamen swaying slightly in the middle of Grant Avenue. They affected both of us with nostalgia for home, so up we went to make their acquaintance. By way of introduction, Gertie, in her delightful confident way, with the words going up and down in the scale, said: 'I am Gertie Lawrence!' We waited in suspense for their reaction. 'I am Gertie Lawrence,' repeated Gertie, 'you know . . . the actress!' They looked at her a little unsteadily; then one of them mumbled: 'Well . . . if you are . . . ssshow ush where we can get shome women!'

It was lucky for me that Gertie and those with her play, were in San Francisco because they lightened by their presence an otherwise uncomfortable month. Hitler was up to one of his tricks and I spent a great deal of my time listening to the radio and buying newspapers and getting angry with Americans for calling Britain 'yellow'. In addition, there was a crisis in the city itself, in the form of a retail store strike. You couldn't walk down the street without passing ten squeaking females with banners announcing: 'This store is unfair to organized labour'; and if you entered a store which was being kept open by a skeleton staff, you ran the gauntlet of a hissing picket of men and women. Their demand apparently was not the question of wages nor the length of working hours; they were on strike because they wanted to control the selection of employees. For fifteen years San Francisco has been bothered by strikes and the effect on the general atmosphere is noticeable; it was strained; cab drivers, waiters, shop salesmen were sullen and unobliging; there was none of the romance and irresponsibility that I'd expected. The long-shoremen have been on strike so often that shipowners have lost patience with them; and if they aren't on strike they deliberately slow their work so as to collect overtime pay. It's no wonder that fewer and fewer ships call at 'Frisco, and instead make Los Angeles the chief port of call on the west coast.

After two weeks I realized I was being even less of a success than in New York. I was ready to admit that it could be my fault, but this could hardly be so when letters of introduction weren't answered; even though the recipients were in town to receive them. I was puzzled, too, why just ordinary politeness was as rare to find as a fly in midwinter. On my third evening in the city I was invited to a charity ball at which the *élite* were predominant. I imagined that it would be an excellent opportunity to get to know people, but, after being there three hours, I had talked to about a score of Americans, all of whom addressed me in monologues, without attempting to draw any conversation out of me. And when it so happened that I was talking to one by the bar, more often than not, it was I who paid for the drinks, not the American. One man did invite me to lunch the following day, but when the bill came, he said he was sorry he had forgotten his money, so I had to pay!

3

I would have gone after two weeks if it hadn't been for the fact I'd rented my apartment for a month; and the remaining two weeks were no better than the first. Much of it I spent in bed; I also wrote some articles for the *San Francisco Chronicle*. In the evenings, if I wasn't at the 'Curran Theatre', I lounged about the bars and cafés of North Beach, downtown of 'Frisco, the district of the old Barbary Coast and Chinatown. Not that these places are any more of interest. By day Chinatown is a spick-and-span shopping centre for the tourists who roam Grant Avenue and Sacramento Street, gazing wide-eyed at the hieroglyphics that decorate shop signs; and by night it welcomes the tourists again, the cafés with whisky and respectable Chinese waitresses, the streets and alleyways with guides who, in addition to their fees, beg for a donation on behalf of their suffering cousins overseas. It was in one of these cafés that I did, however, meet a girl whose companionship brightened a little the monotony of the days.

Her name was Penny. She was eighteen with a figure like that of Ginger Rogers; and her way of living was to show it clothesless three times a day, along with six others of her sex who were nearer forty than thirty, to an audience of sailors of all nationalities, and an assortment of tired business men. She was a chorus girl in a burlesque show. The programme of these entertainments consists of a film with a title such as 'Dangers of the White Slave Traffic', a ten-minute interval when the programme seller urges you to buy a picture book ('but don't look at it now or your neighbour will blush'), and a variety show of vulgar comedians with Penny and her friends.

She had been in 'Frisco two years. She had come down from Seattle where her father was a longshoreman. She hadn't ambitions. She said she was too small for ordinary chorus work. All she wanted was to stick around 'Frisco and earn a living. She didn't really mind standing naked on the stage, though 'Saturday nights are a bit rough.' She liked to laugh; also to cut dates with me. Her favourite drink was hot chocolate and she enjoyed walking along the shore by the Pacific. On the whole she had very little to say for herself; but there was a freshness about her that was as delightful as it was unexpected.

The evening before I was leaving for Hollywood, I'd met her after the show and we'd walked down Vallejo Street to Leoni's, where Leoni, a swarthy little Italian who hated Mussolini, had asked me for a farewell drink. A half-dozen American sailors were lounging against the bar, and another was at a table with two flashily dressed women on either side of him; four other tables were filled, three by a nondescript collection of men in black Trilby hats playing dice, and one by a taxi-driver. It was plain that this gentleman was drunk. His cap was on the back of his head, his green shirt was open at the neck, and he was wailing a song that had no tune to it. We'd been there five minutes before he recognized Penny; then with a whoop like an Indian war cry, he rose unsteadily to his feet with a glass of beer in his hand, and swayed over to us. He was a broad, unshaven hulk of a man with a jaw that stuck out aggressively. Leoni had a hunch that trouble was coming because he darted round the counter to play the part of a nurse remonstrating with a disobedient baby. The taxi-driver, or Ed as he introduced himself, pushed him aside, and leeringly complimented Penny on her performance. 'Do yer

act now, shister,' he spluttered. The sailors were roaring
with laughter. The men in the Trilby hats stopped playing
their dice. 'Do so yourself, buddy,' cracked back Penny.
For some minutes Ed continued to persuade her to oblige
until he had become, in my view, a nuisance. Then it was
that I was foolish enough to say something. I think it was:
'Perhaps you'd better go home now, Ed, old man.'
Anyhow, he swung round to me, repeated what I said in
an exaggerated English accent . . . and threw his glass of
beer in my face.

Two of the sailors grabbed my arms and two others
grabbed his; and while I was held there, he was protestingly
pushed outside. I saw Penny go, too, and when Leoni
came back a few minutes later, she wasn't there with him.
The sailors, pleased with themselves for having so promptly
stopped a brawl, had let go of my arms and I was mopping
my face with a handkerchief. 'Where's Penny?' I asked.
Leoni paused for a second. 'Say, bud,' answered Leoni,
'that guy Ed is Penny's boyfriend . . . she's been standing
him up . . . that's why he was sore.' He went behind the
bar. 'She's taking him home,' he added, 'and she told me
to say thanks and wish you luck.'

I never saw her again. At six o'clock next morning I was
in the Greyhound bus, bound for Hollywood.

4

That same evening I was strolling down Hollywood Boulevard with Miles Mander. Dusk was falling and it was hot,
like an August evening in Regent Street in a heat-wave.
An hour previously the bus, after an uneventful journey,
had dumped me down in Cahuenga Avenue, where Miles
was there to greet me and take me to the Mark Twain
Hotel. I went through the ceremonies of signing my name

and finding my room as quickly as possible. I had the naïve excitement of a schoolgirl in my desire to have my first glimpse of the city. Nor was I disappointed.

Hollywood, as everyone knows, sprawls over many square miles; MGM studios are as far from Warner Brothers as Piccadilly Circus from Watford, and there is no break in the lines of houses separating Hollywood from Los Angeles. But it is in the one mile of Hollywood Boulevard, from Vine Street to Grauman's Chinese Theatre, that you see the highest concentration of Hollywood beauty. It is not the beauty of the film stars, they are in Beverley Hills and the villas off Sunset Boulevard, but the beauty of the extra girls that are waiting for their call to fame. Blondes, brunettes, redheads, in scanty shorts and slacks of orange, white, pink, and blue. Scarlet lips and dark sun-glasses. Figures of Cochran Young Ladies. Painted toenails, sandals and bare legs. On that first evening I saw score upon score of them, perfect examples of that synthetic beauty that is the fashion of the world. And as I stared and marvelled at this cavalcade of sex appeal, I heard Miles say: 'Don't get tied up with these lovely animals. They'll cost you a fortune and you'll get nowhere.'

Circumstances forced me to take his advice during my month's stay. Night clubs are dotted over an area of twenty miles, and as American girls can't sit still in the same restaurant for more than an hour, it would have meant spending in taxi-cab fares alone what would have amounted to an ordinary night out anywhere else. In any case, these extra girls must be seen in the right places where there's always a hope of a director spotting them or a successful film star taking a fancy to them. They are all waiting for the Chance; and, strangely enough, a good many of them have their mothers waiting with them.

They've trekked into Hollywood, the mothers basking in reflected glory, from Missouri, Minnesota, and Texas, after winning the local beauty competition; without brains, talent, or influence, they imagine a miracle will speedily put their names in lights, and even after the first months of disappointment, they still believe with incorrigible optimism that the Chance will come, next week, next month. One such mother and daughter were living in my block of apartments. They'd been waiting eight years and the daughter's bloom of youth was fading. But mother was undaunted. One evening as I was walking upstairs with her, she confided: 'Our little girl Hortense is sure going places some day.'

I wrote an article about the lives of these extras, and to help gather the material, the Central Casting Bureau sent me three girls to interview. The Bureau provides the extras of every film made in Hollywood. Eight thousand men and women are on the books, and only in special circumstances nowadays is anyone else signed on. They are divided into four classes; the £1-a-day class, which is so far from the camera that it doesn't matter what anyone wears; the 30s. class, for which a girl needs two evening dresses and a man a dress-suit; the 45s. class, for which a girl must have four evening dresses as well as smart walking clothes; the 75s. class, for which is needed the wardrobe of any smart man or woman about town. The Bureau keeps a check on the earnings of all the eight thousand, and the result is interesting. Last year four thousand earned more than £150; one hundred and twenty-six more than £400; sixteen more than £500; and only three more than £600. The rest of the eight thousand earned less than £100. Against these figures, you have to bear in mind the cost of clothes. A girl whom I saw, who had earned £650, told me her wardrobe was insured for £1500. It consisted of twenty-four evening

gowns, several fur coats and wraps, twenty-five pairs of
shoes, and ten sports and street clothes. They have to be in
the latest fashion or directors won't want them. She told
me that she pays out an average of £2 a week to keep her
wardrobe in condition and to pay her hairdresser, and the
cost of transport to the studios. Seems hardly worth it,
especially when you learn that out of forty-five thousand
people registered with the Central Casting Bureau in the
last twelve years, only sixteen have got their names into
bright lights; Clark Gable and Janet Gaynor being the
prime examples. Two other girls I saw were the kind that
danced and posed in the mammoth musicals of two years
ago; so now that Busby Berkeley is out of fashion, they are
out of a job. In 1936, a boom year for them, they earned
£600 each, but in 1938 they were lucky to get a £100. They
shared a flat off Highland Avenue near the Hollywood
Bowl: they cleaned the flat themselves, cooked their food,
and made their own clothes. Any day, however, it was on
the cards they'd be called up to play the part of a sophisti-
cated glamour girl. They were hard little realists. The
youngest, aged twenty-one, said: 'Sure I've tried being kept
by a guy but it wasn't much fun. I'd to run around like a
hired motor car. There's more kick in being independent.'
The other, a year older, blue-eyed and blonde, cracked: 'Six
years in this racket and you're a sucker if you sleep with a
man before he gives you the job. Sleep a night with a man
and he forgets next morning what you slept with him for.
"Nuts," I say when they make a pass.' Then she added a
little thoughtfully: 'Maybe it's different with the big shots.'
Both of these girls talked about the Chance that one day
would come their way. Heavens knows how. But they
talked of it like you would talk of the plans you're going to
make next Christmas. Hard boiled careerists; you can't help
feeling sorry for them and the hundreds like them.

Miles Mander has a disarming manner of apparent indifference to his runs of good and bad luck. He has an attractive air of irresponsibility and an attitude of carelessness towards matters which other people make much of. Today he is having greater success on the films than ever in his career, but for a couple of years in Hollywood he frequently didn't have enough to pay his rent. When after a long bout of unemployment he did succeed in getting a big part, he collapsed on the set on the very first day of 'shooting', and was taken to hospital. It was found advisable to operate at once, but the doctor first asked him if he had any money to pay for the fee. Miles, who was semiconscious, didn't answer; the doctor rang up the bank. The bank said Miles had five dollars. The doctor came back: 'We won't operate, Mr Mander, until you get someone to guarantee the fees.' Miles (he was afterwards on the danger list for fifteen days) roused himself from his semi-consciousness to tell the doctor what he thought of the American medical profession. He then phoned Madeleine Carroll, who dashed round half an hour later with the money.

It was a strange coincidence that the man who had the part before Miles was Jameson Thomas, the English star of silent days, who also collapsed on the set seriously ill. He was a great friend of Miles's, and knowing Miles was in need of a job, managed to get a message to him that owing to his illness the job was vacant. Jamie Thomas, though I met him only twice, cut a picture in my mind that I'll never forget. His young wife died in California of tuberculosis, six years before he himself was struck down with it. He had for long been out of work, and he had no money to pay for proper treatment. The Motion Picture Relief, however, came to his aid, paying for a bed in a sanatorium at Sierra Madre, on the outskirts of Pasadena. It was here that I met him, lying haggard and unshaven, in a room whose window faced a wall and where he saw no sun. He had many friends who were wealthy and who were ready to help him, men like Ian Hunter and Ronald Colman, but he was too proud to accept their charity. He wanted them only to bring books which he afterwards returned. None of his friends remember him complaining, but in his last three months he talked always of England. He was being given some sleeping drug which made him dream vividly. He told me that he would dream so vividly of his young days in England that it would take him two or three minutes when he woke up to realize where he was. And then, unconsciously speaking the truth, he used the expression: 'I'm dying to see England again.' But he died there in that little room whose window faced a wall and where he saw no sun; and his friends will remember him as a man who radiated a fineness that made them feel it had done them good to have known him.

5

I had my fill of stars. One of the very great, on an introduction from a mutual friend, gave me lunch with his wife and a famous director. I'll always remember that lunch because, no matter what I said, no one took the slightest notice. Obviously, it was a bore having to ask me to luncheon at all and, once there, why should they bother to make conversation with me? They prattled along about their own affairs and gossip: 'I refuse to play opposite Claudette Colbert' – 'Did you hear that one about the Bradna girl?' – 'Jack caught Claire in bed with Bob,' and so on. I got so annoyed that when the coffee came, and after I'd made another meek attempt to make my voice heard, I rose up saying: 'I'm very sorry I must go now. I'm playing golf with Groucho Marx.' Then, for the first time, they took a look at me. I was worth their attention. Not that I had ever met Groucho Marx in my life. A more pleasant lunch was with Loretta Young. This took place in the studio restaurant of 20th Century-Fox; the tables filled by yellow-face-powdered men and women in garments ranging from modern evening dress to crinoline frocks of the nineteenth century. Loretta herself was in a crinoline of violet and lace frills, looking demure with big round eyes, and teeth that don't look so prominent as they do on the screen. Just as I arrived at the table where she was sitting, Doc Bishop, who was introducing me, was called away, leaving me stranded. Loretta smiled sweetly. 'Do sit down,' she said, 'my name's Young.' The most shining example of modesty I've ever met.

The same day, Harry Revel, the song writer, took me along to see Shirley Temple. He walked me across to her bungalow in the studios, where we found Mrs Temple sitting knitting on the doorstep. She is thin, dark-haired, and fortyish. 'Oh Harry,' she said, getting up 'a whole lot more letters saying Shirley's a midget.' Harry told me later she gets frantic about some of the letters sent to Shirley; she insists on reading all the fan-mail. To me, however, she seemed a sensible woman, the sort of housewife who would always buy the best value at the cheapest price, and a woman who had the pleasant habit of appearing interested in what you're saying. As we were talking, Shirley, earner of £1000 a week, appeared through a doorway. She was in a white party frock, with white socks and shoes. Her hair had a reddish tinge and her eyes were a deep brown. Mrs Temple glanced at her: 'Shirley,' she said firmly, 'you've got a smut on your nose. Go and wash it off before you shake hands.' Shirley obediently turned and went into the bathroom. The following day I was watching her play a scene with Anita Louise. It happens that she is obliged by law to spend a certain number of hours every day learning her lessons; and after each scene she goes to her teacher who times by a stop watch how many minutes she puts in before the next scene is ready. When this particular scene with Anita Louise was over, Mrs Temple cried out: 'Hurry, Shirley ... school!' Shirley pouted her lips and sighed: 'Ooo ... that word haunts me night and day!' It was this same afternoon that I had my picture taken with her. Obviously, Miss Temple didn't want to have hers taken. She sulkily came up beside me, her head reaching my waistline. I wondered what to do to soothe her ruffled feelings. I felt oddly embarrassed, as if the Queen was unwillingly doing me a favour; but I didn't know whether to make my peace with a child of ten or with the Queen. As it was, I looked glum, imagining the grim little face below me; but I shouldn't have worried, Shirley is too well trained – when the picture appeared she had on her face a beaming smile. She redeemed matters for me a few days later, after I had pushed her several times up and down on her swing, by enrolling me as one of her police; as she pinned the imitation gold medal of office on my coat, she remarked gravely: 'If ever I catch you not wearing it, you pay me a dollar!' The last time I saw her, she was sitting by herself in the back seat of their limousine (Mrs Temple always sits in front beside the chauffeur). They were just moving off for home when Shirley suddenly said: 'Oh Mummie, I've forgotten Dinah, can I get her?' and out she scrambled to fetch her doll.

I found it reasonably cheap living in Hollywood. I paid £2 a week for an apartment in Wilcox Avenue off Holly-wood Boulevard and in four weeks I only spent a little over £25; this, however, wasn't achieved without effort. Many evenings I sat at home wishing to goodness I could go out; yet to do so would probably have resulted in my

spending in one night what I'd budgeted for a week. To
go out alone could be all right, as I would linger a long
time over one drink; but as like as not I would meet
somebody and then it would be drink for drink and away
the money would fly. There were some to whom I could
admit my state of affairs; Guv Charlot, for instance, who
to the loss of the English stage now lives in Hollywood.
He and I used to sit on stools in La Conga and watch the
girls and boys enjoy themselves. Myrna Loy with a shiny
nose and dressed like a pleasant, homely housewife. Alice
Faye enjoying absinthe. Joan Bennett dancing cheek to
cheek with Walter Wanger. Jean Parker liking whisky.
Tables of rowdy parties. Guv himself had just finished
being technical advisor to 'Zaza' and he had no idea what
he was going to do next. For that reason he would never
go out of his apartment by day. He said he had to stay by
the telephone in case a producer rang him up. Most people
pretend, as I myself was doing, that they either have more
money than they've got, or that they're more successful
than they are. Guv preferred to joke about his position and
go on smoking his cigars and playing his contract bridge at
6d. a hundred. Once I did hear him say: 'It takes grit to be
cheerful'; and there was another time when I was talking
about the value of prestige. He answered: 'Never rely on
prestige, it's the facts of the moment that count.' So now
Guv, who gave first chances to Ronald Colman, Jack
Buchanan, Gertrude Lawrence, June, Jessie Matthews and
a host of others, is waiting to get a chance himself.

6

I got weary with being shown round the studios. Architec-
turally all studios are the same; the stages, the research
department, the wardrobe department, the music depart-

ment, the carpentry shop, the laboratories. The publicity men insist on showing you everything, and by the time I'd seen 20th Century, MGM, Warner Brothers, Paramount and Radio, my adjectives of praise were worn to shreds; because, obviously, you have to praise each studio above another. The publicity men must have been more bored than I was, but they didn't show it. They placed cars at my disposal, entertained me to lunch, offered free tickets at previews, introduced me to Mickey Rooney, Clark Gable, Spencer Tracy, Adolphe Menjou, Franchot Tone, Joan Crawford; and with the fuss of an art dealer showing me a Gainsborough, one of them let me look at a screen, the other side of which Hedy la Marr was having a bath.

The classic tour of Hollywood studios was made by Cedric Belfrage. Cedric, as anyone knows who has read his books, is a rebel against convention. He writes what he feels, being quite indifferent to the possibility of his remarks bouncing back unfavourably on him. When he was a film critic, he was in perpetual hot water with the film companies. They didn't think they deserved his outspoken criticism since they were paying considerable sums for advertisements in his paper; and especially angry was MGM who, for a long time, wouldn't have anything to do with him. When, however, Cedric went to Hollywood for a month, MGM thought it time to patch up the quarrel; and they decided to do it in a big way. Cedric was invited to lunch by Irving Thalberg, then head of MGM, who afterwards personally conducted him on a tour of the studios. For two hours Thalberg talked to Cedric, while the publicity men hovered in the background quite certain that Cedric had been won over by this honour. But they were wrong. Cedric's next article attacked Thalberg for wasting time – he said that a £100,000 a year man should have something better to do than to be a guide to a £20 a week journalist.

MGM have never forgiven him for this; and in other studios one also doesn't often hear pleasant things said of him. They're scared stiff that at any moment he may lash out on them; especially that now he has made his home in the Santa Monica mountains where he lives with his small daughter Sally, and his wife, Molly Castle. Molly and I were wheeled in our prams, side by side, on the promenade of Blundell sands. Today she is undoubtedly the best English woman journalist, and her Hollywood articles in the *Daily Mirror* the most readable ones of their kind. It was principally due to the two of them that I had such a good time in Hollywood; they spared no trouble so that I might see all that there was to see, and meet not only the blah film stars, writers and directors, but also the others who resemble the normal intelligent people found in any other city in the world. And through them, I met the first American who lived up to my expectation of American hospitality . . . George Volk, the agent, who loaned me his car, invited me to stay with him, entertained me and took endless trouble giving me introductions to various high-ups in different studios. There were many other people who made me feel that Hollywood welcomed a stranger; or at any rate, gave him a chance to find his feet before passing judgment upon him.

7

But scarcely had I found these friends than it was time to move on. I was going to Tahiti.

For a long, long time I'd had my South Sea dream, a picture in my mind of sighing coconut trees, and gentle blue lagoons whose tranquillity would bring a balance to my thoughts and a peace I could not find elsewhere. In my teens, I measured happiness by money, pretty girls and holidays. I imagined that if I had the money to take out a pretty girl and a holiday during which I could do so, I would be forever content. One day, when I do not know, it suddenly came upon me that there was something vastly more complicated which ruled my happiness; and that, to achieve it, I had to find my way through a labyrinth of doubts and fears, until all at once, like coming upon an oasis in the desert, I found myself with peace of mind.

Tahiti, it had seemed to me, would be that oasis; ever since I'd read Rupert Brooke's letter of farewell. 'I was sad at heart to leave Tahiti,' he wrote. 'But I resigned myself to the vessel, and watched the green shores and rocky peaks fade with hardly a pang. I had told so many of those that loved me, so often, "Oh yes, I'll come back – next year perhaps, or the year after" – that I suppose I had begun to believe it myself. It was only yesterday, when I knew that the Southern Cross had left me, that I suddenly realized that I had left behind those lovely places and lovely people, perhaps for ever. I reflected that there was surely nothing else like them in the world, and very probably nothing in the next, and that I was going far away from gentleness and beauty and kindliness, and the smell of the lagoons, and the thrill of that dancing, and the scarlet of the flamboyants, and the white and gold of other flowers; and that I was going to America, which is full of harshness and hideous sights, and ugly people and civilization, and corruption, and bloodiness, and all evil. So I wept a little, and very sensibly went to bed . . .' His words had caught my imagination, and in the years since I'd read them I'd woven round Tahiti my dream of escape, believing that, if by some lucky chance one day I was able to go there, life would become again as simple as when I was a boy.

The difficulty was how to get there. There were two

ways: one from San Francisco by a cargo boat which sailed every six weeks, and the other by a French passenger steamer which passed through the Panama Canal from Marseilles about as often. Unfortunately, the cargo boat was booked six months ahead (it only carried ten passengers), while the French boat was booked up for two months. I was told, however, that if I took the risk of going down to Panama I might be lucky and get a cancelled passage. The risk seemed to be worth taking. I could not imagine myself, once there, not getting aboard. Meanwhile, I had to get to Panama. I wanted to go via Mexico and Central America, but I found there was no regular train or bus service after the Mexican border, and the only way was to go by boat from San Pedro.

And so, on one sunny Monday morning at midday, I boarded the Norwegian steamer *Takanar*, with eight days sailing ahead of me, five days in Panama waiting for the French boat, and then, I hoped, fourteen days across the Pacific to Tahiti.

Chapter Five

PANAMANIAN INTERLUDE

THE 'TAKANAR' WAS 8000 tons, loaded with lead, zinc, fresh fruits and lumber. She had come down the west coast from Vancouver, calling at Portland, Seattle, and San Francisco, before San Pedro; and after Panama she sailed across the Atlantic to Southampton and Liverpool. She did this trip four times a year, there and back, and very seldom was she ever in her native country of Norway.

My cabin was on a small deck directly beneath the bridge. It had a berth with a spring mattress, a wash basin with a cold water tap, a wardrobe, a sofa which would have been another berth had it been occupied, and two windows facing the bows; to reach it I had to walk through the small smoking-room where there was a wireless and three tables and a half-dozen chairs, which were fixed to the floor, so that if the weather was rough they would not slide about. There was room in the boat for eight passengers but this trip there were only three aboard. One was an ex-Canadian civil servant retiring to England, another was a young prelate on his way to be ordained in Panama, and the third was a South American bishop. For eight days we were thrown together, with the same intimacy as if we'd been wrecked on a desert island.

The civil servant was named Harris. He'd been alone on board for a fortnight, and no sooner had we cast away from the dock and were heading for the Pacific, passing far away to our left a squadron of American warships anchored near San Diego, than he buttonholed me and unleashed all his unspoken conversation that had been boiling up inside him.

I learnt that he suffered from heart trouble, had had all his teeth taken out, had lost 45 lb in six months, had been 20th in the King's Prize at Bisley in 1908, should have had a pension after the Boer War but was cheated out of one, that he had lived by himself in Vancouver, and was going to stay for the rest of his life with his brother at Bristol. When I told him I'd been to Hollywood, he said: 'That's the place where they make films, isn't it?' and went on to explain how he'd been to a number of films in the previous few months but couldn't remember the names of them. 'Know the stars though,' he added cheerfully. 'Myrna Low, Tyrone Powell, Loretta Faye.' The bishop was Spanish. He spoke a burbling broken English, little of which I could understand; and he ended every remark with a twitch of his black eyebrows and a giggle. The young prelate had the name of Figaro. He had the head of a guinea pig, with large flapping ears and a pair of black, beady eyes. He told me he had been studying at 'Crompton,' and he said the word 'Crompton' in such a tone of voice that I felt sure I should have known it as I do Paris or New York.

The four of us had our meals with the Captain in the oblong dining-room, which in daylight was darkened by the lumber, piled high on the deck outside. The Captain was a pleasant, round-faced little man with bushy fair eyebrows. He hadn't been to his home in Norway for more than two months in eleven years. His last visit had been three years ago, and during that holiday, he told us, he had married. Coyly he said, in halting English: 'I have not seen my wife since.' There was an embarrassed pause, all four of us thinking of the poor little wife; and it wasn't broken till the bishop, with no reference to any previous conversation, began telling us a tale how he'd once seen a whale off the coast near New York.

After supper I stood on the fo'c'sle listening to the swish as we cut through the water. The sun was setting, and it was very still. To starboard was the glow of the dying sun, pink and gold; but ahead of us was the jet blackness of a thunderstorm. It stretched from the faint line of the Californian coast far into the Pacific Ocean, and we were sailing into the centre of it. The blackness would be suddenly shot with jagged fork lightning or the black clouds would turn grey by a flash like the summer lightning of England. I thought we were in for a big storm, but it melted away as we drew nearer, and only a few spots of rain spattered on the deck. I felt lonely as I stood there, and a little homesick. I thought of the people whose friendship I had shared in the past few months; only to move on, leaving them behind. I thought of Sarah who had telephoned me from New York the night before I sailed; and, as the sun dipped behind the horizon, I wondered whether I would ever see her again. I thought of my mother and father, and the months ahead of me before I would be with them again. I had an acute desire to hear their voices, and, if there had been a telephone aboard, no matter what the expense, I would have put a call that moment through to England. There were many times in the year I was away that I felt like that. I would arrive at some city in which all were strangers; but without fail long letters from my mother and father would be waiting for me; and there was one evening, when I was sitting in my room in Hollywood, when the telephone rang, and I was told London wanted me. I didn't believe it — but a minute later, as clearly as if it had been a local call, I heard my brother Colin's voice. He just wanted to know whether I was enjoying myself. I knew then, even if I hadn't known before, that I was lucky in my family.

2

At meal-times, on the table in front of the Captain, was a dark-coloured cheese which I learnt was goat's cheese and a speciality of Norway. For some days no one partook of it except the Captain, until one evening Mr Harris, who was proving himself a bit of a wit, announced in frolicsome mood that he was going to take some. I offered to do the same, saying: 'I won't let you die alone!' With Figaro laughing and the Bishop grinning as he stirred the bread he had stuck in his coffee, Mr Harris and I each cut a microscopic piece and with great play proceeded to sniff it. Unhappily we had been taking no heed of the Captain; for he had taken exception to our behaviour and, speaking slowly and deliberately with cheeks flushed a deep crimson, and his broken English more broken than ever, he said: 'Thaaat ees foood yooo arre eeeting. Thaat's nottt tooo beee sneeefed aat!' We tried to smother our laughter, like choirboys in church, and Mr Harris turned to me, whispering: 'We've insulted the national cheese!' Even Figaro and the Bishop were laughing, and it was painful to see the hurt look on the Captain's face. 'Eeet's verrry goood cheese,' he added plaintively.

But a much worse scene was to follow. The afternoon before our arrival at Balboa, the Pacific end of the Canal, where I was to disembark, I went to my cabin to pack – and discovered that forty-five dollars I had left in my suitcase had disappeared! I went exhaustively through all my belongings and then got Mr Harris to do the same. I knew that once I mentioned it to the Captain there would certainly be a row. He would naturally consider I was casting aspersions on the honesty of his crew. When, however, Mr Harris found nothing, I went to the Captain, explaining that it was no doubt my fault, that the notes must have caught in the leaves of the book I was reading and, having fallen out, got blown away. He, in his turn, searched every shirt, every envelope and everything else in my two suitcases. And, as he too found nothing, it was embarrassingly necessary to call for the steward. He gave no help; and that evening we had dinner in a subdued strain. Afterwards we went upstairs to the smoking-room, the Captain to play chess with the Bishop, and I to talk with Mr Harris. We had been talking for about ten minutes about my misfortune when the Captain, apparently over-hearing us, banged his fist on the chessboard and stood up. 'Mr Deerek,' he said sternly, 'eef yoo vaant too hearr vaat I'm theenking, eeet ees thees. I veeel tell yooo thaat I theenk yoo neverr haad thee money!'

Now this moment required great calm. I sympathized with the Captain over the position he was in, but here he was accusing me of stealing my own money. I made no answer and he went on: 'But too keep yoo quiet, I, a haard-vorrking maan, veel pay you thee forty-five dollars out of my own money.' The Bishop, with hands clasped and elbows on the table, was staring at the chess-board. Figaro was intently reading a book. Mr Harris had stood up, watching me. 'Thank you very much,' I said to the Captain, 'but beyond that I will say nothing until you've apologized for what you've accused me of doing.' And with that I marched off to my cabin. Once there I saw the humour of it, and also the seriousness; I was left with two dollars sixty cents and my bar bill unpaid. It upset me, too, that the Captain should have his pride so hurt, and when he arrived to say he was sorry, I assured him again that I blamed only myself; though I realized that this couldn't be of much satisfaction to him. We said goodnight on friendly terms, so that when I got up next morning I expected we would be able to discuss the situation more calmly. But this, however, was when the Bishop stepped in. As we sat down to our porridge, amid many a giggle and a twitch of his eyebrows, he made these remarks: 'This is the end of a voyage, so let us make new resolutions . . . we will not be careless . . . we will not drink too much . . . we will not lie!'

The incident had an extraordinary sequel. That morning everybody went through my things again, without any luck. But two months later, when I was in Tahiti, I was looking through my suitcase, and I found, neatly folded in the corner of the suitcase, the whole forty-five dollars! How we missed it I will never know. Nor why it was that I didn't find it for two months, because almost daily in the meantime I had been unpacking and packing that same suitcase. I wrote off immediately to tell the Captain.

3

I landed at Balboa with my two dollars sixty cents knowing that I had to get to Colon, the Atlantic port of the Canal, where a Letter of Credit was waiting for me, before I got any more money. Figaro and the Bishop landed, too, and were met by a covey of clerics who made such a fuss of them that when I went up to bid them good-bye, the Bishop only gave me a nod. Probably he judged me as a sinner, but surely, I thought, here was a chance for him to do a bit of saving. He and his clerics, I saw, had five cars at their disposal; he knew that I was going to the station, and he knew that I had no money; in his infinite goodness he might help the sinner on his way. I hung around for a while, but so much bowing and scraping was in progress that no one noticed me and my two suitcases, hopefully watching. It struck me that if they were to see me struggling along the road, especially if I were in the middle of it, they could not fail to stop; so off I started lagging the wardrobe of a year's travel with me. The Balboa station was only a mile away, but the heat was such that you could have steamed a steam pudding on the pavement, and sweat poured from my brow as if I were taking a shower-bath. Added to my misery, shiny black negroes offered to be my porters at thirty-second intervals, and couldn't for the life of them understand why 'the white fellah' shooed them away. I had gone perhaps seventy yards when a toot behind me warned me of the coming of their reverences. Obstinately I stuck in the middle of the road. More toots. The first car was directly behind me, so I turned to face it, exhaustion written all over my face, heaving my suitcases at the same time to the side. There was His Grace in the front seat, his black eyebrows directly facing me; a faint smile of appeal lit my face, but the man was unmoved; the driver pressed the accelerator and away they went. One, two, three, four cars hurried in their wake, but the occupants were too occupied with themselves to worry about the traveller on the wayside.

The ticket cost two dollars forty cents, which left me with twenty cents to spend in the five hours before the train was timed to go. Balboa was no place to stay, there was nothing more exciting than a few shipping offices; so, having left my baggage at the station with instructions to have it put on the train, off I went on a five-cent ride in a 'jitney' to Panama City, about ten minutes away. By this time I was parched with thirst and, on being dropped off in the square, I spent a further ten cents on a coca-cola;

this left me with five cents which quickly became two when I bought a newspaper. I had four and a half hours before me, so, with the buttons of my shirt undone and my coat on my arm, I started to sight-see. No sooner, however, had I begun walking up the main street, past the window-less shops, than I found everyone in Panama had something to sell. It was amazing. After thirty yards I found I'd collected a procession, a rabble of Indians and negroes, pestering me with Panama hats, lottery tickets, souvenirs, bathing costumes, and a mass of other articles. Worse was to come. I managed to escape down a side street and found what appeared to be a lonely bench. I sat down to read my paper. I had read no more than the headline when a dozen little black boys appeared from nowhere, each with his shoe stool and his cry: 'Shoe shine, mister!' The difficulty was that my shoes obviously needed a shoe shine. They were the shoeshine boy's dream, muddy and shineless. I pretended they were not there, but that only made their cries the louder. So I said sharply: 'Run away, little boys, run away!' Peals of laughter greeted this. A couple got on the seat beside me. 'Only five cents, mister . . . only five cents!' I was at my wits' end. It was impossible to cope with such persistency. Frankness was the only way out. 'Listen, little boys,' I said, 'it's a long story and you wouldn't understand it even if I told you, but the long and short of it is that I'm broke . . . not a dime . . . not a nickel.' And with that I rose from my seat and made for the station. I was both weak in body and bad in temper when finally the train came in. To my luck the purser of an American passenger liner sat beside me. He didn't waste time with words of introduction. 'Have a swig,' he said, proffering me a half-bottle of whisky, 'plenty more where that came from.' I looked at him with astonishment. 'I've read about people like you in books,' I said. 'What part of the States do you come from?' 'My home's in Carolina,' he replied. 'Ah,' I said, 'the Southern States . . . I only went to the east and west.'

Next morning, having slept the night at the Hotel Washington in Colon, an expensive but clean hotel run by the American Government, I visited the offices of the Messageries Maritimes. They told me that the *Ville d'Amiens*, my boat to Tahiti, was not expected for another four days, but, in any case, they said, it was useless my thinking I could get aboard her; they'd just received a wire to say there wasn't a vacant berth on the ship. The news was damping, but it made me the more determined. I told the clerk that I didn't mind how I travelled, in the stoke-hold or the engine-room, anywhere, so long as I sailed to Tahiti. He was a nice little man with a head too big for his body; I departed from him with the arrangement that I should return in three days and, meanwhile, he promised to cable again to the ship.

Colon, if possible, is one worse than Panama. The town straggles unnoticed into another called Cristobal. Colon is under Panamanian jurisdiction, and Cristobal, which is in the Canal Zone, under American. In both, America is supposed to enforce sanitary ordinances, but most streets are slums with a stenching odour of open drains in the sultry, humid heat. The clerk at the bank said on my first day: 'The drains have a bad smell this week because it hasn't rained for some days.' He spoke as if he were explaining why the grass on the lawn had dried up. He didn't seem perturbed. Walk down any street and you see the downstairs living-room of the negroes opening doorless on to the pavement. The bedrooms, ceilingless, like stables. Women and children squatting over basins. Aged gramophones screeching Spanish melodies, no music in the jarring, maddening tone. Children running around in the roadway with black, bare bottoms. Girls sauntering along with thick purple lips. Barbados negroes swaggering with exaggerated waists. Old men limping with jet-black faces, their unshaven faces grey with stubble like mildew. And at night American soldiers from the garrison and sailors from the fleet jam the bars and dance-halls. Panatropes blaring their fox-trots, making the night seem even hotter. Naval police in brown gaiters and white tunics marching through the bars. Military police in wide-brimmed Scout hats swinging thick canes patrolling the streets. Colon . . . where a glass of beer costs 2s. and a whisky 3s . . . where meat tastes like leather, and the hairdresser charges an extra shilling for putting brilliantine on your hair. I never wish to spend five days there again.

The one bright spot of my stay was an evening with Tyrone Power. I'd met him three or four times in Hollywood, and the last time I'd seen him, in the Clover Club the evening before I left, he told me he was due in Panama about the time I would be there; he was taking a flying holiday round South America. Sure enough, on my second evening, he flew in from Mexico City and rang through to my room (he was staying in the same hotel) within a half-hour of his arrival. We just had time for a drink before he rushed off to make a couple of personal appearances, but we arranged we should meet afterwards at the Atlantic Club.

The Atlantic is the Café de Paris, the Rainbow Roof, of Colon. Night after night it seethes with sergeants, able seamen, corporals, petty officers, of the American Army and Navy. The bar and its tables open on to the dusty pavement of Bolivar Street, and the passers-by are tempted inside by the pretty girls, especially imported from New York, that are sitting around waiting to be their hostesses. They are, however, respectable young ladies. The boss of the Atlantic has to deposit a £100 bond with the authorities for each one on arrival; he gets it back so long as there's been no scandal around her name when her contract is up. They live in dormitories above the club which they get free. They also earn 25 per cent on all the drink they persuade their partners to buy, and as the cheapest is 3s. 6d. they don't do so badly.

I was having a drink with one of the girls when Ty Power came in. He looks more manly than he does on the screen, and he has an effortless and charming manner. He takes his success as rather a joke, and it doesn't appear to make him feel any more self-important than if he were a bank clerk. As he stood beside me he was attacked by autograph hunters, and I noticed the way he fixed his charm on each one individually as he signed his name, rather than on the whole crowd as most celebrities do. We got away from them after a while and sat at a table that sided the dance-floor. Every inch of it was jammed with hugging couples. The swing band of negroes yelled and screamed their rhythm. Military police passed to and fro between the tables. Sailors, in their white linen jackets, sprawled over their chairs drunkenly making love to their girl friends. Cigarette girls with bare legs and short skirts sex-appealed their wares; and heat and smoke palled over the room like fog in a monster oven.

We'd been there five minutes when he saw a girl he wanted to dance with. 'That girl over there in a white dress and a red rose on her shoulder,' he said, 'do me the favour of asking her to dance and bringing her over here.' He then explained the drawbacks of being a film star. In his unknown days he'd played the sport of picking up girls. He'd see a pretty little shop-girl and think it a pity he didn't know her; he'd conceive some original way of making her acquaintance, and if he were snubbed ... well, he'd at any rate had the excitement of the chase. 'Now, however, it's different,' he continued. 'There's a rumpus if I'm seen with a girl not belonging to the screen ... and with regard to introducing myself to strange girls ... I must step very warily.' The girl he fancied was dancing with a squat, pug-nosed American marine, but when the music stopped, she left him for a table by herself. I went over to her. She wasn't more than twenty, tall and dark, with wide set-apart eyes, and a generous, full mouth. We danced a couple of minutes and then I took her over to our table. It was the great moment of her life; and Ty fastened all his charm on her, asking all manner of intimate questions. She said her name was Estelle. She didn't much care for gold-digging, but it was so darned easy in Colon where the boys had nothing else to spend their money on except the girls. No, she didn't sleep with any of them; if she were caught doing so she would be shipped straightaway back to New York. Work never ended before six or seven in the morning; and sometimes she made as much as £5 in a night.

Ty danced with her for a while, then suggested that the four of us, I and my girl, a little redhead with green eyes, should go back to his suite at the hotel. This we did. We opened a bottle of whisky and turned on a portable gramophone. We'd been there perhaps a quarter of an hour when there was a knock at the door. Ty opened it, and there in the doorway was the hotel clerk. He was a young, fresh-faced – American. 'Very sorry, Mr Power,' he said firmly, 'it's against the regulations to have ladies upstairs.' We looked at each other foolishly, feeling like schoolboys caught at a dormitory feast. 'But it is all very harmless,' said Ty. 'Maybe,' replied the clerk, 'nevertheless, the ladies must go.' And off they went. I accompanied them down to the hall where Ty said he would escort them home. And the last I saw of him was in the back of a taxi with an arm round each. He flew to Ecuador a few hours later that morning.

4

On the fourth day of my stay, as arranged, I went back to the Messageries Maritimes to see the little man with the head too big for him. He had excellent news. The *Ville d'Amiens* would dock at three the following afternoon – and he'd arranged by cable that I should go steerage. I was jubilant. The ticket, for the fifteen days' journey to Papeéte, port of Tahiti, was only £8, though I had to make a deposit of £30 to ensure I wouldn't become a penniless beachcomber on the hands of the French Government. I could have avoided doing this if I'd taken a return ticket, but it was unlikely I would return. From Tahiti, it was my idea to go to New Zealand and Australia.

Chapter Six

HOOLIGAN CARGO

THE 'VILLE D' AMIENS' wasn't beautiful. Her lines were blunt and solid, and her colour a dark red. She had a single funnel, a white superstructure amidships, and a smaller one astern; the paint on her was worn and patchy, as if she'd faced many a gale since her last refitting. And even from where I stood, in the shade of a warehouse waiting to go aboard, I could see her decks were dark with coal dust. Hunched over the railings of the lower deck were ebony-black Senegalese sailors in blue overalls, and above them on the top deck passengers were queuing up to come ashore, officers in white drill suits standing at the head of the gangway. I was wondering whereabouts might be my quarters when from behind me a reedy American voice, like a thirteen-year-old soprano's half-way to breaking, piped: 'Say, have you got a cabin aboard that ship?' It was a tall, broad-shouldered young man of about twenty speaking. He wore no hat, his brown hair was brushed in waves like an advertisement for brilliantine. His eyes were brown, and his nose flat like a pugilist's. He wore a white shirt, a green tie, and a double-breasted blue suit that fitted his well-proportioned figure like an under-sized glove. 'Say,' he piped again, 'they won't let me and my friend get on that boat. Dammit hell, we just sure must go . . . hide us in your cabin and we'll make it worth while.' His friend was elderly, with a red nose like W. C. Fields, and gold-rimmed spectacles. He was small, with thinning grey hair and a voice like the baa of a sheep. 'Sure,' he bleated, 'we must get on that boat ... we've got friends expecting us in Tahiti ... Dickie Blandy, do you know him?' I told him I didn't know him, nor had I a cabin to hide them in; in any case I wouldn't have helped them, I'd taken an instant dislike to the thrusting egotism of the young man.

I saw then that people were mounting the gangway, so I heaved my suitcases towards it and climbed aboard. An Arab boy came forward to help me, leading me to the steerage along the deck, engrained with soot, until we reached a hatch from which into the gloom below was an iron ladder. I climbed down feet first, finding myself in a messroom, the size of a dining-room in a Kensington house, with two long wooden tables in the centre. At one end, through iron railings, I could see the hold. A car was at one corner and a heap of sacks and a thick coil of rope in the middle. On the other sides of the room, in four compartments, were the bunks, ten of them in each and they were fixed in couples, one on top of each other, with a framework of iron rods like the pieces of a meccano set. On each bunk was a straw palliasse and a rug.

Three men were already in my compartment. Two were tough-looking American college boys who introduced themselves as Ken and Jo; the third was in the fifties with black eyes that peered through rimless spectacles. He told me to call him Doc. At first sight they seemed pleasant enough; and I accepted their offer to return ashore with them for the remaining hours before we sailed. We drank a lot in that time and, when in the evening we got back to the ship, the three of them were pretty drunk and, falling into their bunks, they quickly fell asleep. I wasn't as drunk as they, and I lay awake listening to the clatter of the coaling crane, sweating in the hot, clammy heat. Once I slept, dreaming vividly that I was eating cotton wool and being throttled by it; when I awoke I found my mouth was full of the coal dust that was pouring through the porthole.

I went a stroll on deck after that. It was about two in the morning and still four hours before we sailed. Leaning over the side, watching the coaling, was a little man, dark like a Greek, in a navy-blue shirt, shorts and sandals. 'Hot, isn't it?' I said. 'Yep,' he answered abruptly in a voice of the quality of Charlie McCarthy's. I leant over the rail beside him. I wanted conversation to while away the hours. 'Do you know Tahiti?' I asked. 'Very well,' he answered, as abruptly as before. 'I commute regularly between New York and the Austral Islands. I'm writing a book comparing the Australs with Manhattan.' I was thinking he was going to be interesting, when he said aggressively: 'You're English, aren't you? ... well, did you notice the anti-English sentiment that is sweeping America?' I took the hint and left him. I climbed the ladder to the upper deck. It was deserted save for a couple in deck-chairs; the man in red-striped pyjamas, the woman in a night-dress and a pink dressing-gown. I strolled by them, repeating: 'Hot, isn't it?' They agreed. They were as distressed as I was with the night. They were in the second class and had started at Marseilles; the woman, fair-haired and slim, sharing a cabin with five Frenchwomen, and her husband, a cabin with five men. The food was shocking, twenty people had been treated for food poisoning. They had a house near Bedford where they took PGs in the summer, spending the winter abroad. 'Have you got a card?' asked the wife; and when I said I didn't carry them about at that hour of the night, she brought out hers: Mrs John Tilcote. 'I have a pencil and paper here,' she said. 'Do let us have your name and where we can get hold of you. It would be such fun if you could visit us next summer.' It was odd to meet such county formality on a tropical night.

The hours dragged through. Dawn silhouetted the Cordillera Mountains in jagged blackness. The coaling cranes ceased their clatter. Six o'clock came. *Matelots* stood by the ropes lashed to the quay. Orders rang out. Passengers in dressing-gowns hung over the rails. In five minutes we'd be off. I went below to get my camera, feet first down the ladder. As I reached the bottom, I heard: 'Heh!' whispered urgently in a hiss. I couldn't see where it came from. The room was dark like a cellar. 'Heh . . . you!' I looked through the iron railings into the hold. The sacks and the rope were still in the middle, so was the car at the side. Nobody seemed to be there. 'For God's sake get us some water!' Still a whisper, but I saw now where it came from. It was the young man of the warehouse, his head peering out of the side window of the car. 'We're being cooked alive . . . but we're aboard!' I dipped a glass in a bucket of water that was standing on the table and took it over to him, handing it through the railings.

2

They were discovered, about two hours later, by an Arab boy. They were taken before the captain who, with a kindness which he must have afterwards regretted, allowed them to stay. I certainly had plenty of time to regret it. The young man typified the popular conception of American youth; rowdy, forceful, insensitive, vulgar. I called him Young America. He revelled in practical jokes. One morning, for instance, he woke me up by setting fire to my hair accompanied by his usual shouts of 'Get up . . . get up!' and the slapping of my bottom. He had a never-ending supply of bawdy jokes, and for every piece of food we ate or anything we drank he had a filthy equivalent. Ken and Jo would have been quiet without him, but urged on by his example they were as rowdy as he was. They strutted shirtless about the decks, slapping people on the back and then wondering why they didn't laugh. America and everything in it was, of course, God's own, and an Englishman, in their opinion, had to live there for awhile if he was to become a normal being. 'Look at you,' Ken said flatteringly one day, 'you're as different to the average Englishman as a polo pony from a mule.' Though I was 'different,' I still had a bad time of it. They lost no opportunity at nagging at everything English; and they found a ready ally in Doc. He'd been a dentist, though it wasn't till he was forty that he had qualified to be one; previous to that he'd worked in a telephone company. His first practice was one previously owned by a man very like himself. 'In fact,' he said, 'I chose it because of this, so that most of my patients never would notice the difference.' After a while he decided he wasn't making enough money, so he overlooked the traditions of his profession and began advertising. He organized his skill on a mass production basis, specializing in extractions and false teeth, and ordering the teeth by the hundred from a factory. In his surgery he had three chairs and two nurses. 'Each chair always had a patient,' he explained, 'and after dealing with one chair I would move to the next. The nurse would meanwhile amuse the patient I'd just left until I was ready to return.' In ten years he worked up a practice of 10,000 patients, and then, just as suddenly as he became a dentist, he stopped being one. According to his story, as a sort of retribution for his unethical ways, he gave his practice away to an orthodox dentist who had been one of his rivals. And having settled his affairs he had set out for Tahiti where he planned to spend the rest of his life. He had little to say in favour of England. 'I hate all Englishmen for the way they fed us during the war,' he said; 'when we reached Liverpool they appeared to resent us ... we who had come to save them!' Another time he jeered at England for her respect for tradition. 'That's why you're a decaying nation ... that silly respect for tradition,' he argued. 'What's the use of England as a nation? Why not give it up to the European wolves and move yourselves to Canada? You stick to it for the sake of a lot of silly old monuments and historical ghosts.' I answered: 'Hell only knows what you Americans will do when you've got a thousand years of tradition to respect. You've only a hundred and fifty as yet, but already you respect with public holidays – Lincoln's Birthday, Washington's Birthday, Decoration Day, Independence Day and Thanksgiving Day.'

A motley crowd was aboard. Most were French officials and their families on their way to New Caledonia; and there was a score or more of Jewish refugees going to Australia. Among the travellers to Tahiti was a barman of a Blackpool hotel who had saved £100 to spend a year in the South Seas. Another was an assistant in the dark-room of a photographer's. 'I realized one day,' he explained, 'that war might be upon us before I'd started to live ... so I chucked my job to look for adventure.' In the steerage we had a half-dozen *poilus* and two sailors; and there was a giant of a Swede who spent the days sitting on the bows, staring out to sea, talking to no one. One day I learnt from him that he was a retired postman and, on his pension, he travelled the world. On the sea he went steerage and found it very comfortable; and on land he usually walked. It cost him, he said, about £6 a week. Steerage would have been all right if my companions had been quieter. Breakfast was at seven, lunch at ten-thirty, dinner at five-thirty. Each of

us had the same tin plate for all meals; and the food was
the kind one would only eat if one was really hungry.
There was no bath, and the lavatory, as the drains were
blocked, was an inch deep in wet. I couldn't face it; and on
the first evening I decided to sneak to the one in the First
Class. I waited till eleven, then tiptoed down the passage.
I'd reached the door when from behind I heard: '*Qu'est-ce
que vous faites?*' I swung round. There, hastening down the
passage, was a steward, hawk-faced and thin-lipped, in a
white cotton shirt like a Russian's. '*Allez* ...' he cried
angrily, '*allez* ...' Feeling like a little boy caught in a
larder, I let go the handle and ran away.

The day we crossed the Equator it was so cold that the
King Neptune ceremony had to be postponed. When it did
take place, three days later, it was gloriously hot and
around us was a vast circle of still blue ocean. Soft clouds
were poised in the sky and flying fish skimmed the water
like flat pebbles thrown on a pond. No sooner had the
ceremony begun than a band of people, headed by the
Americans, pounced on the King, Queen, and their
courtiers, and speedily broke up the Court. One after
another the courtiers were hurled into the swimming-pool.
Then Young America picked up Queen Neptune (Mrs
Tilcote) and dumped her in it, too. Next he turned to the
King, a large Frenchman in the First Class, and with
amazing ease lifted him from his throne and began to
stagger towards the pool. Suddenly he slipped ... down he
came with the Frenchman beneath him. There were yells
and screams. Water splashed everywhere. A whistle blew.
An English voice yelled: 'Who licked Napoleon?' – and
then, amid the turmoil, it was found that King Neptune
had broken his ankle.

The steerage was banished to the poop, Young America
was summoned before the Captain, and we were further

punished by being forbidden to attend the dance that was being held that night. To make up for this, as the first and second classes shuffled to the music of a gramophone, the Americans began to cheer and hoot. They gave me a rocket cheer and a train cheer and other strange cheers that are products of the baseball crowds. Then Sid and Tom, two young scientists from Chicago University, got us together and read a murder story they'd written. I was the victim and the story told how the murders were discovered. It was proved that Ken had strangled me with a lady's garter, Doc had burnt my throat away with acid, Jo had stabbed me in the heart, Young America had bashed my head in and someone else had shot me. The story doesn't sound very complimentary to me, but apparently it was. Doc said afterwards: 'Great compliment to you that they should base their story on you.' And when the evening was over, I made a speech in which I said: 'I have a great love for you all, it lies deep in my heart. And it will be with great reluctance that when we arrive at Papeéte, I'll run down the gang plank, seize the first taxi I can find and tell the driver to take me anywhere where I can be certain to be away from you!'

Later, I remember, I went to the bows and stood by the look-out man, and listened to the lazy splash of the waves and marvelled at the Southern Cross. That afternoon I'd been lying there, when between the turquoise blue of the sea and the clouds of cotton wool in the sky, I'd seen, an inch above the horizon, my first South Sea island. Within an hour we'd passed several, flat with coconut trees silhouetted against the sky; they were the fringe of the Tuamotus, and my heart quickened, touched by the expectancy of romance.

3

On the morning of 5 December, I awoke when it was still dark. I'd had but one hour's sleep, for, until long past midnight, the Americans had been more rowdy than ever before. It was the last night aboard and it was their way of telling the world they were happy about it. But I was eager to be fresh to meet the day, and to get away from them, I lugged my mattress up on deck and lay down there. I found I needed a pillow so I went down again into the messroom to fetch one. As I came down the ladder, they saw me coming and gave me a cheer. Then with Young America leading, they dived at me, yelling: 'Let's take off his pyjamas and shove him up naked!'

I was in no mood for college humour but I thought it wiser to laugh with them and hope they wouldn't carry out their threat. When, however, they succeeded in taking them off, and started to push me up the ladder, all my patience of the past fortnight drained from me like water from sand. I've never been a boxer nor a gymnast, but that night I was empowered with the strength of a lunatic. I hit out more wildly than I've ever done before. I slithered myself free from Young America who was holding my arms, kicked him so hard that he crashed against the port-hole twenty yards away, plunged with my left hand repeatedly at Ken, lunged out with my feet at the most vulnerable parts of Jo, and contacted repeatedly with a rabbit punch on Claude, Young America's elderly friend. In five minutes they were at the four corners of the room and the Blackpool barman, who'd been watching, shouted: 'Bravo England . . . revenge for the 4th of July!'

As I sought the torn remnants of my pyjamas, I heard Young America whine: 'Say, we were only having fun . . . damned unsporting of him to hit out like that . . . bloody little Englishman!' I went back on deck, soon to be followed by the others with their mattresses. For a while they were quiet, and then they began a pillow fight which speedily developed into a general brawl. They threw a mattress on to me and jumped on it; and for all they cared, I might have been smothered or had my neck broken. They jumped up and down, up and down, with a motion which Mrs Tilcote described afterwards as being like 'oarsmen in a boat'.

When they'd tired of this game, I lay quite still, bruised and stiff, swearing I would never talk to them again as long as I lived; and feeling as if I'd been transported back across the years to the days of school 'rags'. I'd been like that for twenty minutes when I heard one of them murmur: 'Let's throw Tangye's mattress into the sea!' This was the end. I wasn't going to stick any more of it; and solely to safeguard for myself a peaceful night, I swallowed my anger and said to Ken: 'Let's shake hands, we've been pals too long for our journey to end like this.' He grinned broadly: 'Bravo,' he said, 'that's mighty fine of you, Derek. I knew you would do this. Let's shake hands!' And so, with this manifestation of the old school tie spirit, the matter was ended.

But, as I said, it was still dark when I woke up. I had a feeling of impending excitement, like the first morning of the holidays during schooldays, a kind of tightness in my head. And, as I rubbed my eyes, I suddenly saw, as if only a few yards away, a huge blackness, even blacker than the night. Slowly we were passing it, and each second more of this blackness was coming into view. I left my mattress quickly, and still feeling the cuts and bruises of a few hours before, I hurried to the messroom to collect my things. Then up I went again and ran along to the bows where only the Swede was sitting, motionless as usual. The darkness had turned into grey, and within a few minutes as I stood there, the grey into yellow, and then on the eastern horizon I saw the golden rays of the coming sun.

We were moving at half speed, cutting the water as we would have done a river with no current; or as if we were sailing through a giant mill-pond. Just a cool swish. Each minute the sun was stealing closer to the horizon, and the sky, and the clouds, and the ripples on the water were softening into blues and pinks and mauves and yellows. And the land which was Tahiti was transforming from its blackness into a forest of foliage; each second I saw more of her mysterious valleys, more of her white-streaked waterfalls, more of her jagged mountain tops. I stood there in the bows after all the years of waiting for that moment, secure in the knowledge that she was not failing me, that I was experiencing an exultation of the soul that I would cherish all my life. And as I was thinking this, two things happened. First the sun peeped above the horizon and shot the sky into blazing gold; and then, as I was marvelling, a beautiful scent brushed the air, the scent of the hibiscus and the *tiare tahiti* and the luxuriant jungle of the island. I was moved as I have never been moved before. I wanted to shout and to cry and to laugh. Every emotion crowded inside me and yet struggled at the same time to escape. I stood there murmuring incoherently like a madman.

And, when the intensity of the mood had passed, I found a canoe with a white sail stilled in the water close to us, a native girdled by a red and orange *pareu* sitting motionless in the stern; then further away I saw the surf pounding on the coral, and through the haze to starboard the weird outline of Moorea. Here at last was the land of Gauguin and Rupert Brooke and Stevenson; and here within my sight were the things they loved; and here, too, was the gentleness and tranquillity that filled the dreams of those across the oceans in another world.

Soon we'd reached an opening in the reef, perhaps half a mile in width. I dared not think that we were at our journey's end, because, though I stared through my glasses, I saw only a few shacks, a church steeple, a curling blue smoke, and hazily through the morning mist, two or three masts. But our ship began to turn, edging her way through the pass, and I knew then we were there; that these few shacks, this church steeple, this curling blue smoke, these two or three masts, were Papeéte.

Chapter Seven

TAHITI MERRY-GO-ROUND

I CAME AS AN impatient tourist, fancying the soul of the South Seas would be revealed by a few days in Papeéte and a sight-seeing drive round the island; like the man who fancies the soul of great music is revealed at the first hearing. I was tied to a timetable, I had boats to catch and places still to see. I could not cast off, as I would a coat, the spirit that ruled my world, the world 'of harshness and hideous sights, and ugly people and civilization, and corruption, and bloodiness, and all evil'. I supposed, in my haste, that I merely had to put my foot to the soil of Tahiti for my South Sea dream to come true; that there around me would be gentleness and happiness and laughter; that I, too, would be poised in a frame of mind that denied the existence of time and fear and greed. And so, when instead I found the scars and blisters of white man's sins, I said angrily that Tahiti was no better than the Isle of Man, and booked my passage onward; poor fool, thinking beauty lies on the surface for all to see. For what I found was the din of dance-halls, and women who had their price, and shocking hangovers, and tin-roofed buildings, and raucous tourists. A South Sea island playing the part of a holiday town. Gossip and unrest. Motor-cars on dusty roads, and mosquitoes endlessly biting, and black sand, and smug bungalows.

Such was the beginning, and I will tell of it – and then,

too, I will tell of the enchantment that was mine when I
grew wise.

Pierre drove me to the hotel. Fat, jovial Pierre, who in the
days to come never tired of telling me in a mixture of
French, Tahitian and English, of bedworthy *jeunes filles*
who awaited my bidding. I can see him now, on that first
evening, hailing me in the market-place as dusk was falling,
his cap aslant on the back of his head, the beaming smile
on his round brown face. *'Monsieur,'* he said, *'venez ici à huit
heures. J'ai trouvé pour vous une jeunne fille de seize ans . . . très,
très dounce!'* and he made a gesture with his hand of the
kind of figure I was to expect.

I wasn't there. I was standing on the quay with the little
American, dark like a Greek, who was writing the book
comparing Manhattan Island and the Australs. Since his
first abrupt meeting with me, his manner had softened, and
in the days across the Pacific he had filled many hours with
his stories of the South Seas. The island where he lived
was Rurutu, and he had told me of the ease and carelessness
of his living; and how the simplicity of the beauty, both of
the island and of the people who inhabited it, stirred his
soul, so that, though he was not a religious man, he felt he
was living in a spiritual world close to God. I had envied
his freedom and now I was standing with him, watching
his luggage being taken aboard the battered two-masted
schooner in front of us. But there was no joy about the
parting. Things had changed since last he'd been in the
islands. Zealous officials, anxious to preserve the native
culture from the increasing influx of Europeans, had
banned Rurutu to white folk. It had been decreed that this
far-away island should remain a paradise beyond the reach
of those who would try to spoil her; and so the little
American had to suffer for the sins of others. Luckily for

him he knew the Governor and, with special permission, he was going to stay in Rurutu for three months; but even this didn't ease his disappointment. He spoke no words, in those few minutes before he sailed, for fear he might cry like a child. I watched him clamber aboard, and as the schooner moved away, he stood in the bows, waving his hand slowly in farewell; and because the moon was full, I could see him, and the dozen natives that made up the rest of the passengers, for quite a time as the engine chugged across the lagoon past Pomare's islet to the pass. The air was soft and warm, the scent of *tiare tahiti* touched me as a girl passed with a white garland round her hair, the water lapped against the stones of the quay, and behind me, from the bars, I heard the twanging of dance music. I turned and made my way towards it.

2

Papeéte is one street and a square. There are other streets rambling towards the mountains and along the lagoon, but it is in one street that the world parades and shops and drinks, and it is in the square that it meets at dawn to gossip and to buy the food and produce for the day. They call it a town, but to my idea it is a village. Not a lovely village. White men have done their best to poison it with corrugated iron roofs and misshapen houses. Chinamen, with their money from vanilla and copra plantations, have erected monstrous edifices with garish sheets of tin. And the natives, bowed down by this weight of ugliness, have given up the struggle; you see none of their native houses. And yet there is something stirring about Papeéte. You cannot dismiss it as ugly, as you can Margate or Salford. I was wrong to say 'it.' I should have said 'her' – she is alive; though modernity does its best to throttle her,

Papeéte does not yield without a struggle. Let Robert Keable describe her, Keable the strange Church of England parson, who came to Tahiti to live and write and die there. The author of *Simon Called Peter*, and *Tahiti, Isle of Dreams*. 'She clusters on a bay at the foot of the hills with a wonderful sheet of lagoon before her,' he wrote 'and she never ceases trying to subdue those who would prostitute her. She flings creepers scarlet and purple and gold over Oregon pine and corrugated iron, and she has to do it herself for hardly a soul tries to help her. Be you so kind as but to drop a seed and forget it, she makes of it a flower. Do you build a fence, she transforms it into a hedge. And day and night no power that men have yet discovered can tame or eliminate her sunrises and sunsets.'

She is the gateway of escape. So many has she welcomed who have fled from the madness of another world. Some like me who came in a steamer, and others, like those of the little yachts tied to the quay, who had braved the Pacific to put paid to a dream. Some who were famous like Stevenson and Rupert Brooke and some who were unknown like the schoolmaster from Edmonton and the postmistress from Vancouver. Through the years, Papeéte has watched us come and go, taking and cherishing from each one a fragment of his soul.

The steamer with the mails from the mad world was in, so it was carnival night. From far-off districts they'd come to celebrate this link with the *popaas'* kingdom. They crowded the bars and dance floors, shuffling not to their own rhythms and melodies, but to odd versions of 'Button up your Overcoat', 'I can't help loving you Baby', and others of that vintage, twanged out by guitars and plodding drums and musicless saxophones. Because for fourteen days I'd heard no night-club noise and seen few women, I was in no mood to recoil from it. I watched the men, dark

like Mexicans, in white shirts and trousers with garlands of
tiare tahiti askew on their heads, spilling their drinks and
flopping over the tables; I watched the girls, their garlands
of *tiare tahiti* also askew on their heads, swaying up to me
with slightly bloodshot eyes. The scene was so bewilder-
ingly novel, so utterly different from whatever I'd known
before, that it didn't prick my consciousness that it was
revolting. I sat on a stool at the bar feeling the same
measure of power as a sultan in his harem. These girls,
drunk or otherwise, slim-legged or fat-bottomed are, I
thought, awaiting my bidding. The idea was pleasing.
Some were, of course, gross and ugly, but there were many
others who were young and copper-coloured with bright
shirts, and shorts cut to their thighs, and features that were
fine with the wistful, far-away look of the Polynesian. I sat
there, not wishing to make my acquaintance with any one
of them, finding pleasure by postponing pleasure, and
feeling in the meantime superbly free. I was musing thus
when Ed came in.

'What a mess,' he grunted as he sat beside me. Ed had
been on the boat and was getting married when his South
Sea trip was over; he was the sort of man who would be
true to the girl he left behind and I couldn't expect that he
would feel as I did.

'Look at Jo and Ken over there,' he pointed to a table in
the corner. They were entertaining two women each, and
Ken was standing unsteadily on a chair; 'Drunken louts –
and it's folk like they who have brought the natives down
to this.' His arm swept the scene, his eyes scowling. Ed
was telling an old story, the story of the white man who in
his roaming of the seas was blind in his belief that he could
do no wrong, bringing with him a doctrine to rack the
mind and disease to rack the body. I have no time to tell
the tale of the Tahitian race. How proud and pure that

once they were, with a philosophy of truth and beauty so crystal clear compared with the misguided men with prayer books in their hands who sowed the seeds of doubt and fear. For that sad story of long ago read Cecil Lewis's *The Trumpet is Mine*, most tender of Tahiti books; and marvel with him how, despite the ravages of white man's hypocrisy and pests, there lingers in the air something 'that is as potent and elusive as a dream that leaves you sad at waking. Perhaps it comes from the fulfilment of a hope deep in the human heart, the finding of a way of life the world has lost, the promise that if men so willed they might so live again.' I told Ed this, but he shrugged his shoulders angrily. He was a dreamer and his illusions were shattered. 'They're sky-high with liquor and that's that. We whites are to be blamed but if they'd had any guts they'd have beaten us at our own game.' We said no more. It was not the place nor were we in the mood to discuss the poetry of living. I was too steeped in my South Sea dream for my illusions to be disturbed by drunken natives. I longed for my wakening on the morrow so that my eyes could see and I could feel my dream being realized. I left Ed at the bar and wandered home, drunk, not with wine and spirits, but with the notion that I hung suspended on the brink of something more wonderful than I'd ever known in life.

3

I awoke with the sun blinking through a chink in the curtain on my face. I yawned and stretched out my arms. I'd gone to bed alone the night before; but my hands touched something. I jumped up with a start and looked beside me. There on the other side of the double bed lay a girl, sixteen years old perhaps, like the slim copper-coloured

ones of the dance hall. Heaven knows what kind of a look
I had on my face. She laughed, a childish innocent affair as
if she'd been amused at the antics of a puppy. Then she lay
silent, provokingly unaware of her firm young breasts and
her neat shoulders and her smooth bare skin.

'*Bonjour, mademoiselle,*' I said. Then I added. 'But how the
devil did you get here?'

Her explanation was difficult to understand – a rush of
words, half of which were Tahitian and half were French. I
gathered, however, she didn't think she'd done anything
out of the ordinary. She'd seen me at the dance-hall and
followed me out when I left. She watched me go into the
hotel and then she went to see the manager. It was all so
simple. He was as perturbed as she was that I was without
company and he showed her my room. '*Tu étais seul,*' she
said with a smile, '*et alors je viens!*' She followed her story
with a request for breakfast and a little sheepishly I went
downstairs. Doubtfully I said to the clerk: 'I've got a girl
upstairs . . . charge an extra person for the room.' The
man, clean shaven and young who spoke perfect English,
grinned: 'Oh no, *monsieur*, we don't do that. We do not
mind our customers having visitors at night so long as
they do not sing and be drunk.' I thanked him for the
information and went back upstairs to Rai as she'd told me
she was called. She'd put on skimpy white shorts and a
bright blue shirt; she wore no shoes or sandals. 'You must
walk down the street with me,' she said firmly, after she'd
had her coffee and *croissants*. This, I supposed, was the
price of her visit. She must show off her capture. I visioned
what the street might be like, all my friends being paraded
up and down like peacocks on strings. I shook my head;
and after a little argument and forty francs had been
exchanged and I'd promised to meet her at the Col Bleu at
six, it was decided Rai should go alone. With a degree of

relief I bade her goodbye, and then watched her from my verandah as she strolled, lithe as a child, towards the marketplace.

Later, at the Bourgainville, my friends had other tales to tell. Jo and Ken were as excited as schoolboys let loose in a chocolate shop. They'd got blind drunk, taken three girls by taxi to a moonlit shore and played there while the coconut trees whispered and the water lapped the sand. 'Say,' said one, 'this place sure is the goods . . . but oh Christ, I've got a hangover!' The Blackpool barman was there, too, and his tale was that he'd been lucky enough to hitch up with the telephone girl at the hospital. 'Darned lucky,' he said, 'because she's promised to tell me of all the girls who've got VD.'

Here in the Bourgainville was the Society of the island. They'd come in by cars from Paea and Puna-auia to sip their apéritifs and to gossip. White women were few. The men were English and American, dressed in the manner of Miami and Cannes. They talked loudly of nocturnal adventures while their native girls sat silent and bored beside them. These men had the air of assurance and sophistication in matters of small value that I've never found pleasant. The type that clique around smart parties and Ritzie bars and banter patronizingly with the barman. And to a stranger they pay no attention unless it be a freak produced by one of them. I never bargained to meet their kind in Papeéte. But here they were, escaping from one holiday to another, for, as I found out later, few of them had ever done a stroke of work. One, I remember, was rocking his party into peals of laughter by the simple method of coaxing a dog to sniff the bait of biscuit in his hand, only to reward it each time with a glass of water in its face instead.

The morning left me with a nasty taste in my mouth. I

had the sense to realize that I'd better move out of Papeéte or otherwise I'd be up to no good. I foresaw myself drinking rum punches at twopence a time and being steeped every morning with remorse and a hangover. And, knowing that on occasions I am weakly partial to such a futile, senseless existence, it wouldn't have been long before I'd be wasting my time like the Bourgainville clique. Besides, even though everything was ridiculously cheap, I still hadn't the money to live such a life. I couldn't indulge in luxuries. I had to count every penny I spent. Since leaving Waterloo Station, five and a half months before, I'd paid out £306. That meant I had (including gifts and earnings), £174 and half the world still to see. I decided to try therefore to keep to within £3 a week, and, as the franc was 180 to the £1, I had a good chance of succeeding. The trouble was that I had a certain amount of capital expenditure to make. For instance, it was essential to have a bicycle. Transport in the island consists of taxis and weird trucks that career at irregular times into the distant districts. Most people depend therefore on bicycles to get about on, and so off I went to a Chinaman and bought one for £2 10s. Then, at the police station I found that if I stayed more than two months I'd have to pay a tax of £3. There, too, I was cross-examined, along with other new arrivals, and given a pass-book with the instructions that whenever I moved from island to island I had to notify the police. An irritating restriction until I learnt that no one ever took any notice of it. I had other odds and ends to buy, like a pandanus hat and sandals, and a tropical suit, and a fountain pen, and books; so that all told I spent around £7. Quite definitely I had to find a home in the districts where I could live on bananas and fish and coconuts. The quickest way to do this was to hire a taxi to take me round the island. Ed went shares with the taxi and off we started on the road of bumps and holes with Pierre as our driver.

It was unfortunate that soon after setting out it began to rain. It rained so heavily and fiercely that it blurred our abilities to imagine what loveliness we were passing had the sun been shining. What we saw was, on the one hand coconut leaves and undergrowth the colour of a green tired by many months of a tropical sun, and on the other hand, bays of flat grey water like the Thames estuary on a dull afternoon in February. We might have forgotten the weather if, as the road wound beside the shore, the rain had been falling on beaches of white sand. We could have closed our eyes and pictured the natives and ourselves, basking in the sunshine and lazily swimming in the lagoons. But we couldn't do this because the sand was *black*. Black, like Cornish rock, looking from afar like shores of black mud; bleak, drab, and depressing. Our disappointment is hard to describe. We felt like a man who owned the Derby favourite only to have it beaten by a neck at the finish. We'd come so far, we'd built so many hopes only for them to come tumbling to the ground, as we trundled over the muddy, but bumpy road. The scene was desolate and dreary, and the rain so fierce that it began to leak through the hood; fat, chilly drops wetting our clothes. And it was these that changed our feelings from disappointment to anger. Poor Pierre, we gave him a bad time of it. We let loose on him in a silly facetious way all what we thought about his beloved island, mocking the men who had woven dreams around it, and dismissing the tales of blue lagoons and sunbaked beaches as inventions of foolish liars. Pierre pathetically answered us with murmurs of: '*Attendez pour le soleil, messieurs.*' And then he would halt his taxi and disappear into a forlorn hut, because, after all, I had hired him to find me a dwelling-place far from the noise of Papeéte. He would return with a smile on his face and the information that the native would put me up if I cared. He was puzzled and hurt when I scorned his efforts. I would go nowhere were there was black sand. *'Mais, monsieur,'* he would say, *'le sable noir est très douce.'*

To Tiarei, Mataorio and round by Taravao to Papeari, we went. None of it was beautiful to our eyes, none of it tempted me to stay. Not even at Papeari where old Mauu was whom Cedric Belfrage told me to see and at whose hostelry Rupert Brooke lived, not even when he waddled out to greet us was I pleased. But in any case he had no room; so on we went to Paea and Punaavia. Here were the districts where the white folk lived. For mile upon mile a single line of neat bungalows lay between the beach and road. They were beautifully situated if one judged it from English south coast standards. Nothing separated them from the water save for the beach – and this was black. I don't think Ed felt so definite about this sand as I did; anyhow, he seemed quite ready to take one of these bungalows if he found one that he liked. We stopped, therefore, many times so that he could investigate the insides of those to let. They were good value. They were raised on piles above the ground so that you could crawl underneath; and the windows were large and glassless. There was a lavatory and shower-bath and a kitchen and a double bed; and for all this you only had to pay ten shillings a week. It would have been lovely if it had been down Southsea way, but they were not what I wanted in the South Seas. I had no wish to hear my neighbour's gramophone, nor to have him dropping in continuously for a drink. Ed, on the other hand, was quite pleased, especially when he discovered a bungalow with a patch of white sand as its beach. This was near Rivenac's, the most famous hostelry in the South Seas. For three guineas a week you can have a native bungalow set apart by itself and European food in the main bungalow as well. Pierre showed it to me proudly,

with a smile, as if to say: 'Anyhow, now you can't grumble.'
But I could. The cleanliness and efficiency of the place
smacked like the journey's end of a Cook's tour. The
visitors, what I saw of them, were prim, well-dressed
travellers, the kind that never have the nerve to go anywhere save the most English and American hotels. If
this was the *pièce de résistance* of Pierre's drive, I didn't
think much of it. Nor could I be bothered to look any
more. The rain was pelting down; the weather was more
suited for bars and girls. And so Ed and I told Pierre to
drive to Papeéte. Sorrowful he was, poor Pierre; and
when we offered him a tip, he shook his head sadly: 'You
were not satisfied with our island,' and, as he said that, he
kept his eyes away from us as if our insults had shamed
him.

4

In the next three days I did all those things I swore I
wouldn't do. Every morning I had a hangover; and I even
booked my passage to Auckland by the boat leaving in a
fortnight's time. I was disillusioned, dejected and angry. I
was angry because I'd been deceived all these years by a
dream. Not only had I discovered that the scenery was
bare, like opera without music, but also that the romantic,
copper-coloured women were like the ladies of Piccadilly,
save they dealt in shillings instead of pounds. '*Je ne dors avec
toi que si tu me donnes une robe.*' The 'robe' usually cost five
bob at a Chinese store. Such a life I couldn't stick so I took
the boat to Moorea.

Now Moorea is an island that you can see eight miles
away from Papeéte, lying always shrouded in mist with her
mountain-tops hiding in the clouds. I will quote from
Robert Keable about her:

Shimmering in the heat of the sun lies Moorea, the
Moorea which one wise man of my acquaintance refused
ever to visit, for he said to tread her veritable shore
would be to dispel the magic of a dream. He was right,
for Moorea is one of the most perfect of all the South
Sea Islands. I am myself jealous for the honour of
Tahiti, which, I hold, has to offer all of Moorea and
more – jealous, for so many tourists scarce get beyond
Papeéte, but take the schooner to Moorea, find easy
provision of all island delights, and say that Tahiti
cannot equal them. But the proper function of Moorea is
doubtless that of providing a lovely view for Tahiti, and
all along the western coast you get a glimpse of her
again and again, fantastic and mirage-like in the sunlight,
unearthly in the radiance of the moon, dark, aloof and a
mystery as the sun dies behind her.

It is a horrible journey in the schooner, for she is really
nothing bigger than a launch; and it's jammed tight with
women, babies, cows, pigs, chicken, white men and tourists. And because of the nature of the current, the crossing
is invariably so rough that if you succeed in reaching the
other side without being sick, you can rest assured you'll
never be seasick in your life. I wasn't sick myself, but for
three-quarters of the journey I shut my eyes and prayed,
grey with fear that at any moment we might turn turtle as
a sister launch had done but a few weeks before. But when
at last we sailed into smooth water I felt as Robert Keable
would have expected me to feel after spending a few days
in Papeéte. I was a bum tourist; and here around me was
what I didn't find in Tahiti; the deep blue lagoon of
Cook's Bay, the white sand and the coconut trees, all set
against a background of dense vegetation and jagged mountain peaks. It was a glorious heart-warming sight for me,

and when the launch stopped its engines near into shore in Cook's Bay, and I was told that, if I jumped overboard and waded to three small bungalows lying hidden among the coconut trees, I might find myself a bed, all my first feelings of the South Seas rushed back at me and I was as excited as a child.

The man who directed me and who also accompanied me as I waded knee-deep in the lagoon, was Chateauloup, a French painter. He was grey-haired and friendly, with a quiet polished charm; he had come, so I learnt, to the South Seas seven years before, having left his wife and most of his money in the smart places of Paris. He introduced me to Madame Hildebrand, the little Swiss woman who ran the place. She had but two rooms to let and I had one and the Frenchman the other. It was what I'd longed for; the lagoon, turquoise and still, like glass, the sand soft and white, the rustling coconut trees, some tall and some short like shrubs, and then, walling us in, the silhouette of the mountains cutting into the sky. Through that first afternoon I idled in the water and then wandered in my *pareu* along the beach, disturbing the land crabs into hopping into their holes; and sometimes I stopped – far away in many cities people scrambled in the din of their daily struggle, round and round they went spinning dizzily like a top, some piling up money, some fighting for bread, day in day out, year after year. But here was I hushed in the silence of peace and of untamed beauty.

For two days I was happy; lazily, contentedly happy. This was the kind of life I'd been looking for. I awoke at dawn and plunged into the lagoon and swam slowly into its stillness, while the coming sun bathed the water and the coconut trees and the luxuriant vegetation in a golden yellow. And then, most wonderful of all, was the silence, as if I dared to be where no human being had ever been before; and, as I turned and lay on my back, paddling with my hands to keep afloat and staring up to the misty sky, I pretended I had come to the sacred places of the gods and they were watching me, laughing at the thoughts of the tiny being from the mad world. Blue smoke curled from the midst of the coconut trees at various points of the shore; and over at Chez Hildebrand's a baby son of the house sprawled naked on the sand; and at the opening of the bay, where the lagoon went out to meet the reef, a native in his canoe was paddling with firm strokes towards me.

There came breakfast of coffee and *croissants*, and afterwards, for awhile, I watched Chateauloup trying to put the glories of the bay on canvas. 'I am not much good,' he said, 'I am an amateur. But it gives me a purpose in life . . .' And leaving him I found, further along the shore, two fishermen, diving goggles fixed, ready with their *patias* to swim out into the lagoon. They were at great pains to tell me what they were going to do, not one word of which I understood. But I watched them as they swam, heads submerged for as long as two minutes, and with their *patias* by some uncanny means held poised ready to strike at a fish. Both got one quickly and they held up their *patias*, laughing with joy, the fish squirming on the spikes.

So the day went through, idle in the sunshine, blissfully in peace, until the evening came and Chateauloup and I, sipping our *Pernods*, listened to the natives strumming a guitar and singing in weird musical voices. There was one song I was to hear many times, one they loved above all to dance to, with a wild haunting melody:

> 'Puaa horo te papio
> Ei faahoro ite vahine.
> Ei aha te vahine ruau
> Mea oromoto te araimu.'

'It's about a horse on a merry-go-round,' explained Chateauloup, 'and of the lovers who rode him.' How lovely it was! We sat there clapping our hands to the beats, faster and faster, cheering and laughing, and when it was over we got Madame Hildebrand to fill the players' glasses with red wine, and childishly happy they drank our health: '*Manuia*' – 'Good luck,' they cried. Outside the moon was full and Cook's Bay an ethereal silver. Every so often a soft breeze brushed the coconut leaves and rippled the water. It was called the *hupi*, so Chateauloup told me, the night wind that blows from the mountains. A dream had come true. Here I would stay until I sailed for New Zealand and, if need be, I would cancel my passage and go by the next boat or perhaps the next. I would cut my ties with the mad world. Hell to the rest of the journey! This was where lived my happiness.

5

It was in that spirit I awoke next morning. A lovely morning, the temperature of a high summer day in England; not the damp heat of the tropics, but dry and lazily warm. Chateauloup went off to paint and I basked in the sun, diving into the lagoon whenever I had the inclination. I was lying thus contentedly when around twelve o'clock I was awoken out of a doze by a screaming 'Whoopee!' I jumped up like a startled rabbit. Chateauloup wasn't the kind of man to express his joy like that. I looked around and saw no one. An idea flashed through my head. It couldn't be that ... At that moment from out of the door of the main bungalow, hand outstretched, a grin on his face, and a: 'Say, is that so?' came Doc. Never will I forget it. My peace had, in a second, been destroyed with the same completeness as the bursting of a soap bubble. Behind him were Jo and Ken and a couple of ladies of Papeéte. I stared at them with loathing and disgust. I made no attempt to hide my feelings. In fact, I was downright rude. The memories of those dreadful days on the *Ville d'Amiens* rushed to my head. I let them have it. To Doc I said: 'You're the dullest little man I've ever met and I never want to see you again.' And to Jo and Ken I shouted: 'For Christ's sake get out of here! I come ten thousand miles to find this spot and of all the hellish things you come to spoil it.'

They enjoyed my outburst; and they proceeded to spoil my peace as thoroughly and efficiently as possible. By the time dusk fell they were so drunk that their ladies took advantage of their state to go a-wandering. One came and offered herself to me, but I declined. The other went to Chateauloup. When at last Jo and Ken began thinking of them again, they were nowhere to be found. Jo blamed the state of affairs on to me and he burst into my room, yelling: 'You're sleeping with my girl.' I wasn't, but I'm not so sure about Chateauloup, who had a twinkle in his eye when I told him the story. Both he and I decided to go. It was hopelessly impossible to adjust oneself to their horrible habits.

Chateauloup returned to Papeéte, while I got on my bicycle and set out to ride round the island.

Chapter Eight

FOLLOW THE ESCAPISTS

For the next month I wandered round Moorea and Tahiti, never settling down for more than a few days in any one place. Evidently I expected too much. Whatever lovely spot I found myself in, I quickly discovered some reason to crab it. Either the sand wasn't white enough or the lagoon not deep enough or the island road came too close to the shore. And there was always the problem of finding somewhere to stay; the owners of the *farés* which I liked the most wouldn't have me; and the hotels, well, they hadn't the atmosphere I desired.

There was one at Afareaitu, excellent of its kind, which was kept by a Swiss who a few years previously was manager of a big hotel at St Moritz. His name was known by the rich and famous; princes and film stars had been his friends; he himself was married to the daughter of the proprietor of the best-known hotel on the French Riviera. Yet all the while he was moving amongst this champagne and caviare he was dreaming of Tahiti. One day he divorced his wife and sailed for Tahiti. You should see him now. He has married the native schoolmistress of Afareaitu. He has a bar, behind which he sells the native beer to the fishermen. He has a mother-in-law dressed in a Mother Hubbard and an old straw hat, with bare brown feet. He wears sandals and a *pareu*. One of his closest friends is the local

Chief. But what is so incongruous is that, when you arrive, he greets you as if you'd arrived in his St Moritz hotel. He might have been Ferraro greeting me at the Mayfair, so suave, polite, and charming was he. And at dinner-time he hovered round the table as if I were paying 10s. for the meal instead of 1s.; European food, the best I'd had for months. I'd have thought he'd want to talk a lot as he didn't see many white people, but he was silent about himself. I asked whether he wouldn't one day tire of the natives (he looked only about forty) and want to return to the glitter of his old life. He gave me a gentle smile. 'I'll never cross the ocean again. I have found peace. Here will I die.' Something in the way he said it, the finality or perhaps it was so darned sincere, made me feel sad. Heaven knows why, because he required no pity. He was a man who had moulded the pattern of life to meet his desires; perhaps it wasn't my choice of existence, nor that of most people, but he had the courage to know that it was his; and he was happy.

He had a friend called Peter the Russian. Peter didn't share the same views of South Sea life; he believed there was nowhere in the world more Utopian than Russia. Not that he had been to Russia for thirty years; but the last twelve of these he had spent on a coconut plantation in Moorea, and he hadn't found them to his liking. One evening I was sitting with him in the small bar at Afareaitu; he had red bushy eyebrows, and blue eyes that looked straight at you as he talked. This is what he said:

'It's all a joke in this goddam country – nothing is serious. Natives work when they feel like it. When they've earned money they spend it – quick. How can anyone care for the women? They sleep with anyone because faithfulness isn't in the Tahitian vocabulary. They despise white men whether they're married to them or living with them.

They only marry for the money, which they'll hand out to their relatives. A Tahitian marries one day and cheats on her husband the next. What's the good of that? I've tried living with dozens of them, but they drove me crazy in three days. There was one I was going to marry. She had a shot at trying to make me think she was virtuous. For instance, she wouldn't let our bodies touch when we were dancing. Nor would she let me sleep with her till the wedding bells had rung. She was eighteen and pretty, and she fooled me until one morning three weeks before the marriage date. I was staying in her father's house – he was a Frenchman, her mother Tahitian – and to get to the bathroom I had to pass through her father's room. The mother had gone off to market, so I was surprised to see a woman's body in the father's bed. I looked again and had a bigger shock. It was my fiancée. Incest didn't seem to mean anything to her. When I gave her my mind, she pouted her lips and said: "So what?" How the hell can you live in a country where the morals are like that?'

Nor did he like his manner of living; he believed it would be much cheaper and pleasanter in Russia. This despite the fact that he told me you can buy an estate of several acres in the islands for as little as £100; and that you can build a house for £10! That is what his had cost him and he had a verandah and a large room, half dining-room, half bedroom; a kitchen in an out-house, also a shower and a lavatory. The walls were of bamboo and the roof thatched with coconut leaves, or *niaus* as the natives call them. Looking after copra was his principal occupation, though he kept three cows and a dozen chickens as a sideline. He described to me how every two months he collected the ripe coconuts that had fallen to the ground; then there followed a fortnight before they were ready to be taken to the Papeéte market. This was a fortnight of praying for no rain. The coconuts were cut in halves and left to dry. And when the process was completed, the price he got was £7 a ton; and he was lucky if he had a ton to sell. Peter thought the work too hard and the reward too small. When he sells his plantation, with the money he gets he's going to buy a ticket to Vladivostok.

2

It was when I'd left Afareaitu and was bicycling on my way to Haapiti that I met Gibbins. The track wound parallel to the shore through several small villages where the inhabitants gravely wished me *'Ia ora na!'* ('Good life to you') as I passed. Children stopped their games to stare at the strange *popaa*. Dogs ran barking at the wheels. Sometimes I'd meet, in some lonely glade, a broad-shouldered native, the colour of mahogany, splitting the coconuts that lay around him on the ground. He would stop his work, with dignity raise his pandanus-woven hat, and again I would hear the words of greeting: *'Ia ora na!'* Pigs abounded everywhere, they were not fat and waddling like their European cousins. They had legs as long as terriers and they ran as fast, hither and thither, as I approached. Land crabs skedaddled into their holes, ugly shells crackling their way under the dried coconut leaves. On my right the undergrowth climbed steeply towards the peaks that lay hidden in cloud. On my left the lagoon, cool and serene in the midday sun, dotted occasionally by the canoes of the fishermen, stretched its turquoise calm towards the reef where the waves rolled in a thin white line; and then in the distance there was the misty outline of the Presqu'Ile of Tahiti.

It was in such a place as this that Gibbins lived. I met him as he was manœuvring a cow through the gate of his plantation. And, since white men were few and far between, I got off my bicycle and introduced myself. The reception he gave me seemed to be a little chilly and, as at that moment the cow leapt back on to the track, the situation wasn't improved for me. I watched him whack it with a stick. Then: 'Get in, damn you!' He was an odd sight. He wore Chinese sandals and a red *pareu* wrapped round his middle like a towel, so that from the knee downwards, and from the waist upwards, he was bare; thin, bony legs like gnarled sticks, and a chest that was weedy and yellow like Ghandi's. Seeing him therefore from a distance in his large-brimmed pandanus hat, you would not expect him to have the fierce, peppery face of a *Punch* colonel. His moustache bristled white and furious with a curl like the Kaiser's. His eyes were an icy pale blue. His voice, despite his withered body, as loud as a sergeant-major's. As I followed him to his bungalow, his manner made me feel as if he'd caught me trespassing in the garden of his Camberley villa.

Once there he became friendlier and he asked me to have a drink. I expected him to produce a bottle of whisky and a syphon. Instead he disappeared indoors and returned with two coconuts. He didn't pour the milk into glasses, but, the tops being sliced off, he picked up one and sipped it straight from the shell. It did him good because, after lighting a cherry-root pipe, he began to talk; and as I listened, because of his tone of voice and his style of manner, it seemed we might have been in a London club sipping our port, the old Colonel airing his views on the world.

'Damme, sir,' he began, 'I don't want to be bothered with strangers. They come buzzing round with their news of another world I don't want to hear of. I don't ask them questions because I don't want to know anything about them. I live in a world where a man can do what he wants without pettifogging questions being asked; while you come from a world that is Mad! Yes sir, Mad! I lived in it for fifty years, fought in two wars, and dammit, sir, I got the M.C. at Passchendaele. There's not a capital in Europe I don't know better than I know the palm of my hand. I've lived in America, Mexico, the Argentine. Call me a man of the world . . . that's what I am. I belong to no nation, my brothers and sisters are French, German, Scandinavian, Chilean, they are the people of every country in the world. Some among them I hate, and some I call my friends, but never do I group them in generalization, saying: "I hate the Germans, I love the French, I hate the Russians." I look at the world in detachment, not coloured by flag-waving sentiments. And what do I see? I see in some parts they're burning wheat while a few hundred miles away they're starving. I see them throwing coffee into the sea while millions can't afford to buy it. I see great stretches of land loaded with gold and silver and coal and untold riches while the unemployed hang around the streets and their wives shiver in their rooms. I read of the proud boasts of Ministers of Labour: "The unemployed figures have dropped by fifty thousand. We have less unemployed than any other country." The people cheer. The Minister opens a bottle of champagne. But what of the fifty thousand? Their work aims not at constructing a better living either for themselves or anyone else . . . but for the destruction of what little they already have. For every weekly wage of £2 a man earns he has done his bit to blast to pieces a fellow-being, to shatter a home of another who might, if the world were sane, be his comrade and friend. Do you blame me, sir, from getting away from such crass stupidity?'

He rose and flung his coconut into the lagoon. I heard it fall with a splash, followed by a shriek of laughter. Gibbins shouted something in Tahitian and I saw that he had just missed hitting a canoe in which were two girls, paddling silently and strongly close to the shore. They waved a hand and went on. 'They are the children of the old woman who does my washing,' explained Gibbins as he filled his pipe again. Then he went on:

'Look at England,' he said, 'her politicians excel in pontifical speeches condemning aggressor nations. They talk about the rights of small nations, the brutality of dictators, they ooze the god-like righteousness of the British. Damn hypocrites, sir! And the people are mad to be duped by them. Her flag flies over half the world and she expects everyone to sit back on their laurels like herself! She expects Germany and Italy and Japan to disarm while she continues leisurely to take the fruits of her aggression which she now condemns in others. She utters sweet words of building a better world, but what does she do about it? She lets Newfoundland, the Gold Coast, and thousands of square miles of her territory waste in want, and then rises up hurt and wrathful when some nation, a pauper in comparison, dares to challenge her. She's like the chairman of a large business who refuses to resign though doing no work but still drawing his salary. And the nations that challenge her are like go-ahead young business men who are certain they could do better in his place. They, too, are to be blamed. Germany wants to do in seven years what took England five hundred. They're mad to think that Hitler can do this. Italy and Japan are the same. They're in too much of a hurry. But even if one of them succeeded, the world would be no better off. There will always be rivalry and bitterness and distrust between nations. They have the tortured minds of the inhabitants of Bedlam. There is no rest, no peace. I tell you, sir, when I was part of that world I was the same. My mind was like a bit of refuse on a rubbish heap. I saw no light and I myself was confusion. But here, from this spot where we are now, I see that world as if it were a glass bowl and inside are the fishes swimming round and round, without end and without meaning.'

It was a strange hour that I had spent with him. He had asked no questions as to who I was or as to why I was in Moorea. I had sat there while he spoke as if I'd been one of a large audience listening to a speech he was making. There was none of the intimacy that is usual when two people are alone. But as I said goodbye to him, he thawed a little. 'One day, my boy,' he said, 'you'll find what took me fifty years to find ... that solitude and beauty and the simple things of life are all that count. And you're weak and stupid if you yield to anything else.'

3

When I got back to Papeéte I stayed for a while in Fabian's Hotel overlooking the harbour. I had the corner room with the big balcony, and if ever you go to Papeéte, you should try and get this room. You sit there, on the veranda, watching the world go by beneath you, and when you see a friend you hail him and talk to him as you lean over the balcony. And then there is the view. Just below and across the road a half-dozen sailing boats are tied to the wharf. Perhaps four belong to natives of other islands who have come to Papeéte with pigs and copra to sell. But the other two boats may have sailed the Pacific to reach there. For instance, on that day that I was sitting on the verandah, one boat had come from San Francisco and the other from San Pedro. The size of rowing-boats they seemed to me, the kind that sail on Saturday afternoons in the Solent or in Falmouth harbour. And a little further across the lagoon you see Pomare's islet, where long ago the kings and queens of Tahiti spent their holidays, and which now is the location of the quarantine station. Beyond are the waves pounding on the reef, except for a small opening which is the pass, and through which you will sometimes see the proud sails of a schooner sailing. And in the evening you will be the witness of a more wonderful scene than you've ever known – the sun setting, blazing the firmament into reds and golds and purples until it slips to another world behind the silhouette of Moorea. An old schoolmaster, whose name I've forgotten, was with me on one such occasion. He had come to Tahiti a year previously after retiring from his school in Vancouver. I remember him clearly, gripping the rail of the balcony, his face alight with emotion: 'Look at it, look at it!' he cried. 'How can you fail to fall in love with it?'

I played around, in these days, with several girls, bearing in mind, nevertheless, Fabian's request to me. 'I don't object,' he said, 'to my customers bringing women into the hotel at night . . . but not during the day, please.' I found that conquests weren't so easy as I'd first thought. There was one girl that I liked, called Giselle. She was slim and young, with moods that suddenly changed; one instant she was playing hide-and-seek with the excited laughter of a child, and the next she was silent, staring into space as if the sorrows of the world were on her shoulders. I courted her obstinately and patiently, but she remained always provokingly unattainable. We laughed at the same things, swam and fished together. Because of her I decided to postpone my sailing to New Zealand; I had no wish to leave a romance hanging in the air. Even so I didn't make any headway, she ran always away from me when love was near. So it went on, until one day she said to me: 'I will not sleep with you, because you are soon to go away. I do not want a casual lover. I am not a cabaret girl. If you were to stay and take a house, that would be different. I would be your wife and cook and look after you.'

The girls that the tourist meets are, of course, the prostitutes. There are the others who live in the districts, who are more difficult to possess. I would put them into two classes. In the one there are the girls like Giselle who, if they like a man, will be his mistress for the months he is in Tahiti. She won't ask for money. She'll run your house and share your bed and in return you'll sometimes give her a dress or take her to the bars at night and to the cinema. She'll want to show you off, and periodically you'll have to spend a day with her family. As a companion she'll be rather like a child about the house. She'll have little to say and she'll probably bore you after a time. But she'll have a manner that is refreshing and novel; and when you leave, if you have been kind, she will be standing on the quay weeping tears of genuine sorrow; and maybe you'll feel a brute that you were part of her life for so short a while. To the other class belong, so to speak, the aristocrats of the island. Their virtue is as well guarded as a seventeen-year-old débutante. You must have serious intentions or you're not looked at. The parents of one of these, while I was there, were suing a young man for the seduction of their daughter. They told the Court that the girl was twenty and had never been kissed. To say that the whole of the island was in a furore of ribald excitement would be an understatement. The young man was looked upon as a hero.

One more thing. There is, in Tahiti, no silly prejudices of colour. Because your *vahine* is copper coloured, it won't stop you or her from being invited to the Governor's Ball. The French, thank God, respect the Tahitians as the equals of white men.

4

In ending this chapter, I'm going to present my apologies to Cecil Lewis and borrow from the pages of *The Trumpet is Mine*. It is to tell the tale of Robert Keable. He used to live in a white and spacious house overlooking Port Phaeton and the mountain peaks that rise above the Pari of the Presqu'Ile. A few hundred yards away on the other side of the road is the hostelry of Mauu; Mauu, who was Keable's close friend, and, I believe, gave him the land on which he built his house. Mauu who through the years has known and welcomed the poets and painters of Tahiti. He remembers Rupert Brooke — '*pareu* of Tahiti' they used to call him, because the *pareu* around his middle was always falling down. And out from another century he remembers Gauguin. Gauguin's widow is still alive. He offered to take me to her, but I refused him because I had heard what an American had done to her a few weeks before. He had accepted her hospitality, even stayed in her house, but went away to write an article describing her as an old woman whose work in life was the looking after of pigs. I didn't want her to feel I was looking at her as a curiosity. And, Mauu warned me, she felt humiliated. But here I am getting away from Keable. The man Hall in this story is of Nordhoff and Hall, the writers of *The Mutiny on the Bounty* and *The Hurricane*. But now read on. The year is 1923.

'The author of *Simon Called Peter*, *Numerous Treasure*, *The Isle of Dreams*, and many other books and essays,' wrote Cecil Lewis, 'had always fascinated me, for he was a dramatic example of the call of the South Seas. The son of a Church of England minister, and himself a parson, Keable had left England and his parish, feeling, like many another who has taken the cloth, that although he had a lively intellectual interest in the Scriptures, he had no true vocation to be a man of God. But, with more (or possibly less) character than those who plod on, he had decided to quit. He had come to Tahiti, achieved notable success as a writer, had tried (in who knows what fit of remorse or loneliness) to return to England, but the spell of the island had been too great for him. He had returned to die in the room there opposite us, through whose open door we could see some of his library, still dusty on the shelves.

'The house had remained untenanted for a year or more until Cross, a pioneer pilot in the New Guinea goldfields, also called to the island by the mysterious spell it casts across the world, had taken the house and renovated it. He was sitting in the same room finishing his lunch, and while we waited, Hall talked of Keable.

'He had Bright's disease. His sight was gone, or almost so, and having a contract to write a book a year for a big publisher (and living by it), he was in despair. The isthmus where he lived was fifty miles from Papeéte, and even there, who could help him? It was then that Hall, with characteristic generosity, hearing of his distress, moved in (forsaking his own work) and sat, day after day, at a typewriter taking the blind man's dictation straight on to the machine. Hall told me how one morning, right in the middle of a sentence, Keable stopped suddenly: "Take that sheet out of the machine, Jimmie," he had said. "Start a fresh sheet. I am going to write a Life of Christ."

'Hall had protested he should finish the work he was engaged on, that his contracts demanded it, and so on; but Keable was determined. So they started work. In one month, without looking up a single reference, without pause or hesitation, he completed the book. Only those who have tried to write themselves will appreciate what knowledge and lucidity of mind are required to marshal facts and sequences so perfectly that they can pour out without pause or subsequent adjustment. Such things only happen as a result of a lifetime of meditation.

'Shortly after he died, making his exit after the manner of the chief character in Galsworthy's *Old English*, by drinking a whole bottle of brandy. They had dressed him in his best clothes and laid him on the sofa in his study. His native wife knelt at his head, and all around on the floor sat the neighbours, Tahitians who had known and loved him, singing their mournful songs.

'Hall was gazing through the door.

'"I can see it still, Lewis, the poor chap laid out there, and that girl, lovely she was, with her long hair falling round her feet, and her tears, and all the natives singing away. It was a funny sort of end for a Church of England parson to come to, I thought; ten thousand miles from home; but he had chosen to make it so and, after all, the end doesn't much matter. The girl loved him a lot, in the way they do, you know, and after she wrote home to England to his father to tell the old man – he was over eighty – that she had a son by Keable. It was quite natural, she thought it would please him I expect; but it broke his heart. He wrote to me to ask if it was true; he couldn't believe it. What was I to tell him? How could I explain this place? We don't look on Tahitians as 'natives'; they're our friends and equals. After all, it's their island. We're only interlopers in a way, and many a decent chap has taken a native wife and been happy with her. My own wife's partly native, so I know. Yes, it was pretty difficult to tell him."'

Chapter Nine

A DREAM COMES TRUE

A HUNDRED PEOPLE filled the quay where the *Poti Raiatea*, on her weekly trip to 'Les Iles Sous le Vent', was loading pigs, chickens, cows, cases, and passengers. To a layman the thirty-year-old two-masted schooner appeared lopsided and, as I hauled my baggage aboard, I shuddered at the thought of what might happen if we faced a heavy sea. Below decks she had twelve berths but I had been warned against them – Chinamen, I was told, invariably sat there during the twenty-four hours' journey to Raiatea, vomiting incessantly. I had reserved instead, one of four bunks that were on the open deck beside the ventilators of the engine-room; for the *Poti Raiatea*, besides her proud white sails, had an engine to chug her on her way when the wind was stilled. And that evening there was not a breath of wind to ripple the water. The air was laden with the sweet scent of the *tiare tahiti*. It did not only come from the vegetation of the island but also from the *leis* that most of us had hanging round our necks and from the garlands crowning our heads. Even the poorest natives had these *leis*, dark-skinned natives and their fat wives and little children, who were going to spend the night around me, lying on the deck packed tight like sardines. Up by the bows a score of young men were singing dreamy melodies of farewell with two of them expertly playing guitars. They were going to

Tupai, a lonely island off Bora Bora, where for six months they were to work the copra plantation; and on the quay their families were standing, the women in bright dresses with scarlet hibisci behind their ears, the men silent and dignified, the children clutching their parents' hands. Dusk was darkening the shimmering lights of the dying sun. Already we were late in leaving. The captain was shouting angrily. A new rudder was being fixed, it was not yet in position! The passage of time means nothing to a Tahitian and the workmen proceeded lazily, without notice, to hammer the nails and twist the screws. No sign of impatience on the part of the passengers. And the captain himself gave up his ranting and sat on a case in the hold and opened a bottle of wine. Stars began to flicker. I could scarcely see the faces of those on the quay. The moon in its first quarter rose above the mountains. Ah! the workmen had finished. They walked without haste down the gangplank ashore. Orders were given. Ropes, tying us to the quay, were untied and thrown aboard. We began to move. I had expected the engines to chug but, by some uncanny means, we moved away inch by inch with the strength of the tide. The men were singing the sighing melody of 'Hoi Mai'; and others echoed it back from the quay. How exquisite it was, transposed on the silence of the night. Fainter and fainter were the answering voices. We could see only the twinkling lights of the village. And, as I stood there watching, a native girl beside me murmured half to herself: '*Un joli départ!*'

2

I did not know that evening I would not see Tahiti again. I had planned to spend a few weeks in Raiatea and Tahaa and Bora Bora, returning in time to catch the *Tolten* for

Auckland; and in view of this I had booked my passage in the *Tolten*. I had decided, too, that there was no point in taking my trunk to Bora Bora, and I had with me on the *Poti*, only a sack containing books, a few shirts, a pair of shorts, and a medicine-chest; I also had my typewriter and my bicycle. I didn't know then that I was not to see my suits and chief belongings again till six months later I was back home in England. I had not even said a proper goodbye to my friends.

The night passed uneventfully. We rolled a bit and a lot of use was made by some, of the little grey tin cans. Babies screamed and a fat woman had hysterics; but through most of it I slept. Around one in the morning, the engines broke down, and for an hour the old boat tossed silently at the mercy of the heavy swell. An old native that looked half Chinese and who was lying within a yard of me with two small boys nestling into his either side, saw that I was awake. He grinned in a friendly way; and then, as if he were offering me a cigarette in the European manner, he held out a piece of bamboo. It was for me to eat; and not wishing to offend him I took it. For half an hour I gnawed it, as a dog gnaws a bone, with the strands sticking in my teeth as the skin of an apple sometimes does. Most unappetizing it was and, when I saw him fall asleep, I flung it far over the side.

We reached Huahine at ten in the morning. This was an island the size of the Presqu'Ile of Tahiti with rugged mountains and deep mysterious bays. No white man lives there because water is hard to get. After a couple of hours of unloading supplies, we started off for Raiatea which we could see twenty miles away. The sun was scorching and I sat in the bows with the breeze fanning me with coolness. Beside me was Leon, a pearl merchant who had left France many years ago to make his home in the South Seas. His home, where his native wife lived, was in Tahiti, but he spent several months of the year sailing from island to island. He knew the history of the people as well as the story of his own life; and, in the days that I was to spend in his company, he told me one weird tale after another. On that sunny morning I remember him telling how he had discovered the last work of Gauguin. He had himself written a life of Gauguin from the results of endless questioning of old natives in Tahiti and the Marquesas where he died. In this book he advances his own theory that Gauguin never died a natural death. He quotes the information given him by a score of natives who knew Gauguin in the Marquesas that Gauguin was murdered; murdered by a jealous official who envied his power over the natives. The merits of this story I am not qualified to discuss; but Leon told me how a few weeks after he had finished the book he was in Papeéte market looking at a lot of junk that a native was selling on a cart. Among it he saw a small wooden statue; the native thought nothing of it and sold it to him for fifty francs. Leon took it home, quite certain that he had made a great discovery. It was the statue of a leper, superb in its workmanship. He brought in his friend Gouwe to see it, and Gouwe agreed – there could only be one man who could have created it. Leon sent it to Paris and he was to hear a few weeks later that he had sold it for a hundred thousand francs.

Now Gouwe was himself a painter, and if you go to the South Seas you will see many examples of his work; and Leon, who is a lover of art, believes that one day Gouwe will be a legendary figure like Gauguin. Twenty years ago he was a fashionable painter in Holland. He was rich and successful. He held exhibitions in London and Paris. But within himself he did not feel he was creating the art he was destined to do; and surrendering his fame he came to the South Seas. For awhile he was in Tahiti, then in the Tuomotus and the Australs, until finally he came to Raiatea which for fifteen years he has made his home. Leon pictured him as a penniless old man, too fond of the bottle, living alone in the farthest corner of the island; sensitive and cultured, wrecked with doubt whether what he did twenty years ago, when he gave up success so as to start anew, had been justified by the work he had since produced. 'You must see him,' said Leon, 'because I think you'll meet a man whom one day will be great, but who now is living in pain and squalor and obscurity.'

Utora, where we landed in Raiatea, is an ugly place of tin huts and corrugated iron roofs painted the colours of rust red and offensive greens. It is hot and dusty and smelly. Chinamen abound. Prostitutes grown old do likewise. But this unattractiveness cannot take away its lovely view across the lagoon to Tahaa and the little canoes with white sails that skim to and fro through the water. Nor can it take away the charm of little Fontana, the voluble Italian, one time chef of the Ritz Hotel, London, who greets every stranger who lands there as his lifelong friend. In all my travels, I never met anyone who had such friendliness and kindliness and goodwill as this little man; and why he settled in such an oasis of ugliness I never discovered. But there he was with his shop on the quay filled with Tahitian curios and Gouwe pictures and his smile of welcome. As luck would have it, I found Gouwe with him, on one of his rare visits from his *faré* twenty miles away in Tetooroa.

3

Gouwe greeted me courteously, but I was startled to see that he moved unsteadily as a man drunk, yet in his slow talk he gave the impression of being sober. I mean that, without the clumsy speech of a drunk, he had the actions of one. He was around six feet and looked dirty. He had a stubbly grey beard but, around his lips, it was coloured the brown of nicotine, his cigarettes consisting of drooping little things that he rolled himself. On his face there were three or four red marks like cuts, though they were not open sores but some kind of infection under the skin. Later I heard him speak much of '*mon malade*' and also of his right eye which was going blind. It suffered from a kind of paralysis and, though it wasn't painful, it would close and water when he was tired so that he had frequently to dab it with a handkerchief. That night he dined with me, talking absorbingly of Theosophy and his belief in the transmigration of souls. And at the end of it he invited me to go with him on the next day to his home.

I bought four bottles of wine, two tins of bully beef, and wrapping a few belongings in a *pareu* I set out. There are no buses or cars to take you to his *faré*. The only way is a puffing steam launch that circles the island once a week. Gouwe dozed most of the time, but he awoke to tell me about a house we passed that stood white and lonely in the mountain high above the lagoon. Strange was this story of a woman and two friends, French soldiers of the Great War who, shattered by their experiences in battle, decided to get away from it all. They had no money, but the three of them succeeded, by hoboing across America and stowing away in ships, in reaching Tahiti. The men were engineers by trade and they earned a bit in Papeéte in the electricity works. Then they came to Raiatea. They started their own electricity works and in a year or so the tin huts of Utora blazed electricity at night. The three of them now decided to build a home of their own and they chose the place where this house now stood. Every brick they put there themselves, and not content with that they built a dam and an electricity plant. And because the house was high in the mountain they built a funicular to the lagoon beneath. So here on this island, four thousand miles from any city, these three live in a house of modern marvels set in a scene of lonely beauty and tranquillity.

Gouwe's home was different. We entered a bay that dug deep into the island with dense vegetation bordering the shore and the mountain rising like a wall from the lagoon. And there in the corner of the bay, built out over the water, was the *faré* of Gouwe. From a distance it looked like one of those desolated boat-houses you find on upper reaches of small rivers; and when we got close I saw that the roof of pandanus was tumbling down and there were patches in the walls where the *burao* sticks had rotted away. There was only one room and a verandah, and ceaselessly there was the sound of water lapping underneath. Strewn about the floor and pushed untidily against the wall were his canvases. Nothing had been cleaned for a long time. Cockroaches crawled on the wooden boards, and when I picked up a canvas a bunch of blackbeetles scurried away. That was inside; but outside there was the sweep of the bay and two small islets near the reef, and beyond, the haze of the Pacific.

His food he ate native fashion with his fingers, but in his efforts to be hospitable he produced for me forks and knives red with rust which he spent many minutes trying to clean. His food, he told me, was prepared by a native family who lived a mile away; and for that evening that I was there, a chicken was produced as a special treat. There was nowhere for me to sleep, save on the boards in his room or in a deck-chair on the verandah. He himself slept on a wooden bed without a mattress. The cockroaches put me off the boards, so I chose the deck-chair on the verandah despite the acrid smell of dried urine that came from one of its corners.

But before we slept, we talked much. When I asked him why he had come to the islands, he said slowly: '*J'aime la solitude.*' And he told me how in Holland he had achieved a reputation for painting horses. Always they were wanting a Gouwe horse and he got fed up with it. Then about his drinking. 'When I get drunk,' he said, 'I become a beast. It is horrible. I crawl about the floor, humped like a bear on my hands and knees. I have no mind. I swipe glasses and plates from off the table. I become violent.' He gets up when the dawn is still grey and works through the day till the light is gone. I said something about him being lonely. '*Non, non, monsieur,*' he said. Then he added wistfully: '*Le temps passe trop vite.*' Indeed he gave me an impression that he was aware of fighting desperately against something, death or blindness. He talked repeatedly of '*mon grand tableau*' and the exhibition he wanted soon to hold in Papeéte. 'I want to make fifteen thousand francs,' he said, 'and then go back to Holland for a while ... *c'est mieux pour mon malade,*' he added, pointing to his eye and the marks on his face. '*Mon grand tableau*' was a life-size picture of two natives, branches of bananas on their shoulders, pushing their way through the undergrowth. I know little of the merit of pictures; I have my own valuation of their emotion. And this picture of Gouwe's tremendously moved me. Half closing my eyes I saw the men in dazzling colours thrusting their way through the tropical vegetation; and I seemed also to see something of the tortured soul of Gouwe. A smaller painting I bought and it now hangs in my room; a picture of part of the shore and the lagoon near his *faré.*

He lived in squalor, yet he was gentle and kind and there was dignity about him. When I was leaving he asked me to say goodbye to the two natives who had killed the chicken specially for me. 'They are sensitive people,' he explained. And it was charming, too, when in the early morning I heard in the distance, but coming closer and closer, two children's voices, singing in the hoarse attractive way of the pure native, and Gouwe's remark: '*Voilà notre café* . . . don't show yourself and they will go on singing, right into the room . . .'

4

I arrived back in Utora uncertain what to do next. Leon was still there and he told me that if we wanted to go to Bora Bora, which was forty miles away, we would have to hire a native fishing boat. Otherwise we would have to wait for one of the occasional visits that the *Poti Raiatea* made there. We were standing at the bar of the hotel discussing the cost of it, when up to the side of us and out of the blue stepped an American girl. An elephant could have walked in and we would not have been more surprised. She came right up and introduced herself. Lia Sanders was her name. She came from New York. She'd been in the South Seas for three months and in Raiatea a fortnight. She was a painter and she was alone. She'd heard that we were going to Bora Bora and she wanted to go shares with the boat. Leon accepted her offer before I had a chance to say a word, and off the three of us went to find the captain.

We set sail at noon next day and tied up at the wharf of Vaitapé, the main village of Bora Bora, at nine the following morning. Usually the journey by sailing boat is only five hours, but the day was windless, and when we reached the pass into the lagoon of Bora Bora around midnight, the skipper was nervous of risking the drift of the sea; so we stayed outside and slept under the stars with the deck as our bed.

The dream of many people is to sail the South Seas in their own yacht, but by doing so most of the enjoyment of travelling is missed; because you're stuck with the same company for month after month and have little chance of meeting the types that make the world interesting.

Lia Sanders had a beautiful small figure so that she wore shorts with the grace of a chorus girl. 'Perfectly sculptured,' Leon described her. That very day she said was her thirty-first birthday, though neither Leon nor I believed her; but we thought it funny that a woman should add to her age when obviously she could subtract from it without fear of contradiction. She had travelled in many parts of the world; in Afghanistan, China, Java, Europe, Finland. Wherever she went she took her paints and easel and on her return to New York she held an exhibition of what she'd done. She had a real talent for watercolours and drawings, working at a terrific speed with bold, decisive lines. She had a knowledge of many subjects and there was richness and variety in her thoughts. She had a zest and confidence in life. She never stopped asking questions, nor painting pictures, nor swimming, nor writing in her diary; and after a little while her activity jarred a little. Leon and I wanted her to relax and be peaceful for a bit. She had been married very young but was now divorced; yet she still spoke with great love of her husband. 'I have no children,' she said, '. . . that is the great sorrow of my life. If I'd had, they would have provided me with the fullness of life.'

It was hot that afternoon we three sailed from Utora, and we sat on deck using the sail as a shelter from the sun. Lia would sometimes perch herself on the bowsprit, looking easy to fall, and once she dived into the water and hung for a while to the rope they threw her from the stern.

The crew were four natives who couldn't speak French. Soon after starting I wanted to give them a bottle of wine, but Leon said: 'If you give one now they won't stop drinking until they've finished every bottle we've got. Wait until the journey's over.' That's a trait with the natives. Supposing you produced a demijohn, they would never leave until it was dry.

We talked most about Leon, Leon and his attitude to women. He was an odd mixture of cruelty and naïvety. He said that he had never loved any woman, never had said the words: 'I love you.' If his wife slept with another man he would divorce her, however slight and temporary the affair might be; but he himself could have as many affairs as he liked. This was a strange doctrine for Tahiti, because there was none who believed a native wife could remain virtuous for always, according to Western ideals. Moreover, he despised native women and admitted that he'd been a rotten husband. Yet he said that if any man made love to his wife, he would shoot him. He was a strange jumble of inconsistencies. He had told me that no woman, white or coloured, could provide companionship; yet with the naïvety of a schoolboy, he said a few hours after meeting Lia, that he had met the one exception. That was his opinion for a few days and then back he went to his old ideas.

Close to the shore of Tahaa we went, wild and beautiful, and white sand lining the edge of the lagoon and, oh, the colours! We ate pineapple and spluttered the pips of watermelon on the deck and had *pâté* with our bread and drank red wine and realized that, though we were all violent individualists, we shared sensitiveness and love of beauty, and we knew that for that day alone we were the luckiest three people in the world.

Heaped in a pathetic mass on the cabin top was the

skipper's wife, who was a terrible case of *féfé*. She lay below in a fever for a long time, but when she somehow heaved herself on deck she showed the usual curiosity of the native in the lives and belongings of a *popaa*. She asked blunt questions in a simple way. She could not understand the relationship of us three. She wanted to know to which of us, Leon and me, Lia belonged. And when Leon explained that *popaa vahine* was on her own, she asked quite simply whether Leon and I were mahus (homosexuals)!

The night was too beautiful to sleep through. We lay on the deck, a million, million stars above us, and Lia pointed to the three of Orion and then I learnt where shone the little group of the Pleiades; and the moon, huge in its gentleness, shimmered the Pacific in an ethereal silver. When the dawn came, in orange and gold, it was so still that two of the crew had to heave on an oar to get us through the pass into the bay. Oh, God! how lovely it was . . . the great rock of Bora Bora thrusting its silhouette into the blaze of the dawn and all around us the dreamy peace of the lagoon.

We stayed in the local hotel and were not happy. A Belgian of the Bourgainville clique was there and we quickly got tired of his company; also a fat-lipped Frenchman from whose room at night came the squeals of his *vahine* whom he was beating with a stick. The same girl in the daytime had a mad-making habit of consistently playing on the guitar at every possible moment the same bar of music. And though the food was good, the rooms were stuffy and small so that one tossed and sweated as one lay abed at night. I went off round the island to find something better, but I came back without news. And I sadly believed that I'd been deceived again, and that it was the same as I'd found in the other islands – noisy people in lovely places. So I decided to go, to return to Papeéte, and I even had carried my sack to the cutter when suddenly I changed my mind. There was an island a mile across the lagoon, small, with a hump in the middle and a solitary coconut tree on the topmost point. White sand, I could see, and coconut trees bordering the water. The natives, when I questioned them about it, said it was impossible to stay there as there was no water, and the mosquitoes were terrible; besides, only one native family inhabited the island. Something within me urged me to see for myself; and I fetched Lia and Leon and the three of us borrowed a *pirogue* and across the lagoon we sailed.

5

The island of Toopua, they call it. And it is my island. Beaches of white sand and sudden bays and inlets, and deep, deep water so blue and clear that staring from a canoe into the depths you see another world of many coloured fishes swimming lazily among a forest of luxuriant vegetation and rocky mountains. There is a legend to the name. Toopua means branch of the *pua* tree, and long years ago it was told that if you went to the island and found a branch and brought it back with you, you would draw the island to Bora Bora so that it joined.

When the keel of our *pirogue* grated against the beach, Hélène was sitting on the sand beneath the shade of the *burao* tree, her breast bare outside her dress, unconcernedly feeding Marceline. We were at a corner point of the island that faced north. There was a view of half a circle, beginning with the far-off reef and the open sea, and then the islet where the fishermen's nets were hanging to dry, and the blues of the lagoon with the songs of the natives as they sailed by, and the village of Vaitapé hidden in the coconut trees, and the mountain climbing the sky; and there was the white beach that fell steeply when it touched the water so that when we bathed a few steps took us out of our depth. So harsh these sentences sound; but what they try to say does not belong to words, it belongs to the symphony that is found in the silence of imagination, of a dream long longed for, and at last fulfilled.

Hélène didn't mention money when we asked whether we could stay there. She beamed a smile of welcome and said that if we went back to the hotel for our things, she would have the hut ready on our return. Dear Hélène! No trouble was ever too much for her. She was tall and young with a fine row of white teeth and silky black hair that fell in two plaits to her waistline; and though she never had seen much of the world, she had the serenity and wisdom and competence that reminded me somehow of my nurse who had been long in our family; as if evil had never knocked at her door and that goodness had been her companion from the first hour of her life. Vetea, her husband, could not speak French as she could. He was that rare specimen, a pure Tahitian. Broad-shouldered, the fine features of pure breeding, and a laugh that forced you, in its good humour, to laugh with him. And then there were the children, Albert and Marceline; no children of my acquaintance were so full of fun and jokes and games as these two. Naked they ran around, and Marceline, just one year old, as sturdy on her legs as if she were three. I loved those two.

Our hut was the bedroom of the family, and on our arrival they moved over to the other hut thirty yards away where Hélène did her cooking and they ate their food. Neither was a hut in the ordinary sense of the word. Ours had a floor of white sand and the walls were upright *burao* sticks through the chinks of which, at night, you could see the stars twinkling on the water. The roof was not tin nor made of planks, but coconut leaves matted together, or *niaus* as the natives called them. There was no door. The white sand that was our floor stretched a few yards to the lagoon. There was a mattress, the size for a double bed, and it lay propped a foot above the ground on flat wooden sticks; and, because we were three, Hélène had borrowed, from her mother-in-law, a single mattress which she put beside the double one so we could all sleep together; but, as it happened, Lia preferred sleeping alone on a rug on the shore.

Hélène cooked the food. Sometimes we had bully beef and tinned peas bought from the Chinese store at Viatapé; but mostly it was fish prepared in queer native ways; *poisson cru* was the favourite, raw *operu* fish soaked in lemon and coconut sauce. One night we sailed in Vetea's *pirogue* to the reef to catch lobsters with a big oil lamp we had. How careful we had to be or otherwise our fingers could be caught in their pincers! We envied Vetea in the quick confident way he would stoop, clutch an unsuspecting lobster, and hurl it in a bucket before the poor thing had a chance to attack him. We had a big catch to take back to Hélène. And I remember, when we were softly swishing through the water close to our corner point of the island, the moon was paling our beach and the two huts aslant to each other, and it seemed to me that I was very young again and that someone had led me to fairyland.

Leon was the first to go. He never liked the complete primitiveness of our life. We had no bath, no lavatory, and for water Vetea went over to Bora Bora for it every morning with two tin cans. Besides this, I think he carried a weight in his mind so that whatever he did, wherever he went, he never had peace for long; as if early in life he had got off on the wrong foot and he had never been able to change step. I was sorry to say goodbye to him. He had shared with me moments that would remain precious all my life.

So Lia and I were left together. And we were as different as a mouse from a horse in the way we spent the days. I would laze and bask in the sun and ramble round the island. It took about an hour to walk round, lovely white beaches and rocks to climb and always the lagoon to plunge naked into whenever I felt inclined. At one point Tabu Island is but a hundred yards away, the island that gave the name to the lovely film I'd seen a decade before. Long years ago a battle had been fought there and because many were killed the King of Bora Bora declared it 'Tabu' out of respect to the fallen. No one must live there, but when Murnau, the German who made the film, fell in love with the island, he did so despite the warnings of the natives. They nod wisely now when they talk of him; first the negative of the film was burnt, and then, a year later, he was killed in a motor accident.

And when I'd get back to our corner point, I'd find Lia feverishly active as if she were racing against time, in this place where there was no time. Even when the weather was bad she would sit outside busily painting until the rain smudged her colours; and then she would come into the hut and start sketching the face of one of the natives. They were thrilled by her. They would canoe over from Viatapé and group themselves behind her, silently watching. Great was the honour when she picked one out as a model. But, if it were a girl, though she herself would sit grave and motionless, her girl friends would giggle and chatter with the nervousness of schoolgirls in the presence of a film star. And if Lia wasn't painting she would be getting Vetea to show her how to spear fish with a *patia*. Water goggles tied round her head, for an hour on end, she would be diving under the water and flinging her *patia* at fishes that darted always away. And the questions! How weary I became of her high little voice piping one query after another. If only she would have rested quiet for a while yielding serenity where serenity reigned. Virile young American womanhood. How is it that nine-tenths of them have the same characteristics? Purposeful, obstinate, bossy. There was the evening when we'd canoed over to the other side to have a meal at the hotel. The sky grew dark and threatening as we ate; and when we'd finished and were wanting to return, sudden gusts of wind bent back the stems of the coconut trees with their force. We knew it was only the beginning of a storm that would soon be with us. And I, knowing that the wind would blow waves six feet high on the lagoon, was against the risk of being sunk by them. Not so Lia. She was certain she could cope with a cyclone and off she started alone. A native saw her and jumped in a canoe after her. '*Matai aita maitai*' ('Wind no good'), he shouted and succeeded in bringing her back. And there was the time she bought dress material as a present for Hélène. She didn't think of asking what colour Hélène liked. She made her own choice, saying when she brought it back: 'I couldn't stand anything else they had.'

And then she, too, was gone.

Chapter Ten

TOOPUA

ON SATURDAYS I would go over to the hotel for my meals because Hélène and Vetea were Seventh Day Adventists and Saturday was their Sunday. It was empty now save for the Administrator of Les Iles Sous le Vent who was on one of his periodical visits to Bora Bora; in fact, he and I were the only white men in the island. Alain Gerbault was, however, expected and, from what I gathered from his talk, the Administrator was anxious to get away before his arrival. It was all a matter of the village green. Gerbault preferred Bora Bora above all the other islands and deemed himself the most important man who went there. And on his last visit he had taken it upon himself to order the removal of two large trees from the village green, because their absence, he considered, would provide a better football field for the natives. The Administrator was angry that he hadn't been consulted; and now had ordered twelve little trees to be planted about the village green so that football games would be a thing of the past.

Perhaps you don't remember Alain Gerbault. In France he is a figure of legend like Lawrence of Arabia. In the Great War he was one of the Allies' greatest pilots and afterwards he achieved world renown as a tennis player. Then he gave up playing tennis and started to roam the world in a tiny yacht. He was the first man to sail the

Atlantic alone; and for fifteen years he has been roaming the Seven Seas, frequently reported missing, but always turning up in the end. I saw him in Papeéte, bare-footed, a *pareu* around his middle, preferring to talk to natives than to white men, loping along the front or playing billiards with the fishermen in a saloon near the harbour. There is a tale that is told of him of an occasion when he was invited to a Governor's reception. He appeared as usual, bare-footed and bare-chested, and the *pareu* around his middle. Fellow-guests were horrified and watched the Governor to see what he would do. But the poor fellow was impotent, Gerbault had hanging round his neck an Order higher than any of the Governor's. I spoke to him once or twice and left him always with a feeling I would like to know him better. Once I found him poring over a catalogue from a London yachting firm. 'I am looking to see what I shall give myself for a Christmas present,' he said in his faultless English, 'that clock with a ship's bell, or that knife with a cork which never sinks.' His home is his yacht. He never sleeps ashore. When he so wills to see another island, he weighs anchor and sails there. For money he depends on the books he writes, but he needs very little. If ever a man was free, it is he.

I, too, was free in those days, when the sun lulled the hours in tranquillity, and Marceline sneaked into my hut to pull the cloth from the table, and the coconut trees whispered to each other, and Hélène shouted that my dinner was ready, and the lagoon lapped the white beaches of my island. Minutes were not known, days not counted. I rose when the dawn filtered through the chinks of the *burao* sticks and slept when the stars filled the heavens. A sort of coma, I think it was, like the moments between a dream and the wakening; worries of yesterday didn't matter, those of tomorrow didn't exist; only the hazy, wonderful present.

Maéva was with me then. Slender, child-like Maéva with the far-away eyes. What mystery, what sorrow could lie behind them in one so young? But when she laughed and played, she had the spirit of a child that knows no trouble, the abandon of a fawn on an April morning. Out of the darkness she would come to me; the shadow of a canoe on the water, the gentle sound as it touched the beach, and there she was, a ghost of the islands, running bare-footed towards me. Slim, supple body. Soft scent of *tiare tahiti*. We would lie in the warmth of the night, and I, closing my eyes, would say a prayer to the heavens – let me be aware of each single minute, none to escape, so that whatever the years may bring I will remember.

We would be up when the Morning Star still shone in the east and the dawn was a mirror of soft yellows in the sky. She would ask me what I wanted for breakfast. Was it a red fish or a black fish or was it a white one with big blue spots? A red fish I would say, and she would take the *patia* and run naked into the lagoon. Half an hour she might be there, swimming and plunging, till the dawn had become a glorious spectacle of golden loveliness and thin wisps of smoke curled from the coconut trees of Vaitapé and the call of the *pu* echoed across the water as the Chinaman told the island he had bread to sell. Then she would reappear, triumphantly holding a red fish, and perhaps others of other colours, and wrapping her *pareu* tight around her, she would deftly clean it and light a fire and we would watch it together as it cooked. Vetea would be up by this time, ready to sail over to fetch the water; and Hélène would be busy scrubbing Albert and Marceline. Maéva would wait until I had eaten and then, with a shy kiss, she would run to her canoe. '*Ia ora na*, Derek,' she would cry, and across the lagoon she would be paddling. Perhaps half-way across she would pause. '*Ia ora na,*' she would cry again. And I would echo back the words: '*Ia ora na*, Maéva!'

I never saw where she lived, and this was strange because they usually wish to parade a *popaa* before their friends. Perhaps it was that she knew I was soon to go and that she was sensitive to the humiliation that might be hers if she were mocked for loving a *popaa* who said goodbye so quickly. Perhaps, too, this was why she came and went with the suddenness of the wind. I never knew when she would appear. In the stillness of the night or in the sunshine of the afternoon, she would come and go with the inconstancy of a dream. When first I saw her she had come over to watch Lia paint. I noticed her then because she had a wistful slender beauty that was a contrast to the usual heavy type of Bora Bora. And afterwards, when she had gone, I remember Hélène coming to me and saying, as if she were passing on a message: '*Maéva m'a dit qu'elle t'aime.*' Such was the naïve way that love was born.

She had never been to Papeéte and she talked of it as a little Cornish girl will talk of London. Papeéte for her had the glitter of Piccadilly and Shaftesbury Avenue; the cinema had the glamour of the Palace Theatre. Of the world outside, it was too big for her imagination. '*Est ce que c'est vrai,*' she asked, '*que les gens en France ont besoin d'argent?*' Sweet child of the faraway eyes! Your riches are around you. Bananas hang in clusters on the trees and fish in abundance await you in the lagoon, coconuts by the hundreds are there, ready to be turned to the score of uses you have for them. Wild pigs and chickens. Hunger you will never know. And if you need the help of man, to repair the *niaus* of your roof or to build a swift canoe, your people will be there with smiles, proud they can be of use to you.

What a long procession of the good things in life you have to teach us; who send our priests to you to spread the mess that we have made of life. What will God say on the Day of Reckoning? Who will He salute? We who hypocritically and self-consciously push forth His Gospel or you who have never known ugliness, who 'love thy neighbour' with hearts unsullied by doubt and fear and greed?

We would take the canoe, Maéva and I, each with a paddle, and glide softly through the water, I in the centre and she in the stern to do the steering. How cunning she was in dodging the coral rocks that lay secretly a foot beneath the water close into shore; and how clever the way, with the sureness of an expert, she would find the narrow passes of the reefs that circled every islet! Hot work it was after a while and we would lift our paddles and the canoe was stilled. Now for a swim. Off would come my pandanus hat that hid my head from the glare of the sun, and my *pareu* would fall at my feet as I stood poised for a dive. Splash! Hands, head, body, feet, the water caressing me like cool silk. Down into the depths, my eyes open, smarting with salt, seeing the coral in a distorted mirror that from above was shaped so beautiful. Nothing is so pure to the senses as the naked bathe; the coolness of water on warm bare skin. I turned and twisted and kicked out with my legs. Free I was! free like the fishes that darted quick from the interloper. Free as the birds in the skies. Joy raged in my mind. I needed to shout to the heavens. Up to the surface, then. A little puffed, but enough in my lungs to yell to the gods, defiantly maybe, that here in the world they looked down upon, a soul had found Elysium.

'*Tu es fou,*' laughed Maéva. There she was, a few feet away, splashing the water with the palm of her hand. Her black hair, wet from a dive, clinging about her neck and her small sun-coloured shoulders. '*Fou* I may be,' I shouted back, 'but I'll beat you to the beach.' No answer from her then. She was off with two yards start, not the quiet crawl of the professional swimmer, but with arms working like the sails of a windmill and legs churning the water like the twin screws of a steamer. How she went so fast was a mystery. I buried my face in the water and moved my legs and arms in the way I was taught at school, automatic and easy it comes to me, but each time I turned my head for air, Maéva had gained a foot. Shorter of breath I got, rhythm was broken. Splash, splash, splash ahead of me. No use. She'd won. She was standing with her hands on her hips with the water only up to her knees and her laughter pealing across the lagoon. '*Fou j'ai dit*,' she said.

Oh lovely days! They stand with the sparkle of jewels out of the mists of time. Vanity and ambition and selfishness were not my comrades then. Mean actions, thoughtless words, were driven from the corners of my mind. I was sure of myself, I was the captain of my soul.

One afternoon we lay on the beach of Tabu. Two miles away, perhaps, we could see the pin-pointed figures of the fishermen on the reef; high above us two birds, snow white against the blue of the sky, were hovering and swooping with the grace of gulls. A whisper of a breeze rustled the coconut trees, making a sound like soft rain on leaves. Out in the lagoon a school of porpoises played lazily together, and such was the stillness that we could hear their snorts as they sniffed the air. Maéva was idly chucking shells at the canoe that lay half clear of the water, not listening, nor understanding if she had done, to my monologue in English.

'Do you know, Maéva,' I was saying as a coconut fell

with a thud behind me, 'I'm going to be quite different when I go from here. I've been a person without principles who yielded to the whim of the moment and was always getting into trouble because of it. I've been ready too often to scratch the surface of life, shying away impatiently when faced by problems that, if they were to be overcome, required more than just my casual acquaintance. Momentarily, maybe, such evasion has given me ease; but it's been an ease that has as quickly died as the sparkle of champagne, making my happiness a thing of fits and spasms, neither profound nor peaceful, ready at any moment to be killed by worries so trivial that on looking back upon them I am ashamed. But I'm not going to be like that any more, Maéva. I'm going to have a set of rules which will steer my life like a rudder steers a ship across the sea. I'm going to fashion a shield of spiritual strength that will protect me from vanity and desires and meanness. I'm going to be untouched by the hurts and mouthings of this wounded world I live in. I'm going to be complete in myself; wherever I go, whatever hateful circumstances I may find myself in, I'm going to have the power of a soul at rest. Like an oasis that in the dry desert is sufficient unto itself, and yet gives forth strength to those who pass its way.'

A handful of sand banged down on my tummy. '*Mamu mata nehenhe*' ('Shut up kind eyes') laughed Maéva. She was sitting with her small bare thighs on her heels, and her knees in the sand; and she was looking at me with a smile that had tenderness and mischief and pity all in one. '*Quelle bêtise tu parles!*'

I was angry when you said that, Maéva, and I gave you a little smack. That made you angry too and you pouted your lips and went off in a huff down the beach. And the day was very nearly spoilt.

But listen to me now, Maéva:

> There's wisdom in women, of more than they
> have known,
> And thoughts go blowing through them, are
> wiser than their own.

Nonsense you had called my words and you were right: as I knew then you were right, deep in my heart. I spoke with the foolishness of the faint-hearted who on New Year's Eve roll forth a catalogue of dreary resolutions. I was blinded by the gentle spirit of happiness in your people and the wonder of the world they lived in. My soul was quietened like the stillness of a pool above a waterfall and yet glowing with an emotion as if I'd heard great music after the silliness of a dance tune. I could see with the detachment of a star looking down from the heavens, the pettiness and the conceit of man, his waste and his cruelty and his futility. I could see myself wandering aimlessly like a butterfly on the wind, fired for the moment with the ardour of youth, but heading for a destiny with no purpose, no end. In the silence of your islands I felt I could conquer myself, and march forth with power and with faith, so to find a new world.

That's what I supposed I could do, Maéva, as I listened to the sigh of the reef and watched your faraway eyes and heard the cries of sea birds and marvelled at the shadows of coral beneath the turquoise blue of lagoons.

And then, one day, reality stepped in, bleak and grim. The South Seas were not my journey's end. I'd said I'd go round the world, and I knew that if I didn't there might be a restless, thwarted feeling within me for the rest of my life. So I set about planning to return to Tahiti, where I knew a boat was sailing for Auckland in a week's time. The difficulty, however, was how to get there in time. The local policeman in Bora Bora informed me that the *Poti Raiatea* wouldn't be calling at the island for a fortnight and that I'd have to be in Utora in four days' time to catch it there if I were to have any chance of reaching Tahiti before my boat sailed. Further complications presented themselves when I learnt that the *Teriora*, the only sailing boat of the island, had gone to Moapiti, a little island thirty miles away, and that it depended on the wind whether she got back with enough hours to spare to take me to Utora.

There was, however, another possibility. Into the loveliness of the Bora Bora bay was coming the *Stella Polaris*, a super yacht which at that time of year did an annual cruise of the South Seas with a cargo of American millionaires. To the exact minute the local policeman knew when she would be sailing through the pass; the owners had notified him six months previously and they had charged him to present an exhibition of native dancing an hour after they'd dropped anchor. The time she was expected was seven o'clock on the morning of February the seventeenth.

The notion of travelling in her hardly crossed my mind. In the first place I hadn't the funds and in the second I wanted to return to Papeéte to collect my trunk and a letter of credit of £50 in the custody of the bank, which was all the money I would have till I reached New Zealand except for £2 cash. So I sat down and waited for the wind to blow the *Teriora* back from Moapiti.

Each morning I'd be up early and asking Vetea what he thought of the weather, but there was always either no wind at all or it was blowing from the wrong quarter. Three days slipped by and there was still no *Teriora*. I can't say I was very perturbed; and I meandered through the hours with the same idle irresponsibility as in the days behind me. Perhaps it was not quite the same, for my mind was working in terms of civilization again, timetables and

LSD. And this made me think a great deal of my family and gave me a certain homesickness; for I knew that what had been my experience would have been loved by them and I felt there was a loss in my own enjoyment because of that. To my father, the South Seas was a lovely memory, but to my brothers, Colin especially, stuck in their offices, it was only a dream. There were moments when I would have given days of my life if they could have been at my side.

The fourth day dawned so still that not even the coconut trees rustled and the lagoon was like a pond with the water too lazy to lap the shore. By midday I knew there wasn't a chance of the *Teriora* arriving in time, and I realized that I would have to stay another six weeks in the islands till the next boat for New Zealand left Tahiti. The only alternative was the *Stella Polaris*, but I didn't see how I could do without my clothes and money and, besides, I didn't know her itinerary and where she could take me.

She arrived as punctually as the Cornish Riviera Express steams into Paddington, on 17 February at seven a.m. White with graceful lines, she sailed through the pass and into the bay and dropped anchor two hundred yards from the wharf of Vaitapé. The whole island population was awaiting her, and I was there too, the only white man, clad in my *pareu*, bare-footed and bare-chested, wearing my pandanus hat. Large motor launches were quickly lowered, loaded with passengers, and raced to where we were standing. Spruce, white-uniformed sailors made them fast and out of them jumped the millionaires; cigars, wives, cameras, daughters, horn-rimmed spectacles, green and yellow checked plus fours, chewing gum and all. They swarmed on the wharf and the village green, buzzing round the natives as if the latter were exhibits of a picture gallery. They studied the local wares on sale and offered half the price they were asked. They played ring-a-ring-a-roses round a girl in a dance skirt and gave their versions of a Tahitian dance. One wit, I remember, stood among a group of naked children, solemnly pointing to each one, saying; 'That's a boy . . . that's a girl!'

But amid this tumult I found a friend, a cruise official who remembered I'd written about the *Stella Polaris* a year before. I told him my tale and with bouncing American goodwill he said he would try and fix something with the Captain and the cruise manager. Ten minutes later he was back and beamed on me the news that they'd take me to Suva for £10 instead of the official rate of £30; and then from there I'd be able to get a boat to New Zealand. I was, of course, delighted and profuse in my thanks; and I hurried away to collect what baggage I had and to make my farewells. They were very incomplete. I had only an hour before boarding the *Stella Polaris*. I canoed back to my island and, with Hélène and Maéva at my side, I bundled my belongings into my kitbag. There was no time to feel sentimental. I was as unmoved as if I were going to the hotel for dinner. I wanted my toothbrush and razor blades and where was my spare typewriter ribbon? It was all so oddly matter-of-fact. I remember thinking I ought to be stifling sobs and making poignant remarks; or composing in my mind farewell lines like those of Somerset Maugham's:

The breeze was laden still with the pleasant odours of the land. Tahiti was very far away and I knew I should never see it again. A chapter of my life was closed, and I felt a little nearer to inevitable death.

But none of these things were the case. Even when Maéva gave me two necklaces she'd made from the shells on the shore, I gave her only a light kiss; my emotions seemed unaware that at that moment I said farewell to love. And when Hélène presented me with one of the beautiful dancing dresses of the islands, my first reaction was how on earth I was going to travel with it.

I left them both there on my island, waving my hat to them as Vetea paddled me to the gangway of the *Stella*. And when the *Stella* weighed anchor and turned slowly in the bay and made for the pass, I still could see them on the beach, fluttering two white handkerchiefs; but Vetea was close to us, his canoe bobbing in the wash like a cork in a fast-running stream. Then, for the last time, above the murmur of the engines, I heard him singing out the words: '*Ia ora na!*'

Perhaps it was well I left so suddenly, and that I had no time to be stupidly sentimental. And yet I wish it had not been so. Through the years I will cherish the days I dwelt in the islands, and I feel I owed them something more than the casual wave of the hand in goodbye. It is like the lover who, after his love has gone, suffers sorrow because he knows he could have been more tender. Weeks later I got a letter from my father which he had written, unaware of my change of plans, and thinking I was leaving in the way I would have wished.

'I can't resist sending you a line on this your very last day in Tahiti,' he wrote, 'for I know how you will be feeling. It is now about 4 a.m. with you, and you will have had your last dance, and in a few hours the farewell *tiaré* will be round your neck, and you'll be waving farewell and promising to return again. And if you are wise, you never will return again, for it will never be quite the same as on this, your first visit. Many a time when fog envelops London, you will recall memories of the waving palm trees, the sighing of the sea on the reef, the fantastic shapes of the mountains, and the merry maidens' voices. And one day you will somehow and somewhere get a whiff of the scent of the coconut mingled with that of the *tiaré*, and in a flash you will suddenly be transported in spirit back to that happy isle. The memory of it will be a blessing to you for ever.'

Chapter Eleven

PROUD TO BE BRITISH

No sooner had we cleared the pass than the cruise official and the purser came to me with faces like pall bearers at a funeral. They brought the news that, after looking up the ship's rules and regulations, they'd found they couldn't take a passenger at a reduced fare. Something about the clearance papers; they were cleared with details of the crew from the authorities at Papeéte to those at Raratonga; and so they couldn't sign me on without risking a heavy fine. Any other way was equally impossible for reasons I couldn't understand. I couldn't see why they couldn't have found it out before we started. They were eloquent in their apologies and offered to take me to Suva for the normal price of £30. Even permitting me to do this was a special kindness on their part, they told me; an attitude which made me even more annoyed. But I also, if I wanted, could get off at Utora where the millionaires were to watch a display of 'fire-walking' for a couple of hours.

Whichever I did was considerably inconvenient. I had five shillings in my pocket (the rest of the cash had gone in paying Hélène at the rate of 1s. a day – I had also given Vetea my bicycle) and therefore, in any case, I'd have to cable home for money. If I paid the £30 and went to Suva, my budget would have a big hole in it; I'd expected it would only cost me £16 to reach New Zealand. But my budget would also be affected if I stayed on six weeks for the next boat, and my timetable too; I didn't want to be away more than a year. I couldn't decide what to do. I paced the deck and puffed furiously at cigarettes. I changed my mind a dozen times. No doubt it would be cheaper if I got off at Utora, but doing so would miss my seeing Raratonga, Pago Pago, and Apia, places which the *Stella* was calling at *en route* for Suva. Besides, I argued, if I stayed in the boat I was sure to be specially treated and given a very good time. What finally influenced me to stay, however, was none of these things. I happened to find that there were three heiresses on board, each of whom had a face and a figure worthy for the first line of an Earl Carroll chorus.

The boat was like a superior private hotel on the Bournemouth sea front. There was no privacy. Everyone knew at what time anyone else went to bed, and there was no corner that evaded the scrutiny of each passenger who had a walk on the deck before turning in. If, during the day, you were in one person's company for an hour, you could see that in every deck-chair you were the subject of comment. The millionaires and their wives all wanted romance for themselves, but the next best thing was watching someone else, or inventing a romance about someone else. Since therefore the cruise had been in progress a month when I arrived, scandals raged like tornadoes. The heiresses were supposed to be doing all sorts of things with waiters and bandsmen; there being no young men otherwise aboard. And the more mature women had properly tied themselves up with each other's husbands. Number One romance was between a widow of seventy and a retired sugar-candy king. They'd get tipsy together each evening, take part for a while in the dancing, and then retire to a certain corner of the deck to coo under the moon, apparently unaware that the rest of the company were watching. This sugar-candy king talked to me about his love for the widow, explaining that it was a rebound. He told me that his own wife had run off with a younger man. Then added confidentially: 'She's at her change of life, you know. Perhaps when that is all over, she'll change her mind.'

I was thought to be a 'genu-ein' beachcomber, so that I came in for a full share of attention. Certainly I must have looked odd, wandering bare-footed round the deck with very little else on; while the rest wore what Fifth Avenue shops imagined were the mode in the South Seas. One millionaire after another asked me for my story and each one got it more and more embroidered. I thoroughly enjoyed myself; and I shamelessly made use of my inventiveness as a means of getting free drinks.

Attention from the cruise management was, however, not forthcoming. They allotted me a poky little inside cabin with no windows at all – this for £3 a day on a millionaire's luxury yacht! As it happened, the *Stella Polaris* was built for cruising in cold northern waters, not in the tropics; and the design of all her cabins assured their occupants the maximum of heat and the minimum of air. The millionaires were paying around £2000 for the three months' cruise, besides current expenses, which must have been colossal considering the cocktail parties they gave and the curios they bought in bulk at each port.

The cruise management must have felt I was a pauper in comparison with these lavish spenders. In fact, my first four days aboard were most embarrassing as I had no money at all, and though I knew there would be an answer to my cable in time, I could feel doubt growing each day in the minds of the management as to whether I was completely bogus or not. It was with glee that, one evening, I was able to inform them that £50 had been placed to my credit at the ship's agents. Meanwhile I had also cabled the Consul at Papeéte to forward my luggage to Sydney together with my money; even so I knew that the odds were against my ever contacting them, as I would probably have left Sydney by the time they arrived. Anyhow I paid over the £30 and, by the end of the voyage, another £5 for tips and my bar bill. I had therefore £15 when we sailed into Suva, which had to keep me there five days and also pay for my ticket to Auckland. It was so little that the Suva passport authorities wouldn't let me land until, after an hour's arguing, they produced a police sergeant who escorted me to a booking agent's where he watched me buy a third-class ticket to Auckland for £7; then they were satisfied they'd be able to turn me out of the Fiji Islands if I spent the rest of my money. As it happened, however, I was lucky; and I went away from Suva with more money than I had when I arrived; but that'll be told in a moment.

For six days of the voyage the weather was most untropical. A high wind that sent the boat lurching from side to side. And it was so bad at Raratonga that we were unable to land. There is no wharf or lagoon to shelter in there; the boat anchors a half-mile from shore and you go the rest of the way by launch. I wasn't therefore able to verify the proud boast of a New Zealander I met in Tahiti who said: 'Raratonga is a damned sight better place than this hole. The natives are taught to respect a white man there – and they damn well get off the pavement when one comes along.'

From there we went to Pago Pago (pronounced Pango Pango), which has earned renown as the spot where Somerset Maugham wrote *Rain*. It must have been on such a day as we arrived that he had his inspiration. It was like a shower-bath, turned full on. Hour after hour it fell unceasingly; and the ninth day in succession, somebody told me. The inevitable native dances were held under cover. Broader of face and body than the Tahitians the natives seemed to be. Obviously they'd taken after their American masters in a love of gold. One naked little boy, in a corner of the warehouse where the performance was taking place, did a roaring business, despite the bad light, by posing for his picture. Each time a millionaire produced a camera, the little boy chirped: 'Me don't stand still till you give me dollar!'

An afternoon was our allotted time there and then we left for Apia. To the dismay of the cruise management we arrived two hours late, so our visit was cut down to three hours. Off went the millionaires to Stevenson's tomb like a pack of hounds. That was the sort of excursion they'd be able to brag about to their heart's content when they got back home; and surely this Jules Verne journey, under the wings of trained nurses, had no other purpose than to provide them with subjects to brag about? For what was left of their lives they'd be able to say unctuously to their old cronies: 'When I was in Tahiti ... when I was in Apia.' As it was, after spending a couple of hours in a South Sea island they'd say: 'What a horrible place compared with Raiatea'; and 'How unfriendly the people of Pago Pago are.' Ugh, what ants!

I spent my time in Apia talking to Olaf Nelson, a big, double-chinned half-caste with a deep musical voice who has twice been deported by the New Zealand Government (who control this part of Samoa) for his nationalistic activities among the people. Samoa used to be German and the New Zealand Government keep a watchful eye that there aren't demonstrations in favour of going back to Germany. As it happens, there's not much to fear of this because, Olaf Nelson explained to me, the average Samoan dislikes the Germans as much as he does the New Zealanders: what he wants is Samoa for the Samoans, and he includes American Samoa in that as well. When Nelson has been in trouble it's because he's been urging for wider powers to be given to the natives. In this he has succeeded in achieving a great deal, and as he said to me: 'We're quite satisfied with the Government at the moment.' What he couldn't understand, however, was why the New Zealand Government had allowed a Nazi school teacher to come to Apia to teach the children of the thirty-six Germans in the islands; especially as he flew the Nazi flag over his school. I couldn't understand myself and I had no time to find out; sitting in Olaf Nelson's office I heard the *Stella's* siren and I had to rush back.

2

And so to Suva. I stood on the quay and waved my handkerchief at the millionaires as the *Stella* moved away. I was quite sorry I'd been left behind. Some of them had been very charming, and it was going to be dull and quiet after the noise of the past ten days. I had taken a room in the cheapest hotel, and there I had to stay till the New Zealand boat left in five days' time. My first impression of Suva had not been favourable. The heat was the kind that kept one's clothing perpetually clinging to one's body; and the natives were fuzzy-wuzzies with none of the attractiveness of the Polynesians. There were many white women, but the climate gave them no help; one and all seemed to be flat-chested and their faces were tight-skinned and without colour. The men, too, looked tired, as if every movement was an effort. There was none of the irresponsibility of Tahiti. Here was a country where white men ruled and dressed for dinner and looked upon the coloured man as a servant.

It was in gloom therefore that I left the quay and wandered back to the hotel. For the life of me I couldn't see how I was going to fill in my time. I hadn't the money to go on any excursions, and so I couldn't see myself doing anything else than hanging around the hotel lounge. It was a dreary spot, with the Fijian equivalent of aspidistras and a green parrot with a persistent shrill whistle, and prints on the walls of Wellington at Waterloo and a setter carrying a pheasant. And the chairs were hard.

I got back and found a letter awaiting me. This was a surprise as I knew no one in the islands. And what I found inside made me call for a drink. Neatly folded around a card were two crisp £5 notes!

'Happy birthday and good luck,' was written on the card — and it was signed by one of the heiresses! I was thankful the *Stella* had already sailed. There could be therefore no question of my returning them: at the same time I was grateful that anyone should think of giving me such a gift and be so tactful as to hand it over after they'd gone. I wasted no time in sending an ecstatic cable to the *Stella*.

The situation was now considerably changed. I was able to buy several things that would help me to look a little more respectable when I arrived in New Zealand. I got, for instance, a white gabardine suit made for me. It cost 30s. at an Indian tailors. Then there were shirts, and a pair of shoes; and I was able to instruct a solicitor to draw up a power of attorney in the name of the British Consul in Tahiti, a procedure I'd learnt was necessary if the Consul was to get my money from the bank. But as the charge for this was £3, it was soon that I'd little of the £10 left. In fact, I had none to spare which might have enabled me to see more of the Fiji Islands than Suva. Despite my good fortune, I still had to loaf around the hotel.

Since I knew nothing of Fiji, I decided to fill the hours by finding out something about it. So, from the local newspaper editor, the publicity officer, and the chief of the local BBC I discovered such facts as that Indians, Fijians, and Europeans each have five representatives on the Legislative Council; that these are more an advisory body than anything else since Fiji, being a Crown Colony, is governed by benevolent despotism, e.g. the Governor. The main problem, however, facing the Colony is the ever-increasing Indian population. In the 1936 census there were ninety-eight thousand Fijians and eighty-five thousand Indians, but though the birth-rate of the two races is about the same, the Fijians have a higher mortality rate. In the not too far distant future therefore there will be more Indians than Fijians; as it is, the Indians, being harder working and cleverer, have ousted the Fijians from many spheres of the economic life of the islands. What people are wondering is what is going to happen when they are no longer the minority.

Other scraps of information I collected included that about the gold mine, though only discovered in 1931, which was now producing a £1000 worth of gold a day. And that though the Berlin and Rome radio stations were easily heard, Daventry was so faint that no one could be bothered to listen to it. And that the Japanese were fortifying the Caroline Islands which were only two-days' sailing from Suva. It was here in Suva, incidentally, that I first knew people who were in real fear of the yellow terror, in much the same way as Londoners fear air raids. Fiji, so the locals thought, would provide an ideal base for the Japanese as a jumping-off ground for an attack on New Zealand. The armed forces in Fiji, so they said, were hopelessly inadequate for defending the islands and the Japanese would have no difficulty in overcoming them. As it is today, however, Japanese are forbidden to enter the islands just as they are forbidden by the French to enter the Society Islands.

After these five days in Suva, I left by the *Niagara* for Auckland. It was an uneventful journey. In a burst of extravagance, knowing that £100 was waiting for me at Auckland, I changed my third-class ticket to a first-class. It gave me a cabin to myself and an Australian steward who preferred grousing to working; so bad-tempered was he that when I asked him to press my trousers he told me to go and do it myself. He accused Australia of being riddled with graft, and the union bosses, both there and in New Zealand, to be racketeers who had no regard for the men whose welfare they were paid to look after. He said that the cost of living in Australia had risen a £1 a week in one year and that both countries were heading for bankruptcy. The rulers, he said, had no idea of ruling, yet resented advice from Englishmen and Americans who might know better. Always at the back of their minds, however, was the secure knowledge that if bankruptcy did come upon them, they would be helped out of it by loans from the old country.

3

I heard more sentiments like these when I reached Auckland. From the first small shopkeeper I met, a tailor who sold me a tie in his shop a few hundred yards from the quay, I heard these words: 'We are too young to govern ourselves. We want a Colonial Government.' He surprised me. I fully expected a somewhat arrogant 'we can manage better without you' sort of attitude, both on the part of New Zealanders and Australians. But what this man said was typical of what I later heard from small wage-earners of both countries; though I don't mean to be misleading by coupling New Zealand and Australia together. Each has her own problems and each is profoundly jealous of the other; it is only their common attitude to the Mother Country which I found the same and which surprised me.

The tailor went on to talk to me about wages. Wages have risen with a jump since the Labour Government came into power. Laws have been passed making union membership compulsory for those over eighteen; and a sliding scale of wages has been introduced into every trade and business of the country. A male clerk of twenty-three, for instance, now gets £4 sterling a week compared with 45s. in 1936. The same for a shop assistant. Eight hours is a working day, and overtime is paid at time and a half for the first four hours and double time afterwards. Road labourers get £3 10s. sterling for a forty-hour week. A farm labourer gets £4. Maidservants get 26s., with board, for a forty-eight-hour week. Warehouse workers used to get 45s. and now get £4 a week. As far as waterside workers are concerned, no one knows what they earn. They are scheduled to have 2s. 8d. an hour for a forty-hour week. Then there is the overtime which they arrange for themselves day after day. My tailor friend told me that he numbered several, among his acquaintances, who were collecting £20 every Friday, who were running cars and renting houses in the residential area of Auckland.

'Everyone is in favour of higher wages,' he said, 'so long as there is plenty of money to pay them; but many of us who have even benefited are now wondering how long it will last. The Government have placed so many restrictions on business, profits have so fallen, and the cost of living so increased, that we can't help thinking that these fine days may end in bankruptcy.'

There is no doubt what the business leaders think.

Those whom I saw were filled with gloom – like those the world over when profits are not effortlessly filling their pockets. They admitted that the idea of the Government to make the country self-supporting was admirable in theory, but they were quite certain it couldn't work out in practice. The chief reason was the small population of New Zealand, which is only one million four hundred thousand. No firm could therefore build a factory and make it pay. For instance, an electric light bulb factory, with only thirty employees, would supply the needs of the whole country in six months. A steel factory, with a minimum organization of staff, would produce enough steel in three months. A motor-car factory would turn out enough cars in four months. And so on. Besides this lack of a market, the factories are faced with exceptional overheads owing to the high level of wages.

Then the business men have hard things to say of the Government's control of their money. The banks are controlled by the Government and not a penny of a private person's money is spent without them knowing it. They allege that it is as hard to get a New Zealand pound out of the country as it is to get ten marks out of Germany. In this respect I can support them. My £100 sterling was waiting for me when I arrived, but when I informed the bank manager that I was taking all but a few pounds of it to Australia, he explained that I would have to fill up various forms and receive the permission of the Government before I could do so. I got the permission after eight days, but I was luckier than some other tourists. An Englishman from India had £300 left after spending six months in the country, but when he applied to take it home with him, he was informed he couldn't take more than £20. And there was a London woman who was refused permission to take £500 of her money back to England.

I was lucky to have my uncle living near Auckland and it was thanks chiefly to him that I learnt so much in so short a time; and my own sketchy opinion of the situation was that it wasn't as bad as people made out. Certain aspects such as those I've just mentioned I didn't like. Also the fact that if a newspaper attacks the Government, the unions call a strike in the paper concerned; that sounds too much like the other end of a dictatorship. The Government, however, have had the courage to try something new, to make a gigantic experiment. Its supporters admit that adjustments will have to be made, but they're confident that a balance will be secured in time. Then, they say, New Zealand will be the envy of the world because her people will have a higher standard of living than any other nation. If, on the other hand, the experiment fails, because of the war or for some other reason, they do not feel they will suffer, because, as a union secretary put it to me: 'We know that Britain will not let us sink into inflation and bankruptcy.'

4

This reliance on Britain I found in Australia as well. It was the confidence of a rich man's son who knows that if he gets into trouble, his father will help him out; not that he intends to ask for help unless he absolutely needs it; only, unlike an orphan or a poor man's son, he has a background behind him in which he can shelter if it comes to the worst. Neither Australia nor New Zealand have any intention to shirk their end of the partnership. That's old news, the war has proved that. But when I arrived in Sydney, since it had so often been drilled into me that the Empire was breaking up, I believed it to be true; and on every side of me I expected to hear words of determination to steer clear of European entanglements at all costs; and if Britain got mixed up in a war, well, that was just too bad. Within five minutes of my landing, however, on that sunny morning when the world's newspapers were screaming Hitler's march into Prague, the driver of the taxi which was speeding me to my hotel shouted over his shoulder: 'We have to slam that man from the face of the earth some time or other, so why don't we get on with it now?' I was to hear plenty more of that kind of talk, from labourers, business men, shop assistants, railway porters; and it was always the word 'we' that they used, never 'you'.

Strangely enough they weren't at all impressed at the appointment of the Duke of Kent as Governor-General. I found them hypersensitive as to what the old country thought of Australia, and they imagined they could see in this appointment a double meaning; as if Britain doubted the loyalty of Australia and was sending a Royal Duke to win her over. They argued they couldn't be any more loyal than they already were and Royalty in the country could only result in snobbishness among the wealthy; while the poor would look upon it as a waste of time and expense. As for myself, I'd hoped to make some money out of the Duke of Kent; and that there would be one or two letters from London commissioning me to write articles on his home, etc. I was, however, needlessly optimistic. There wasn't a line.

Sydney was so hot that you could have fried eggs and bacon on the pavement any hour of the day. Thinking that by having a smart address I'd be more likely to impress the local newspapers, I took a poky little room on the top floor of the Australia Hotel. Again I was out of luck. I was quite unable to bluff them into hiring me to do anything. They proffered the old story of being willing to read anything I cared to submit, but this I was too lazy to do;

firstly because I couldn't risk the inevitable expense which I'd have to pay out when collecting material, and secondly, even if an article was accepted, payment was very small. I had worked out that I could spend £20 in Australia and not a penny more. That would leave me with £25 for the fare to Japan, £40 for the fare across Siberia to England and a measely £10 to spend on the way. I had, however, yet to find out whether I could get a visa for Japan and another visa to take me through Russia. Many people had warned me that, since I was described on my passport as a journalist, neither Japan nor Russia would want me. I was, therefore, fully prepared to find I'd have to go home by another way; and I'd already made up my mind that this would be via America. Luckily, on my first evening in Sydney I met the Japanese Consul-General at a party and he assured me that he would be only too pleased to give me a visa. 'The more Englishmen to see my country, the better,' he said. But whether I got a Russian visa would have to remain in doubt until I saw the Soviet Embassy in Tokyo.

I therefore booked a second-class ticket on the *Kamo Maru*, leaving Sydney on 2 April. The price of £25 was reasonable since it was a five weeks' voyage, and the boat was calling at Brisbane, Thursday Island, Davao, Manila, Hong Kong, Shanghai and five ports in Japan before reaching Yokohama; I could, however, if I wished, either break my journey at any port on the way or get off at Kobe and have a free train fare to Tokyo. How I was going to live within my £10 pocket money I refused to think; but I had a feeling that somehow it would be all right.

Meanwhile, in addition to my Suva gabardine suit, I'd bought a pair of grey flannel trousers and a double-breasted blue flannel coat. These I wore every day (and continued to do so till I reached home two months later) since gabardine suits seemed to be out of fashion in Australia. On occasions, unfortunately, I was invited to parties where evening dress was worn; and then I appeared in my white gabardine trousers, my double-breasted blue coat, a white shirt and a black bow tie.

On the first occasion I arrayed myself like this, I'd been invited out to dinner at Princes. This is a dance restaurant equal in its band, its food and the glamorous women numbered among its customers, to any top flight restaurant in London or New York. I confess I had come to Australia in the same condescending mood as a Londoner goes to Manchester. I expected the women to have bad skins, dowdy clothes and voices you could cut with a saw; and the men to be bronzed Tarzans who, in scanty shorts, lounged the day through on the beaches. Quite wrong of course I was. At Princes that evening one girl after another had a figure and looks of a film star; and wore her clothes with the chic and poise of a young American rather than the gaucheness of an English débutante. The men, too, were like any of the young men about town seen around Fifth Avenue and Mayfair; and yet a dozen I met of both sexes had their homes hundreds of miles away in the bush and a visit to Sydney was as much an adventure as a Londoner's visit to Paris. Later in Melbourne it was the same. And in both cities, except in Hollywood, I had never seen such a universal slimness of figure and prettiness of face among typists, shop assistants, waitresses and usherettes. Their knowledge of clothes and make-up leave the English far behind.

Yet you quickly sense the inferiority complex they have of English people. The whole nation suffers from it and the mirror of the affliction is in the newspapers. They are like English provincial newspapers except they are four

thousand miles away from London instead of a hundred or
so. All the page lead stories are London stories; and, like as
not, any story on Australia is dated from London. In the
gossip columns London is always being mentioned, either
concerning someone who is going to London or someone
who has come from London. People talk about a trip to
London in the same way as a film-struck girl talks of a trip
to Hollywood. Those who have done it can dine out on
their experiences for years to come and affect a snobbishness when the name of a famous politician crops up, like
the schoolboy who knows the captain of the school cricket
eleven in the holidays; even though they've never even
seen the man. And, of course, the most popular sales talk
of a shop assistant is to say that the article is the latest
thing in London.

5

For ten days in Sydney I kept to the minimum expense
while at the same time appearing as comfortably off as
possible. The pretence was beginning to bore, but for
good or for evil I imagined I'd more chance making
money by looking prosperous than by looking down and
out. At a cocktail party I met an English theatrical producer
who at one time in London was as well known as C. B.
Cochran. He buttonholed me in a corner and expounded a
grandiose scheme to bring out world-famous actors and
actresses to Australia over a period of two years, thus
coinciding with the stay of the Kents. He explained that he
had already £20,000 as backing, and that his next step was
to persuade such people as Noël Coward, the Lunts, and
Charles Laughton, that it was worth their while to spend
three months touring Australia. In this he thought I could
help by writing an article on the theatrical possibilities of

the southern hemisphere; and so that he might explain his plans more fully, he invited me to lunch at Princes the following day.

As we sat down at a sofa table and we were looking at the menu, I heard him say: 'The lunch is on you.' He said it in the tone of voice as one says: 'The lunch is on me.' And so the words didn't sink into me and instead I replied: 'Oh no, don't be silly . . . let's each pay for our own.' This offer I made in half-hearted politeness, hoping he wouldn't accept it as I'd spent my quota for the week and I would have had a sandwich lunch if he hadn't asked me to Princes. After we'd ordered the food, he said: 'What would you like to drink?' I looked at the wine list and with his help chose a Liebfraumilch. It was very good and expensive; and as we sipped it and ate the excellent food, he told me of his past successes and failures in London. How he had lost £300,000 two years previously but how he had since redeemed his losses in Australia. If only he could succeed in signing a half-dozen big names for an Australian tour, he would make so much money that he would return to London and put on bigger shows than ever. He talked with a kind of boyish enthusiasm that was charming; and what with the wine and the good food, by the time the coffee came I was beginning to like him. At that point he asked the waiter for cigars and two Biscuit Débouche's 1889; before they arrived however I offered him a Player's. He looked at it and said: 'Oh, I must smoke Craven A,' and he called the cigarette girl for a packet, telling her to put it on the bill. For three-quarters of an hour more we were together as he told tales of his exploits in the theatrical world, and then he called for the bill. Without a flicker of an eyelid he took a glance at it and pushed the plate over to me. It was done with such an air of confidence that I lost my senses. Without a murmur I brought forth my notecase and paid for it. He continued talking to me as if nothing unusual had happened and didn't stop until we'd walked up the stairs to the street. Then he paused, and looking at me said: 'I'm going to make an extraordinary request . . . I'm going to see my lawyer at six-thirty . . . but until then I've only fourpence . . . could you, old man, lend me £1?' That was the last straw. Feebly I said I hadn't a £1 but would two bob do? Apparently it would, because with a gay: 'Thanks, old man,' he pocketed the coin and went off.

The next day I went off to Melbourne for the weekend. I arrived in time to get to the opening night of the Russian Ballet and to see Baronova, Gregoroeva and Anton Dolin among others, dancing to an orchestra which was too small to drown the squeaks of the floorboards. Afterwards I was taken to a party for the performers, and when Sevastianov, Baronova's husband, heard that I might be going to Moscow, he asked me to give a message to his sister who is an actress there. Most interesting person present however was Stuart Menzies, now Prime Minister of Australia, but then in the wilderness after resigning from the Attorney-Generalship. In actual fact, ten days after my seeing him, Lyons the Premier died; and a few days after that Menzies had taken his place. Amid the chirrup of ballet talk, he told me that it was his conviction there would be no war for two years. But if there was, we need have no fear of the Empire not standing together. He assured me that both Australia and Canada would be even more warlike than the English. 'There is a deep conviction in every Australian's heart that once we take the lone road, we are lost.' He is a big man, over six foot in height; though his hair is thin and white, his face does not look old. He has a deep voice with only a slight Australian accent. He has a way of fixing his whole attention on you when he is talking or when you are talking to him. He is surprising both critics and friends by the way he is holding his office. Most people thought he was the one man in Australia for the job but few thought he was strong enough to keep the members of his Government in harmony for long.

From Melbourne I went to Canberra. It was a night train, and at Goulburn at eleven o'clock I had to change to the small branch line that runs to the capital. Just as the train was about to pull out a man tumbled into my compartment, his necktie askew and his face perspiring. 'Heaven knows what the reporters will say after that!' he gasped. I looked intelligent, pretending I knew exactly who he was, and asked: 'Were they unpleasant?' He smiled, a nice smile of a man who had seen a lot of life and who had always kept his sense of humour. He looked about forty, a lean bronzed face which made his eyes startlingly blue. He reminded me at once of Lord Nuffield. 'Oh no. They were all right,' he answered.

For twenty minutes we talked on various topics of the day. He appeared as interested to hear what I had to say as he was to talk himself. I tried hard to discover from his remarks who he might be but without result; until at last I said to him: 'I suppose this scare talk of war on the part of the Government is just the old dodge of taking the people's mind off the social problems of the country?' There was a pause. He coughed. 'Oh no, it isn't,' he said, 'and I happen to know. You see, I am Minister of Defence!'

His name was Brigadier Street. More than anyone it is he that should have the kudos for the state of preparedness on the part of Australia. In a quieter way than Hore-Belisha he effected a number of reforms in the Australian army over the past three years. I asked him whether he thought Japan to be threatening Australia. 'Not yet,' he said, 'their hands are full for some years to come. But we must never forget that Darwin is nearer their Caroline Islands than it is to Sydney.' He is dead now, killed in an aeroplane accident; but not before he had laid the foundations of Australia's great war effort.

I spent two days in Canberra. I went over 'Yarrumla,' the residence of the Governor-General where the Kents were to live, a lonely, uncomfortable house which the Government were making great efforts to improve; in fact they'd budgeted £20,000 to be spent on it. And for the rest of the time I meandered about the spacious avenues and parks. It is more like a health spa than a capital. No houses line the roads except the few official residences of those connected with the Government. The station with its wooden fence reminded me of Bodmin Road in Cornwall.

In Canberra at the time was the British Air Mission, one of whose members was Sir Donald Banks who had already achieved remarkable results in the organization of aeroplane factories in Canada. I'd met him once in London with my brother Nigel, and as he was on the same train going back to Sydney I sat with him for a while. Most of what he said I have forgotten, but there was one sentence which he said so decisively that I noted it down. 'We have two wars to fight,' he said, 'first we must beat Germany . . . and then Russia.' He spoke with the same matter-of-fact conviction as one talks of winter following autumn. It chilled me with fear, the first time for many months that reality of the sores in the world were once more in my mind. I remember when late that night I reached my hotel I left my bags and then went out again to walk along the deserted streets. The world was caught in a trap from which there was no escape. It was no use deceiving oneself. If not this year, then the next. Perhaps it would have started even before I got back. And for a fleeting moment I thought of cancelling my passage to Japan and taking the first boat home.

Chapter Twelve

WHO LIKES THE JAPANESE?

I WENT ABOARD the *Kamo Maru* with only the barest necessities in my small suitcase. I had arranged for my diary, letters and photographs to be sent home; and I left instructions that when my trunk from Tahiti arrived, it was to be sent home, too. I had with me my camera, though I was fully prepared that at some time or other it would be confiscated. This was because I had no liking for the Japanese and viewed them with considerable suspicion.

In the second class I was the only passenger. I had to myself a double-deck cabin in the stern, all the second-class deck space, the dining-room, and the lounge; and there were four Japanese stewards who had nothing else to do except to look after me. When I remarked upon this unaccustomed luxury to the tubby, round-faced purser, he laughed. 'Generally at this time of year we are full – but now no one likes us!' And he burst into laughter again as if the boycott was a huge joke.

We edged away from the wharf at noon, 2 April. Japanese music blared from the loud-speakers and passengers hurled coloured-paper streamers to their friends on the quay. In a few minutes we were out in the middle of the harbour of bays and passing slowly under the Bridge which all Sydney people refer to as 'our bridge'; and which every visitor gets bored to tears with because of the scores of times he's asked his opinion of it. My answer was always perfectly frank. I neither thought the harbour as beautiful as that of San Francisco nor the Bridge as fine as the Golden Gate.

I had my lunch alone. It was excellent, consisting of grilled thrush and Spanish chestnut pudding; and the first meal of some forty I had on the voyage at which no dish was ever repeated and which provided a standard of food unequalled by any British line. Always there was a menu in a cover of lovely Japanese coloured designs (different for each meal), and at this first lunch there was also a booklet, a guide to the Japanese language presented to me with the compliments of the NYK. I got busy with it in an effort to talk to the stewards. I was greeted with shrieks of merriment. My pronunciation was quite astray and they tried hard to improve it. So the game went on, until in a pause one of them, quite out of the blue (we hadn't mentioned politics), said in his best English: 'Japan so small and so full. Australia so big and so empty!' And then laughed in a merry way as if he'd said something very funny.

2

For ten days we hugged the Barrier Reef, never out of sight of the Queensland coast, and passing islands so close that we could see the colour of the sea-birds perching on the rocks. A canvas bathing pool had been rigged up on the fore-deck, and in the blaze of the day I would cool myself in the water; when I got out it was so hot that I was dry in five minutes without touching a towel, and as I walked the deck it seemed that my feet were on hot coals. I would hang over the side and watch the porpoises, their brown bodies glistening in the sunlight, leaping and plunging in a hectic race to keep up with us; or I'd join the squat sailors in the stern who were throwing their fishing-lines in the churn of our wake.

I was allowed to wander pretty freely in the first class, making a friend there of an Australian marine engineer named Jefferies who was on his way to Hong Kong to take up an appointment as chief engineer of a newly-built coastal steamer. He was a huge fellow with a mouth like Joe E. Brown; and he had tales to tell of the Southern Seas that were not half exhausted after twenty days of his companionship.

One or two were about Errol Flynn. Flynn was adventuring around New Guinea when Jefferies first met him. Flynn was at the time recruiting natives for the New Guinea Gold Fields. Black-birding, it's called, and the price is £20 for every native who will accept a two-years' agreement to work in the mines. Flynn wasn't having much success until one day, in front of a Chief, he played the disappearing and reappearing coin trick – producing coins from behind his ears and out of his mouth, from the tummy of the Chief and the seat of his trousers. The Chief was amazed, quite certain it was a miracle. And so Flynn, taking advantage of the situation, held up the bamboo stick he had in his hand and explained that if the Chief had the stick, each time the moon was full he could do the same. The Chief forthwith took Flynn at his word and in exchange for the stick gave him fifty boys. Which meant a £1000 into the pocket of Errol Flynn.

At another time he wanted to make a film of the South Seas with Jefferies, but changed his mind when he bought a half-share in a Salamara hotel. Once he bathed naked for a bet on a Sydney beach and when a policeman arrived to arrest him for indecency he explained that a shark had bitten off his trunks; and so convincing was he that the policeman let him off.

There was a German aboard who, though an Aryan, was a refugee from the Nazis. In the sobriety of the day he would talk of his hate of Hitler. 'Only the youths are with him,' he said, 'we older people hate him. We felt last September that you should have called his bluff. We used to say: "If only Eden was Premier and not Chamberlain."'

But in the evening as he sat drinking beer with Jefferies and me his Teutonic upbringing was too strong for him. 'England,' he would say, 'will be beaten in a few months if a war takes place with Germany within two years. She will be committing suicide. She is a dwarf compared with Germany's strength. Even her navy is not as powerful . . . for Germany has secretly armed all her merchant ships so that her fleet is both more modern and larger than yours.' He was on his way to Manila, he told us, having left his wife and small daughter in Sydney. He had invested a large amount of his savings in an NYK ticket which he had paid for in Germany with the marks he couldn't take out of the country; and so he was using up the ticket by wandering around in NYK boats. He had already been to Japan and, à propos of this visit, he said to me one day: 'What a pity your people and mine can't get together – because it is in the East that the danger lies. The West will need all its strength to defend its existence.'

It was difficult to believe this when talking to the Japanese on board. They were gay and amusing companions and showed an astonishing naïvety in their efforts to be liked. Not having known any before, I was surprised to find that I felt as much at ease with them as with my own race. One among them was a young Consul official returning to the Foreign Office in Tokyo; he attempted to alter my anti-Japanese outlook.

'It is not easy for us in Japan to forget how you took Hong Kong and established yourselves in other parts of

China,' he said. 'Hong Kong became yours after a war caused by the refusal of the Chinese to allow you to import opium from Burma. You excuse yourselves by saying that that was long ago and two wrongs don't make a right; but you make no effort to make amends by returning the conquered territory to its owners. If you are like that, why shouldn't other nations expand as well?'

Such questions, if I want to be honest, I find difficult to answer. I can readily put myself in the place of a foreigner who boils with rage over our superior, sanctimonious attitude. And you'll find our behaviour in China, if you look into its history, quite shameless.

'You conveniently forget, now that you've condemned Japan as an aggressor nation,' he went on, 'that ever since the first Englishman landed in China, the Chinese have been trying to get you out. The memories of most of your people are so short that they do not remember that in 1927 five battalions of British troops had to be sent to Shanghai to restore order; and the Kuomintang published a declaration at the time to herald the "revolutionary struggle against British imperialism".'

I had to admit that my memory was very short, and that most of what he told me was new to me. In England we think of the Chinese as peaceful, easy-going people who love us as brothers; and as far as I was concerned I never even considered the possibility of the Japanese having a case for their actions. I was beginning to learn.

3

We spent a morning at Thursday Island, a weird shell of a place which once upon a time roared with the swashbuckling lives of pirates, pearl merchants, adventurers and gamblers. We'd left the ship in the outer bay and came to the wooden wharf by a launch manned by three coal-black aborigines. A half-dozen pearl luggers were anchored nearby, and we could see the little Japanese divers squatting on the decks; for the Japanese are easily the best pearl divers in these parts, a fact which is a never-ending source of chagrin to the Australians. But though pearl diving still goes on, there is none of the prosperity of the old days. The main street was like the deserted set of *Barbary Coast* I'd seen in Hollywood. The saloons that once were filled with noise and drinking, perhaps a score of them, were boarded up with faded signs of 'For Sale' nailed to the rotting wooden walls; and if you looked closely you could see dim posters proclaiming the date of the opening night of some Mae West of long ago. It was indeed a city of the dead.

As I was returning to the launch, I passed two men sitting on the kerb; I'd hardly noticed them until I heard them speaking the broadest Scotch to each other. Their clothes were bedraggled to look at; and they wore caps which was strange for this part of the world. I stopped to have a word with them and they told me that they were brothers who, eleven years before, had left their native Highlands to seek their fortune in Australia. They'd done everything from gold-mining in Kalgoorlie to sheep farming in New South Wales, and they'd always remained together. Nor had either of them made a fortune. In fact, they just hoboed from Darwin, and for a month they'd been in TI without jobs. 'Only white trash can get jobs,' they explained. Now they had a plan to go to the Solomon Islands and they were hanging around for some boat which might be travelling that way. Maybe a month they'd have to wait, maybe six. They were a forlorn couple, and when I gave them five bob they were as grateful as starved dogs being given a bone.

For six days after leaving TI we touched no port, nor saw no passing ship. We were on a lonely track of the seas, sailing first through the Torres Strait, then the Arafura Sea south of Papua, and through the Banda Sea, dotted with islands of the eastern arm of the Netherland East Indies. No wind stirred the calm of the waters. Sometimes we'd see a giant shark leap at the sky from the depths and fall back with a splash that sounded like the crack of a whip. We'd twist and turn among the islands, so close to them that we would wave at the natives of the many that were inhabited. Often they'd sail out to meet us in their canoes with snow-white sails, and we'd throw at them anything that was handy; picture magazines, an old hat, or even cracked plates the dining-room steward found. Even more beautiful was it at night when the moon flooded the sea in silver and painted the islands in ghostliness. Jefferies said that he always considered this journey the loveliest sail in the world; and I would have agreed if I hadn't known Tahiti and Moorea and Bora Bora and Toopua.

At last we reached Davao, the hot and dirty port of Mindanao, the second largest island of the Philippines. It lies at the foot of a range of high hills and at the far corner of a deep bay that cuts into the island. Its streets are long and dusty, and its shops and bars are windowless like those of Panama. It is no advertisement for American colonization. There are only twenty Americans living there. They have apparently surrendered this rich and fertile island to the Japanese, of whom there are ten thousand in the district of Davao alone. This place is, in fact, a danger spot of the world. The Japanese, working much harder and more skilfully than the Filipinos, have collared the hemp and sugar plantations; and observers say that it is only a matter of time before they will be instructed from Tokyo to appeal to the Japanese armed forces 'to come to their help.'

This isn't likely to be before 1946, when the Philippines are promised complete independence by the United States. Then anything may happen, and now that the prospect of Japanese domination is facing them, the Filipinos are regretting like hell they've made such a fuss to become independent. It is difficult to see what they now can do about it. They aren't energetic enough to develop their country by themselves because, as a member of their Government put it: 'The Filipino does not work enough, he does not work continuously, he does not work scientifically . . . and, what is worse, many Filipinos do not work at all.' Nor can they hope to defend it without the aid of America, and in the event of America not coming to their help the Japanese will not be able to resist the temptation of marching in with a 'New Order for the Philippines.'

We had a day and a night in Davao, loading hemp from lighters, and then we sailed up the coast to Manila. Japanese swarmed on the boat here, and we set off for Hong Kong with two hundred in the steerage and every cabin full both in the first and the second classes. My companion was a garrulous American of sixty years, with eyes that squinted at right angles to each other. In the three days and nights he told me of a score of shady incidents he'd been mixed up in, in Manchukuo and Japan; and he seemed to think that the Japanese wouldn't want to see him any more. He'd been staying three months in Manila, and was on his way to Shanghai. A knapsack was his only luggage, and there were holes in his shirt, and a patch in the seat of his trousers. He earned a meagre living by teaching English. He gave me certain advice of the ways of the Orient. 'Chinks will nab anything they lay their damned hands on,' he said on the second morning, looking round to see no one was peeping through the porthole. 'See here, I keep my dough in this specially made strap . . . on the groin.'

We crossed the China Sea uneventfully, arriving off Hong Kong in a dense fog. We hung around for a couple of hours, bleating like a lost sheep, until it lifted a little, and we could slowly nose our way through the mass of islands that guard the entrance of the harbour. We could see the gun emplacements and the barbed wire that zigzagged round the cliffs, and we were so close that we could see the Chinese written characters forbidding anyone to land. Outside the purser's office, and in other parts of the ship, there were notices forbidding anyone to take photographs. It was difficult to believe this was so. I counted thirty Japanese in the stern, all with their cameras, hurriedly snapping pictures of the fortress they would so like to possess. They showed a disregard to officialdom that, in Japan, would land a foreigner in gaol. When I was in Tokyo two American students were arrested for taking photographs of Yokohama from a Japanese liner. And the two contrasting incidents upheld my American companion's opinion of the nation: 'They grin like Cheshire cats in a foreign country and get away with murder. But in Japan they treat a foreigner as a criminal before he even thinks of a crime to commit.'

Chapter Thirteen

ORIENTAL KALEIDOSCOPE

To write of the Far East in a single chapter is as absurd as copying out the Bible on a penny stamp.

I found Hong Kong as complacent as Stratford-on-Avon; and this surprised me, as from a distance I'd come to the conclusion that at any moment the Japanese might attack it. There appeared to be no air-raid shelters, no plans to evacuate the population, and no talk that these precautions were necessary. When I asked what would happen if it was besieged, people shrugged their shoulders, saying: 'We'd last three months in any case.'

The fighting abilities of the Japanese were rated very low; and it was considered that the commanders, if faced by swiftly-changing tactics of British soldiers and sailors, would be as useless as aeroplanes without wings. So I asked Graham Barrow, Reuter's correspondent in Hong Kong, why, in that case, the Chinese were being beaten.

'The Chinese being beaten?' he replied. 'You won't find that idea among us who are covering the war.'

To a layman this was difficult to believe. All ports were in Japanese hands. Every big city had been surrendered – Peking, Shanghai, Nanking, Hankow, Canton. And the Government had taken refuge in Chungking, one thousand miles from Nanking, where they were when the war started. I would have thought that the Chinese were on the run;

but what Graham Barrow had said I found to be the view of the greater proportion of European business men and newspaper correspondents I met.

Naturally, I tried to find out how it was, considering the circumstances, that China was going to win the war. But the answers were vague and conflicting. I would be told that the Chinese military leaders were soaked in graft, that they were incompetent, that they wouldn't co-ordinate with each other, and wouldn't take advice from any European adviser. At the same time, I would be told that the withdrawal was strategic, forcing the Japanese to lengthen their lines of communication, and enabling the Chinese to harass them day and night. I would be told that the Chinese were incapable of winning an offensive victory in the field, and yet the time would come when the Japanese would withdraw to the coast. To an outsider, who knew nothing of the Chinese character, it seemed that Graham Barrow and his friends were wishful thinkers. But when I was in Tokyo a Japanese diplomat put in a sentence what they were driving at. He said: 'When I was in Peking, last month, an old Chinaman whom I have long known came to me saying in all seriousness: "We Chinese know that your invasion of our country is only a passing phase of a century or so."' The remark cleared the fog in my mind. Even if in the next year or two there is a 'peace,' from the Chinese point of view it will only be a truce. It will not be the end of the war. They will reorganize their forces and strike again. They will give the Japanese no rest, no time to consolidate their gains. With the persistency of mosquitoes in a tropical swamp, they will bite and bite until in weary desperation the Japanese withdraw. Perhaps in ten years. Perhaps in a hundred. The time does not matter.

From the British outlook, if the army remains in power in Japan, it is best that the war should drag on and that stability does not come to China. Likewise from the French, or the American, or the Italian. An American merchant in Shanghai was one of several who explained to me why. 'Our trade,' he said, 'has of course suffered considerably, but we are at least still keeping our heads above water. If the Japanese licked the Chinese, and if they were really able to organize the territory they occupy, it wouldn't be long before they turfed us out. After all, there is no military force to oppose them except a few hundred soldiers in Shanghai and a few score in Peking and Tientsin. Once they did, one couldn't expect America to send an expeditionary force to rescue us; and Britain obviously couldn't do much. Then, on the other hand, supposing the Chinese licked the Japanese, it would be silly to think they would be content with that. The Chinese are anti-foreigners, Japanese or Europeans, and they would soon swing round from their present policy of courting us to that of driving us away. We who have lived here for many years do not forget the Chinese boycotts and armed demonstrations against us. In 1937, during the Shanghai fighting, many were convinced, among them myself, that if Chiang Kai Shek's forces had succeeded in driving the Japanese into the Whangpoo, the Chinese would have swept through the International Settlement. Mind you, it was a very near thing. The Japs had only four thousand troops defending the Hongkew area against Kai Shek's army of fifty thousand. The Chinese even got through to the Bund, and it was only rank incompetence on their part that turned imminent victory into defeat. But it would be humbug not to admit we were thankful when the Japs got the upper hand.'

2

My father came to my rescue in Hong Kong with a cheque; and this considerably improved my financial position, coupled with the discovery that, before leaving for Japan, through certain Chinese exchange dealers I would be able to get 27 yen to the £1 instead of the official 17. I stayed therefore a few days in Hong Kong before taking an Italian liner up to Shanghai. The liner was crammed with Jewish refugees who were following the Russian influx into Shanghai of twenty years before. They were an ugly, pathetic sight. Their future was as blank as a man who has been sentenced to life imprisonment. Already ten thousand were quartered in camps outside the International Settlement in the Hongkew area, and prospects of employment were practically nil. A thousand of these, I was told, were professional men but only two hundred had found employment of any kind. The story of how the Russians sank to accepting coolie wages has often been told. Whether the Jews will do the same remains to be seen. Their trouble is made doubly worse by the already large number of Chinese refugees in the International Settlement. That they may overcome their difficulties by cunning Jewish methods is suggested by the story of a friend of mine. He had a flat to let in the Avenue Haig, and as flats are at a premium in Shanghai, he knew he could get a good price for it. When, however, a forlorn Jewish refugee, with his wife and four children, called on him and begged for a reduced rate, he was moved to pity and let them have it. A week later, having left behind a picture, he went back. Instead of the Jew in the flat, he found an American. And it transpired that the Jew, having got the reduced rate, went the same day to the American and rented the flat to him for a hundred dollars a month more.

Shanghai is a flat, dusty, smelly city, with a tense atmosphere; at any moment, as you walk along the street, you expect a hold-up and to hear the crack of shots. Danger, excitement and a certain romance is in the air. Ten minutes after the liner docked I was in a launch, talking to an American river police sergeant, on my way to the Customs. Suddenly he nudged me. 'See that guy with a coat over his arm?' His thumb pointed to a dark young Russian, as good-looking as a film star. 'I'll call him over. He's a pickpocket.' The young man answered the call. 'Had any luck today?' asked the sergeant. 'No,' answered the man, 'no luck at all. I have only just started.' He spoke good English and the sergeant let me talk to him. It seemed the most natural thing to talk of his exploits, despite the presence of the policeman. 'Sometimes,' he explained, 'I do quite well on this launch as the people go to the Customs. I am one of a gang and we share what we collect.' The sergeant laughed. 'Anyhow, come into the lavatory. I'll have to search you. If, as you say, you've had no luck, I'll let you go.'

Pickpockets, you see, are as insignificant lawbreakers in Shanghai as cyclists without rear lights are in England. The daily task of the police is to deal with gunmen who operate on a far bigger scale than ever was the case in the wild days of Chicago. Several lose their lives every year, and yet there is no national honour attached to their bravery. They are serving an International Settlement. They don't die for their country.

Over four hundred Britishers are in the Force. They're all sergeants, either detectives or policemen, and they have about four thousand Chinese under them. There are White Russians and Sikhs as well. The Chief Constable is Major Bourne, who won the M.C. in the Great War. Two policemen patrol the grounds of his home day and night; and his two children can never go out without a guard for fear of kidnappers. And yet, he and his wife appear as indifferent to danger as if they were a retired couple in Budleigh Salterton. I went with them to the police sports. The stands were crowded with Europeans and Chinese. Mrs Bourne was to present the prizes, and just before she mounted the dais to do so she said to me: 'I often wonder what I would do if someone on such an occasion as this tried to shoot me.' The day before, the wife of a police sergeant was actually faced with this problem. She and her husband were in a tram in the Bubbling Well Road on their way to the cinema when a bullet smashed the window beside them. The sergeant was out of the tram in a second and was firing at a coolie that was running away. He missed, but after reporting the matter, the two of them went on to the pictures. The Chinese have a nasty habit of revenging themselves on the police for relatives that have been arrested (you can hire an assassin for a couple of pounds, it is said). Shortly before I arrived, the chief Chinese detective of the Force, a man named Lo, had been assassinated. He himself had been a bandit before he came over to the side of the law; and with him he had brought fifty thousand 'dudies' or followers, which is the other name for them. These 'dudies' looked upon him as their leader and acted as informers. For several years, since they were in every kind of Shanghai life, they were able to tip him off before any plan to kill him succeeded. He, however, had a girlfriend whom he liked to visit unaccompanied by his guards; and on one such visit his 'dudies' failed him. As he came away from her apartment he was greeted by a hail of bullets. A gang, whose leader he had arrested, had got their revenge.

The work of the police is made more difficult by the Japanese. A diplomat's patience has to be added to their qualifications. On the second day I was there a prominent British educationalist was killed, along with a Japanese sentry, as a result of a collision between his car and a Japanese-owned bus in the Japanese area of Hongkew. The man's wife and a British police sergeant were seriously injured and taken to hospital for treatment. They were at once put on the danger list, but this didn't stop a Japanese officer thrusting his way to where they were lying and interrogating them in an offensive manner. An assistant commissioner of the police tried to reason with him, whereupon the Japanese officer hit him in the face.

3

It is difficult to understand why the Japanese are so unpleasant in China. Vere Redman, who was *Daily Mail* correspondent in Tokyo and who has covered for his newspaper many phases of the war, says there are two Japanese nations; the one which is in China and the other which is in Japan. 'There must be something in the air of China that makes a Japanese into an unfeeling bully,' he told me, 'because there is no more courteous and friendly person than he when he is in his own country.' I discovered this for myself, and also that the great majority of the Japanese population are ignorant of the brutality and conceit of their army. And that the intelligent civilians who do know are ashamed. I had lunch in Tokyo one day with Yukichi Iwanaga who was head of Domei, the news agency, until he died a few weeks ago. He was responsible for the dissemination of Japanese news to the whole world, not only to Japan. He was on the same level as the Minister of Information. I was asking him why the Japanese people permitted their army to disgrace the nation, and he replied: 'They don't know of any of the beastly things that happen.

It is my job to hide the truth, and I tell you, it disgusts me having to do it.' I remember he went on to talk about Hore-Belisha. 'I wish,' he said, 'we could get someone like that to turn out our generals.'

Look, for instance, at a little publicized example of their obnoxious activities in Shanghai. Stretching out of the International Settlement into the districts are roads which come under the jurisdiction of the Municipal Council; in other words it has extra-territorial rights over them. A hundred yards off the roads, the Japanese-sponsored Chinese puppets take over control. If, therefore, a crime is committed on one of these roads the criminal has only to run a hundred yards for him to be free form the pursuing Municipal Police; and it is very seldom that the puppet police ever catch him, let alone hand him back to the Municipal Police. Such lack of co-operation is alone enough to anger the Europeans; but it is made much worse by the practice of the Japanese to let opium dens flourish in these areas, while in the Settlement itself the Municipal Police naturally forbid them.

I was taken to one of these dens by Kenneth Selby-Walker, Reuter's Special Correspondent. Incidentally, never will I allow that my countrymen in far-off places are frigid and inhospitable. I didn't know Selby-Walker from Adam until I rang him up and introduced myself. He promptly came round to see me, and while I was in Shanghai he and his young wife continuously entertained me and went to endless trouble to assure that I saw all I wanted. Such friendliness I found whenever I met Englishmen during my journeys, and the coldness I had been led to expect to find in them I found only in Americans. But as I said, Selby-Walker took me to one of these dens.

It was not as sinister as I expected. The building was called 'The Hollywood,' off Jessfield Road. The chief amusement in it was bahjeu and roulette. The gambling was pretty high, and, to protect their customers against bandits, it had been necessary for the proprietors to have built two gun-turrets at either end of the outside of the building. One of the guards, we were told, had shot the other the night before by mistake. Inside, it was the size of a dance-hall, with paper partitions dividing one gambling room from another. At one end were the small rooms of the opium smokers, and the sickly, pungent smell of the opium pervaded the whole place. What I noticed most was the child labour. There were children of nine or so, hurrying to and fro like waitresses in a restaurant. Not only were they employed in the gambling rooms, but also in the job of preparing the pipes of the opium smokers. I looked in at one of these small rooms and saw a little boy, squatting beside an old Chinaman and stirring the sticky mess of opium in a bowl. It was an ugly sight. It didn't say much for 'The New Order in Asia' and yet, when I later told Japanese of what I'd seen they were frankly horrified. Sotomatsu Kato, for instance, who is now Ambassador at Large to China, and whom I met in Hsinking, said: 'I deplore such things as much as you do.' This was the diplomat's way of saying he blamed the army; but more of that later.

The notorious Shanghai night-life, after a quiet spell for the first year of the war, is now as wild as ever. Down in Blood Alley are the cheap, bawdy dance spots, where no evening passes without a fight. They are the Mecca of the American marines, the Italian, French, and British soldiers and sailors. I was down there one night, listening to a British Tommy. He had a hate against the Italians. 'Those bleeding Ities,' he said, 'their idea of an evening's sport is to go from bar to bar, 'alf-dozen together sort of thing, lookin' for one of us or a Froggie, and then tryin' to beat us up before our pals get wind of them.' Tourists are taken to the Alley so as to see a side of life that hasn't changed for thirty years. The Alley is where the word 'Shanghaied' was born. But there are dozens of other places to go to. Russian and Chinese dance restaurants with Filipino bands that have the rhythm and the music of first-class Western bands.

Or there are the small, soft-lighted clubs where only a piano plays, or a piano and a violin. Russian and Chinese dance hostesses sit side by side. The Russians are tall, and would be elegant if they were dressed in Parisian clothes; but as they are, they look drab, and tired of life. The Chinese, on the other hand, are small with exquisite figures, wearing the national dress in many coloured silks; close fitting, high collar, short sleeves, and a slit in the side of the skirt so, as they walk, you see a slim bare leg from the knee to the foot. At threepence a time you dance with them, the Russians gloomy and silent, the Chinese dumb and emotionless.

Brothels abound like public houses in Glasgow. The first evening in my hotel the house-boy asked: 'Want nicee Chinee ladee?' Out in the streets they were hanging about, always accompanied by an *amah*. This old lady might be the girl's real mother or she might have bought her as a child. At any rate, if you wanted the girl, you didn't discuss money matters with her; you argued with the *amah*. The Russians were herded together in gloomy houses. The one I visited was kept by an elderly American woman, and the girls, over whom she presided like a nurse in a nursery school, were worn and fat and unappealing. She wasn't at all upset that I and my friend went away without being customers. 'You must come again,' she said cheerfully, 'all my girls are guaranteed clean. I haven't had a case of venereal disease for five years. On that occasion a policeman claimed he got ill from one of my girls. So I gave him £50 as compensation!' The brothels in Japan are licensed and supervised by the police. The Japanese have a realistic outlook towards sex. They do not pretend it does not exist, nor do they feel it should be indulged in furtively. The army in China, for instance, have girls following after them in groups as well organized as any military unit. It may seem funny to Western ideas, but it stops homosexuality and other vices which are inevitable when young men of any army are forced to live for a long time together.

4

The army, however, though it may be a platitude to say so, is the evil thing of Japan. Never having suffered defeat in war, it is puffed up with its own conceit, and is convinced that its duty is not only to fight for Japan but to rule it as well. It is responsible for assassination, insolence, bribery, and brutality; and whenever it is pricked by conscience it excuses itself by saying it represents the Emperor and he, being the Son of Heaven, can do no wrong. If the Emperor only knew what sins were committed in his name, he would probably abdicate. He is a fine man, who has already shown his dislike for the revolting methods of his soldiery, by standing out against the pact with Germany, whose soldiers have similar ways of behaving. It is said that he favours Japan coming to terms with the democracies; and there is no doubt of the presence of an influential group of statesmen who are in agreement with him. Such men, if they were in power, would be as honourable in their diplomacy as a British Government. They would respect our rights as conscientiously as we respected theirs. Honour, decency, and justice would be once again the policy of the Japanese people.

There are signs that this group of statesmen are increasing their power; the nation is growing tired of the vapid boasts of the army. A prominent Japanese diplomat talked to me of how Britain could strengthen their hand. 'Your country,' he said, 'have a knack of casting its friends into the arms of its enemies. Look at Italy. She has always been at heart a friend of yours, yet by tactless and useless acts, you drove her to the side of Germany. Same with Japan. Though you blame us for everything, I assure you the antagonism shown by our people towards you is a great deal owing to your clumsy diplomacy. For instance, since the war began you've lodged nearly a thousand complaints at our Foreign Office about damage done to your property in China. Every time, even if so much as a slate on a roof is damaged, your Ambassador calls with a note, stiffly worded with a hint of threats. Can you imagine how you would feel if America did this to you when you were engaged in a life and death struggle with Germany? You would boil with anger. And if America took no action to carry out her threats or see that her demands were settled what else would happen? You would lose respect for her word, just as we have lost respect for yours. For twenty years your country and mine were close friends and allies. The Japanese people are still at heart closer to Britain than to any other nation. If you would realize that, and would direct your policy towards strengthening the position of the moderates in Japan, rather than feeding the extremists, and by them I mean the army, with ammunition to use against you, your country and mine could become allies again, and our common interests established on a lasting basis.'

The mass of the Japanese people are obviously bitter towards us. Propaganda has made us the scapegoats for the army's failure to subjugate China. Even though the United States, being in a stronger position than ourselves, has been able to be correspondingly firmer in her policy towards Japan, I didn't meet a single Japanese who was anti-American in the same way as he was anti-British. Rightly or wrongly, it was thought that Britain was to blame for America's firm attitude. And it was firmly believed that China would not be fighting if it were not for the support being given her by Britain. As Major Akiyama, the army spokesman, said to me in Tokyo: 'It is certainly true to say that at any rate the youth of Japan now feel their country is fighting Britain, not China.' That the Japanese feel so strongly about us, seems to suggest that perhaps we are a little to blame. Such a view was expressed to me by an Englishman who had lived a long time in Japan. 'It is a pity,' he said, 'that our Foreign Office hasn't been more realistic. They should have realized from the beginning that our position was extremely weak in the Far East. And instead of adopting a Palmerstonian attitude, they should have been clever enough to have kept on friendly terms with Japan while at the same time being friendly with China. After all, the Germans have done so; they have been supplying China with arms while coming to terms with Japan. Where they have succeeded, why couldn't we?'

5

I had hoped that my stay in Japan would be made the more exciting by finding my movements were being shadowed. I went long walks down deserted streets and lonely parks, but never once caught sight of a suspicious-looking follower. Nor on my arrival at Kobe in the *Shanghai Maru*, a boat that was crowded with returning army officers and soldiers, was I even questioned at length; nor during my stay did I once discover that my baggage had been examined. The only time the police took any notice of me was after I'd been to the Soviet Embassy for my visa through Russia. As I came out through the gates, they took my name and address, and inquired my business. I was a little disappointed at this lack of attention.

For the most part, however, they're as suspicious of foreigners as mice of cats. You cannot, for instance, buy the Official Guide to Japan as produced up to 1933; the maps then printed might give secrets away. When, in a train, you're passing a port you might as well be in the Piccadilly Tube for all you can see; high boards beside the track hide the ships that might be there. A friend of mine bought picture postcards of Japanese aeroplanes in a stationer's shop; he was promptly taken to the police station as a potential spy. I wanted to have a look at one of the big cotton mills, but I was forbidden to do so because I might have discovered some secret process to take back to Lancashire. And then, of course, all foreign books and newspapers are strictly censored, so that on the bookstalls you can only buy the rosy Japanese point of view.

Thanks, however, to my friends in Domei, I was allowed to see a paper factory; and despite the fact that economic figures are forbidden to be disclosed by law, I learnt some wage figures that were interesting. For instance, in this factory which, like everything in Japan, was as clean as a dairy, the men worked eleven hours a day, seven days a week, for 1s. 6d. a day; and the girls, for the same length of time, at a 1s. a day. These figures in Western ideas are the next thing to slavery; and it seems impossible that anyone could work for such wages with a good heart. It is obvious, however, that under such conditions Japanese industry can turn out goods far cheaper than those of the Western world. It puts us in a hopelessly unequal position. We can and do, of course, impose high tariffs to bring them nearer the level of our goods, but that, after all, is only a synthetic trick of keeping our trade. Nor does it answer the question put to me by our Japanese industrialist: 'Isn't it wrong,' he asked, 'that you should deliberately keep away from your working people the kind of articles that at our prices are within their pockets, but at yours are beyond them?'

It puzzled me why the Japanese workers accept such working conditions. After all, they have scarcely any time for home life or recreation; and you would think they would get tired of their ceaseless labour. The answer lies in Shintoism. Shintoism is the worship for the Emperor, and it has the same meaning as the Nazis' worship for the State. It is a most convenient gag to suck the last drop of energy out of the population for the benefit of the Government. The factory girl at her 1s. a day is not working for herself; she is working for the Emperor. Every hour she is beside her machine she has spent to bring more glory to the Son of Heaven. Such a state of affairs is the answered prayer of industrialists the world over . . . but how long is it going to last in Japan?

Education is the pride of the nation. It doesn't matter how poor a toddler may be, he goes to school; and, if he has brains, because of State-supported schools and universities he can go on learning till he is twenty-five and more. Not unnaturally this education is sowing the seeds of doubt in the minds of the young working class. Like in Britain in the middle of the nineteenth century, they are beginning to ask themselves why they should work so hard for so little profit. Mass action to improve conditions may be a long way off; but, with increasing regularity, news seeps through to the Europeans in the capital, of strikes that have to be quashed by the police; maybe these disturbances are straws in the wind of what is to come. While the war lasts and providing it doesn't last too long,

Shintoism will maintain its power over the people, but afterwards who knows? Certainly in the minds of progressive Japanese a change in the way of things would not be unexpected. One of their best-known journalists said to me: 'The working class are being awakened. Not only by education, but by the cinema as well. They are at the same stage as yours were fifty years ago.' Then he added, with a disarming giggle, typically Japanese: 'Perhaps in ten years . . . we will be in the soup!'

6

Among the little things of Japan I'll remember, will be the pink, bare feet of the slum dwellers, as if they'd come straight from a hot bath; and the paradoxical sight in dustless, spotless Tokyo of men urinating in the gutters. There'll be the rowdy drunkenness in the streets off the Ginza at night. The feeling as you enter a shop, this being the exact opposite in China, that the salesman will not try to cheat you. The politeness of everyone. The European cooking which is as good as in Paris. How half the girls wear the national kimono and obi, and the other half Western clothes as chic as the girls in New York. The bells of the newspaper sellers. The enthusiastic audience at the embarrassingly bad 'leg show' at the Takarazuka Theatre.

I'll remember, too, the unshaven clerk at the Russian Consulate who kept me waiting a fortnight for my visa while he telegraphed to Moscow. The other Russian at the Intourist to whom I paid the £40 for my journey to Paris. The sleeping berths in the night train to Shimonoseki that were open without privacy on to the corridor. The *geisha* who had the one beneath mine, and the young officer who asked me to lend him my sponge. The clean grey kimono and slippers provided with each berth. The wash-place that had no door. The silent group in black, two old men and two old women, who the following day sat motionless at one end of the long carriage, each with a white square box on the knees – the ashes of their soldier sons killed in the war. The endless miles of plains and hills and valleys, no yard of which was uncultivated, resembling a vast kitchen garden. And then my last memory of Japan, the yells of: 'Banzai!' as loud as the yells of American college boys at a football match, that came from a troop train halted in the ill-lit station of Shimonoseki, as I hurried, a suitcase in either hand, with the bustling crowd towards the midnight boat for Korea.

Chapter Fourteen

THIS COUNTRY DOESN'T EXIST

Two BEEFY American marines scowled at me when I reached my cabin. They were taking the diplomatic mail from Tokyo to the American Embassy in Peking. They had no wish to have a stranger in their company; and for some minutes they argued with the steward in an attempt to get me moved. They had no luck as the boat was full; so, taking no chances, one of them went to bed with the chain of the heavy-looking black bag locked round his wrist.

We parted at seven the next morning when we landed at Fusan. They took the train for Peking and I found myself the only European on the one for Mukden. My Trans-Siberian connection didn't leave for a week, and I'd planned to stop there a night or so and also at Hsinking, the Manchukuo capital, and at Harbin. The carriage was without compartments, like those of the London Underground. Each seat had been reserved and mine luckily was a corner one. It meant that for the following twenty-four hours I at least had the window to rest my head against. My legs, however, were painfully cramped as I had no more room than if I'd been sitting in a General omnibus, and if I stretched them even a little bit, they got entangled with those of the two passengers facing me. One was a quaint little Japanese who was off on a fishing holiday to some river near Mukden, and the other a fat, thick red-lipped

Korean woman with rosy bare feet, a blue kimono and gold obi. Beside me, who, during the coming hours, persistently overflowed into my own square foot of the seat, was the woman's husband. He looked like a bandit. Slits of eyes set in an oval, unshaven face; dirty yellow teeth, a smell like a latrine, and a black skull cap. He would snore loudly, and drop his stubbled face so that it rested on my shoulder. I had no alternative but to stick it out; and for the whole of that night I didn't get a wink of sleep.

The other passengers were mostly returning soldiers of the Kwangtung army, which is the watch-dog of Manchukuo. I had three of them sharing my table for dinner. They had only two bottles of Kirin beer between them, but it was enough to set them singing and to make them feel brotherly towards me. Arms were flopped round my shoulders, and the health of Britain was drunk, and by picking out isolated words from my Japanese dictionary I made a speech in praise of Nippon which resulted in prolonged cheers of 'Banzai!' Back in the carriage they shrieked songs which reminded one of the jungle, and which is the habit of Japanese when they're tight. Across the gangway in the four seats parallel to ours were three shy little *geishas* who giggled like schoolgirls whenever anyone spoke to them, and a Mongolian schoolboy who sucked oranges; and in other parts of the carriage were six Japanese of university age who would take it in turn to practise their English on me. It was exceedingly boring correcting their grammar, but I kept my patience. If you're in a foreign land you can do a lot of good for your country by being polite.

2

The railway wound in and out of the hills, past primitive villages with cottages round like big mushrooms and made of mud and straw; and men working in the rice fields dressed in long white coats like Finnish ski troops, and wearing tall hats like those of the witches in *Macbeth*. We passed Taikyu, and Keijo which is the centre of the Japanese administration of Korea; then through monotonous hilly country to Heijo that has a history dating back to 1122 BC. Darkness fell and I grew tired and bad-tempered. The carriage was smoky and stuffy. The bandit sagged against me, using me as a pillow, his skull cap falling off his head into my lap. The soldiers still made their noises. My legs ached. The bandit's wife snored. And the moment that I fell into a doze the train reached the Yalu river which divides Korea from Manchukuo, and we were at the frontier town of Antung.

Squat Manchu officials entered the carriage. They began their search of baggage and scrutiny of passports at the other end to where I was. They seemed to be casual, as if they wanted to complete their tiresome duties as quickly as possible. In ten minutes they'd looked at the baggage and passports of forty people without raising a query. And then they came to me. Four of them there were, oval yellow faces, black eyes blinking through inch-thick glasses, caps like Winston Churchill's yachting cap, and yattering together like monkeys in a zoo. I had already opened my suitcases and, as they foraged through my shirts and books and handkerchiefs, I pretended with my smiles that they were doing me the greatest favour by being so thorough. They scanned my books upside down and shook out my vests and pants for all to see. They took my camera to pieces and told me to empty my pockets. And having spent a quarter of an hour in doing this one of them began, in English, to ask me questions, but in such a parrot fashion that I was sure that he neither understood the questions he asked nor the answers I made. 'Where are you going?' 'What have you written for your paper?' 'Where were you educated?' 'What is your father's profession?' 'Why are you going to Russia?' and a whole lot of others. When they seemed to have finished I went out on to the platform to walk up and down in the darkness. The cross-examination had been easier than I'd expected. This was due, I thought, to my willingness to help and my care not to show impatience; after all, Custom Officials are only doing their job and the point of resenting their investigations, as many travellers do, seems to me pointless. And as I was thinking this, the English-speaking little man stopped me, saying: 'Come back to the carriage, please.' He led me not to my seat, but to half-way down the carriage, so that when he stopped everyone had a chance to watch and be impressed by his mastery of English. He waited for the silence of his audience as a *prima donna* waits before beginning her song. The eyes of Mongols, Koreans, Japanese soldiers, and *geishas* were fixed on us. The sense of their expectancy that a European was going to be made a fool of filled the carriage with the same reality as the smoke and the stuffiness. He then began. 'Where are you going?' 'What have you written for your paper?' 'Where were you educated?' 'Why are you going to Russia?' 'What is your father's profession?' . . . All the questions he had asked before. I had no alternative but to answer them pleasantly. He was obviously anxious for me to lose my temper, and I refused to oblige him. And when he came to the question: 'What do you think of China?' I made an obscene snort which made our audience roar with laughter and so pleased the little man that he shot out his hand, saying: 'Goodbye and good luck!'

3

For seven more hours I sat cramped in my seat. I got no sleep, and when at last we arrived at Mukden, I felt that if

I lay down on a bed I wouldn't get up for twenty-four hours. I bundled my suitcases in a droshky pulled by an emaciated horse, and set off at one mile an hour for the Yamoto Hotel. I arrived there, only to find it full. Not a room to be had. I went to another hotel. The same result. I was told that they weren't Japanese that filled the rooms, but Germans. They swarmed everywhere. Engineers, insurance agents, journalists, motor-car salesmen. And after the second hotel had turned me down I was advised to go to a third hotel called the 'Kleining' that was run by a German. There I was shown a room, but I hadn't been in it five minutes before the Chinese boy knocked at the door and said he'd made a mistake. 'You're English,' he said, 'not allowed here.' I refused to go before I had a bath and a shave, and having made myself look a little more presentable, I set off to see the British Consul.

Perhaps I should remind you that Britain doesn't recognize Manchukuo, and that, therefore, our Consuls at Mukden and Harbin are not officially there; nor is the country itself, which the Japanese, in nine years, have transformed from being corrupt and bandit-ridden into being safe and civilized. Thus, thanks to this ostrich-like policy of ours, Britain has few interests, which results in the Consuls having correspondingly little to do compared with Consuls elsewhere. It couldn't, therefore, be on the plea of overwork that the Consul at Mukden was unable to offer me a cup of tea or a cigarette; or, since it was lunchtime, invite me to his table. After talking to me for a few minutes he made no secret of the fact that I had interrupted the peaceful routine of his day, and taking the hint I went away. It was the first time in my travels I'd come across the music-hall example of an Englishman's manners in a far-away country.

Since there was no room for me in Mukden, the only

thing to do was to take the train to Hsinking. Here again I
had difficulties. You have to reserve your seat on the crack
'Asia' express, and I found that every seat had been reserved. Luckily a young German overheard me at the
booking office and he explained that if I bought a platform
ticket no one would stop me going on the 'Asia' platform;
and, once there, I could get on the train and pay my fare
when the ticket collector came round. He said that the
collector might be angry, but if he was I had no need to
worry; the 'Asia' went non-stop to Hsinking, so he couldn't
turn me off. I took the German's advice and, beyond a few
cross words from the Manchu collector, the journey passed
off without incident. It was a strange train to find oneself
travelling in; streamlined and air-conditioned, with a look-
out car for the first class like those of the crack American
trains. There was a fair sprinkling of Europeans, but the
majority were Japanese business men and soldiers; and it
was odd to find in the dining-car, amongst all this yellow,
two exceedingly pretty White Russian girls as waitresses.
Still odder was the patrol of six Japanese soldiers, who,
with fixed bayonets, continuously walked up and down the
train. Such patrols are on every train in Manchukuo, not
because there are frequent attacks, but because the Japanese
believe that it is best to take no risks. We got into
Hsinking after dark, where once again I was to find the
only hotel full. I was tired beyond belief and had no care
where I went; and finally I came to rest in a Japanese
ryokhan on the top floor of a house that had a dirty
staircase leading up to it like that of a Whitechapel office
building. Before entering I had to take off my shoes and
put on slippers, and then I discovered my bed was a
mattress on the floor with crumpled, used sheets; and the
room itself was an inside one with no windows. Even so I
slept for twelve hours.

4

Japanese like to say that Manchukuo is to Japan as Egypt is to Britain. Both the smaller countries, they say, are independent, both have their own Royal house, and both are dependent on the bigger countries for protection. This, however, is wishful thinking on their part, for to say that Manchukuo is any degree independent is a pure myth. True they have a Manchu Emperor and the titular heads of Government departments are Manchus, but to think these gentlemen have any power is sheer nonsense. Each department has an Under-Secretary of State who is a Japanese and who makes the decisions; and the Manchu Prime Minister is himself subject to the control of the Director of the General Affairs Board, a Japanese called Naoki Hoshino, who tells him what to do. Then in the departments themselves all the best jobs go to Japanese. According to John Gunther, in the Department of Public Peace 82 per cent of the personnel is Japanese; in the General Affairs Board 72 per cent; in the Foreign and Home Office 63 per cent; in the Courts 87 per cent; in the Bureau of Capital Construction 88 per cent; in the Metropolitan Police Board 65 per cent; in the Department of Public Welfare 61 per cent; and in the provincial governments at least 60 per cent. It can hardly be said, therefore, that Manchukuo to Japan is like Egypt to Britain.

Why the Japanese should maintain this pretence of being innocent 'lookers-on' is difficult to understand. It is, however, an incredibly naïve attempt to curry favour in foreign countries, an attempt they are repeating in China with no better success. With the passionate sincerity of crusaders, they believe their method absolves them from being branded as aggressors and conquerors; and they are at a loss to understand why countries other than Germany and

Italy do not agree with them. It is not as if in Manchukuo they have something to be ashamed about, as if they were bad conquerors who wreak vengeance on the conquered like the Germans in Poland; Britons and Americans who, conveniently forgetting the history of their own countries, cry out from afar that Manchukuo should be given back to the Chinese, might alter their opinions if they took the trouble to discover for themselves what the Japanese have achieved in nine years.

Sitting in a corner of his long room which overlooks the grounds of the Emperor's Hsinking palace that is taking five years to build, Naoki Hoshino talked to me in broken English about their achievements. 'First,' he said, 'we had to bring law and order to the country. We found the only way to do this was to make every village a walled fortress. The inhabitants work in the fields by day and return to safety at night. And thus the bandits, unable to get food or ammunition, either give up being bandits or retire to the mountains. By this method we have practically wiped out banditry. And another thing that has helped us is the development of roads and railways. In 1932 there was a thousand kilometres of railways; in 1938 there was ten thousand. In 1932 there was three thousand kilometres of roads; in 1938, fifty-one thousand. At the same time we have set about to educate the masses. We are opening schools everywhere. In 1932 six hundred and sixty thousand attended primary schools; in 1938, one million five hundred thousand. In another five years all these figures will be doubled.'

The figures are certainly impressive. The production of them also cost a mint of money. It is estimated that £140,000,000 will have been invested in the country by 1942, and a cash return on the money is still a long way off. As Hoshino frankly said to me: 'We have no money to pay for goods we buy from foreign countries. We can only barter.' This suits Germany, who is providing the machinery to develop the resources; resources that are so extensive that no one, not even the Japanese, knows the sum total. It certainly contains large deposits of coal and iron, tremendous timber regions, a considerable amount of gold, excellent agricultural land, and soya beans that vary in their utility from being food to the Chinese and Japanese to being fuel, fertilizer, soap, and a hundred other things to industrialists. One important product the country lacks is oil. Japanese prospectors are exhaustively searching for it, and although a field has been discovered, it is only a very small one. Western powers should certainly pray that the prospectors meet with success, because if oil is found in Manchukuo, Japan will no longer look hungrily at Borneo and the Netherlands East Indies.

5

The problem that hangs over Manchukuo like the sword of Damocles is Russia. Japanese make no secret that they're terrified that Russia may attack; just as they make no secret that when they have firmly entrenched themselves in Manchukuo they intend to attack themselves. Sotomatsu Kato, who, as I've already said, is now Ambassador to China, and who, when I was in Hsinking, was Counsellor of the Japanese Embassy, said to me: 'The Russians have a magnificently equipped army which at the moment we have no wish to fight; though we have learnt from Russian soldiers who have deserted to us that the morale among the troops is not high.' The truth is that the Russian army is highly mechanized and the terrain of Manchukuo is favourable to such warfare; but the Kwangtung army, though it is supposed to be superior to the Japanese army in China, is hardly mechanized at all.

I got a taste of the nerviness of the Japanese when I arrived in Harbin. My arrival coincided with the first of three nights of black-out and ARP exercises. I hadn't been in my hotel half an hour when a Japanese sergeant and a White Russian acting as an interpreter called on me. They asked the same silly questions as the Manchu on the train, but in addition they tried to discover the hidden reason why I had landed in Harbin the very evening when these ARP exercises were taking place. Apparently, they thought I had come all the way from London to learn what Harbin looked like without lights. And during the following three days I had a suspicion, for the first time since I'd set foot on Japanese territory, that I was being followed.

When the old Chinese Eastern railway was still in Russian hands (the Russians sold it to the Japanese in 1934, after having given it partially back to the Chinese ten years before that), Harbin had the reputation of being the richest and gayest city of the Orient. Today it is a dead end of poverty. You still can see the large mansions and the impressive bars and hotels; but their walls are cracked and unpainted, and window-panes are broken. It has an air of faded, battered prosperity; like a man who was once rich but who now, though still wearing his fine clothes, stands begging, beaten by the wind and the rain, in the gutter. There is no hope in the hearts of the White Russians who live there. Even if they had money, they could not take it out of Manchukuo; for the Japanese forbid them doing so. They cannot therefore even make the journey to Shanghai or Tientsin, which towns, strangely enough, are the Mecca of most. One feels sorry for the drawn-faced and haggard elderly men and women, but it is the girls one really pities. There are many of them in the shops and the cafés working at coolie wages; and they are pretty and astonishingly cultured, speaking perhaps French, English, and Japanese besides their native language. They have no future, and not much of a present. They're lined and old before they're thirty. And they don't even have the advantage of their sisters in Shanghai of becoming prostitutes; for in Harbin there is no one to pay them.

Chapter Fifteen

PRELUDE TO HELL

I LEFT THE SAD, gloomy town on the first day of June. The train rattled for eight hours across the monotonous plains to Manchouli. We passed one after another of walled villages, and concrete pill-boxes guarding the ends of bridges. At each station, as we arrived and as we departed, the stationmaster and the soldiers on the platform stood at the salute, as if the Emperor himself was among the passengers. At Hailar, soldiers came into the compartments and drew the blinds, then stood in the corridor with fixed bayonets and the door open, so that we should not spy on the Japanese secret fortifications that border Siberia. They had forgotten the lavatory, however; and I went along there. As a result I couldn't understand why they were making such a fuss. All I could see were endless miles of undulating plain, and, once or twice close to the railway, I saw several Mongol nomads on tough long-haired ponies and wearing their orange cloaks and sheep fur caps.

Across the frontier it was different. I could have understood the Russians wishing to hide from the gaze of foreigners the gun emplacements, the aerodromes, the trenches, the fields of barbed wire, that stretched all the way inland to Lake Baikal. Yet, they neither made us pull down the blinds nor did they patrol the corridor. We might have been in a train in England, so free were we.

Though before we got into it we had trouble. At Manchouli the Japanese put us through the usual questions, adding one particularly naïve one: 'Are you going to speak favourably of Japan when you're in Europe?' I answered I'd do my best, but I added that I'd take away a better impression of Japanese rule if they forbade the sale of forged bottles of Johnnie Walker whisky at the station bar; for, just previously, I'd been offered a bottle of the said brand, same size, same coloured labels, but with the name spelt 'Johnnie Wacker'. Having been dealt with by the Japanese, we now had to face the Russians. We got with our luggage into the Trans-Siberian train which took us in ten minutes to Otpor, the Russian frontier town. Out we had to get and once again go through the performance of having our luggage searched and of being asked silly questions. My camera was sealed, together with the suitcase I wasn't going to need during the seven-day journey to Poland; and my money counted so that I couldn't indulge in any currency tricks. And when they had finished with me, and finished too with the score of other Europeans, men and women, who were my travelling companions, I got back into the train and waited for two hours after the appointed time of departure before the train started.

2

I was travelling 'soft' class, which is the Russian equivalent of our second; and at first sight it looked as if I was going to be very comfortable. Admittedly the carriage was so old that one of my companions had travelled in a similar one in 1911, but the compartment was the size of an English first-class one; and if, as I imagined, only one person was going to share it with me I had no reason to grumble. Most of my companions – they were Shanghai business men

and their wives, British, Swedish, French, and German —
were travelling first class; two or three 'hard' (the bunks
are of wood) including an Irish woman missionary who
had taught for twelve years in a school near Mukden; and
four others like myself who were 'soft'. When the train
steamed out of Otpor, no one had appeared to share my
compartment, and since my fellow Europeans were all
fixed up, it meant that at some future station I would be
joined by a Russian. With a certain misgiving I wondered
what sort of a Bolshevik he would turn out to be.

I was unduly optimistic to expect only one. In the early
hours of the following morning the train pulled into Chita,
the town where one section of the Trans-Siberian railway
branches to Vladivostok; and I awoke to find the dirty,
sullen car-attendant shaking my shoulder and telling me by
signs that he was going to make four berths in my compartment by pulling out the backs of the two lower ones.
Without much pleasure I watched him fixing them, and
then with still less (the space between the two pairs of
berths was no bigger than that of an English third-class
sleeper), I made room for two uniformed soldiers, an old
woman of seventy with a shawl round her head, and a
pretty little girl of four. They gave me no greeting and in
fact, except for the little girl who stared, they took no
notice of me. As they brought in their luggage, I clambered
to one of the top bunks, deciding that I would be more
independent there than in a lower one. For a long time I
tried to go to sleep, but when finally I succeeded, I was
soon awake again; for the little girl lying with her grand-
mother in the berth beneath mine was crying out in a small
agonized voice: 'Mamma! Mamma!' She was going to do
this regularly every night all the way to Moscow.

I paid for my meals by coupons which I had bought
with my ticket; I got what they called first-class coupons as

opposed to second class, since I was told that with them I could indulge in an endless supply of caviare besides having a bottle of mineral water a day. As it happened the caviare ran out on the third day, and as far as mineral water was concerned I never even saw a bottle. The meals were invariably late, sometimes as much as two hours, and when they arrived they never varied from either leather-like steaks or tough, stringy chicken. Black bread with two pats of butter accompanied them, and at dinner there was cheese; though you were warned that if you took it, you wouldn't be allowed to have eggs for breakfast next day! My comrades in the compartment never went to the restaurant car, buying their food instead at the stations we stopped at. And I would lie in my bunk, my nostrils filled with the smell of garlic and fish, that seemed to be their favourite dish.

Most of my time I spent in my bunk. There was little else one could do. I would lie there in a doze, with the train jerking and rattling like a motor-car that has no tyres. I couldn't speak to my comrades as there was no language to speak to them in. But we used to smile politely at each other, and one of the soldiers used to loan me his newspapers, so that I could look at the pictures. They were ruddy, fresh-faced, decent-looking young men with curly, dry, brown hair which they had an almost feminine interest in combing; one of them used to join me and the little girl, who was called Alla, in a game of hide-and-seek up and down the corridor. There were many children on the train. They were extraordinarily attractive and healthy-looking, and they had no fear of strangers; and the hours would pass in hectic games with them. It didn't seem possible that they would grow up like their sullen, pinch-faced mothers and fathers who looked as if they were fifty when they were thirty.

Every station we arrived at was crowded. We would look at the people as one does animals at a zoo. 'They seem to be in a better state than five years ago,' said an Englishman who had done the journey before. But that was scarcely a compliment. Their clothes were like the rags that film producers dress the crowds in in films of the French Revolution, and their faces had the same grim, smouldering hardness. Look as carefully as we could, we never saw a smile nor heard a laugh. Outside each stationmaster's office there was a large glass picture-case containing photographs of both men and women of fierce, criminal types; or what we thought were criminal types. But when we asked a Russian on the train who could speak English whether he could discover what crimes they had committed, he looked sternly at us. 'The photographs,' he said, 'are of those who have earned honour in their town by working harder than their comrades.' The stations were dirty and battered-looking, as if they'd been waiting ten years for a new coat of paint. And they were surprisingly small. Omsk, for instance, had but three platforms, smaller, therefore, than Wimbledon Underground station. Irkutsk had four. And yet these are two of the chief towns in the Soviet. Still stranger was the sight of Sverdlovsk, which was the scene of the murder of the Tsar, though in those days it was called Ekaterinburg. We reached it as dawn was breaking. I was woken up by a large woman who was taking the bunk vacated by one of the soldiers who had got out. She was standing by the window, hissing sobs, and in the half-light I could see her shoulders heaving up and down. And then through the window I saw her lover, a huge man in a heavy coat with fur collar and cap, standing looking at her, grimly silent. The pair of them stood like that for the half-hour we were in the station; and for the life of me I couldn't understand why they didn't prefer to stand by the carriage and talk.

As for myself, I pulled on my shoes and went out into the cold early morning for a stroll. There was a pale light behind the black of the Ural Mountains that surround the town, and a pall of smoke lay over the roofs and about the tall chimneys of the factories. Here was the centre point of the wealth of Russia, and from this junction was despatched to the four corners of the country thousands upon thousands of tons of coal and minerals. One would have thought, therefore, to see a station and rolling stock worthy of their importance. Yet the station, like Omsk and Irkutsk, was no bigger than that of an English small town; and the wagons, passenger carriages, and engines that were halted in the sidings were the kind that disappeared from the Great Western before the Great War. I do not see how Germany can make use of them. They are like ancient Parisian *fiacres* which, if they were loaded too heavily, would collapse. Even their Russian masters have found their age a hopeless drawback in their attempts to put the Russian railways on an organized basis; so one can hardly expect the Germans to fare any better. True, the Germans are fine organizers, but no amount of organizing can bring modernity to ancient trucks; and it's the rolling stock that is the root of the Russian transport problem. And then, of course, even if the Germans had them to spare, they cannot bring their trucks to Russia because of the difference in the gauge. Whatever the German propaganda machine would like the world to think, it will take years, besides costing millions of pounds, before materials to Germany can be transported in an amount commensurate to the need.

3

And then Moscow. We arrived at ten on a Sunday morning; but I was awake at daybreak, and got up to stand in the corridor to watch the flat, outlying country, and to notice with surprise that soldiers stood with fixed bayonets on every bridge the train passed. I had my last shave in the dirty lavatory at the end of the corridor; and listened for the last time to the raucous sound of music and propaganda that screeched from the loudspeakers which were fixed at intervals along the carriage. The Russian Intourist representative had warned us that the waitresses and car-attendants would not accept tips; and this was true if you offered them anything when one of their comrades was present. It wasn't true however when they were alone. They took what they could get.

We had fourteen hours before the train left for Warsaw and we were all taken, shepherded by Intourist officials, to the Hotel Metropole by Underground. The Moscow Underground is the pride of the Soviet; and admittedly if one stayed in it and didn't go above ground one would be impressed by the achievements of Communism. The trains are as good as the Piccadilly Tube, and the stations miniature marble palaces. But they only make the cobbled streets and the ugly buildings the more dreary and drab by contrast; and then, of course, they make the Hotel Metropole (the Ritz of Moscow) look as dilapidated as a disused cotton mill. My first meal there was interrupted by the rain that dripped from the glass dome of the huge dining-hall on to my table. One naturally had to wait for an hour between each course; but the time passed quickly enough because of the amusement one had in watching at the other tables what in fact was a cartoonist's conception of Bolsheviks come to life. Moustaches, those peculiar shirts, coupons, and all.

As soon as I reached the hotel, I rang up Denny, who's been Moscow correspondent for the *New York Times* for five years. And while I was waiting for him to come round, I went out for a walk; though with dramatic seriousness the Intourist official warned me I should not go without a guide for fear of the Ogpu asking for my passport. I saw the great walls of the Kremlin, and the Red Square seemed a quarter of the size I expected it to be; and many shops whose windows were bare of goods. When I got back, Denny was waiting for me. We sat down in the lounge, and had been there but three minutes when he leant across to me, whispering: 'Say, one of the boys has just sat down beside you. We'd better go out into the car.' It was very film-like, very exciting, and very absurd. I laughed as I sat in the car beside him. 'When you've been here as long as I have,' he said, 'you can smell an Ogpu boy a mile off. Do you know all the contacts and friends in official circles I knew five years ago are now dead or missing? Do you blame me for feeling nervy?' He took me a sight-seeing drive round the city, and talked meanwhile about the Soviet. 'Heaven knows why you Britishers are trying to get a pact with them,' he said, 'your Foreign Office must be damned badly informed or else they'd know the country is dead rotten. Wages are going down and cost of living going up. Do you know the average wage is now lower than it was in Tsarist times? And production and transport is so bad that the people don't know from one winter to the next whether they're going to have enough food to fill their bellies. Stalin, I can assure you, is not playing your game. Supposing you find yourselves fighting the Nazis, he certainly won't come to your help whatever pact he's signed, unless Russia is attacked. It's absolutely impossible for Russia to wage war ... such a thing would irreparably dislocate production throughout the country, and then it would be only a question of time before there was revolution. Who the leader of it would be, I can't say. Stalin has been very thorough in his purges.'

What has happened since has proved how phoney were the negotiations between us and Stalin. And now, thank heavens, it is Hitler who has to deal with his trickery.

I, in my turn, had to deal with the trickery of one of his subjects on my return to the hotel. The Ballet was performing at the Opera House, and though all tickets at the box office had been sold, I was informed that if I went along to the entrance I would find people auctioning them, in the manner of Covent Garden touts. I went to the exchange clerk and asked if he could change £2 into roubles. I explained what I was going to do, and asked him whether, if after all I couldn't get a ticket from a tout, he would give me back my £2. He said he would.

I ran across the square to the Opera House, but finding the touts were asking too much money, I hurried back again. I wasn't away more than ten minutes; but when I asked the exchange clerk for my £2, he looked blandly at me. 'It is against the law. I cannot do it,' he said in English. It was useless reminding him of his promise, or calling the manager of the hotel, or demanding the head of the Intourist Bureau to do something for me. They all looked woodenly at me, obstinately repeating it was against the law to hand the money back to me. At length, I became so angry that I cared neither that I was in the land of the Ogpu, nor that I was in the public lounge of the Metropole. I told them exactly what I thought of them, their damned Trans-Siberian railway, and the wretched mess they'd made of their country. And as the people in the lounge began to stop their chatter and watch, I finished off with the sentence: 'You live in the most uncivilized, uncouth country in the world.'

Not a very gentlemanly scene; yet I'm glad I made it.

4

The loss of the £2 was a bad blow to my finances. I now had only £7 to last me to London, and I wanted to stay both in Warsaw and Berlin. I reckoned that since that day long ago when I'd set out for Southampton and New York I'd spent £502; so that I'd collected £59 from gifts and earnings during the course of the journey. I'd had good value for my money, but the lack of a little more had many times been irksome. Perhaps I should have earned more and that I was lazy not to have done so; yet gathering stories entails capital expenditure and this I couldn't afford to risk unless I was certain the article would be sold. It is very difficult to arrive in a strange town and begin immediately to earn a living. If you're ready to stay a long time, you may pick up a routine job; but if you're only passing through, it is next to the impossible to find a temporary one. The days of the wandering adventurers are gone for ever. The world is too cluttered up with labour regulations and laws forbidding travellers to land in countries without first proving to the authorities they have enough money to support themselves.

Entering Poland was like entering a farmer's house after a visit to the pigsty. The moment we crossed the frontier at Stolpce we found a station that was painted snow white, well-fed looking peasants, and railway officials who were smartly dressed and obliging. The train, too, was as fine as the Royal Scot. And when a splendid-looking young officer in a flowing cloak and three-cornered cap gave me an example of Polish politeness by saluting me and asking if he could share my compartment (it was empty but for me) I felt delight that Poland was our ally; the pride of the

Poles for their country seemed to me to be physically alive, and each individual wanted to show it off to a stranger. I remember a sentence of the young officer's as I said goodbye to him at Warsaw's station. 'When we fight,' he said, 'we will not be fighting for riches. We will be fighting for the lanes and fields of Poland.'

After I'd booked my room at the Europesci off the Pilsudski Square I looked for a journalist who would short cut my study of the political situation. And I was lucky to find Alex Small in the hotel, roving European correspondent of the *Chicago Tribune*. His views were brief and to the point: 'Hitler ought to have pulled the chain the day he marched into Prague,' he cracked, 'now whatever he does won't catch the Western Powers napping. He's sure to come into Poland, and there's nothing to stop him. The Polish staff are so damned slow-witted that they'll be running round in circles. Do you know they still think a cavalry division can beat a motorized division? They've got no defences around Warsaw, no system of air raid precautions, and not even an air raid shelter. For the past week I've been pestering the authorities to tell me what they're going to do in the event of an attack on Warsaw, and all they do is to look wise and murmur: "Everything is prepared." Hell, when Germany starts, I give them five days before they've captured the city. France and Britain will turn the war into a long-drawn-out affair, and Germany won't be able to stand it. She won't get any support from Italy. I've just come from there, and the country is in a mess and will remain so for years. But mark my words, if you get tied up with Russia God help you. She'll double-cross you at the first opportunity. Your Government's crazy to be dickering with her.'

I had been for so long a far-off spectator of the European scene that I had grown accustomed to viewing it with the same dispassion as one does the pieces of a chess-board. The fear that chilled men had for me been dimmed by distance. War belonged to history, not to the present; not to me and my friends and the places I knew and loved. But, as Small talked, I felt myself slipping back into reality, as if I were forsaking the escape of a dream for the cold facts of the day; and as the winds of fear blew through my heart I remembered a scene that I'd been a part of, a long, long time ago.

I remembered the lagoon, cool and serene in the midday sun, dotted occasionally by the canoes of the fishermen, and stretching its turquoise calm towards the reef where the waves rolled in a thin white line; and then, in the distance, the misty outline of the Presqu'Ile of Tahiti. Old Gibbins, his moustache bristling white and furious with a curl like the Kaiser's, was beside me on the verandah, the two of us sipping the milk from coconut shells. A man of the world he once had been; he'd won honour in battle and served his country well. But I remembered the words he used, as he told me of his renunciation of the thing called civilization. 'There'll always be rivalry and bitterness and distrust between nations. They have the tortured minds of the inhabitants of Bedlam. There is no rest, no peace. I tell you, sir, when I was part of the world I was the same. My mind was like a bit of refuse on a rubbish heap. I saw no light and I myself was confusion. But here, from this spot, I see that world as if it were a glass bowl, and inside are the fishes swimming round and round, without end and without meaning.'

5

Warsaw had a happy, Ruritanian atmosphere in those days. Officers in splendid uniforms strode along the streets.

Women were smartly dressed, and children looked clean and healthy. Food in plenty filled the shops, and the cabarets at night were packed. The antiquity of the buildings and the churches brooded a peace over the city; and the old bridges, across the Vistula, a quiet loveliness. I could not have believed that within two months they would be a shamble of ruins. Nor, when I left the city in the train for Berlin, could I believe that the rolling fields and snug farmhouses we passed could so soon have been turned into a battlefield. In all that I saw there was something permanent, something so good and solid that it didn't seem possible that the evil in man could touch it.

There were no complications facing me at the German frontier. I was neither questioned nor was my baggage searched. Someone, a few stations later, came in with a 'Heil Hitler' and sat down. I was taken so much by surprise that I said 'Heil Hitler' too. When I told the story to a friend in Berlin, he said: 'When they do that to me, I answer "God Save the King"!' I followed his example on the next occasion. Another passenger was a well-dressed middle-class woman who told me she had two sons in the army. But she added a sentence which was to be several times repeated to me while I was in Germany. 'None of us want war,' she said, 'we do not want our loved ones killed . . . *und der Führer, er weiss das!*'

I didn't get the opinion that the Führer shared the same view when I saw the Unter den Linden and the Wilhelmstrasse next morning. Paul of Yugoslavia was arriving on a ceremonial visit, and huge flags, alternately Nazi and Yugoslav, hung at twenty-yard intervals from every building. Aeroplanes roared over the roofs. Steel-helmeted troops rushed about in lorries, and high Nazi officials raced hither and thither in black open Mercédès cars. For five hours before the procession I wandered among the crowds watching the legions of marching girls and boys who had been called from the schools to swell the chorus of cheers with their unbroken voices. Bands were spaced at hundred-yard intervals, fat-bellied, big-mustachioed trumpet players, and a huge fellow to beat the big drum. Little flags were handed out to all and sundry by smooth young party men. Black-shirted storm troopers with magnificent physique lined the streets, each alternate one facing the crowd. And yet despite this pomp and circumstance, all of which I had read so often about before, there was an atmosphere of goodwill that was unexpected. Jokes among the storm troopers, bursts of laughter from the crowd when a civilian lost his way and was escorted across the cleared street by a policeman, and remarks such as: 'Oh, dear, how much longer have we to wait?' When at last the great moment arrived it was over in exactly thirty seconds. First Hitler and Paul flashed by, after the manner of: 'That's Shell . . . that was!' and then followed, in speedy succession, Ribbentrop with a nasty, self-satisfied grin on his face; Goering, red and bloated; and weedy Goebbels. The bands drowned any lack of cheering, but there wasn't one around me, for either Ribbentrop or Goebbels, though Goering got more than his chief. The crowd yelled: 'Hermann!' with the same sincerity as we cheer the King.

When it was over I joined Ronnie Panton, the *Daily Express* Berlin correspondent. Here was an example of the British hospitality that I'd seen so much of. He'd never met me before that day I arrived in Berlin, but not only did he volunteer any information about Germany, but also he took me to his home for dinner and afterwards showed me the night spots. He believed war was inevitable. He said that the Wilhelmstrasse was quite incapable of believing that we were ready to fight them. Hitler had in any case gone so far in his Polish demands that he could not now draw back.

'There is no sign of political upheaval here,' he said, 'and so long as the going is good Hitler will stay. But all of us correspondents are convinced of one thing. If there is a war, and Germany gets a major defeat, the present regime won't last three months after it. Wishful thinking, however, that the country will disintegrate by itself is sheer nonsense.'

Panton was in Copenhagen when the Germans marched into Denmark. He had no chance of escaping. It can be only hoped that the Nazis won't try to revenge themselves on him for the stories he has written condemning their regime.

I went on from Berlin to Cologne, where I had spent five years of my childhood during the time my father was serving in the Army of Occupation. Shortly before we got into the station a man in my compartment started a conversation with me by asking: 'Are you a Swede?' (Oddly enough, an SS man in Cologne, of whom more later, asked me the same question.) On learning I was English he began the usual talk of: 'We don't want war'; and he pointed to a scar on his face, saying: 'I got this when one of your submarines torpedoed my ship . . . but I don't bear you any grudge because of it.' He asked me what I was going to do and what I was going to see during my few hours in the town. I told him I was going to visit my old home at Bayenthal Gürtel on the Üfer, and also the Opera House where we used to hear the great singers of Germany night after night. We said goodbye at the station and I thought no more about him. I took a tram down the Rhine front to the Bismarck statue and surveyed the vacant plot of ground where once stood our house, and then returned to the Dom Platz with the intention of finding my way to the Opera House. My memory was bad, and I stopped a man to ask for directions. It was as I was speaking to him that the SS man came up. He said that as he himself was going that way he would escort me. For half an hour I walked beside him through the streets, discoursing in German about current events. He, too, said no thinking German wanted war. 'We have so much to do inside our country,' he said, 'that we cannot worry about taking other countries.' He was polite and most friendly towards me; but when we reached the Opera House he gave me a surprise. He smartly clicked his heels and bowed stiffly. Then he said in the most perfect English: 'It's been a great pleasure to be of help to you. Goodbye!' I gaped at him. 'Hell,' I said, 'why have you been letting me struggle with my German?' He looked at me, almost fiercely. 'In Germany,' he said curtly, 'we speak only German.'

I watched him for a second as he crossed the Sachsen Ring before I turned into the Opera House. I had taken about a dozen steps when suddenly from behind a pillar appeared the man of the train. He took off his hat and smiled at me with such an air of surprise that for a second I thought it might have been just a strange coincidence that he was there. 'This is a pleasure,' he said in German. 'We must celebrate our meeting. Come with me to the café.' He took me upstairs and over a glass of lager he oozed propaganda. Again I heard about this wish for no war; and about the trust of the people that the Führer wouldn't lead them into it. And, cunningly, he told me that the people derided Goebbels, and that Goering was just a nice hail-fellow-well-met sort of man; and that Ribbentrop was hated. He was lyrical in his praise of what Hitler had done for the people . . . the slums cleared away, holidays with pay for all, opera seats at prices low enough for the poorest working man, etc., and he ended with the words: 'Can you possibly believe that a man who has done all that would now lead his country to destruction? Because war would mean destruction whether we conquered or lost.'

He would not let me pay for the drinks, nor would he let me pay for the taxi in which he afterwards took me to the station. 'I want in my own small way,' he said, 'to show friendliness to your country.' It was a good thing that he did. For I had run out of money. My funds had at last come to an end; and I had had to wire home for £5 to be sent to Paris so as to pay for my ticket to London.

6

Not only £5 was waiting for me when I reached Paris. My mother was there too. I came into the hotel in the Rue du Colisée which I had given as my address, and there she was, sitting in the lounge. That sudden sight of her will remain vividly in my memory all my life. I'd been a long time among strangers, among people whose companionship, because of its brevity, could never be much more than frivolous and superficial. And if on occasions I'd met someone who shared my outlook, and who laughed at the same things, no sooner had we become friends than it was time to move on; on to a new city where I had to start all over again. Such was the penalty of travel.

So when I saw my mother I felt how a dumb man would feel if he were suddenly able to speak. I was able to unload the multitude of thoughts and experiences that only someone who knew me intimately could possibly be interested in; and for three hours I lived again my journey across the world. Then afterwards, when we'd had dinner, we strolled out into the warm June evening down the Champs-Élysées across the Place de la Concorde to the Avenue beside the Seine.

I remember her asking me how I thought I'd benefited from my year away and my reply that it would take months and months before I'd know how much I'd got from it. 'At the moment,' I said, 'I cannot see it in perspective. It's like looking at a large painting a yard from the canvas. Or like being a man who has just read the Bible for the first time from the beginning to the end. He is confused by its riches, and it will only be after study and contemplation that he will separate the truths, so that they become clear in his mind. In the same sort of way I hope to discover what this journey has done for me.'

Then, I remember, she asked me what I was going to do next. And I didn't answer at once. On that day I'd set out for New York my mood had been a holiday one; and the weeks that followed in America had been lighthearted, and the things I had done could hardly be described as being very serious. And then, too, in the South Seas I was only a casual adventurer with no cares on my shoulders, and with a sense of irresponsibility that kept me unaware that the force of history might interrupt the independence of my life. True, I was conscious of the wounds of the world, but I didn't believe they would ever affect me personally; just as a racing-car driver believes that accidents will happen to others but never to him. I imagined that in the immediate years to follow I would be able to go on fulfilling my way of life. I did not imagine that my independence would be cut into pieces by the ravages of war.

But gradually, as my journey led me from New Zealand to Australia, from China to Japan, from Manchukuo to Germany, there grew a heaviness of heart within me. From looking objectively on the scarred scene of the nations' quarrels, I awoke to being aware that my life was a unit in the quarrel, that I would have to face the hell that was coming with the same realism as a small boy faces a beating. And as I stood there with my mother, beside the gentle, idle peace of the river and the dark shadows of the old bridges that stretched across the water to Montparnasse,

I saw in my mind the strutting, threatening figures of Berlin, the myriads of uniforms, the planes roaring low over the roofs; and I knew there was no escape. Like millions of others I was caught in a trap; but unlike millions of others I felt I was able to say, no matter what future there lay before me, that I had lived.

But I answered my mother's question by saying it was too soon to know what I would do next, there being no object in burdening her with my gloomy thoughts; and then, taking her by the arm, I said: 'There's at any rate one thing I can tell you. I've come home a bit of a jingoist. I know now that Britain with all her faults is the best of the lot. And tomorrow, when I see the cliffs of Dover, I'll have the proverbial tears in my eyes.'

And by heavens it was so! When next day, on the far horizon, I saw the thin white line of cliffs, I had a lump in my throat. And just as when I'd left I'd had a brandy to stop me making a fool of myself, so had I then.

A Gull on the Roof

'PUBLISHERS ARE APT to be cynical when they are offered a manuscript which is different,' wrote Charles Pick, Managing Director of Michael Joseph, when choosing the Michael Joseph Spring Book in the *Sunday Times*, 'but when we read *A Gull on the Roof*, I scrambled on the Cornish Riviera Express, contract in hand.'

Jeannie and I were waiting anxiously for him at Penzance station. We had already waited a long time for this moment.

I had, for instance, waited five years before starting to write *A Gull on the Roof*. I wanted to write a book which reflected the in-depth feeling we had for our new way of life. I did not want to write a book which skidded over the surface. I wanted to avoid appearing like those city-orientated people who decide to live in the country but who bring their superficial values with them, thus destroying the real reason for living in the country.

I write very slowly. Sometimes I write in long hand but normally I use a portable typewriter which I have had for years. A word processor would never suit me. It is too inanimate. A typewriter can be a collaborator, a friend, and can cope with emotional hiccups. I will, for instance, read a page which I have typed, and find it to be nonsense. I then get rid of my disgust by tearing out the sheet of paper, crushing it in my hand and throwing it into the wastepaper basket. It is a wonderful way of purging oneself. Each time I write a book, there will always be a full wastepaper basket.

I finished *A Gull on the Roof*; it had taken two years for me to do so. Jeannie patiently proceeded to type a fair copy. We carefully assembled the pages in order, wrote a hopeful little letter to the agent, and, having wrapped it up in brown paper tied with string, set off to St Buryan post office to post it.

Day after day went by and there was no response except for a routine acknowledgement. Three weeks, four weeks, and then disaster. The agent replied that he had received a very disappointing judgement from his professional reader, and that he was doubtful about finding a publisher, but he would do his best. We were in despair. We were broke at the time; the daffodil season was being a failure; hopes of financial survival were waning. At this point, a gleeful agent wrote to say that a publisher, so small that I had never heard of it, was prepared to offer a £50 advance. We were at such crisis point that I was tempted to accept. I remember walking up and down the flower house where we were bunching daffodils, discussing with Jeannie what we should do. Both of us had the same reaction. We *believed* in *A Gull on the Roof*. We would not succumb to a petty temptation. And we were right.

Eventually the typescript was read by Michael Joseph, a

publisher I had admired ever since I had read Richard Llewellyn's *How Green Was My Valley*. Thus here we were waiting at Penzance station for the arrival of Charles Pick, the managing director. But there were problems.

We had no electricity in our cottage, no telephone, and we already had a guest occupying our spare room – Sir Alan Herbert (A.P.H.), wit, Member of Parliament, playwright. Where, therefore, could we put Charles Pick?

'In the flower house on a camp bed,' I said.

'You can't put your publisher on a camp bed,' said A.P.H. 'You must cosset him, flatter him, give him plenty of hospitality ... remember he has your future in his hands.' Then he added, 'I will be happy to sleep on the camp bed in the flower house.' And so he did.

A.P.H. did much to help make that weekend a success. The ambience was there for friendship. Michael Joseph have been my publishers from then on; and for Jeannie's three hotel novels.

To Jeannie

Introduction

I sat down in our house overlooking the Thames at Mortlake and felt a soft, caressing rub against my ankle. Monty was saying in his feline fashion that he sympathized with me over the apprehension that was in my mind.

> The humble earth must ever fly (wrote A. P. Herbert)
> Round that great orange in the sky;
> But, Monty, with devotion due
> The home of Tangye turns round you.

An animal, as one grows older, plays the role of the teddy bear in childhood. He stirs those qualities which are best in one's character and is one's patient confessor in periods of distress. So it was with Monty. He was, for both Jeannie and myself, the repository of our secret thoughts.

My apprehension that evening was in reality an ally of the caution I had discarded; for in the morning we had set in motion our decision to leave London in favour of the bath-less, paraffin-lit two-roomed cottage called Minack and six acres of uncultivated land on the coast between Penzance and Land's End, I had completed the settlement of my own affairs and Jeannie had handed in her resignation to the Chairman of the Savoy Hotel. Our livelihood now depended upon the creation of a flower farm from this desolate, beautiful country, aided not by any practical experience, but only by our ignorance as to what lay ahead.

Jeannie's position at the Savoy was the epitome of a career girl's ambition, but it was because she was not career minded that she performed her duties so well. As Public Relations Officer of the Savoy, Claridge's, Berkeley and Simpsons, she had a high salary, a large expense account and a multitude of friends. Her salient task had been to promote goodwill, and that was achieved not only by organizing efficiently the daily routine of an office, but also by endearing herself to the great variety of people who pass through an international hotel.

'Absolute nonsense!' said the Chairman when she saw him, 'you're obviously tired and want a rest. Take six months holiday with pay' . . . then added: 'When you come back you will want to stay with us for ever.'

I could understand his scepticism for he had no knowledge of the months of reasoning which had brought us to this moment. He could only comprehend the fact she was throwing away a career of distinction in favour of a wild adventure which, after a short while, might appear as a misplaced enthusiasm.

He could not be expected to appreciate the sense of futility which perforce invades the kind of life we had been leading. The glamour and hospitality act as a narcotic, doping the finer instincts of living, and in the grey hours of early morning you lie awake painfully aware that you live in a flashy world where truth and integrity for the most part are despised, where slickness reigns supreme.

We found the pace too fast and any material rewards poor substitutes for the peace of mind which was sacrificed. The world of politics, journalism and entertainment in which we moved requires a ruthless zest for professional survival if you are to do so, and this neither of us now possessed. It is a world in which you cannot live on prestige alone for it is only the present that counts. We had come to distrust both the importance of the objectives and the methods used to achieve them; for it is a world in which acclaim, however transitory and gained at whatever moral cost, is valued in the same currency as the conquest of Everest.

The atmosphere corrodes the individual and it had been corroding Jeannie and me. The moment of self-criticism, the shame we felt for our arid minds, slipped into oblivion as soon as we were in the splash of another party, in a cuckoo land of mutual admiration and sudden rip-roaring friendships.

There was no decisive occasion when we decided to leave. It was a host of occasions mingled into one, so that one day we suddenly realized our life was a spinning top, dizzily circling on one spot. We saw our fate, if we remained, in the men and women around us who had taken no heed of the barrier between youth and middle age, braying prejudiced views, dependent on values that toppled upside down, propping against a future which repeats endlessly the present, resembling worn playing cards. We could either drift on, or start again. We could either suffer the illusion our life was a contented one, remain within the environment we knew too well, or seek a freedom in a strange one.

We had been playing the game of looking for somewhere to settle whenever we had taken our holidays in Cornwall. We wanted a cottage with a wood near by and fields that went down to the sea, distant from any other habitation and remote from a countrified imitation of the life we were wishing to leave. Somewhere where we could earn a living and yet relish the isolation of a South Sea island, be able to think without being told what to think, to have the leisure to study the past, to live the present without interference.

It is a game which is perfectly harmless so long as no place you see fits your ideal. Once the two coincide the moment of decision arrives and it is no longer a game. This is what happened when Jeannie and I found Minack.

Chapter One

We HAD SET OUT, one May morning, from the inn in the Valley of Lamorna to walk westwards along the coast. We were on a week's holiday and as usual the carrot dangling before us on the walk was our imaginary home.

Lamorna was once the centre of quarrying and its beauty was incidental. The great blocks of granite were blasted from the cliff face beside the little harbour, transported in long wooden wagons pulled by teams of horses up and down the hills to Penzance where they were cut into the required shapes and shipped for building purposes all over Britain.

The name means valley by the sea, and it is now a sleepy wooded valley possessing the ethereal beauty, the lush vegetation and shimmering colours, the away from it all atmosphere which tempts people to believe that here is their earthly Nirvana. In the summer, of course, it erupts with a lava of holidaymakers yet, and this is the charm of Lamorna, there is no strident attempt to exploit these visitors. There is the inn, a small hotel, Ernie Walter's filling station and café, Daniel's place down in the Cove; and though a few cottages advertise bed and breakfast in their windows, one feels this is done out of courtesy rather than a desire to earn a living. Lamorna, then, is a pilgrimage of the day tripper and though the narrow road on a summer afternoon is choked with cars, charabancs and dust, the evening comes and the valley is silent again. In winter it is always silent except for the wind in the trees and the echo of the surf in the cove, and it becomes a valley to cure a cynic. The air is sweet with the scent of the violet plants which climb up the hillsides in neat cultivated rows, and as you walk along you will meet a picker, a basket of violets or anemones in either hand, taking them home to bunch. Or in the early spring when cities are still shivering, you find the valley a factory of flowers with every inhabitant a picker or a buncher, sharing in the hectic race to harvest the daffodils before those 'up along' come into bloom. During the war growers had to surrender a large part of their daffodil ground to the growing of vegetables, and so they threw their bulbs at random in the woods. The effect in spring is as if the constellations had left their places in the sky for Lamorna woods, a myriad yellow lights peeping from the undergrowth, edging the sparkling stream beside moss covered boulders, struggling through twining, unfriendly brambles.

The path we walked along was only a shadow of a path, more like the trodden run of badgers. Here, because there was no sign of habitation, because the land and the boulders and the rocks embraced the sea without interference, we could sense we were part of the beginning of time, the centuries of unceasing waves, the unseen pattern of the wild generations of foxes and badgers, the ageless gales that had lashed the desolate land, exultant and roaring, a giant harbour of sunken ships in their wake. And we came to a point, after a steep climb, where a great Carn stood balanced on a smaller one, upright like a huge man standing on a stool, as if it were a sentinel waiting to hail the ghosts of lost sailors. The track, on the other side, had tired of the undergrowth which blocked its way along the head of the cliff, for it sheered seawards tumbling in a zigzag course to the scarred grey rocks below. We stood on the pinnacle . . . the curve of Mount's Bay leading to the Lizard Point on the left, the Wolf Rock lighthouse a speck in the distance, a French crabber a mile off-shore, pale blue hull and small green sail aft, chugging through the white speckled sea towards Newlyn, and high above us a buzzard, its wings spread motionless, soaring effortlessly into the sky.

Jeannie suddenly pointed inland. 'Look!' she said, 'there it is!'

There was never any doubt in either of our minds. The small grey cottage a mile away, squat in the lonely land-scape, surrounded by trees and edged into the side of a hill, became as if by magic the present and the future. It was as if a magician beside this ancient Carn had cast a spell upon us, so that we could touch the future as we could, at that moment, touch the Carn. There in the distance we could see our figures moving about our daily tasks, a thousand, thousand figures criss-crossing the untamed land, dissolving into each other, leaving a mist of excitement of our times to come.

We stood outside the cottage and stared; a Hans Andersen cottage with the primitive beauty of a crofter's home, sad and neglected as if it were one of the grey boulders in the wild land around. The walls seemed to grow out of the ground, great rocks fingering up the sides until they met the man placed stones, rough faced granite slabs bound together by clay. Once upon a time, it appeared to us, there might have been upstairs rooms and perhaps a roof of thatch; but now the roof was an uncouth corrugated iron jagged with holes, tilting so steeply that it resembled a man's cap pulled over his eyes; and prodding defiantly into the sky above it, as if ashamed of being associated with such ugliness, was a massive lichen-covered chimney. The poky windows peered from the darkness within, three facing the moorland and the sea, and two either side of the battered door which looked upon the unkempt once loved tiny garden. We pushed the door and it was unlocked. Wooden boards peppered with holes gnawed by rats covered the floor, and putting my hand through one of them I touched the wet earth. The walls were mustard yellow with old paper and though the area of the cottage was that of an old fashioned drawing-room it was divided into four rooms, matchbox thick divisions yielding the effect of privacy. At right angles to the door in a cavity of the wall beneath the chimney, an ancient Cornish range seared with rust, droppings of rats dirtying the oven, brandished the memories of forgotten meals. Above, the sagging thin boards of the ceiling drooped in curves, rimmed grey in patches from rain dripping through the roof. A cupboard faced the door and inside broken crockery lay on the shelves, a brown kettle without a lid, and a mug imprinted with a coloured picture of King George V and Queen Mary side by side. Musty with long absence of an inhabitant, lugubrious with the crush of the toy sized rooms, the cottage seemed yet to shine with welcome; and we felt as if we had entered Aladdin's Cave.

Outside we stood by the corner of the cottage, the battered door facing climbing ground behind us, and looked down upon a shadow of a valley, gentle slopes, heading for the sea. Beyond was the Carn where we had stood, cascading below it a formation of rocks resembling an ancient castle, and in the distance across the blue carpet of sea the thin white line of breakers dashing against the shores of Prah Sands, Porthleven and Mullion. A lane drifted away from the cottage. On its right was a barn with feet thick walls in which were open slits instead of windows and on its left was a tumbled-down stone hedge, holding

back the woods we had seen and the jungle-like undergrowth, as policemen try to hold back a bursting throng.
The lane led down to a stream, dammed into a pool by the
density of the weeds which blocked its outflow, and then,
a few yards on, petered out in a tangle of brushwood and
gorse bushes. We could see that the cottage was only
connected with civilization by a track through a field.

There was another track which led towards the sea and,
as it broke away from the environment of the cottage, we
found roofless outbuildings, bramble covered stone walls,
with blackthorn growing where once stood men and cattle
sheltering from the weather. The track broke into a huge
field, or what we could see by the hedges was once a field
but now had grown into part of the desolate moorland,
then fell downwards to the top of the cliff. It was no
ordinary cliff. It did not fall fearsomely sheer to the sea
below but dropped, a jungle of thorns, gorse, elderberry
trees and waist high cooch grass, in a series of leaps to a
rugged teaspoon of a bay; and as we stood there, somnolent
gulls sitting on the rocks far below, we saw in our minds a
giant knife slicing pocket meadows out of the rampaging
vegetation, refashioning the cliff so that it resembled the
neat pattern of daffodil and potato gardens that were
grouped like hillside Italian vineyards at intervals along the
coast. We saw in our minds not only a way of life, but also
the means by which to earn a living. It was the sweet
moment when the wings of enthusiasm take flight, when
victory is untarnished by endeavour, the intoxicating instant when the urge for conquest obliterates the reality of
obstacles, dissolving common sense, blanketing the possibilities of failure. We had found our imaginary home. If we
were able to possess it the way stretched clear to our
contentment.

Details about the cottage were told to us back at the inn.

Mrs Emily Bailey who was then the innkeeper, and Tom her son who nursed the adjoining market garden but who now has taken her place – these two listened patiently to our excitement. It was the habit of holidaymakers to lean over the bar expounding their hopes of packing up jobs, seeking an answer as to where they could escape; and these words of good intentions were as familiar to Tom and Mrs Bailey as the goodbyes at the end of holidays, a part of the holiday as splits and Cornish cream, a game of make-believe that was played for a fortnight, then forgotten for another year.

The cottage was on the land of a farm which belonged to one of the great Cornish estates. This Estate rented the farm to a large farmer who lived a few miles from Land's End who, in turn, sub-let it out on a dairyman's lease. This lease was a relic of those days when Estates had difficulty in finding tenants for their farms. An established farmer would rent an unwanted farm, stock it with cattle and hire out each cow to a man of his own choosing who would occupy the farmhouse and farm the land. Hence this man, or dairyman as he was called, had no responsibility to the Estate for he was only a cowman. The responsibility of upkeep lay in the hands of the absentee farmer who, in this case, was a man called Harry Laity. As I lay awake that night he loomed like an ogre and, determined to call on him on the morrow, I experienced the same queasiness as I had felt before the interview for my first job.

We took the bus to a hamlet called Poljigga and found ourselves deposited at the end of a drive a mile long; a dusty, pot-ridden drive with the farmhouse eyeing us in the distance. We were absurdly nervous. Jeannie whose success was born from her ease with spangled names, and I whose duty it had been to have a weekly solitary interview with the Secretary of the Cabinet, walked along that drive, nervous as children visiting the headmaster. An over-sophisticated approach, a crude remark, sincerity sounding shallow because of lack of confidence, could batter our hopes for ever.

'What on earth do I say?' I said to Jeannie.

My passport, I thought, could be that I was a Cornishman. My ancestors had come from Brittany at the beginning of the fifteenth century, being descended from the Breton family of Tannegui du Chatel whose ruined castle still exists in the north-west corner of Finisterre. The Tangyes lived in obscurity in various parishes of West Cornwall until my grandfather, Richard, was born at Illogan near Redruth. His parents kept the village shop, and farmed a few acres near by where my great-grandfather followed the plough in Quaker dress and broad-brimmed hat. Richard and his brothers became engineers, and breasting the waves of the industrial revolution their inventiveness quickly brought them fame and fortune. Their success, they used to say, dated from the occasion when Isambard Brunel's huge vessel the *Great Eastern* obstinately refused to be launched from the dock at Millwall where it was built. Its length was nearly seven hundred feet, its breadth more than eighty, the height of the hull sixty, whilst its five funnels were a hundred feet high and six feet in diameter. It was intended to carry four thousand passengers, a crew of four hundred besides a mighty cargo – but there it was wedged high and dry on the stocks. It was then that the Tangye brothers produced their new invention the hydraulic jack, and to the excitement of the watching crowd, the vessel slid into the water. 'We launched the *Great Eastern*,' said Richard, 'and the *Great Eastern* launched us.'

My father was trained as a lawyer and he belonged to that group of men and women who, though without personal ambition, perpetually give their services to the community in unpaid but responsible jobs. He was, among other appointments, Joint Chairman of the Cornwall Quarter Sessions, a Deputy Lieutenant of the County, and organizer of the Cornwall Special Constabulary until he died in 1944. He was easy among people and they could always endear themselves to him by enthusing over the loveliness of Glendorgal. Glendorgal, now a hotel kept by my brother Nigel, was our home on the north coast of Cornwall near Newquay and it has the most beautiful position imaginable; the house is low and rambling and stares up the wild north coast past Watergate Bay and Bedruthian Steps to Trevose Head in the far distance. Below the house, so close that you can throw a stone into it from the dining-room, is a sandy cove which is itself a dent in Porth Beach. Across this beach is Trevelgue Island, historic for its ancient burial grounds, though it is an island only by the length of the footbridge which connects it to the mainland. My father had a great love for this island but just before the war circumstances forced him to sell it. The buyers were the local Town Council and I remember the wrangling which went on during the negotiations. It centred round a public convenience. My father was aware of the Cornish habit of erecting ugly cement blockhouses in the most prominent situations without any regard to the visual effect on the beauty spot concerned. The island had always been open to the public but the Town Council, now that they were buying it, believed they could improve its amenities. They intended to erect a blockhouse on the island which would remain for ever a silhouetted sore against the view beyond. My father was adamant that this should not be done, and though in the end he won his point, it was only by sacrificing a large amount from the sum the Council had been prepared to pay.

My father delighted in affectionate surprises. When I was returning to London by train he would see me off at Newquay station, then race in his old Wolseley car the three miles to Quintrell Downs where he would stand at the railway crossing waving his pipe as the train rushed by. I remember another time, after my twenty-first birthday week-end, I and my friends had said goodbye to him at Glendorgal before returning to London by car and then found him, one hour and a half later, nonchalantly strolling on the Tamar Bridge at Launceston accompanied by Lance his old English sheepdog; by a round-about route he had raced to the bridge to say goodbye again.

We walked apprehensively along the Laity drive, happily unaware that this was the first of our visits on the same errand. We were nervous, as actors are before a performance, but in our hearts we did not think we could fail. Our zest would smother the awkwardness of the introduction and, because we were accustomed to meeting strange people, we would soon be at our ease. We were wrong.

Harry Laity, whose robust enjoyment of life we were later to appreciate, eyed us as if we had escaped out of Broadmoor. We saw him first in the yard outside the farmhouse watching the cows being brought into milk; and I began to explain our mission while he stared at the cattle as they passed. I soon became aware that our presence was a nuisance and my confidence ebbed. This was not a situation which either of us had foreseen, and was not one that smooth manners could dissolve. We were out of our depth. The gambits on which we were accustomed to rely were as ineffective as a saddle on a wild pony; and as I stood there awkwardly beside him our plans, which to us seemed so important, became deformed, diminished by their reception into a scatterbrained foolishness.

The cattle disappeared to their milking, and he led us

into the house and to the dining-room. Jeannie and I sat down with Harry Laity opposite, the bare dining-table like a frozen lake between us. I sat there and began to describe – defensively, falsely jovial – my Cornish background, our longing for a Cornish home, our plans for Minack. He stared at us, his eyes giving no clue to his thoughts, puffing a cigarette, replying to my leading questions with grunts and monosyllables. His attitude was unnerving. I began to overstress our case. The more unresponsive he was, the more talkative I became. I slithered into sounding like Uriah Heep. I felt myself acting like a gold prospector who, having found gold, was cunningly pretending he needed the land for another purpose. Handsome Harry as he was known in the neighbourhood was suspicious. He could not be expected to understand why I pleaded as if our lives depended upon his decision. It was beyond his comprehension why two people should wish to leave London for such a derelict, isolated, unwanted place as Minack.

We went away and waited, and visited him again. We wrote carefully worded letters. We enlisted the help of mutual friends to put our case. We sat in our Mortlake home endlessly discussing the tactics which might penetrate

the obstinacy of this man who held our future in his hands. We were at the door as soon as the postman knocked. Nothing. The weeks dragged into months. Silence.

And then, one November morning, we had a message to call on Harry Laity the next time we were in Cornwall. Jeannie was in bed with flu, but it was she who proposed we should take the night train to Penzance.

Chapter Two

THE BLESSING OF enthusiasm is its ability to deceive pleasantly. When Harry Laity told us we could live at Minack, it seemed that now the major obstacle had been overcome, our other problems would be solved without effort. And yet, the victory achieved, doubts soon began to enter my mind.

'We're intending to live in a wilderness,' I said to Jeannie, 'we have little in the bank and we haven't a clue as to how to grow anything. The world is littered with people who would *like* to do what we are wanting to do. Common sense stops them.'

We were, for instance, brushing aside the fact that we would have no legal security at Minack. The cottage, and a vaguely defined area of land, had been offered us at a low rent by the tenant of the farm but not by the Estate which owned it; hence we had no lease, yet in our zest to secure occupancy we had promised that all improvements would be at our expense. We convinced ourselves that once we had moved in, no one was likely to turn us out; and that conventional legal niceties, if pursued, might scare Harry Laity away from having anything to do with us. Long afterwards he told us we were right in our guesswork. He let us have Minack because he expected we would stay six months, then creep back to London, leaving a redecorated cottage behind.

The cottage, then, was now nominally ours though it was eighteen months before we were able to set off along the Great West Road to live there; but during this interval, as we continued our rackety life in London, there remained in our minds the picture of Minack, snug, untamed, remote, giving us the same sense of protection as a deep shelter in an air-raid. Whenever we had the time we dashed to its safety.

Our first visit was a week-end in November when we introduced Monty to his new home. When I first met Monty I was allergic to cats, or rather, as we had never kept cats in our family and knew nothing about them, I pretended to be. He had been found, the last of a litter from a tortoiseshell, by Jeannie's mother in a hairdresser's at St Albans, and brought to Jeannie at the Savoy not long after we had been married. One day I walked unsuspectingly into her office and there on the floor, like a miniature foal trying to control its legs, was Monty. It was a few months after the battle of El Alamein.

I feigned my displeasure and as it was to be my task to take him back to our house overlooking the finishing post at Mortlake, I insisted I would drop him over Hammersmith Bridge. But we passed the bridge and he was still in the basket, and though I swore he would only be a kitchen cat, he slept that night on our bed. From that day he shared with us doodle-bugs, rockets, a bomb on the house, wore a light blue ribbon each Boat-race day, sat for hours at night on the window-sill waiting for our returns, made many hours happy with his purrs, and was always universally admired.

To call him a ginger cat would be a mundane description. The postman at Minack, when he first saw him, called him red – after the red cats of Zennor. There is a legend that a woman many years ago came to the village of Zennor, on the North coast of the Land's End peninsular, and announced she was going to breed tigers. The local authorities, not unnaturally, stepped in and forbade her to do so. The woman thereupon declared that if she could not breed tigers she would breed a red cat as fierce as a tiger; and now if you go from St Ives to Zennor it is the strangest fact that nearly every cat has a tinge of red. But Monty was not red. He had a snow white shirt front, magnificent whiskers, white paws except for a front one which had a puddle of orange on it, while the rest of his person was covered with a semi-Persian fur the colour of bracken in autumn. 'Like a fox,' a farmer said, 'and you'll have to be careful when the hounds are around.'

We had left London after lunch on a Friday and in the back of the car were a mattress and blankets, a Valor Stove, other camping equipment, and Monty in a wicker basket specially bought for the occasion. The basket was my idea. I had visions of Monty escaping from the car and disappearing into the countryside; but by the time we reached Andover he was clearly losing his temper, miaowing his head off and clawing at the sides of the basket in fury. 'Perhaps he wants a walk,' I said. We found a quiet spot off the main road, carefully lifted the lid, and fitted him with a blue harness and lead which had also been bought for the occasion. His fury swept the quiet spot like a storm and he would not budge as I pulled at the lead. 'Let him be,' said Jeannie, 'let's get back in the car and let him sit on my lap.' In a few minutes he was purring contentedly and staring with interest out of the window at the passing scene; and the wicker basket and the lead and the harness have now been for years in the attic as a discarded monument to my foolishness in treating him as a cat who did not know how to travel. He came several times by car before staying at Minack for ever, and once by first-class sleeper. I was at Minack on my own and was expecting Jeannie down for the week-end. I was on the platform at Penzance when the night train drew in, and I saw her waving excitedly from a window. I went up to the door of her carriage and she said: 'Come and look what I've got in my sleeper!' I opened the sliding door, and there on the bunk was Monty. She had been dining at the Savoy when she suddenly had the whim of bringing Monty with her. She rushed back to Mortlake, found him by torchlight walking along the garden wall, wrapped him in a rug and carried him to a taxi. At Paddington he behaved like any prudent conspirator as he was smuggled into the train, and Jeannie awoke every now and then during the night to find him purring peacefully beside her. He stayed on with me for a few days after Jeannie returned; then we drove back together to Mortlake.

It was nearly midnight, on that first visit, when the three of us reached Penzance. A gale was blowing in from the sea and as we drove along the front cascades of spray drenched the car as if coming from a giant hose. We crossed Newlyn Bridge, then up steep Paul Hill and along the winding road past the turn to Lamorna Valley; then up another hill, Boleigh Hill, where King Athelstan fought the Cornish ten centuries ago. Rain was whipping the windscreen when we turned off the road along a lane, through the dark shadows of a farm, until it petered out close to the cliff's edge. I got out and opened a gate, then drove bumpily across a field with the headlights swathing a way through a carpet of escaping rabbits. This, the back entrance to Minack, was the way we had to use until the bramble covered lane was opened up again; and after I pulled up beside a stone hedge, we still had two fields to scramble across in the darkness and the rain and the gale before we reached the cottage.

I lit a candle and the light quivered on the peeling, yellow papered walls. Everything was the same as the day we first pushed open the door; the ancient Cornish range, the pint sized rooms with their matchbox thick divisions, the wooden floor peppered with holes – only it was raining now and above the howl of the gale was the steady drip, drip of water from the leaking roof.

We didn't care. The adventure had begun.

The phase in which daydreams had to be turned into facts had also begun. The romantic, escape-from-it-all atmosphere in which we had battled for the possession of Minack was now dissolving into the uncanny realism of victory. I had the same sense of living in the third dimension as the day when I enlisted in the Army and exchanged emotional patriotism for the discipline of the unknown. We could no longer talk of what we were going to do, we had to act; and the actions increasingly enmeshed us in a condition of living from which there was no turning back. As our first visit was succeeded by others, individuals entered our lives who pushed us forward linking our future with their present, as if they were pylons of a bridge. First we had looked for a bolt-hole from the kind of life we were leading, then we relished the emotion of its discovery, now we met the responsibilities of success. We found ourselves faced with a challenge that defeated our brittle egos, that was only to be accepted by the selves within us who found tranquillity in integrity.

Ashley Thomas was the carpenter in our village of St Buryan. Tubby, twinkling eyes, always wearing a peaked cloth cap to cover his bald head, he reminded Jeannie of Happy in Snow White and the Seven Dwarfs. His family had been carpenters in St Buryan for over two hundred years and craftsmanship was his second nature. And along with his tradition of skill was a quixotic nature akin to the carpenter of a neighbouring village who, after years of never sending out a bill, piled them all in his yard a few weeks before he died – and set them alight. Ashley Thomas never sent out an account within three years of the work being completed; then he would present it most courteously in person while the account itself was a masterpiece of script, a scroll it should be called, in which every nut, nail and inch of wood was meticulously tabulated.

Ashley Thomas looked around the debris of the cottage, notebook in hand with a pencil behind his ear, and promptly provided the assurance that order could soon be created. Our plans were not ambitious. A new roof, that was essential; the thin boards of the ceiling could remain but the matchbox thick divisions had to be ripped away providing us with one large room in which to live and a small one that would be our bedroom. The Cornish range was useless so a modern stove that both cooked and gave warmth would be its substitute. The rat-gnawed planks covering the floor would be torn up and in their place a damp-resisting cement flooring would layer the earth. The mustard yellow paper would be peeled off the walls, and the crater-pitted slabs lime-washed white. The battered front door would be removed, replaced by one divided in half, like that of a stable. There would be no sink or bath and the lavatory would remain an Elsan, posted in a hut like a sentry box thirty yards from the cottage. Water, until we could sink a well, was going to be a tricky affair. We would have to collect the rain from the roof into a water-butt or fill a jug from the stream; but in the summer the stream dried up, and if the water-butt was empty as well, we would have to go three miles to the village tap in St Buryan square. 'Never mind,' said Ashley Thomas looking at Jeannie, 'it's lovely at Minack in summer and lack of water won't worry you . . . but how you'll stand it in winter I just don't know.'

While Ashley Thomas provided the guiding hand within, Tom Bailey from the Inn at Lamorna, acted as adviser without. He arrived at the cottage on a drenching afternoon when the sky seemed to have changed places with the sea. Clad in oilskins and sou'wester he looked as if he had come from a lifeboat. 'Come on,' he said, 'let's walk round' – and he said it as if the sun was shining. Tall and spare, Tom was the man the villagers called on first in times of trouble. He had the dark cadaverous Cornish good looks with a watch in his eyes like that of a sailor, as if much of his life had been spent staring at the signs of the weather in the skies. He had been head gardener of a neighbouring estate before he began his own market garden, and his lifetime experience of growing was at the disposal of anyone who sought it. He was gentle in his manner and never dogmatic, and the advice he gave came hesitantly as if he considered it an insult to correct, however ignorant might be his listener. And he had the gift, despite his knowledge of technical difficulties, of fanning enthusiasm instead of blighting it with past evidence of personal failure.

'That'll make a nice meadow,' he said, looking at the bog which sided the wood below the cottage. It was the second of our brief visits and, despite the rain, we had spent the morning in this bog channelling an escape route for the water using a broken cup and a trowel. I do not know what we expected to achieve except to re-experience the pleasure of bucket and spade on a sea-shore. The task ahead was enormous and though Tom was right, and it did in the end make a nice meadow, it took two years of experimenting and two hundred yards of underground drain pipes before it was dry enough to grow a crop. Then we grew violets and sent away to market five hundred bunches in six months.

'That's yours?' He was looking at the ancient building bordering the lane, half of which was a stable, half a general purpose shed. It was not ours, only the roofless, age-stricken buildings came within our agreement. 'It's John's,' I replied.

John also was a new arrival – as Harry Laity's dairyman he had come to live at the farm at the top of the hill and was our nearest neighbour. The land he worked dovetailed into ours. We, of course, had accepted the uncultivated land. His consisted of the weirdly shaped, beautiful meadows that bordered the cliff and ran down to the sea's edge, and the green fields which lipped the pocket garden of the cottage. He had called one morning when we were cooking breakfast on the oil stove.

'You're John,' I said, and shook his hand in welcome. He was squat and powerfully built like a miner. He had a round face with skin coarsened by the open air. His eyes were grey and they looked at me as if he was saying to himself: 'I wonder how long these people are going to stick it here.' He wore an old raincoat and a mottled brown cloth cap aslant on the back of his head, showing his black hair tinged with grey; a cigarette hung out of the corner of his mouth and he fiddled a foot with an imaginary stone. And as I talked with him I suddenly became aware of a warning emotion within me for which my town conception of a country life had not prepared me. There was a hint of a challenge in his manner. It was as if I had had a punch on the nose to remind me we were amateurs who had a hazy, paradise notion of country life that had no relation to reality. We did not belong. We were as out of place in the kind of life we were intending to lead as John would have been in the Savoy Grill. I could see him wondering what mystery had brought us here. Why, because we possessed smooth ways, did we think we could exist in a land where skill was the product of generations of struggle? We were typical city dwellers who had the conceit to believe it would be easy. He had seen them come and go before, and we would be no exception. There would be the customary froth of enthusiasm as we put the cottage in order, the showing off to up-a-long friends, the token effort of manual work, the gradual boredom with discomfort. Anyhow *she* won't last. Then, and I could sense the question revolving in his mind: 'Who will get the cottage?' His visit had a salutary effect on us for it promised the stimulus of battle, the realization that we were going to be watched and judged and expected to fail. He was another pylon of the bridge.

We led Tom Bailey to the little wood, a forest of blackthorn and elm tree saplings with grey boulders heaving up in groups between them. 'Cut them down and dig up their roots,' he said, 'and by dodging them boulders you'll have three, maybe four meadows out of here. They'll be sheltered . . . be all right for daffodils.' And all this time we were pestering him with elementary questions. What varieties of daffodils would be best for us? How do you grow them? What about violets . . . and anemones . . . and potatoes? We left the wood and took the path to the big field and the cliff, into the scrub, the waste-land smothered with gorse and brambles where one day, we hoped, the crops would grow which Tom described to us. 'Mind,' he said, 'everyone will tell you different and no season is ever the same . . . but this is how I find it.'

There are several thousand different varieties of daffodils and narcissi but only a comparative few are recognized in the markets as established commercial successes – such as the yellow trumpet King Alfred, Magnificence, Carlton, Rembrandt, and a hundred or so others. Some of these are early varieties, some middle season, some late, and the aim of the grower is to have a succession of blooms from the end of January to the end of March, usually ending up with the white narcissi such as Cheerfulness, a double white bloom with an exquisite scent. The normal custom is to buy bulbs by weight which means the bulbs will be of different sizes – most will flower the first year but others will take a year or so to reach flowering size. If you buy by numbers you can expect all the bulbs to flower the first year but, quite apart from it being a much more expensive way of doing things, you run the risk of the bulbs taking a rest the following year with the result you pick few flowers. In any case bulbs are expensive. Cornish growers usually buy their bulbs from Holland or the Isles of Scilly and the price, of course, varies according to the variety; normally, standard types such as King Alfred, cost about £150 a ton. The big growers plant bulbs with a plough, placing them two or three inches apart within the rows; the small growers, in their cliff meadows, use a shovel and, when the time comes to dig them out, a special clawed digger. Seven tons average the acre and a good yield per ton is 28,000 flowers.

When you have bought and planted your stock the hazards begin. A gale may blow up during the week the blooms are ready to be harvested, and although they are always picked in bud the damage incurred as the buds rub against each other in the wind may result in all your efforts ending up in the compost heap. Then there is eel-worm and the bulb fly, two pests which are as common as household flies and one of which is usually the answer to home gardeners who wonder why their bulbs have disappeared. Eel-worm, microscopic in size, wriggles through the soil attacking a plantation like an invincible army, burrowing into the bulbs and destroying them; and after such an attack, since eel-worm hangs around feeding on certain kinds of weeds, you have to leave the ground empty of bulbs for seven years. 'In fact,' said Tom, 'once you have eel-worm in the soil you seldom get completely rid of it. You can only check it.' Yet if you have the luck not to have eel-worm there is nothing to stop the bulbs being attacked by the bulb-fly for it is on the wing every year. There is a small bulb-fly and a large one but they both look like any other flying insect of the spring. The fly lays its egg in the neck of the bulb and the larvae proceeds to mature within the bulb, feeding on its tissues until it is destroyed into a sticky mess. Hence bulbs should be dug up every three years and given hot water sterilization treatment before being split from each other and replanted in September; an hour of this treatment will kill the larvae of the fly, three hours the eel-worm. If the bulbs are cared for in this way they will increase considerably in numbers; if they are left as they are generally left in a garden, they will gradually die away and the capital you have invested will be lost. 'The trouble is,' said Tom, 'there always seems something more urgent to do than digging up bulbs and planting them again.'

The flowers are picked when the buds have dropped at right angles to the stem, and they are brought into the packing shed and put into pails of water. If the weather is cold, there has to be a gentle heat in the shed to help burst the buds open. Then, when their petals are spread they are bunched and sent away to the markets. Every grower has a salesman in each of several markets and he is charged ten per cent on the sales plus a market charge for the handling of each box. Some growers have their own boxes, others hire boxes from the salesmen. In any case the grower pays the railway freight charges to whichever market he sends. In fact a grower has to pay twenty per cent in commission, boxes, market charges and freight, out of any price he receives for his flowers.

Tom said that violets provided his bread and butter. They are a cheap crop to grow because each year's stock consists of the runners pulled off the previous season's plants. They are planted in May and June, fifteen inches apart and about the same distance between the rows. The plants have bushed out by September and have begun flowering by the end of the month, continuing to do so through the winter months to April. There is an average weekly picking of twelve dozen bunches for every thousand plants – twenty violets and two leaves making up a bunch. Up to fifteen thousand plants go to an acre but, Tom warned, such was the time and labour involved in picking and bunching, no small grower could manage such a number. He himself usually had four thousand plants, growing a variety called Governor Herrick which, though it has very little scent, is prolific in flowering and lasts very well once picked. He had no use for the pale-coloured, sweet-scented Princess of Wales because it was difficult to grow, bloomed scantily, and fetched no higher price in the market.

Anemones are more difficult to grow and more expensive, but they are as much part of a Cornish market garden as bacon in a grocer's. The type most in demand in the markets is the De Caen variety, single blooms of multi-colours, and although some growers sow seed, the majority plant corms early in July. Seed is cheaper to buy but this economy is cancelled out by the extra labour involved. Good corms cost around fifteen shillings a thousand and eighty thousand go to an acre – the whole crop being ploughed into the ground at the end of the season. Their flowering period is the same as violets but they are liable to downy mildew which can devastate them, especially in a period of muggy weather when soft misty rain covers the Land's End peninsular – and as the spores of this mildew stay in the soil, anemones must not be grown in the same ground more than once in four years. 'Last year,' said Tom, 'I lost the lot because it was so wet before Christmas.' Frost, of course, sometimes damages them but as Tom explained, a frost hard enough to wipe out the plants seldom strikes West Cornwall. Anemones like a lot of lime in the ground and corms must be planted after the ground has been firmed, only a couple of inches deep and the same distance apart; and you must allow at least twenty inches between rows to enable the pickers to walk up and down without bruising the foliage. Mice sometimes do a great amount of damage. They nip off the buds as they break ground, then carry them off to the hedge where they tear off the petals and eat the heart of the flower. You can find little piles of these petals around every anemone field. The flowers are picked when the bud is just beginning to break. You must on no account send flowers to market which are 'blown' or full open, and this is very difficult to prevent in warm weather. If all goes well you should be able to send throughout the season an average of four dozen bunches a week for every five thousand corms you have planted.

Tom tempered these details with caution. He told us not to accept them as the gospel of the expert because the problems of market gardening were as numerous as a football permutation. Every season provides a different set of circumstances, and there is always an element which no one has ever experienced before. You are at the mercy of gluts and the weather, and they can knock you for six just when you think the season is going to be a good one.

We were now standing in the middle of our big field. It used to be called the cemetery field because at the bottom of it, the old cows and horses of neighbouring farms used to be buried. We were standing at the ridge half-way down

– the top half sloped fairly gently, the bottom half suddenly dipped below the ridge until it levelled out just before the cliff. 'That top piece,' said Tom, looking at the upper half, 'that wouldn't take long to break if you had someone to help. Then you can hire a man with a plough and work up the land, then get a few potatoes in by March. Couldn't expect much but it would clean the ground and be a start.'

The growing of new potatoes held a fascination for us. There was past enjoyment of their flavour and the prospect of producing a crop so far ahead of the rest of the country that it had the merits of a delicacy; besides, stories had been told to us of small fortunes being made out of the pocket cliff meadows between Penzance and Land's End – 'the earliest potato land in England' it was called. Potatoes appeared easy to grow. In fact they seemed to be the answer to the amateur's prayers – hard manual work but no specialized skill, the warm climate and high prices ensuring a handsome profit. They would be the first corner stone of our income, so we then thought, as soon as we had the cultivated land in which to grow them. Hence Tom's suggestion suited us well.

Seed potatoes are delivered in the early winter and the varieties have names like Sharpe's Express, Home Guard, Arran Pilot, May Queen. When the seed arrives the potatoes are picked out and carefully placed eye-end up side by side in special wooden trays. They stay like this indoors until planting time, and by then they will have grown shoots a couple of inches long. The larger potatoes are then cut between the shoots so that there are two or even three sections which can grow on into plants. The planting is done in February and early March and, given good weather, the crop will be ready to draw at the beginning of May; and for every ton planted three or four tons should be harvested. The work, because the meadows are steep and small, has to be done by hand labour. Turning the ground in the autumn, planting the seed, digging out the crop – is all achieved by the use of the long-handled Cornish shovel. The seed potatoes are carried down the cliff, the harvest up. Thus every stage is identical to that in use a century ago; but we gladly accepted the prospect of what, in due course, would be our wearisome task, because of the anticipated financial returns. We were assured that whereas a ton of seed potatoes cost £20, the cliff early new potatoes sold at an average of £70 a ton. It seemed to us we had found an El Dorado.

We looked expectantly at the land in which Tom proposed we should grow our first crop. It was late in the year to order the seed so there would not be time to 'shoot' them in the trays, and they would have to be planted 'blind'; but the first step was to find someone to take charge, to prepare the land, plant the potatoes and then look after them. That evening we went up to St Buryan village to seek the advice of Jim Grenfell, a Pickwickian figure who presides at the inn with the slow measured courtesy of the days of coach and horse rather than of motor cars. Jim soon found Harry, a rabbit catcher; and Harry, over seventy, wiry with bright blue eyes and a drooping white moustache, promised that if we left our problems in his hands, all would be well.

That spring as we toiled in London, we thought of our growing potatoes as one might think of a racehorse in training for a great race – and on each visit to Minack we dashed on arrival to stare at their progress. They developed so green and flourishing, five hundred weight had been planted and Home Guard was the variety, that we began contentedly estimating what our profit might be; and when Harry proclaimed the crop would be ready to draw the following week, I promised to come down and help. I left

London at three in the morning and reached Penzance at ten – and on arrival I called at the wholesaler who had promised to market the crop.

'I've just driven down from London,' I said, with the rush of the journey still filling my ears, 'and I'm going on now to start digging the crop. You can expect me back this afternoon with a load.'

'Driven down specially from London?'

The man glared at me, and threw the stub of his cigarette viciously on to the pavement outside his shop.

'You must be mad . . . there's a glut of potatoes. They're not worth a penny a pound.'

In August Tommy Williams entered our lives and became the last pylon of the bridge. I met him first striding down Market Jew Street in Penzance one Saturday afternoon, wearing a Harris tweed suit, a smart trilby, and smoking a cigar. He looked more like a wealthy farmer than a labourer who had spent his life around a cowshed, and I understood why I had been told I could not fail to recognize him if I saw him. He was very tall with a fine, thin looking face and brown eyes which gazed gently at you except when, and this I later found often to be the case, he became roused; and then they would resemble those of an excited evangelist. He lived alone in a caravan near St Buryan and on the walls hung pictures which he had bought in local curiosity shops. 'I have a Constable,' he said proudly that first day I met him, 'a genuine Constable . . . and a Stradivarius!' His eyes gleamed. 'It's broken but it can be mended!'

Shortly before my encounter with him – after a particularly rowdy argument with his employer – he made it known throughout the district that he would do no more regular work, only casual work and on days which suited him. This attitude admirably coincided with mine as I was looking for a man who would work two or three days a week at Minack throughout the winter so that, when in early spring we came down permanently to live, the foundations of our future endeavours would have been laid.

He was undaunted by what he found he had to do. With eyes of knowledge instead of wishful thinking he mapped the whereabouts of meadows in the undergrowth. He was impatient to slash the saplings and the brambles which blocked the lane. He talked of rebuilding the old roofless buildings and rerouting the course of the stream. He rushed out his plans as if he was drawing zest from the prospect of showing others what he was capable of achieving when left on his own. And then, during the winter, he sent us progress reports:

'I am pleased to inform you that I have trimmed down all the hedges round top and bottom. I have burned the trimmings and been around the field hedges and put back all small stones. I have cut the trees back around the two home meadows and stacked branches around hedges to keep out cattle. The little potato house meadow will be a nice meadow when I've finished breaking it. I have the thorns around the hedges for fences and windbreaks. There is quite sunny weather at Minack between showers. Well, that is all for the present. Tommy Williams.'

Then came the final report at the end of March, a few days before we were due to arrive:

'I have moved the stones in the front garden so that there are four beds instead of two. I have borrowed wallflowers from my cousin. They are in flower and taken well. Also primrose plants from the cliff. Makes the garden cheerful and I hope you will be pleased.'

And we *were* pleased.

Chapter Three

JEANNIE'S FRIENDS looked out of their own personal windows and judged her decision according to the view they were accustomed to see.

'My dear, what are you going to *do* all day?'

'If *only* I had the same courage!'

'Are you *sure* you're not going to miss all the fun?'

'I'll take a bet you're back in six months!'

Those in the tight little world of parties, American Bars and gossipy sensations, disliked the idea of one of their number deserting – the justice of their lives was being questioned, an end had come into sight when they felt only safe in prolonged beginnings. Hence they interpreted her decision by complicated explanations, and gained satisfaction in their certainty she would soon be back.

Those who had never tasted the flavour of mixing with celebrities found her decision incomprehensible. She led the life of a modern fairy princess yet she was giving it up. She must be out of her mind, and they looked at her as if she were an oddity in a zoo.

There were others who envied her. These, captured by their own success, could only reason that she was showing the courage they believed they lacked themselves. Courage, in their view, was required if you are going to break the routine of butterfly pleasures – whereas Jeannie only saw in her choice a way of escape. We were both, in fact, taking the easy way out towards reaching our personal horizon of living time slowly.

We first met one evening at the Savoy in an air-raid. I had written a travel book called *Time Was Mine* and my first words to her were abrupt: 'You're just the person I have been wanting to meet. Can you manage to get my book on the bookstall?'

I had written in this book of a man called Jeffries, a weird mountain of a man, whom I had met on a Japanese boat sailing from Sydney to the Far East, and who, as it proved, was a link between me and Jeannie. I used to sit on deck till late at night listening to the stories of his nefarious life, leaning over the ship's rail, the soft breeze in our faces, watching the passing shadows of the islands along the Barrier Reef. It was the spring of 1939 and he was on his way to a job in the shipyards of Hong Kong.

'I once studied with Cheiro the astrologist and palmist,' he said on one occasion. 'He told me I would never be any good, but then I was never able to tell him his judgement was wrong . . . you see, I worked out on my own that he would die when he was sixty-eight. And he died on his sixty-eighth birthday.'

As it turned out many of the prophecies Jeffries made to me during the voyage were proved false by events. There would be no war. Chamberlain would be Prime Minister for a further five years and so on. But one evening he asked whether I would be prepared to have my own hand read. I was not very keen because I had always remembered the distress of my mother who, when she was thirty, was told by a palmist that my father would die when she was forty-one. She said it was the most agonizing year of her life for she never could get the prophecy out of her mind. However, I agreed and we sat down in a corner of the deck lounge, glasses of saki on the table beside us, and I watched Jeffries study my palm in his ape-like hands. Later I wrote in my diary what he said – among other things that I would marry in 1943, that my wife would be smaller than myself and dark, and that her initials would be J.E. . . .

Jeannie arranged for my book to be on the bookstall and in celebration I asked her out to dinner. The River Room, with its windows bricked up against bomb blast, was the Savoy restaurant in those days and we sat in a corner while the band of Carroll Gibbons played to a crowded dance floor in the background.

I happened to ask her whether she had any other Christian names beside Jean. And she said: 'The awful name of Everald.' I looked at her across the table. 'Do you mind saying that again?' She appeared puzzled. 'My full name is Jean Everald Nicol.' Two years later in 1943, we were married.

The American *Look* Magazine called Jeannie 'the prettiest publicity girl in the world'; and when it was announced she was leaving the Savoy, the newspapers wrote about her as if they were saying goodbye to a star. A columnist in the *Daily Mail* described her as slim, colleen-like, with green eyes and dark hair

'. . . who seems so young, innocent and delicately pretty that you couldn't imagine her saying "Boo" to the smallest and silliest goose. But Jean has said "Boo" to all sorts of important people including tough American correspondents.

'For ten years she has been a key woman at that international rendezvous of film stars, politicians, maharajahs, financiers, business men and what have you – the Savoy Hotel.

'She is about to quit the post of publicity boss or

public relations officer for the Savoy, Berkeley and Claridge's. Her job consisted not only of keeping those hotels before the public but in stopping indiscreet stories from appearing in the newspapers and sometimes in protecting timid guests from the glare of publicity. Now that is a job requiring tact, intelligence and charm, and Jean has all three qualities.

'Who stopped the story about the colonel (with D.S.O.) who was working in the kitchens of the Savoy from getting into the papers? Jean Nicol. Who arranged Dior's first interview in this country? The same girl. When Ernie Pyle the famous American war correspondent (they made a film about him) was going off to his death in the Pacific he had his last lunch in London with Jean. He told her sadly: "I'll never see you again. There's been too much luck in my life, and it's exhausted."

'Close friend of Danny Kaye, Tyrone Power, Gertrude Lawrence, Bob Hope, Bing Crosby . . . there isn't a famous name in the past decade that doesn't know Jean.

'Well, she is going to retire for she thinks that ten years is enough to spend in the glare of London's West End. And she is right.'

We left Mortlake on a sunny April morning when the tide was pushing its way up the river, creeping into the inlets of the riverside like an octopus feeling with its tentacles. On the steps of the Ship, beer mugs in hand, a group stood ready to wave us goodbye. On their right loomed the Brewery, and on their left an empty space, an elm tree, and the house with the roof like a dunce's cap which we were leaving. The act of departure spares only the light hearted, and as I carried out our belongings, sticking them in the Land Rover, I found myself thinking of that ardour seven

years before with which we came to this house; for it was
with this ardour, dressed up in new clothes, that we were
going away. I looked up at the windows and thought of
our happiness which would always live within the rooms;
the unfinished sentences of gay conversations, raised
glasses, sweet moments when endeavour had met its
reward, affection like suffused sunlight warming the company of friends. I saw poised in my mind the fragments
of other people's lives, lost perhaps by them, for ever
attached to me . . .

Bob Capa, the wayward brilliant photographer, who was
killed in Indo China was there, leaning against the door, his
sombre face brightened by a stick of bombs falling across
Duke's Meadows, cigarette drooping from his lips, quietly,
with broken accent calling: 'Coming nearer, coming nearer'
. . . a startled A. P. Herbert on a November night, whisky
glass in hand, hearing the S.O.S. on the *Water Gypsy's*
hooter; the tide had gone out and the crew had awoken when
she tilted on her side . . . George Slocombe on a winter's
afternoon standing with his back to the fire, red-bearded like
an apostle, praising the virtues of France . . . Baron hitching
a camera under his withered arm before photographing
Monty; 'Come on Monty, give us a smile' . . . Gertrude
Lawrence, a cockney again, boisterously shouting the Cambridge crew to victory . . . Carroll Gibbons drawling the
song *People will say we're in love* as he played at our small piano
. . . Alec Waugh standing on the steps looking at the empty
river: 'Your last Boat Race party . . . it was the best.' We had
come to this house believing it would be our home for
always, yet here we were setting off again, packing away past
hopes and ambitions, disappointments and victories, buoy-
antly confident that we now knew better. 'A chapter of my
life was closed,' wrote Somerset Maugham when he left
Tahiti, 'and I felt a little nearer to inevitable death.'

We were aware, too, that departure meant a crack in the lives of those who cared for us. Jeannie would no longer be calling in to see her parents nor would I be able to have the almost daily, hour long conversations with my mother. I was never unsettled by age difference with either of my parents. My father kept a perpetual eye on his own youth, and so never grew old in his approach to me and my two brothers. My mother's philosophy had been to hold up a mirror to the happiness of the three of us, and gain her own in the reflection. When I was a schoolboy I said proudly to a small friend: '*My* mother would walk five miles with a heavy suitcase if it would help me or my brothers.' The childish boast always remained true.

The canvas hood of the Land Rover bulged like a kitbag ... an armchair, suitcases, books, pots and pans, blankets, a camp bed, an ironing board. They piled high behind us as we sat ready to start ... my mother whom we were taking to my aunt's house on the way, Jeannie with Monty on her lap, and myself at the wheel. And as I let out the clutch and slowly moved away, we could only laugh with those who were waving us goodbye.

'I hope you'll get there!' was the last I heard as I turned the corner.

I was on the road to the West again, a road which from my childhood had been part of my life. I used to drive to Glendorgal, our family home, as casually as I drove from Victoria to Kensington. My father saying: 'When in 1903 I drove a car to Cornwall for the first time, a donkey and cart actually passed me on this hill.' My mother: 'Three weeks after my first driving lesson I set off for Glendorgal. We had a puncture at Honiton but there was no garage anywhere near and we had to send to Exeter to find someone to repair it.' And myself: 'Here at Amesbury we had a smash with a Baby Austin ... on my twenty-first birthday week-end we drove through the night and had breakfast at that café . . . I bought an evening paper at this corner shop and learnt the *Royal Oak* had been sunk . . . the car broke down here and I spent the night in that gateway . . . I was gonged on this stretch . . .' Scores of incidents so vivid in my mind that it seemed to me, as I travelled this road again, that I had 'time regained'.

The full moon was waiting to greet us at Minack, a soft breeze came from the sea and the Lizard light winked every few seconds across Mount's Bay. An owl hooted in the wood and afar off I heard the wheezing bark, like a hyena, of a vixen. A fishing boat chugged by, a mile off shore, its starboard light bright on the mast. It was very still. The boulders, so massive in the day, had become gossamer in the moonlight, and the cottage, so squat and solid, seemed to be floating in the centuries of its past.

I said to Jeannie: 'Let's see if Monty will come for a walk.'

He came very slowly down the lane, peering suddenly at dangers in the shadows, sitting down and watching us, then softly stepping forward. His white shirt-front gleamed like a lamp. He sniffed the air, his little nose puzzling the source of the scents of water weeds, bluebells and the sea. He found a log and clawed it, arching his back. He heard the rustle of a mouse and he became tense, alert to pounce. I felt as I watched him that he was an adventurer prying his private unknown, relishing the prospect of surprise and of the dangers which would be of his own making. We paused by the little stream, waiting for him to join us; and when he did, he rubbed his head affectionately against my leg, until suddenly he saw the pebbles of moonlight on the water. He put out a paw as if to touch them.

'I'll pick him up and carry him over.'

But when I bent down to do so he struggled free of my

grasp – and with the spring of a panther he leapt across, and dashed into the shadows beyond.

'Well done!' we cried, 'well done!'

This little stream where it crosses the lane as if it were the moat of Minack, halting the arrival of strangers, greeting us on our returns, acting as the watch of our adventures, was given a name that night.

Monty's Leap.

We awoke the following morning to the sun streaming through the curtainless windows, to the distant murmur of the sea, to a robin's song hailing another day, and the delicious sensation that there was no frontier to our future. If our watches stopped what did it matter? An hour, a day, a week could pass ... there was no barrier to which we were advancing, no date on a calendar which glared at us from a distance. No telephone to shiver us into expectation. No early morning noises, a far off factory hooter, the first rumble of traffic, the relentless roar of a Tube ... no man made alarms to jerk us into the beginning of another day. No newspaper shoved under the door. No clatter of milk bottles. Time to think, time to read. Go down to the rocks and stare vacantly at the sea. Perform insignificant, slowly achieved tasks – weeding the garden, mending a bolt on the door, sticking photographs in an album – without conscience nagging us with guilt. Take idle walks, observe the flight of a raven, the shifting currents of the sea, the delicate shades of moss. Travel the hours on horseback. Timelessness, isolation and simplicity creating the space which would protect us from the past. The hazy happiness of the present guiding our future.

I got up, collected a jug and went down to the stream. I had invited Monty to come with me but he would not budge. I picked him up and put him down in the garden, but within a second he had rushed indoors again. He behaved in this manner for several days, hating the daylight and only venturing out in the dark, and then if we accompanied him. It was difficult to understand his behaviour for on his previous brief visits, though he had never wandered far, he had always kept his nerve. A week later, however, he gained his self-confidence after meeting a baby rabbit face to face outside the front door. He seized it by the neck, brought it into the cottage while I was having breakfast, and deposited it at my feet – alive. Henceforth every tuft of grass was a potential rabbit and every capture brought to us for our admiration; and instead of having to lure him outside, we used to spend much of our time searching for his whereabouts.

While I fetched the water Jeannie went up to the patch of ground where we had fixed up a wired run for the chickens. We had always kept chickens at Mortlake where they lived in a disused air-raid shelter and in a run that was messy with mud. Now they had a house of their own and, although the site was open to the four winds of heaven, they had grass to scratch, legions of succulent insects to peck, and farm chicken food to eat instead of the sticky mash which used to be their diet. There were ten of them (I had made a special trip in the Land Rover and they had laid six eggs on the way) and they were delighted with their new home. The eldest was called Queen Mary and although she was too old for egg laying, we had brought her to Minack because we did not have the heart to kill her. But the Cornish air, in due course, worked a miracle and she began laying again; and a year later we gave her a set of thirteen eggs to sit on, from which she proudly hatched one chick. Their devotion to each other was pretty to watch until the chick grew into a cockerel and to its duty of ruling the roost; and then Queen Mary, perhaps exhausted by motherhood, began to ail, and had to be put away.

I stood the jug of water on the table and lit the two valor stoves. The coal stove, in place of the Cornish range, always went out overnight; and so breakfast was cooked with a kettle on one oil stove, a frying pan on the other. Then, while Jeannie got on with the breakfast I walked up to the farm for the milk.

It was not a pretty farm; indeed it was not a single farm but a collection of ancient buildings including three cottages which were allotted to three different farmers. The grey stone buildings were juggled together without any design of convenience for the farmers concerned. A cowhouse of one was opposite the tool-shed of another. A barn alongside one cottage belonged to the one opposite. Decrepit buildings, cracked windows, mud and muck on the ground – yet they were a monument to centuries of humble endeavour and this, I found, gave pleasure.

I was looking around for John when an old woman, a battered grey felt hat pressed down over her ears, with a lined face like that of a Rembrandt portrait shouted: 'He's in the shelter, Mister!' Mary Annie lived with her daughter in one of the cottages, and all her life had been spent among these buildings, working a man's day on the land. She was kind, friendly and happy, and if anyone had suggested she would have been better off in an old people's home she would have laughed in their face. The spirit of Mary Annie was as indestructible as the boulders in the moorland that she could see from her cottage.

I found John sitting on a stool milking a cow. Farmers are silent and solemn people when they are milking, and as they are likely to be performing this task for two hours every morning and evening they have plenty of time for contemplation. Doubtless their thoughts roam over the crops they are growing but I guess they are thinking of those of their neighbours as well. If they do not wish them ill, they at least derive comfort if the crops are not as good as their own. At any rate some of them do; and I confess I developed the habit myself, when our potatoes were 'cut' by frost; of hastening to look at other people's to discover if they were as damaged as our own.

'Lovely morning,' I said cheerfully.

John replied with a nasal sound like 'urr,' but without any rolling of the r's. It is a sound with which I have become very familiar. It is uttered by any farmer who does not want to make conversation or commit himself to an answer, and it is emitted on various notes of the scale. If, for instance, a tone of surprise is required, the note is high with a slight cadence. If agreement is to be signified but without it being overstressed the note is in the middle; and if it is necessary to make clear that any conversation is unwelcome, the 'urr' becomes a grunt.

'How are your potatoes looking?' I asked. This enquiry, during growing time, is the Cornishman's substitute for enquiring after anyone's health.

A low 'urr.'

I hung about for half a minute, then asked if I could help myself to the milk and I would pay him at the end of the week. The 'urr' came out in the middle of the scale. Then, as I was going through the door, I heard him say, 'Cubs are makin' a mess of them taties down cliff and I be setting traps.' Fearing for Monty, I was immediately on my guard. 'Whereabouts?' There was a pause. 'They won't harm yer cat,' he answered without me having to explain what I was thinking.

In one direction stretched the lane to the main road, nearly a mile long with its surface straddled with cart-made craters; in the other the lane to Minack, rough like the dried-up bed of a river. Tommy Williams had cut away the undergrowth of the last one hundred yards and we could now drive up to the cottage in the Land Rover. Cars could reach the farm buildings but they could not get any further, and in time the lane became known as our chastity belt. We could not be surprised by visitors and, if tempted to go out, so bad was it even for a Land Rover, we usually had second thoughts about going.

I walked happily down the lane carrying the milk in a tin can, marvelling at the way the hedges on either side unfolded the view of the sea like a tape. First a pin point of blue, then stretched as if it were a few inches long, growing longer and longer as I went down the hill until I reached the bottom and the hedges fell away and I looked upon the vastness of Mount's Bay.

I was singing when I came up to the cottage, breakfast ahead of me, and a lovely day at our mercy. Jeannie was waiting at the door, a jug in her hand.

'You clot,' she said, 'when you filled this jug you filled it with tadpoles.'

The tadpole problem remained until they grew into frogs. I used to crouch beside the stream with a jug and a cup, flicking the tadpoles out of one and emptying the water into the other. It was a laborious way of fetching water, and more so when we needed water at night, and then Jeannie would gleam the torch on the swimming black spots while I repeated my methods of the day-time.

We were, in fact, leading the life of two campers, and the prospect of continuing to do so appeared to stretch far ahead. The cottage was sparse of furniture. We had no bed and we slept on a mattress laid on the floor. Our pride was a fitted carpet in the sitting-room but with it we had only one armchair, a divan, a table and three kitchen chairs. We saw no reason to grumble. We had left our furniture behind for the very good reason it was earning us money.

The house at Mortlake which we ourselves rented unfurnished, had been let by us to a young Embassy official and his wife. The profit we derived was to be our income at Minack, and we therefore took care to see that our tenants would be satisfied. He was a solemn young man, and neither he nor his wife had been away from their native land before; and when, after a lengthy inspection of the house they expressed their desire to rent it, I proposed that it first should be vetted by the chief of his department. The chief arrived, inspected and gave his blessing both to the house and the rent; and as the young man wanted to move in as quickly as possible, he and I came to a gentleman's agreement that he could take possession without waiting for the formal agreement to be signed.

Hence, although we were now without furniture we did have a small income ... but not for long. Three months after the young man had moved in, just as the lease was about to be signed, he moved out. I contacted his chief and also the Embassy concerned, but with no result. A gentleman's agreement was not a valid document. Thus Jeannie and I suddenly had our income cut off, had an empty furnished house on our hands, and were three hundred miles away from superintending its reletting. It was a worrying situation until I said to Jeannie: 'Look, we've been compromising by keeping the house. At the back of our minds we've been thinking we *might* want to go back. We won't and we know it. Let's give it up.'

Early one late summer morning we got out the Land Rover and drove up to London; and by the following day we had seen our landlord, given up the lease and sold him the fittings, and had arranged for some of our furniture to be sold, some to be transported to Minack.

The incident was a warning that escape is not an end to itself and it sharply removed from our minds the pleasant reflection of its achievement. London was no longer our home. It was now vital to make a success of the apprenticeship in the way of life we had chosen to follow; and it is the story of this apprenticeship that I am ready to tell.

Chapter Four

APRIL PASSED, the potato season drew near and the inhabitants of the district, including ourselves, began to develop the mood of prospectors in a gold rush.

Three and four times a day Jeannie and I inspected the land which Tommy Williams had planted with one and a half tons of seed – the small meadows he had cut out of the top of the cliff, and the upper part of the cemetery field. The sight fascinated us. We stood and stared at the dark green leaves, hypnotized by their coarse texture, greedily calculating the amount of the harvest; then we would bend down and tickle a plant, stirring the earth round it with our hands, and calling out when we found a tiny potato . . .

'Need a nice shower,' Tommy would say, 'and they'll treble in size within a week.' Or in the lane, I would meet John who, in answer to the inevitable question: 'How are the taties looking?' would say gloomily, 'Been known for a gale to come at this stage . . . blast them black and only the weight of seed been lifted.' It was not only the size of the harvest which was at stake, but also its timing. There was a rivalry among growers as to who would be the first to draw, like jockeys at the starting gate; and the information that was circulated was as inspired as that on a race-course. I would go up to Jim Grenfell's pub at St Buryan in the evening and listen to the gossip.

'Bill Strick was cut by frost last night.'

'Over at Mousehole they look handsome.'

'Nothing will be going away until after Buryan Feast.'

'William Henry starts drawing Monday.'

These rumours and false alarms increased as the pace of excitement grew faster every day, and by the end of the month the inevitable question had become: 'Started drawing yet?' The disinterested – the postman, the man at the garage, the proprietor of our St Buryan grocers, put the question as a matter of politeness; our fellow growers, whether neighbours or others living a few miles away, jerked it out as if they were apprehensive we might spring a surprise. Our land, having never grown potatoes before, might upset the balance of prestige . . . supposing Tangye was first to draw? Of course, we caught the fever ourselves and went staring jealously at meadows other than our own, and asked repeatedly: 'Started drawing yet?'

The mounting tension had an effect similar to the concern of a general who feels he is being pushed into battle before he is ready. There was the pressure of local prestige on the one hand, hard economics on the other, and the economics were very confusing.

Supposing the price on a certain day at the beginning of the season was 1s. a pound but a week later it dropped to 8d. a pound. In that week the crop may have doubled in size and you would therefore be receiving 1s. 4d. a pound. On the other hand the increase in weight would cost more labour and more in freight, and require twice as many chip baskets; and in any case the price might have dropped to 6d. a pound and the crop failed to increase as expected. Moreover for the early potato growers like ourselves whose crop is grown in the cliffs, there was always the shadow of the farmers. We had to hand dig our crop with a shovel, while they careered through their fields with tractors towing spinners. These spinners threw out the potatoes so fast that with sufficient labour a farmer could send away ten tons in a day; and so our economic survival depended on clearing our crops before they began.

There was the bewildering problem of marketing. No difficulty existed about finding a salesman, the problem was which salesman to choose. Several had visited us representing different firms and different markets but their methods of approach were the same; they smiled winningly, talked jovially, and then offered us identical terms. We had to pay 9d. for each chip basket (chips were used at the beginning of the season), pay the freight charges and ten per cent commission on the gross sales, and had to trust to luck for the price obtained on the morning our consignment arrived in the market. With this information I was able to calculate approximately how much each ton of potatoes we sent away would cost us. One hundred and sixty chips were required for a ton – £6. Each chip was scheduled to contain 14 lbs. of potatoes but another 1 lb. was required to allow for shrinkage in transit; if the price, then, was 8d. a pound, we would give away £5. The charge for freight to the Midlands or London (and it had to be a passenger train in order to travel overnight) was another £10 a ton. There was paper to put in the chips, string with which to tie them, and the cost of taking them to Penzance station – another £5.

Thus we had to pay £26 a ton, or about 3d. a pound out of the price we received in the market – in addition to the ten per cent commission. Then there was the cost of the seed, fertilisers and labour involved, all of which had to be covered before we made any profit ourselves. From the purist's point of view all new potatoes should be in chips because they travel and keep much better than when they are in sacks; but the 56 lb. sacks cost only a shilling, the shrinkage required for each sack is only an extra 2 lbs. and these are despatched by freight train instead of by passenger train. Hence there would be a stage during the season when the potatoes had begun to arrive in the market in bulk with the consequent drop in price, when sacks would replace the chips.

One Monday morning Tommy Williams came striding up the lane while we were sitting on a rock sipping cups of coffee, idly watching Monty stalk a mouse in the grass. Tommy was now working the first three days of the week for us, another two days for John; and thus his loyalty to the potato meadows was divided. On this particular morning he had an evangelist look, his chin thrust out, and his tall figure in ragged working clothes like a prophet on the war-path. 'John's told me he's starting to draw this morning,' he rushed out as if he had brought news that war had been declared, 'we must go down the cliff at once and see what ours are like. You bring the chips and I'll take the shovel.'

We swallowed our coffee and off we went, Tommy with the shovel over his shoulder, I with a bundle of chips, and Jeannie walking hopefully behind. The weather was perfect. The sea was smooth as a pool and flecked with gulls swimming nonchalantly like ducks; and as we trudged down the cliff the old steamship *Scillonian* sailed past outward bound to the Scilly Isles, cutting through the water as gently as a yacht. Tommy brought out the telescope he always carried with him. 'Got a car on board,' he said importantly. In the summer she sailed to and fro to the islands every day, and in the winter every other day in each direction except when the Scilly flower season was at its height. She was a friendly sight and she became, as her successor has also become, a timepiece. 'Has the *Scillonian* gone past?' I would call out, or Tommy or Jeannie.

Her course took her parallel to our meadows a half mile
out, a sea green painted hull and a yellow funnel; and
sometimes in a storm when the sea was running mountain-
ous waves we would watch with our hearts in our mouths
as she lurched toy-sized among them. Then Tommy –
brutally – would roar with laughter; 'I bet them passengers
are feeling bad.' In fair weather she berthed at Penzance, in
bad she made for Newlyn, and as she was the link between
the Scilly flower growers and the mainland markets, her
skipper sailed her in seas when she might have been
expected to remain in harbour. There was one occasion
when, after leaving the islands, a gale so fierce blew up
that when she reached Mount's Bay she was three hours
late and it was dark. The skipper, a Scillonian, unexpectedly
decided it was too dangerous to enter Newlyn harbour,
and chose to spend the night steaming to and fro across
the Bay, sailing out the gale. There was wry laughter in the
Scillies when this was known. The Government, a few
weeks before, had announced that the Scillonians were to
be liable for income tax – and off the boat the following
morning stepped two sick-looking Inland Revenue
Inspectors.

We reached a meadow at the top of the cliff and I cut
the string of a bundle and singled out a chip while Tommy
banged the edge of the shovel on his boot in the manner of
an acrobat calling attention to a special trick. Then, with
Jeannie and me standing expectantly beside him he stabbed
under a plant and turned it upside down. Several little
white potatoes connected together as if by a string lay in
the soil. Tommy said nothing and moved to another part
of the meadow and stabbed again. The same thing
happened.

'Look's like we're going to be disappointed,' he murmured, 'we'll try the May Queen over there. They should

be ready.' We walked over to the meadow which was steep and fringed with bluebells. Tommy turned over one plant, then another, picked up the stems and shook them, and ran his hands through the soil. We were out of luck. The May Queen were no better than the Pilot we had tried first. 'Marbles!' Tommy snorted with disgust, 'just marbles!' We gathered up the little white things for ourselves, cross and disappointed, and trooped back silently, disconsolately to the cottage. As Tommy put away his shovel he looked at me, his eyes no longer blazing, and grunted: 'Don't say a word to anyone in the village about this. Keep your affairs to yourselves. Some of them are a mean lot and they'll be pleased.' I nodded solemnly in agreement.

Our village of St Buryan stands on high ground three miles from the coast on the road to Land's End, and the church spire is a beacon to ships far out to sea. It is a sturdy village of neat granite cottages with grey slate roofs and no pretensions about being quaint. It is a business-like village and makes you feel that it prides in brawn and courage rather than in brain and guile, in the basic virtues rather than those which are acquired. Until a year or so ago there was no main water and the village supply was tapped from a spring in the square opposite the inn; so that when you stood in the bar looking out of the window, you watched the inhabitants filling their pails of water as their ancestors had done patiently for centuries before them. It is a village which challenges the sensibilities and yet soothes them, as if it were an integral part of the gales which lash it and the calm which follows. It is not a village in which to live and be idle, for work conscientiously performed is the yardstick of value. It is generous both in spirit and in pocket, for no worthy cause fails to meet with success; but if it is willing to like, it is also quick to distrust, and slow to forgive. It is, in fact, a village of character.

The name comes from that of an Irish girl saint and is pronounced Berian. How she came to the Land's End peninsular is obscure, but in ancient days Irish pilgrims used to travel to the continent by way of Padstow and Mousehole. The object was to avoid the stormy passage around the 'corner' of England by landing at Padstow, travelling overland to Mousehole and embarking in another ship for France. It is believed that in the sixth century she was one of these pilgrims. In any case the shrine of St Buryan existed in the tenth century when King Athelstan swept into Cornwall to drive out the Danes who garrisoned the county and the Isles of Scilly. His final great battle in Cornwall was at Boleigh Hill, two miles from Minack, and he afterwards rested his troops at St Buryan before setting out from the beaches of Sennen near Land's End to invade the Isles of Scilly. On the day before he sailed he worshipped before the shrine and vowed, if the expedition was successful, that he would as a thank-offering build and endow a church.

The original church decayed into rubble during the fifteenth century and at the beginning of the sixteenth the present one was built. It is a beautiful old barn of a building, and in a village whose limited number of inhabitants are divided between Methodists and members of the Church of England, it has the effect of a cathedral. In a corner of the church is a collection of ancient finds that have been made in the district and which were gathered together by a remarkable old man named Croft who was Vicar of St Buryan when we came to Minack. It seemed that Croft was as much interested in the past as he was in his parishioners and he spent much of his time seeking the history of the parish from ancient documents and in leading groups of earnest archaeologists in excavating from the soil the traces of Stone Age settlements.

A few months after our arrival, a mason repairing a wall in the cottage had discovered a cavity, neatly roofed with small stones, which he explained was an old oven dating back some five hundred years. A few days later I looked out of the window and saw an old man struggling slowly up the steep path to the door. 'The Vicar's come to call!' I cried out to Jeannie, and Jeannie in those few split seconds between the sight of an unexpected visitor and his arrival, rushed round the room picking up papers and hiding unwashed plates. 'Why didn't he warn us?' she moaned, while I wondered how I was going to explain why I never went to his church. I ushered him into the room and he sat down on the sofa, panting from the exertions of his walk. He sat silent until he had recovered himself then, with a gleam of excitement in his eyes, looked at me and said, 'I've come to see the oven!'

The trail of archaeologists used to irk the inhabitants of St Buryan and there was one old man, many years ago, who became a hero to the village for the trick he played on a group. He was a specialist in stories about Athelstan's Battle of Boleigh which, he declared, had been handed down from father to son in his family from generation to generation; and so sincere was his note of authenticity that historians never failed to bring out their notebooks in excited belief. The fields where the battle is supposed to have been fought are known as Gul Reeve which is the old Cornish for 'red field'; and as neither the soil nor anything else in the neighbourhood is red, it has always been presumed that the name is derived from the blood which flowed. Near by is a farm and the old man declared one day to a group of believers that the dead of the battle were buried in a long trench in a field adjacent to the farm buildings. He knew the exact position having carried in his head the number of paces from each corner of the field that led to the trench, details which had been told to him by his father. A score of men dug for two days and not a bone was found. The archaeologists were angry, the men who had done the digging happily pocketed their pay, and the old man grinned. 'If mistake there be,' he said, 'it be due to father.'

On these same Gul Reeve fields stand, some distance apart, two massive upright stones which are known as the Pipers. They are, in fact, Peace Stones, representing the Conqueror and the Conquered, erected presumably after the Battle of Boleigh. But during the centuries in between they acquired the name of the Pipers so that they might dovetail into the story that the elders of St Buryan told their children about the circle of nineteen stones known as the Merry Maidens which stand in a field a few hundred yards away on the other side of the road. The elders told the story as a warning against playing on Sundays. The nineteen stones were nineteen maidens of the parish who were lured by two young men to dance on a Sunday afternoon; and while the girls tripped daintily hand in hand, the young men played their flutes – until there was a flash of lightning and they were all turned to stone.

Our post came from St Buryan, and the telegrams from a sub-post office at Lamorna. Our first postman had an eccentric sense of delivery and his route to the cottage across fields and over hedges was to him an unwelcome steeplechase. Letters, therefore, sometimes reached us two days late, sometimes three, sometimes not at all. This waywardness fitted our mood until one morning I received a writ for an unpaid account without ever having seen the letter of warning which preceded it. The telegrams also came across the fields, and the authorities awarded the sub-postmaster with a special bonus of sevenpence for each delivery. Usually they were from Americans who had arrived at the Savoy to find Jeannie had left, and a telegram would arrive asking us to lunch the following day as if the distance between Minack and the Strand was that between Chelsea and Kensington; or else it would be a request for us to telephone at some inconvenient hour as if the charge was a fourpenny call and the call-box in our front garden.

After a sequence of such requests I made enquiries about installing a telephone, half-hearted enquiries which were more of a gesture to conventionality than a desire to have one; and made in the confident belief that the cost of installation with its half mile of wire and poles would in any case be prohibitive. I was surprised when the Post Office informed me that the cost would be twelve shillings and sixpence and the installation immediate; and the Post Office was surprised when it received my letter explaining I had changed my mind and did not want one after all. We still have no telephone and although it is sometimes irritating to drive two miles to the nearest call-box, we are spared the far greater irritation of a menacing ringing bell.

A month after our arrival, and when the tension of the impending potato season was reaching its climax, we received a telegram, 'Expect me tomorrow night' and signed 'Uncle B,' – the nickname by which many knew Baron, the photographer. He was to be our first visitor and the first to pose a problem difficult to solve. If you earn your living from the land you have to work regular hours like anyone who goes to an office, but unlike the office worker, you do not have the security of an office building to shelter you from your friends. A further difficulty is that most people who visit Cornwall are on holiday with time to spare and an inclination to look up old friends or to stay with them for a night or two at the same pressure of gaiety as in the days of their former acquaintance. On our part although we usually quailed at the prospect of visitors, we surrendered when they arrived and suffered penitence for the lost hours after they had departed. Our real difficulty arose when such visitors arrived in sequence throughout a summer, each an old friend regained from the past, each deserving the full attention of a merry reunion. It was on such occasions, and those when we paid rare visits to London, that our ego of sophistication reasserted itself leaving that of the peasant to provide the remorse.

The gusto of Baron was that of a roaring gale which eventually exhausts itself into stillness. He pounded every twenty-four hours like a punchball, working, playing, loving, talking, drinking, dazzling his friends with his wit, kindness and a great gentleness. His behaviour was often outrageous. He once asked me to introduce him to Mike Cowles, proprietor of the American magazine, *Look*, and I arranged that we should all meet at Claridge's for drinks. After an hour and there was no Baron, Jeannie suddenly turned to me, 'Heavens,' she said, 'it's Thursday!' Thursday was a notoriously unreliable day for Baron as it was the day of his weekly Thursday Club luncheon. Another half hour and we saw him beaming smiles at surprised strangers as he weaved his way towards us. 'Jeannie, Jeannie,' he cried, 'forgive me, forgive me!' And he thereupon knelt down in the dignified foyer, clasping his hands together in mock prayer. A few days later I was with him in the Savoy bar when Mike Cowles passed by and I waved. 'Who's that?' asked Baron. I told him. 'That's the very man I want to meet,' he replied, 'do introduce me.' I put down my drink and looked at him. 'I have done so already . . . we all spent an hour together the other evening at Claridge's!'

Our spare room at Minack was a chicken house which we had bought and converted. We had erected it adjacent to the cottage with its floor lifted clear of the soil by pylons of stones, and the windows looked out on the croft and Mount's Bay. On the floor was a rug, and the furniture consisted of a camp bed and chest of drawers. We had painted the walls white and there was little sign of the hut's original purpose except a small hatch door at ground level where the chickens should have come in and out. Baron was delighted. 'Just the place for an old rooster like me,' he said. He stayed with us on that occasion for twenty-four hours and during that period we visited every pub in the district. We ended the first evening at the Tolcarne in Newlyn where Gracie Thomas rules tough seamen of many nationalities in the manner of a kind headmistress. We had been there ten minutes when I saw Baron was the centre of a group of French fishermen who were roaring with laughter. '*En avance à bateau,*' he called out when he caught my eye, and off we all went to the French crabber in the harbour and spent two hours of drinking from a demijohn of wine.

We waved Baron goodbye and felt no nostalgia for the life he represented. We were enjoying a honeymoon with the primitive and tasks that could become monotonous – fetching the water from the stream, filling the paraffin lamp, cooking, cleaning, lighting the stove – possessed the brisk pleasure of the unusual. When I first knew Jeannie she could not even boil potatoes, and the first meal she gave me consisted of cinder-burnt chops due to the fact that she was unaware that frying required fat. She now had a file bulky with recipes and it was not long before she added two more – those for Cornish cream and home-made bread. She collected four pints of milk from the farm, poured it into a bowl and allowed it to settle for a few hours. Then she put the bowl on the edge of the stove where there was a gentle warmth and left it overnight. On the first occasion she tried this out I watched her, as excited as a girl going to a first night, skim off a thick layer of yellowy cream and then, with the confident air of a farmer's wife, serve me with thunder and lightning – treacle and Cornish cream on slices of bread. A few weeks later I had a pain in my side and I said to Jeannie, 'I believe I've got appendicitis.' I was nervous of going to the doctor and put off doing so until the pain or 'feeling' became so persistent that I had no alternative but to make an appointment. As I entered the surgery I visioned the hospital, the operation, the convalescence which would keep me incapacitated throughout the potato season. The doctor examined me and poked my side, then asked, 'Have you been eating a lot of Cornish cream since you came here?' And with his question the pain disappeared.

Jeannie's mother sent the recipe for the bread and it was such a success that we never bought a shop loaf again. She makes four one pound loaves out of three pounds of wholemeal flour and three teaspoonfuls of dried yeast. While the yeast is dissolving in a cup of warm water, she mixes half the flour, a tablespoonful of brown sugar and one of coarse salt in a warmed basin. To this she adds the dissolved yeast, about one and a half pints of warm water, mixes it all into a batter and leaves it on the back of the stove for fifteen minutes. The rest of the flour is then emptied into the mixture and kneaded for five or ten minutes – after which the dough is cut into four sections, put into warmed, greased bread tins and left to rise on the back of the stove until the dough has doubled in size. Finally the tins go into a piping hot oven for about three-quarters of an hour, and the sweet smell of baking fills the room.

My mother had arrived to stay when we dug our first potatoes. She came loaded with gifts for the cottage including dust cloths, saucepans, detergents, a pair of sheets, and a water filter. My mother was never thrusting either with her views or with her presents, and when out of a packing case she produced the water filter, she very softly said, 'I was thinking of the tadpoles, dear.'

It was on the first evening of her stay that she saw the square figure of John leading his horse and cart, piled high with potato chips, past the cottage. She was irritated that he should be meeting with potato success while we were sitting back and waiting, and she urged that we were not showing enough confidence in our meadows. I explained that we had planted our seed later than he had done, that our meadows in potato parlance were considered later than his, and that in any case Tommy had warned us to wait another week. My mother, however, had the gambling instinct inherent within her and she insisted that no harm would be done if I collected the shovel and the three of us went down the cliff to try a few plants.

The bright light of day had gone from the cliff when we reached it and the sun was dipping to the sea on the other side of the Penwith peninsula. The shadows of the rocks were enjoying their brief passage of life before dark, and the sea was dotted with the waking lights of the pilchard fleet. I poised the long-handled shovel and cumbersomely jabbed it under a plant, lifting the bundle of earth and tossing it to where Jeannie was standing. She stooped, shook the sturdy leaves, and ran her hand through the soil. And there, gleaming bright in the dusk were six potatoes, each the comfortable size of a baby's fist.

Jeannie and I were up at dawn the following morning and I drove the Land Rover over the shoulder of the cemetery field and down to the top of the cliff. It was a heavenly morning with a haze hiding the horizon, the first swallows skimming the landscape, the white parasols of the may trees pluming from the green bracken, and the scent of the bluebells mingling with the salt air of the sea. In the back of the car we had a spring balance weighing machine and a tripod on which to hang it, a bundle of chips and a ball of binder twine with which to tie the cardboard tops when the chips were full, a pair of scissors, the shovel, a box full of salesman's labels with printed addresses of different markets. It was a lush moment of hope blissfully blinded from the realities the years would see.

Chapter Five

DURING THE DAYS that followed, smoothly dressed salesmen appeared on the cliff, watching me dig and ache my way through a meadow, bantering me with news of prices better than their rivals.

'We paid 8½d. home at Bristol,' one would say, and then another two hours later would announce: 'Manchester is strong. We expect 9d. tomorrow.' They served too as the errand boys of news from other potato areas and I would clutter my worries over the prices with the threats that these areas, so much larger than our own, would soon be in production. These treats became progressively worse in their nature, beginning gently with: 'Marazion starts next week,' edging dangerously to 'Gulval are opening up their fields,' or the generalized black news that 'the farmers begin Tuesday': and growing to a climax with 'Jersey are at their peak' or 'Pembroke has a bumper crop,' and then, most disastrous of all: 'Lincoln has begun.' If you have not cleared the cliff by the time Lincoln stream their potato lorries to the markets, you might as well tip your potatoes in the sea. Nowadays these threats have become internationalized and one goes dizzy with the news that Covent Garden is flooded with Morocco, Birmingham with Cyprus, Liverpool with Malta; and it is only when you hear that France has Colorado beetle and has stopped sending that you have a glimmer of hope.

Tommy Williams, during the three days of the week he worked for us, dug in one meadow while I struggled in another; and at the end of the day he would have forty full chips to my fifteen. The Cornish shovel has a long handle like that of a rake and, until one becomes accustomed to it, is a most unwieldy instrument to use. You do not dig as if it were a spade, but scoop under the potato plant using your leg just above the knee as a lever, the left if you are right handed, on which you poise a section of the long handle. As I lunged away my mind rattled with the absurd game of guessing how many potatoes would be under each plant. A meadow of potato plants is seldom uniform, some have squat stems, some thin, some elongated as if they were trying to reach the sky instead of making potatoes among their roots. The ideal plant has a tall firm stem with the shine off the top leaves while the bottom ones are yellow – these are called 'going back' and the fattest, most numerous potatoes should be under them. But, as usual, the dogma of experts was frequently at fault, and I dug plants with squat foliage which had many fine potatoes, some with copy-book stems which had few, and some with green leaves and plenty of shine which had plenty. Sometimes I would be digging a meadow where the crop was light and it seemed to take an age to fill a chip. In another, where the crop was good, the chips seemed to fill on their own and I would shout: 'Lovely samples here, Tommy!'

Tommy's mood varied according to the meadow he was in. If it were large enough for Jeannie to follow behind him, she in blue shorts thrusting her hands in the soil and dropping the very small ones in one chip, the rest in another, and he shirtless in patched brown trousers and wearing a sun-drenched Panama hat, he would treat her to endless dissertations on the problems of the world and his theories on their solution: and from the meadow I was in I would hear the drone of his talk with the gentle voice of Jeannie interrupting every now and again. If he were happy and in a meadow by himself I would suddenly hear the roar of his bass voice, startling the placid cliff with the fragment of a hymn. 'When I start singing in Chapel,' he once told me, 'the congregation stops singing so that they can listen to me solo.' The *Scillonian* was always subjected to close scrutiny. 'Got a tractor on board,' he would say severely, as if it had no right to be there. Or he would spy through his telescope a group in the stern: 'Look to me like Indian students.' And this remark would provide the excuse for a monologue on British policy in India.

Sometimes this telescope annoyed me, for there were days when it seemed more a part of him than his shovel. 'Every time I look at Tommy,' I would say to Jeannie, 'he's staring out to sea.' And Tommy, unaware of my annoyance, would call out: 'That's a Frenchy coming in,' or 'Never seen that white crabber before,' or, if there was a liner on the horizon, 'That's the *Mauretania* bound for Cherbourg.' His diet came from tins and when Jeannie, sickened by the jellified mess of meat he ate for dinner day after day, offered to warm the tin in the oven, he replied, 'It's proper as it is, thanks very much.' There were occasions when he would work for nothing. 'I know what your expenses are,' he would say to me, 'but I want to break the back of this meadow and I won't charge you.'

He did not seem to be happy working for John. 'Mark my words,' he warned, 'I don't think I'll be with him for long.' And sure enough a couple of weeks later Tommy came raging into the cottage. 'It's all over between me and him,' he shouted, and poured out a torrent of detail which was difficult to follow. From then on he worked for us full time, but the row which parted him from John seemed to irritate. He proceeded to carry on a pin-pricking feud with

John, sometimes to my embarrassment. One morning I found him planting a clump of lilies in a piece of ground in front of the cottage. 'Where on earth did you get those from Tommy?' I asked. 'They came from the wood,' he replied without looking up, 'and they belonged to my sister.' Tommy's sister had been married to the man who had the farm before John – and he had been killed in his barn by a falling bale of straw. 'I like to think they are hers.' This same line of reasoning governed a later occasion at the time of the flower season when I saw Tommy climb over our boundary hedge and pick a bunch of wild daffodils on the other side. 'You can't do that,' I shouted. 'Oh, yes, I can,' he shouted back – and then I caught sight of John a little way off, silently watching, his cloth cap on the back of his head, a grass stalk in the corner of his mouth like a pipe. I strolled up the field to him, anxious to disclaim any part in the affair. 'I'm very sorry about this, John,' I said, 'Tommy was over the hedge before I could stop him . . . here,' I began to fumble in my pocket, 'here, you'd better have 1s. 6d. for the bunch.' I held out the money and John, like a magistrate's clerk accepting a fine, thrust it in his pocket. 'As you like,' he said, and then turned away.

Tommy's roughness was balanced by his tenderness for birds and animals, and I have seen his eyes soften in wonderment at the sight of a young robin being fed by its parents. Once I saw him half-way up a tall elm, climbing with one hand while the other held a tiny object. 'A baby owl,' he shouted down at me, 'I won't be a minute before I put it back in its nest. You look at the bottom and you'll see two mice its mother must have brought it during the night.' There was the incident of the fox cubs who chose one of our potato meadows as a playground, gambolling at night among the green plants and crushing flat the leaves and stalks. It was the custom in the neighbourhood when this sort of thing happened for the farmer to set traps; and I have seen of an early May morning four cubs each in a corner of a meadow with a leg caught in a gin. I remember how curious it seemed to me that they did not appear frightened, as if it were still part of the game they had started to play in the night; and they waited there as the sun rose until the farmer, in his own good time, arrived to knock them one by one on the head. We, however, were prepared to leave the playground as it was, losing the potatoes to the cubs, but Tommy, on the other hand, was more practical. 'We can't afford to lose the taties,' said he, 'and we mustn't hurt the cubs. I know a way of persuading the vixen to move them to another earth. You leave it to me.' He never told us what he did though I can guess. In any case the meadow was never used as a playground again.

An hour before Tommy was due to go home, he and I used to begin carrying the chips up the cliff. We carried them one in either hand, a hateful, exhausting, back-breaking task, forgivable when the price was high, but when it began to dip I used to mutter curses, as I climbed, against the city dwellers who had no notion of the endeavour that lay behind the potatoes on their plates. Jeannie and I were too tired to weigh them in the evening, and we would have a meal and go immediately to bed, falling into a revolving kaleidoscope of dreams – potatoes with human faces, crushed haulms served for lunch at the Savoy, the *Scillonian* in the guise of a whale, stinging nettles dancing like a chorus, running a cross-country race on a magic carpet which never moved, Tommy looming out of the sky like Mephistopheles. We awoke as tired as when we went to bed, limbs aching, our minds fogged by our dreams and the prospect of another day of chain gang labour. I would get up and put the kettle on the paraffin stove and when it had boiled replace it with a saucepan for the eggs. Then, breakfast over, we would walk along the path to the top of the cliffs where the chips in neat rows awaited their weighing, and suddenly, as if an icepack had melted miraculously before our eyes, we became aware of the glory of the early morning. We looked down on to the sea, glittering from the sun which rose above the Lizard, spattered with fishing boats hurrying to the Newlyn fish market like office workers scurrying to town. A cuckoo flew past, topping the undergrowth, calling as she went. A cormorant perched on the rock that is called Gazell, its black wings extended, drying them against the softness of the breeze. High in the sky a wood pigeon courted another, clapping its wings, then swooping silently and up again, and another clap as sharp as a pistol shot. Around us bluebells brimmed the green grass and foxgloves pointed to the sky like sentinels. Meadow sweet and may blossom clung the air with their scent. A woodpecker laughed. And the sea, sweeping its cool tranquillity to the horizon, lapped its murmur against the rocks below us. Here was the heightened moment when the early morning, unspoilt like a child, is secure from passing time; and when a human being, sour with man-made pleasures, awakes to the sweet grace of freedom.

I weighed, while Jeannie tied the cardboard tops to the chips with binder twine, and while we worked we worried where we would send them. 'I think Birmingham,' I would say, and then, a few minutes later: 'Of course that Scots salesman did say Bristol was very good.' Jeannie would suggest Covent Garden. 'After all,' she reasoned, 'the West End restaurants surely want Cornish new potatoes and should be ready to pay a decent price.' But a few moments later: 'What about Glasgow – the man with one arm said it topped all the other markets last week.' 'All right,' I would reply, 'We'll send to Glasgow.' There would be a pause while I hooked another chip on to the crook of the spring balance. 'Of course, there's all that extra freight to think of,' Jeannie would murmur. 'Oh, hell,' I would answer, 'let's send to Birmingham.' We would pack the chips into the Land Rover, make out the invoice and despatch note, and I would drive to Penzance station. And there, as I waited my turn to unload, doubts would arise again for I would see some farmer of great experience and ask him where he was sending. 'Liverpool – I always send north at this time of the season.'

Our indecision could be blamed on inexperience, but as the years passed the guesswork has continued. Growers despatch their produce to the market, and then, like punters, hope for the best, and storm with irritation when they back the wrong town. There is no way of gauging the see-saw of demand. A salesman said to me once: 'Cardiff is going to be very strong at the beginning of next week. I'll take all that you can dig.' We hired extra labour and sweated through the week-end until we had one ton of potatoes to despatch on Monday and off they went to Cardiff. Three days went by and I received no sales returns – and when sales returns are delayed, it is usually an ominous sign. They came a week later and the price, as by then I had expected, was disastrous. I did not see the salesman again till the end of the season when he appeared at the door to ask for seven chips, the balance of those his firm had sold me and for which I had not paid the price of 9d. each. 'They're broken,' I said truthfully, but grimly, remembering Cardiff. 'Well,' he said, 'you'll have to show them to me, or pay.' That was enough. I burst. Jeannie and I had worked for a month in the manner of peasants of a hundred years ago, and we were exhausted both with potatoes and salesmen. 'Get out of my sight,' I yelled, 'go down the cliff and find them yourself.' I have never seen him again.

There are the same lottery selling methods for flowers. Except on special occasions such as Christmas, Easter and Mothering Sunday, no one seems to have a clue when flowers will or will not be wanted. I have had a telegram from a salesman at 10 a.m. saying, 'Market is glutted,' and another, two hours later from the same man saying, 'send all you can.' There was one February week when the weather in Cornwall reminded one of the Alps. The St Buryan road was impassable with drift snow, no buses could climb the hill out of Newlyn, and the flowers, of course, were unpickable. Yet we ourselves did have a meadow of Magnificence daffodils growing close to the sea which were bravely coming into flower although the ground was white around them. 'We ought to get five shillings a bunch for these,' I said to Jeannie. We proudly picked, bunched and packed them, two boxes with fifteen bunches in each, and then set about thinking how we were going to get to Penzance. We had been cut off from the main road for five days, but, propelled by the excitement of our achievement, we spent five hours digging away a track for the Land Rover; and when we reached the station we were greeted as conquering heroes by the porters. 'Nothing going away at all,' said Owen, who was head porter on the flower train platform, 'nothing at all.' Three days later we received our sales returns and scribbled across the bottom were the words: 'Sorry, it's too cold for the buyers.' The price was sixpence a bunch.

There are, too, the hazards provided by British Railways. I have known a consignment of our potatoes take a week to reach Newcastle by freight train and three days to Bristol. During a period when the price is swiftly falling day by day, such delays mean financial loss for which we can claim no recompense. It is, however, when our flowers are delayed that Jeannie and I are most enraged, and the fury is the more violent because one is impotent to do anything about it. We have pursued the arduous task of growing the flowers, then picked, bunched and admired their exquisite freshness in the packed box – only to learn later that they never reached the market in time for sale. There was the time, on a Tuesday, when we sent forty boxes of Wedgewood iris by the special flower train to Hull. The engine of this train broke down, the truck containing our flowers was put in a siding, and none were sold till the Thursday when a shipload of Guernsey iris swamped the market and brought the Wednesday price of twenty-five shillings a box down to five shillings. Thus we had lost £40 through no fault of our own and, as usual, we could claim no compensation – for British Railways absolve themselves from blame provided the flower boxes reach the station of destination within thirty-six hours of the original arrival time. The fact that the scheduled service has failed to deliver them for the next day's market is immaterial.

Such frustrations, however, lay ahead, for during that first summer we had beginner's luck; and when the potato season was all over and the meadows were strewn with the withering tops of the plants which a month previously had looked so green, with a broken chip lying here and there, an unused sack and the crows poking in the soil among the untidy desolation for the potatoes which had been left behind, we estimated we had made over £200 profit. This figure, minute against the background of a year, inflated our expectations owing to the comparative ease with which it had been gathered. If, with so little land yet under cultivation, with only thirty hundredweight of seed, we could make that sum of money, surely in another year we would have room for four times the seed and make four times as much.

My mother, who had rejoined us for the last week of the potato season, was delighted with these calculations: she had spent most of each day standing in the field holding open the sacks for us to fill, making the professionals smile by her ardour, but saving time and temper for Jeannie and myself who had not yet mastered the knack of tipping a basket without spilling the potatoes. Her gaiety, however, was tempered by increasing concern over our water supply. There had been no rain for a month, the water butt was empty, a pencil-sized trickle was all that was left of the stream, and Jeannie had been forced to discover that soap does not really lather in sea water. My mother, naturally, was unable to adjust herself to the situation, and I used to drive to the village tap at St Buryan, fill up a milk churn I had bought and bring it back for her use. It was inevitable that sooner or later we would have to sink a well, and in view of the drought it seemed best not to waste any time.

'Tommy,' I said one morning, 'we're going to dig a well. What do we do?' Tommy, of course, rejoiced in a question which gave an opportunity for a display of his knowledge and he proceeded to inform me of his personal theory that all spring water in the Land's End peninsular came from Switzerland, that the snow in the Alps melted through the crevices to deep underground, and then slowly crept during the course of hundreds of years across Europe and under the Channel to Cornwall. As often happened, he spiced his imaginative discourse with a practical point. 'You can get a subsidy for sinking a well, I fancy,' and so, at his suggestion, Jeannie and I paid a call at the dingy Penzance offices of the local branch of the Ministry of Agriculture. We had been there once before.

It was shortly before we came to live at Minack and we wanted to seek the advice of the then Agricultural Adviser as to how we should grow potatoes and whether he could

arrange for a soil analysis of our land. We were ebullient
with enthusiasm and naïve with our questions, but the
grizzled-faced man greeted our fervour with: 'We don't
want anyone else growing potatoes down here . . . you'll
be wasting your time and your money.' Incensed at such a
reaction to our zest, I said to Jeannie, 'Come on, let's go,
we don't want to spend any more time with this moron.'
We went back to Minack and the next morning as we were
sipping coffee on rock outside the door, a neat Homburg-
hatted gentleman, dressed in a double breasted black suit
and wearing shiny black shoes, suddenly appeared. 'I have
come to test your soil,' he said solemnly, in the manner of
a doctor who might say, 'Let's hear how your chest
sounds.' We were delighted, and as I led the gentleman to
a meadow we required tested, I found myself feeling
ashamed that I had left the dingy office so abruptly. We
came to the chosen meadow and our friend bent down, ran
his fingers through the soil, then heaped some into a little
canvas bag. 'Oh,' he said, 'this *is* a kindly soil . . . I should
say this is a *very* kindly soil.' There was a note in his voice
which made me suspicious, and a few minutes later I asked
him how long he had been with the Ministry of Agriculture. He smiled at me blandly. 'Only three days,' he said,
'I've just been transferred from the Ministry of Labour.
They change us around a lot, you know.'

I was sceptical when I arrived at the dingy office once
again and I was thus prepared for the Alice in Wonderland
conversation which followed. 'The Ministry,' said the girl
clerk, 'cannot grant a subsidy unless a sample of the water
has been passed by the County analyst, and you may not
start work on the well until an analysis has been approved.'
I looked at her limply. 'How can I have a sample of the
water analysed if I have not got the water?' She smiled
primly. 'That's what we wonder too.'

Our next step was to find the source of water on our land and this could only be done by a water diviner or dowser. The mysterious gift of dowsing defies scientific explanation and if you are not born with it, it can never be acquired. Its use is of immemorial antiquity, but not until Elizabethan times is there any record of its first practical use in Britain; and then some merchant adventurers finding the Germans using it in the Harz Mountains for the prospecting of minerals, introduced its use into the tin mining industry of Cornwall. Scientific instruments can now, of course, trace minerals underground but they still cannot trace water; and whether you live in a cottage or belong to a great oil company planning a reservoir in the desert, you have to pin your faith on the man who communes with water. But a dowser not only has to possess the instinct to trace water. He has to have the sixth sense to gauge the depth underground of the spring, its strength, and its course within a foot or two. There are many stories of dowsers who have judged wrong, of wells that have been sunk at great expense only to produce no water, and my own particular sixth sense on this occasion warned me that unless we were very careful we too might be unlucky.

Our first dowser charged five guineas and displayed such showmanship that he made us feel like natives witnessing black magic. He was a Londoner, who had come to Cornwall a few years before and he had, so he told us, made a lifetime study of water divining. 'I've developed a method,' he said proudly, 'that has made water divining almost scientifically accurate.' We gaped in belief as, opening his suitcase, he produced numerous gaily coloured little flags, and a dozen or so forked hazel sticks. 'Now leave me alone,' he said, 'I need to get in the mood.'

We left him and promptly went inside the cottage to watch from a window, and in a few minutes he rose from his prayer-like position and began to shuffle down the lane, his head bent, his hands holding the hazel stick. Suddenly he stopped, took a flag from his pocket, dropped it and then shuffled on. He stopped again, dropped another flag, then came back to the point where he had started and went off in another direction. It was an hour before he called us to join him, and then he proceeded to give us a lecture as to why, under a pink flag forty feet from the cottage, we would find a spring strong enough to flood St Buryan. 'But how,' asked Jeannie meekly, 'are we to sink a well so near the cottage when there are rocks to dynamite?' 'Ah,' said the man, 'that's not my problem.'

It was not only for this reason that we decided to seek the advice of a second dowser. That evening we were in Jim Grenfell's pub when someone said: 'That fellow may be wrong . . . now the man you want is old John Henry. He's never been wrong in his life and he's nearly seventy . . . he'll find you a spring if anyone can.' I was still cautious and during the following few days I asked other people in the district. 'Oh, yes,' everyone said, 'John Henry is the dowser you're looking for.' The Cornish, like the Irish, are adept at providing those remarks which, they sense, will bolster your personal hopes; and in this case no one wished to tell me that old John had given up regular professional dowsing and that, as he himself later put it: 'I be afraid my sticks have lost their sap.' It was so apparent I wanted our dowsing to be a success that to cast a doubt on my hopes would have been an offence.

The old man had kindly blue eyes wrinkling from his gnarled, weather-beaten face, a character who was so much the countryman that the mind, in his company, was blind to any conversation other than that which concerned the open air. I told him about the other dowser and pointed out the spot where the spring was supposed to be. 'The trouble is,' I said, 'it's so near the cottage that I don't see how we could sink a well.' The old man stared at the soil deep in thought, then pulled his forked hazel twig from his pocket, steadied himself as if he were trying to anchor his feet on the ground, and began to dowse. I looked at Jeannie and smiled. I felt I knew what was going to happen; and a moment later the old man swung round at me crossly. 'Minerals,' he snorted, 'not water.' For the next hour he wandered about while we followed as if we were in the wake of a sleepwalker. Sometimes he would stop and the stick would dip, but never, it seemed, in a way that satisfied him. 'Look,' I would cry out hopefully, 'it's dipping!' But the old man only replied by smiling mysteriously. And then we went up to the crest of the hill above the cottage to a point a few yards from the wire netting of the chicken run. Once again he steadied himself, held out the stick horizontally, gripping it as if he were afraid it might catapult from him. It dipped . . . quickly, strongly as if it were making a smart bow. The old man broke into smiles. 'Here's your spring!' he cried out triumphantly, 'come and feel for yourselves!' I first held the twig by myself and nothing happened; but when he clasped my wrists a power went into that stick as if it were a flake of metal being sucked by a magnet. 'Now there's a strong spring,' said John Henry, 'and you won't have to go more than fourteen or fifteen feet to find it. You can be sure of that.'

Fourteen or fifteen feet. It seemed simple. Jeannie gaily waved goodbye to the old man expecting the water to be gushing into the kitchen sink within a month.

Within a month – the chickens having been moved to a place of safety – there was a hole in the ground seventeen feet deep, eight feet square, and the bottom was as dry as soil in a drought. Its creators were two miners from the Geevor tin mines at St Just, Jack Tregear and Maurice Thomas, and they were as distressed as we were; while old John hastily called in again by me when the fifteen feet limit was reached, nervously scratched his head and said: 'If you go another foot there's sure to be water.'

It was all very well for him to lure us downwards, but for how long were we to pour money down a hole chasing a spring which might not be there? And yet we had gone so far that the tantalizing prospect existed of a spout of water waiting to be released within a few inches of where we might stop. We were, of course, given plenty of advice. 'Ah,' said a neighbour, 'you should have had Visicks the bore-hole drilling people. They reckon you have to bore one hundred feet to get a good supply. They charge thirty shillings a foot, but' – looking lugubriously down our hole – 'they do get results.'

One hundred feet! And here we were at seventeen feet wondering whether to call a halt. The miners had hoped to complete the work within their fortnight's holiday and at their charge of £2 a foot I had expected the well to cost £30. But from the beginning the plans went awry. Instead of being able to dig the first few feet with pick-axe and shovel, the miners came across solid rock within a foot of the surface. Dynamite had to be used and dynamite meant the laborious hammering of the hand drills to make the holes in which to place the charges. Three or four times a day Jack and Maurice would shout 'Fire!' – and scamper a hundred yards to the shelter of a hedge while we ourselves waited anxiously in the cottage for the bangs. One, two, three, four, five, six . . . sometimes a charge would fail to explode and after waiting a few minutes the miners returned to the well to find out the reason; and there was one scaring occasion when Jack, at the bottom of the shaft, lit a fuse which began to burn too quickly. He started scrambling up the sides, pulling himself by the rope which Maurice held at the top. These events added to our distress. The well was a danger besides being a dry one.

I was now paying them by the hour instead of by the foot and the account had reached £50 without value for money except the sight of a splendid hole. It was a hole that taunted us. It laughed at us. It forced us to lean over the top peering down into its depths for hours every day. 'Now let's go and see how our hole's getting on,' Tommy Williams would say as often as he felt I would not mind him dropping the work he was doing. The miners had carved a rectangle and the point where John Henry's stick had dipped was its centre; the sides were sheer, the slabs of granite cut as if by a knife. We would stare downwards and when our eyes had grown accustomed to the dark we would gaze at the veins which coursed between the dynamited rocks; the veins through which, if a spring was near, the water would flow.

The miners would make hopeful comments and Jack would shout up from the depths: 'The rab here feels damp.' By now the hole had become a talking point in the district and monotonously I would be asked, 'Any luck yet?' It became, too, the reason for a walk and in the evening or at the week-end neighbours and far neighbours would lope towards it and add their opinions as to its future. 'Now I reckon you'll have to go thirty feet before you strike water,' said one. 'My cousin Enoch found plenty at twenty,' said another. 'In Sancreed parish,' said a third, 'there are two wells within a mile of each other forty feet deep and never a drop of water from either.' Tommy Williams would comment about these remarks with acid sharpness. 'That fellow,' said he about one who prophesied we were wasting our time, 'is worried about his own water, he's frightened we might drain his.'

We were down twenty feet, then twenty-two, then twenty-five. By now, made frantic by the tortoise pace of the hand-drills, we had hired a compressor and the drills to drive into the rock. It speeded the blasting but there was still no sign of a thimbleful of water. Twenty-six feet. Our money was falling into that hole with the abandon of a backer doubling up on losing favourites; and sooner or later we would have to stop. But when? We now had planks across the top and a winch to pull up the debris after each blast, and back we brought old John Henry to stand on the planks so that we could see again the reaction of his hazel stick. Down it dipped, relentlessly, a powerful character staunch to its original opinion. 'If you go another foot . . .' said John.

It was that evening I met the manager of the Newlyn Quarry to whom I described the nightmare in which we were involved. He was a young, Rugby three-quarter type of man who considered my story as a challenge to himself and his organization. 'I have some compressor equipment and some new drills I want to try out,' he said with a light in his eye, 'we'll bring them out next week-end and we'll have a helluva bang.' The following Saturday a caravan from Newlyn wormed its way through gates and across fields to within a few yards of the hole. A shiny new compressor with a tractor to power it, the manager and his foreman, two quarry men in snow white overalls and polished black helmets who moved speedily about arranging the equipment with the expectant air of conjurers before a children's party. By Monday, I said to myself, we will have water. By Monday the hole was thirty feet deep and my friend had offered to return the following week-end.

Down the hole the next Saturday went a quarry man, the compressor started up its whining roar, the drill spat like a machine-gun, and the dust began to rise, blanketing the bottom. I hung around with the others bemusedly chatting, dazed like a boxer after a fight. 'When I was a child,' I was saying to the foreman, 'I started to dig my way to Australia . . .'

Suddenly from the murk below us was a shout. 'Water! I've struck water!' We let out a cheer which may have been heard across Mount's Bay and I ran around shaking every-one by the hand like a successful politician after an election. Water! It was as if I had won a football pool. I ran down to the cottage where Jeannie was patiently kneading dough on the kitchen table. 'They've found it!' I cried. 'Water! . . . old John Henry was right!'

But Jeannie was going to wait a year for her bath and her indoor wash-basin. For one thing our money had gone down the hole. For another, the water turned out to be a 'weeper' which seeped into the well at a gallon or two an hour. And the third reason was that the rains had come. The water butt was full.

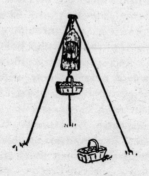

Chapter Six

MONTY HATED the proceedings of the well, and the bangs frightened him into remembering the bombs, flying bombs and rockets which were the companions of his youth; and into remembering the night when, the dust of the ceiling in his fur, he hid terrified in the airing cupboard at Mortlake while Jeannie and I frantically searched the neighbourhood believing he had bolted after a bomb had blown the roof off the house. Thus Jeannie, as soon as the miners shouted 'Fire!' always sat beside him, stroking him, until the bangs were over.

But his contentment, these events apart, was a delight to watch and as the months went by he quietly eased himself into the comfortable ways of a country gentleman. He hunted, slept, ate; then hunted, slept, ate. He never roamed any distance from the cottage, but sometimes he would disappear for hours at a time and we would walk around calling for him in vain. He was, of course, curled up in some grassy haunt of his own and he would reappear wondering what all the fuss was about, and although the reason for our searches was mainly due to the simple curiosity of wanting to discover the whereabouts of his hiding places, we also possessed secret fears for his safety. He was, after all, a London cat and therefore could not be expected to have the intuition of a countryman; and we were prepared to appear thoroughly foolish in any efforts we made to protect him. Our concern was due to three reasons – the fact that the colour of his fur made him look, from a distance, like a fox; rabbit traps; and because we knew that sometimes foxes kill cats. And if, by our behaviour, it looked as if we possessed neurotic imaginations, the future proved our fears were justified.

There was, for instance, the young man with an airgun whom I saw emerge from our wood and begin to stalk, the airgun at the ready, up the field at the top of which Monty was poised beside a hole in the hedge. 'What are you doing?' I yelled, running towards him; and the young man who, in any case, had no right to be there, halted for a moment, looking in my direction and began to make grimaces as if he were trying to tell me to shut up. Then crouching, he began to move forward again. 'Stop!' I shouted again, 'what the hell are you up to?'

I reached him panting, and he stared oafishly at me. 'Have you any chickens?' he said bellicosely. 'I have . . . but what's that got to do with it? You've no right to be here.' He looked at me with disdain. 'I was doing you a favour. I saw a cub at the top of this field and if it hadn't been for you I could have shot it.' At that moment Monty sauntered down the field towards me. 'A cub?' I said. The young man went red in the face. 'It looked like a cub!'

Monty was given the freedom of the window at night and paradoxically, though our fears for him were bright during the day, they were dulled at night. We were deluded, I suppose, by the convention that cats go out in the dark and that a kind of St Christopher guards them from danger. Then one day a neighbour told us he had found the skeletons of three cats outside a fox's earth not half a mile from the cottage. 'There's a rogue fox about,' he said, 'so you'd better look out for your Monty.' A rogue, by its definition being something which does not pursue normal habits, earns odium for its whole species. Badgers, for instance, are generally supposed to be chicken killers but there is unchallengeable evidence that they are not; it is the rogue badger who has brought them their bad name. So it is with foxes – only the rogues kill cats; but once a rogue gets a taste for cats a district will not be safe until the fox is killed. But even after this warning we did not interfere with Monty's nocturnal wanderings. We were aware of the rebellion we would have to face if we tried to stop him, and so we preferred to take the easy way out and do nothing at all. He was agile, he could climb a tree if attacked and, as he never went far, he could always make a dash for the window.

Then one night Jeannie was woken by a fox barking seemingly just a few yards from the cottage, and this was followed by a figure flying through the window and on to the bed. The following night we were determined he should stay indoors, and we gave him a cinder box and shut the bedroom door; and a battle of character began. He clawed, battered and cried at the door while Jeannie and I, trying to sleep, grimly held to our decision that he should *not* go out. At dawn we surrendered. 'After all,' argued Jeannie, as if cats cannot see in the dark, 'it is light enough for him to see a fox if one is about.' Our bed lay against the wall which contained the window, and the window was so placed that with my head on the pillow I could watch the lamps of the pilchard fleet as it operated in Mount's Bay; while beyond, every few seconds, there was the wink of the Lizard light. Three feet below the window was the rockery garden and the patch of trodden earth on which Monty jumped when he went out on his adventures – one moment he could be on our bed, the next outside.

On the night after our attempt to keep him indoors, he

was curled asleep on the bed and the window was open. Jeannie too was deep asleep and I was dozing, when suddenly through my haziness I heard Monty growl like a dog. Instinctively I put out my hand but he was on the windowsill before I grasped him. I fumbled for the torch and switched it on. 'What's the matter, Monty?' I murmured, 'what's outside?' I leant forward so that I was half out of the window with my torch shining downwards . . . on to the head of a fox. There he was so close to the wall that he was touching it, so large that in the first startled moment I thought he was an Alsatian dog. 'Quick!' I shouted irrationally, 'a fox is after Monty!'

But before Jeannie was aware of what was happening the fox was away, gliding down the lane like a ghost, only pausing a second to look back, its eyes meeting the beam of my torch like two phosphorescent pin-points. Monty was still growling and struggled to free himself from my hold. 'What's happened? What's happened?' Jeannie called sleepily. 'Only this,' I replied, 'Monty has seen for himself why he can never go out again at night.' And he never did unless we accompanied him. As for our method of keeping him in, we had a carpenter make a frame of wire netting which we fixed to the open window at night. Thus we had our fresh air and Monty could continue to sleep on the bed. He was perfectly satisfied.

A dividing line between a townsman and a countryman is the attitude to rabbit traps; a townsman abhors them and a countryman considers them a necessity. Today the gin trap is banned by law and only a specially designed trap can be used legally which fits in the entrance of a rabbit hole and kills the rabbit instantly as soon as it comes out. But since myxomatosis rabbits have changed their habits and instead of using the burrows they lie out in the undergrowth of the open ground; hence gin traps are still in use, illegal though they may be. Our district is still free of rabbits and we hope we may never see them again; but one day they probably will come back and we may live again the summer nights when, with the background of the murmuring sea, we would lie awake waiting, waiting, for the curdling screams that inevitably would pursue the hours until the trapper arrived to collect his harvest.

And yet I found myself, possessing as I did, the intellect of a townsman and the way of life of a countryman, in a quandary. The rabbits showed no appreciation of our efforts to be nice to them, and they ate our anemones, violets and lettuces with the same abandon as they ate those of our neighbours. We bought hundreds of yards of wire netting, but I found they used it as a rope ladder, climbing up it and into the meadow on the other side; or sometimes I would find a hole in the wire neatly made as if by wire cutters, and then I believed the story I had been told that cliff rabbits had teeth as hard as steel, and the intelligence of monkeys. As a townsman I admired their cleverness, but as a countryman I became infuriated by their destruction of my livelihood; and so I reluctantly began to trap.

I used to set the traps at dusk, go round to see them with a torch at midnight, and again soon after dawn. The object of these tactics was, of course, to curtail the sufferings of my victims, but the result was hideous to witness; for the brief period of their pain had not sapped their strength, and when the light of the torch announced my coming they darted crazily this way and that within the circumference of the chain which joined the trap to its anchor in the ground. Each time they rushed to escape, winnowing their terror, the gin bit deeper, while I myself, the amateur executioner, fumbled in my attempts to take a firm hold so that with a jerk I could break their necks. Such incidents, etched into the grotesque by the shadows cast by my torch or turned into a Wagnerian Valhalla in the still soft scent of the dawn, gobbled the zest I had to protect our crops.

Then one night I forgot to set my alarm clock and slept peacefully until within an hour of the time Tommy was due to arrive for his day's work. I jumped with horror from my bed and hurried in my pyjamas to the eight traps I had set the night before. Five were undisturbed, in two others were full-grown rabbits each of which must have struggled hard through the night because their trapped feet were gouged red by the gin's fangs, and in the eighth was a sight I will never forget. By some horrible chance two baby rabbits had been trapped together, and as I approached they were knocking each other as they tried to escape, giving the appearance – had I not known what had happened – that they were playing. I killed them and went silently back to the cottage. 'Jeannie,' I said, without telling her what I had seen, 'Hell to the crops, I'm never going to set a trap again.'

The incident was still vivid in my mind when a week later, as we were finishing supper, we heard the tap, tap, tap of the trapper's hammer in John's field above the cottage which ran towards the sea. It was a May evening and although John and I were still on speaking terms, there was a simmering friction between us that seemed certain sooner or later to erupt. 'I do think he might have warned us,' I grumbled, 'we might easily have been out for the evening and then what would have happened to Monty?'

The custom of a trapper was to ring a field with traps two or three days running, leaving them open during the day and setting them afresh in the late afternoon or early

evening. Sometimes, however, a trapper was not so conscientious and I remember an occasion when traps on a
neighbouring land were set at midday on Sunday and were
not visited again until breakfast time on Monday. I was
waiting when the trapper came down the lane in his car.

'Good morning,' I said, and then without wasting any
time: 'I believe you went to Church yesterday evening.'
The man looked at me doubtfully. 'I went to Chapel . . .
I'm a Chapel man.' 'Well wherever you went,' I replied,
my voice rising, 'your aim was to give thanks to God and
yet . . . at that very time you were allowing His creatures
to suffer agony at your hands.' The man stared at the
ground. 'Come here,' I ordered, and led him to a rabbit
which was hanging head downwards from a trap set on
top of a hedge. 'That rabbit was caught at one o'clock
yesterday afternoon,' I said, 'and had I not heard its cry it
would have taken several hours to die in agony . . . and
you were in Chapel!' My anger, of course, made me
pompous but it had an effect. A few months later I saw the
man again. He had given up trapping.

Passion, therefore, was always waiting to come to the
surface when traps were set – that of Jeannie was born of
imagination, mine of experience. And so when we heard
the tap of the hammer in John's field there was the growl
of anger within us, the dread of the coming night with its
screams, the nag of knowing Monty was in danger. On the
second evening, a couple of hours before sunset, Monty
was sitting in the front garden, sphinx like, eyes half closed,
his burnished fur glossy in the light of the ending day.
There was no hint he aimed to wander. His white whiskers
sprayed his lion cub head, his tail curled round his body so
that its tip gently flicked his front paw. He was at peace,
utterly secure in the small world we had found for him.
Then I looked through the open door and he was not there.

'Where's Monty? He was outside five minutes ago.' We had panicked often enough before, and been calmed, and made ourselves feel foolish that love should exaggerate fear; and yet the instant of warning repeated itself each time with the same spasm of fright. I ran up to the field and stood on a bank.

The young green corn was brushing the soil, and far out to sea aslant to the Lizard a liner was making for Cherbourg. A raven grunted overhead, flying heavily westward towards the sun, and a charm of goldfinches fluttered chirruping before me, then dived out of sight behind the hedge on my right. A buzzard lazily glided, and silent in the heavens a jet traced its plume. It was very still and only the sea whispered. Suddenly across the field a hundred yards away near the gap pencilled by barbed wire which led to John's cliff, I saw Monty's tail flapping in prisoned puzzlement, as if a hand at ground level was feebly motioning a welcome. 'Jeannie,' I shouted, 'Monty is in a trap!'

I led the way across the field yelling: 'Monty, we're coming!' . . . absurdly frightened, my mind racing with stories of trapped cats. 'It's easier to kill 'em,' a trapper once told us, 'than to get 'em out of a trap. That wild they be.' And I felt enraged that a threat guarded against had yet materialized, that even with all our care Monty could still be trapped. Irrational thoughts, I know, but such are often the companions of distress.

He was lying quietly on his side, his little front paw with the white smudge on it squeezed in the gin; and his yellow eyes gazing up at me as if my presence alone was enough to make him believe the trap would release him. Then, when in those first few seconds I did nothing, he uttered a little cry, a querulous cry as if he were cross.

'You'll hold him firmer than I can,' Jeannie said when she reached us, 'I know how to open the trap.' I grasped his soft body, limp as a fur stole while Jeannie, her knees in the green corn, put her hands on the gin. It would not budge. 'It's rusty,' I said, 'look, it's coated with rust.'

It was as if Monty understood the significance of my remark because he began to cry and struggle and scratch, and try to bite his paw free. 'Hold him! For goodness sake hold him or he'll pull his paw apart!' At that instant he slipped from my hands, lashed out with his three free legs, tugging at the trap with his fourth, claws like knives ready to rip anything within reach. There was blood on Jeannie's wrist.

'Something's wrong with the trap and we'd better get him back to the cottage.' I had the crazy idea that once there I could rush up to the farm for help. 'Pull the peg out of the ground,' I said, 'then take the weight of the trap with the chain while I hold him.' He had become exhausted and was still again, except for his panting which made his body heave like bellows.

We began to walk, a miserable trio, across the field . . . Jeannie with the chain, I holding him in front of me like a tray, the paw and the gin between us.

'What about your wrist?'

'It's only a scratch. Nothing deep.'

We were nearly there. The lump of the chimney bulged at eye level, the height of the field parallel with the roof, the open door now below us waiting. Suddenly Monty gave a twist with such vicious strength that he caught me unawares. He slipped from my hold, and like a macabre juggler I went this way and that in an effort to regain him. 'Keep the chain up!' Miraculously Jeannie succeeded so that the weight of the gin went along with his paw. He had his terror and pain but she saved him from the awful wrench of the weight, and in those few seconds of success I had grasped him firmly again and he was still and limp in my hands.

'I'm going to put him on the ground.' His little pink tongue frothed as he panted and sweat damped his fur and he lay on his side so quietly that he might have been asleep. The next instant I seized the trap, gave it the wrench of a maniac – and it opened. He stretched in the green corn for a minute shuddering with exhaustion; and then Jeannie picked him up and gently carried him home.

Our sweet relief very soon turned into unreasonable anger. Unreasonable because it was nothing to do with us what people did on land under their control. Unreasonable because we had learnt to our cost that rabbits steal with the same effect as a thief putting his hand in the till. Unreasonable because trapping, however much we might disapprove, was the main method of checking the rabbit plague. Our tempers, however, were flaring and only action could bring abatement.

'I'm going to throw that horrible trap in the sea!' Jeannie had bandaged her arm and Monty was still lying exhausted on the sofa.

'All right,' I said, 'and I'm going to find John.' I tramped up across the fields to the farm and the breeze cooled me and told me to be calm – Monty was safe and there was no point in adding to distress. And then I thought of the scratch on Jeannie's arm, and Monty's panting little body and the sound of the screams of the rabbits at night – and when I reached the farmhouse door I was angry again.

Only John's wife was there, peeling potatoes in the kitchen, and his small son who eyed me silently, suspiciously from a chair by the window as I told my story. 'I know nothing about it, Mr Tangye,' said John's wife, 'nothing at all. You speak to John about it.'

I returned to the cottage to find Jeannie had completed

her mission. 'I didn't throw it in the sea,' she said doubtfully, 'I threw it over the hedge into the brush . . . we can always get it back if we *have* to.' My own interview had damped my temper, and I was now wishing it had never taken place. I had fired a shot without the compensation of seeing it land on the target – and John was warned. I was now in any case not sure of my ground; and it seemed to me on reflection that inner forces were at work within us to use the incident as a tilt at John and the attitude he represented. If we were desiring a peaceful life and to be left on our own, this was not the way to go about it. I awaited John's coming.

He came thundering up the lane soon after breakfast the following morning. Cap askew, his face red as a beetroot, squat and powerful as a gorilla, he advanced on me with arms swinging as if his intention was to knock me down. 'What right had the cat to be on my land?' he shouted at me when he was still twenty yards off. 'What right had you to trespass on my land to let him out?'

He was now ten yards away.

'What right had Mrs Tangye to throw my trap away?'

He was now five yards away and he had scored a point.

'I tell you what, mate,' and he had now stopped, thrusting his face at mine, 'from now on you go your way, I go mine. When I come down here I won't speak to you.'

He swung round and stamped away.

Chapter Seven

THE WINDS CURL Minack in winter. In the beginning while we sat snug in the cottage a sense of security acted as a narcotic against the roar outside. A book, a pipe, the scent of a wood fire, Monty on my lap, there was comfort in joining the ghosts who had listened to the same rage, in sheltering within the walls that withstood centuries of siege. Then as we passed through the shoals of first enthusiasm, facing the reality of the task we had undertaken, tension replaced comfort as the winds blew.

I am afraid now when the westerly comes galloping over the hill behind the cottage and charges with thundering hoofs into the elms that edge the wood; when the northerly steps aloofly along the valley, chilling its visit with frost; when the easterly bites from the Lizard, mouthing the sea and ripping our cliff which puts up a hand to stop it; when the southerly brings the rain and the storm which binds the sea and land in gloom. For all are our enemies. Those from the east and the south carry salt as they blow, salt which films over flower petals and leaves and burns them papery white. That from the west savages the crops like a madman, that from the north shivers black the plants in its way. I have learnt now the wisdom of Tommy's advice when, at the start, he said to me one day: 'We'll have to have good hedges if we're going to save our crops, and the sooner we start planting them the better.'

I remember at the time that I was grateful to Tommy for looking ahead. The evening before, a man in a pub had asked whether we had yet packed our bags. 'Everyone roundabouts,' said he facetiously, 'is sure you'll never stay. You won't stand Minack in winter . . . oh no! Minack's all right in summer. But winter . . .!' Only the seasons could prove to those who were watching us that we were not flirting with the life we had chosen, and that we belonged to the land they loved; like recruits to a battle-proved battalion we had to wait to earn respect. Meanwhile our ways were sure to be smiled at, and our failures seized upon as evidence of coming surrender; and so when Tommy countered the prophecies of our departure by discussing the planning of hedges for the future, his unconscious gesture gave us unreasonable pleasure. But the advice itself made me apprehensive.

There were so many other tasks to perform, so many other things on which to spend our limited capital that it seemed a dreary prospect to lay out time and money on hedges which would take years before they became effective. I know now that my attitude was that of an amateur who is unable to believe that the conquest of the land is only achieved by monumental patience. I was in a hurry. My chief concern was to earn sufficient money from immediate crops to secure our survival. I had no time for the laying of foundations and my faith depended on the years ahead looking after themselves; and yet my instinct conflicted with my inclination and I knew that I should listen to Tommy. 'All right,' I said to him half-heartedly, 'I'll find out what we ought to do.' I proceeded to find out, then discarded my findings, and compromised with a plan of my own; and the result is that even today I am ashamed of my hedges.

Hedge planning is in effect the mapping of a market garden, and that was another reason why I was shy of it. What kind of a map did I want? I did not know. I was not a man sitting at a desk drawing up a blueprint with skilled experience behind him. I could see no further ahead of me than potatoes and more potatoes, interspersed with daffodils, violets and anemones, and I possessed a sublime faith that a vague number of these would provide our living. What number, I had no idea. Nor the ground space which would represent an economic unit. Costs in relation to turnover were a mystery to me and thus prospective profits, if any, were a blank figure. True I tried to find out, but the growers I talked to were loquacious about their contradictory methods of growing yet dumb on finance. They looked prosperous in their fashion and I was not to know that at this particular time they had passed the peak of the war and post-war years and their profits had begun a diminishing slide. The Horticultural Advisory Service of the Ministry of Agriculture were helpful on the techniques of growing but they too were silent on how to make a market garden pay. I suppose I was expecting too much of them because Minack, in the eyes of an expert, was a folly, and no professional market gardener would ever consider embarking on the task Jeannie and I had set ourselves. We were aiming to make a market garden out of a home, instead of a home out of a market garden.

It was a coincidence that the Ministry of Agriculture itself was establishing a vast experimental horticultural station from one hundred acres of farm land thirty miles away at Camborne at the same time as we were scratching our heads over our own few acres. Rosewarne, as it is called, is now a showplace of planning achievement and there is not an aspect of horticulture – except how to make it pay – that is not investigated. Similar experimental stations, including those maintained by large private firms, exist all over the country, and in the past few years they have developed into being an industry within an industry. Vast sums of money are spent, hordes of scientists and manual workers employed, bevies of reports are issued – while the humble grower who provides the purpose for all this effort remains in the earthy reality of shortage of capital, higher costs and falling prices.

Progress is the scientist's justification, and in the horticultural sphere this means the conquest of the soil and plant diseases, and the production of larger and better crops. This praiseworthy aim is pursued without any thought of likely economic results and thus a scientist's howl of success may be the grower's toll of doom. Daffodil bulbs have in the past been checked from over-production by the fly which lays its eggs within them in the spring, the larvae of which eats and destroys them. Today there is a chemical which, if the bulbs are dipped in it before planting, will secure them from fly attack for at least two years; and this is resulting in a staggering increase of daffodils for sale in a market which is already overloaded. Glasshouse lettuce, unless very skilfully grown, has in the past suffered much from botrytis, a fungus which rots the leaves and stem; now a dust has been produced which can result in a 100 per cent cut of a crop instead of, perhaps, 70 per cent. Rosewarne, among its other activities, is engaged on the conquest of downy mildew on anemones, a disease which attacks large quantities of plants every season and which prevents anemones, as a precautionary measure, being grown in the same ground more than once in every seven years. From the scientist's point of view this would be a conquest worth achieving and hence a mammoth effort is being made to do so; but here again a victory for the scientist means a bell tolling for the grower. 'You know,' said a backroom boy to me gleefully, 'when we succeed . . . anemones won't be worth growing in Cornwall, they'll be so easy!'

Of course, the claims of the scientists do not always prosper in practice, and this adds to the grower's bewilderment. The trade papers bellow with wares of hybrid names promising myself and my colleagues a grower's paradise, luring us to buy concoctions that are found wanting within the year, leaving us with half-filled tins. During the battle of the bulb fly the scientists produced a smelly dust which, they assured us in extravagant language, would kill the menace if dusted over the bulb meadows at fortnightly intervals during April and May, making five applications in all. I bought the dust together with an expensive dusting machine which hitched weightily on my back and was operated by my hand pumping a lever, energetically as if I were a boxer pommeling an opponent. April and May was potato time so I had to be up at dawn marching over the dew filled meadows with the smelly dust spoiling the sweet scented air, exhausted by the energy involved and in any case sceptical whether the effort would be worth the result. It was not. I conscientiously performed my duties for two seasons, then discovered the whole idea had been discarded as worthless by the scientists, leaving me with memories of ruined early mornings, a dusting machine which is now rusted with disuse, and a sack of the smelly dust which seems too expensive to throw away.

Growers, like punters, are gullible and are only too anxious to believe that these dangling promises will provide the profits which are so elusive; hence the chain of scientists, manufacturers and horticultural merchants exercise the same hypnotism as Littlewoods. One autumn I decided to grow spring onions and I had gone through the preliminaries of preparing the ground and sowing the expensive seed when I was advised to use a pre-emergence weed killer. This tempting concoction would spare me the task of weeding throughout the winter and assure a bumper crop at harvest time; and all I had to do, so I was told, was to spray the ground a couple of days before the spring onions were likely to emerge. The timing was important and so was the weather. By leaving the spraying to the last possible moment, I would kill the maximum number of weed seedlings which had grown faster than the spring onions; on the other hand, according to my directions, the weather had to be dry and the sun hot – as if I were able to arrange these factors as easily as opening the weed killer tin. I scratched the ground daily until I saw the seeds had germinated, then looked up at the sky, decided it was going to be fine, and brought out the sprayer. Unfortunately the weather took no heed of the manufacturer's directions and within a few hours there was a sharp heavy shower; and the spray instead of staying on the surface was washed into the ground – and that was the end of my spring onions.

Some sprays are so dangerous that the operator must wear a spaceman's suit when using them. Some, drifting on the wind from a neighbour's field, creep through the open windows of greenhouses and destroy the tomato plants. I have used a spray to kill greenfly on lettuce, and have killed both the lettuce and the greenfly. A spray to kill aphis on brussel sprouts was being spread from an aeroplane when some of it wafted into a country lane bordered with blackberries – police set up road blocks at each end of the lane while the blackberry bushes were forthwith cut down, carted away and burnt. I have never used slug pellets since a friend's dog, finding them scattered in his garden, ate them as if they were biscuits, and died. One season we had a plague of mice eating the anemone buds and, bemoaning the fact to a merchant, I was recommended a liquid which, when sprayed on the ground, killed the mice when they walked on it. 'What about other animals?' I asked, 'cats or dogs, I mean.' 'Oh them,' said the merchant, as if nothing else mattered so long as the mice were killed, 'it wouldn't do them any good either.'

A time came when we had a greenhouse at Minack and the first crop we grew were April sweet peas which had to be dusted with a special powder throughout the winter as a protection against mildew. Sweet pea plants need endless attention, and during the countless days we spent in the greenhouse Monty used to be our companion. We were amused by his presence and innocent that he ran any risk; and indeed we considered the greenhouse his playground so that when the weather was stormy we put him inside so that he could exercise in comfort. One March day we had driven over to Newquay and did not return until seven in the evening when, as so often happened, the tiger-like face of Monty staring from the bedroom window welcomed the lights of the car as we came up the lane to the cottage.

Inside we gave him the usual vociferous greeting and Jeannie, anxious to appease the long absence, doled out the boiled fish on his plate. He made to go towards it, halted, began to stagger, then fell down. Jeannie's back was turned and I alone was the witness. 'Jeannie!' I shouted as if I were calling against the wind, 'what's happened to Monty? He's had a stroke!' Panic can easily seize me and as quickly be defeated, just as my temper can flare and fade. Here seemed the threatened instant of finality, the wink of the eyelid that makes the past unreal, love silenced, the agony of leaning on memories threaded like gossamer. And then, quite suddenly, I was calm again. Monty had got to his feet and was weaving towards the bedroom door, crying, and I bent down to hold him, then picked him up in my arms and saw that his eyes were glazed, unseeing and circling in their sockets, control abandoned. 'I'll get the vet,' I said firmly, 'if he's in he'll be here inside the hour. I'll get the Land Rover out and go up to the farm and telephone. I'll put Monty on the bed and you do what you can to keep him quiet.'

Within the hour the vet was leaning over Monty, sounding him, taking his temperature, talking to him in a quiet Scots accent, and by his presence alone making us feel the worst was over. 'His heart's sound,' he said, puzzled, 'and I don't see any sign that he's had a stroke and yet ...' I suddenly thought of the sweet peas and the mildew powder, and I ran out to fetch the tin. There was no mention of poison on the label but when the vet read the analysis he put out his hand and stroked Monty. 'Here's the trouble, old chap,' he said, 'you've been going into the greenhouse and the dust has been brushing off the plants into your fur, and after all these months you've absorbed it into your body. You've got a bad dose of slow poisoning ... that's what's wrong with you!'

The treatment was bicarbonate of soda every four hours for the next forty-eight and Jeannie and I took it in turns to watch through the night. On the second night, it was shortly before dawn, Jeannie, who was in charge of the difficult task of emptying the spoonful of bicarbonate down his throat, was just about to go off to sleep after giving him his dose, leaving me awake in a chair beside him, when there was a noise from the bed on which Monty was lying. We looked at each other. The crisis was over. The noise from the bed was a purr.

I am, then, suspicious of those who feed from the struggles of growers. Conventionality provides them with a mask of altruism towards us, but it is a thin mask. So vast is the industry that now exists on the perimeter of the once basic one of growing, so many are the ramifications of subsidized bodies that thrive on horticultural research, so huge is the number of men and women whose salaries depend on these sources, that the role of the grower has become that of the guinea pig – the purpose of his existence belongs to others.

I once pinned one of these highly paid gentlemen in a corner in an effort to extract from him a practical programme for a mythical market garden. He was well qualified to give me the advice and I had a simpleton's belief that he would provide an answer. 'Supposing,' I said earnestly, 'you were offered £5,000 on condition you gave up your job and spent it on planning a market garden in Cornwall. How would you set about it?' The man looked at me in astonishment, then roared with laughter. 'Good heavens,' he said, 'I'd forget the condition and put the money in Consols!'

Of course, like all who are prejudiced, I am being unfair, expecting too much, forgetting the occasions when those whom I attack have helped. I rely, for instance, on John Davies, Horticultural Advisory Officer for West Cornwall in the same way that in the old days one relied on the family doctor. If a plant shows signs of a mystery disease, if I want soil samples taken, if I want bulbs tested for eelworm or basal rot, if I just want him to walk round Minack and to listen to his comments, then John Davies will be at my service. And Rosewarne has helped me personally, though it seems to me the expenditure lavished on it far outweighs its usefulness to the ordinary grower.

It is like a wonderful department store where none of the goods are for sale; packing sheds, bulb stores, machinery buildings, heave into the sky like jet liner hangars; an elaborate oil heating apparatus pipes heat to the greenhouses and offices; pedigree cattle and pigs are kept solely for the manure they produce; tractors of the latest design fuss over the land, labourers swarm like bees where mechanization is impotent; dutch lights and cloches of various shapes and sizes cover an area like a frozen lake. The whole is laid out with the vision of a Capability Brown – avenues and cross sections, myriads of plots where groups of similar flowers or vegetables are grown under different conditions, their progress of growth meticulously noted. It is a vast laboratory, like the site of a space rocket where no expense is spared yet it would be a shambles without a master mind of organization. One is envious. One feels if one could hitch a particle of the skill and money expended to one's own particular programme, the cares would dissipate. I look at the hedges, thousands of yards of them running sturdy and thick across the open land and marvel at the shelter belts of trees now twenty feet high; and then I come home and stare at the wispy things which represent our hedges, the long gaps between them, the trees which have remained obstinately stunted, tangible evidence of disappointment.

I can plead the excuse of expense. I found that escallonia, the type of hedge planted at Rosewarne, cost £160 for every thousand eighteen inch plants, that other suitable hedge varieties were around the same price; and so, as I was unable to afford rooted plants I had to use my initiative to take their place. There were already around Minack patches of elder and privet, and at my old home of Glendorgal there were hedgerows of tamarisk. All three stand up to salt winds but, compared to escallonia, they have disadvantages; privet sucks the ground of its goodness and nothing will grow satisfactorily within a few feet of it; elder, when fully grown, is often attacked by woodworm and decays into a petrified hedge; while tamarisk usually leaves an unwelcome gap of two feet, through which the wind rushes, before the feathery foliage branches out. But they were free. That was the point which appealed to us, and we gaily treated the difference between cuttings and rooted plants as of no importance whatsoever.

I asked for advice and the advice I received was of the kind I wanted to hear. 'Just stick 'em in the ground,' said an old gardener, 'no need to concern yourself. They'll take.' Tommy, too, was our ally, and for an encouraging reason; he had pushed elder branches into the ground where, the year before, he had dug the meadows in the cliff and now each was a vigorous little plant of its own. It seemed, therefore, that success was limited to the labour involved, and so we proceeded to collect a load of tamarisk branches from Glendorgal, and added hundreds of privet and elder from Minack. It was autumn. It took a week to stick them in the ground, and the winter to find that only a hundred or so had taken. Rabbits were partly to blame for they used the thin cuttings to test out their teeth, nipping them neatly like secateurs, even ignoring the stinking paste I smeared on the bark to check them. Yet the cuttings which escaped their interest fared no better and when in the spring, in irritation, I began pulling them up to see what had happened, the few inches that had been stuck in the soil were as dead as a walking stick. 'Let's put some more in now,' said Tommy, 'they might grow on through the summer.'

We painstakingly collected a further pile of cuttings and once more laboriously stuck them in the ground; and as a gesture to conventional methods I bought a hundred rooted plants called New Zealand Ollearia. Our defeat, on this occasion, was caused by a hot, dry summer; there was not enough moisture to excite the cuttings nor to satisfy the Ollearia, and when autumn came round again the Ollearia had been cut by half and the cuttings had gone the way of the winter ones.

I was beginning to lose patience. At this point, however, I learnt of a chemical solution in which the cuttings could be soaked, which would hasten the growth of the roots. I decided to give it a chance, and off we went collecting cuttings again. We tied them in bundles, dropped them in the tin bath specially bought for the purpose, and waited the required time for the chemical solution to perform its magic. Then, instead of sticking the cuttings haphazardly in an embryo hedge, we arranged them a few inches apart in a meadow. Now, I said to myself, I have at last done the right thing and by the spring we will have several hundred rooted cuttings to transplant. Unfortunately it was the coldest Cornish winter of the century and for a month the ground was frozen like cement. None of the cuttings survived.

This tale of misfortune, I now realize, need not have happened had I been more methodical. The soil does not accept impatience, short cuts, or the attitude of take it or leave it; and it rewards only the careful. The weather is a market gardener's standby excuse but it also covers a multitude of his sins. Hedge plants, like roses, need weeding and watering and the fact that there may be hundreds of them does not hide this necessity. I now know that it is my fault that hedges do not ring Minack. They bored me. There were so many other things to do. They grew too slowly to capture my imagination; and once I stuck them in the ground I forgot them. They could look after themselves.

Jeannie spent the first winter locked in the chicken house we used as a spare bedroom, writing 'Meet Me At The Savoy.' There was the camp bed used by her father in the 1914 war and now strewn with her papers, the rug, a second-hand kitchen table with her typewriter, an upturned box as a chair, another box where a paraffin lamp hissed at night, except when the winds blew and then it was silent against the roar outside. 'Where's Jeannie?' some friends who had called would ask. 'In the chicken house,' I would answer, 'here's the key. Go and see if she wants to be let out.'

This apparent brutality, I say in self defence, was at her suggestion because she was aware that incarceration was the shortest way to completing her book. She had no one to help her in the cottage, and though it was small and though I did what I could, the eyes of a woman saw work to do; and so if she had freedom of movement the mind would fuss and time be wasted. Thus I would clean and light the stove, make a gesture of dusting the two rooms, do the shopping, provide a snack lunch and endless cups of tea; and then in the evening Jeannie would emerge to cook the dinner.

She performed this tiresome task quite unconcerned that the world she had left on her typewriter was a gay and glamorous one, while reality was that of a peasant. The essence of marriage is ease of companionship and this the two of us shared. Our professions had forced us to mix with people as a duty, and it was a duty which we often enjoyed; but neither of us were ever dependent on mass companionship, the sickness of being afraid of being alone. And now that time was ours we saw no virtue in leaning on conventionality; attending gatherings whose purpose was to hide the boredom of those who gave them. We kept to ourselves. We did not have to escape to pleasure, for pleasure was watching Monty jumping Monty's Leap or noting the time the woodpecker went to bed in the hole of the elm twenty yards from the cottage, or wondering what bird called a piping cry at dusk, or opening a parcel from the London Library, or becoming aware of the colours of lichen, or that of old stones, or rejoicing that we were both so lucky. We would have dinner with the candlelight flickering the white walls, and discuss what she had written and what she planned to write on the morrow, and I would give an account of what I had been doing during the day. And then we would clear the table and cover it with newspaper, for there was still work to do.

Violets waited to be bunched.

Chapter Eight

WE HAD PLANTED the violet runners in June – six thousand Governor Herrick in the top half of the field, the cemetery field where we had cropped potatoes; and two thousand Princess of Wales in the meadow walled by elms near the cottage which we whimsically called 'Gee's Meadow' at the request of Gertrude Lawrence. 'It would give me a nice warm feeling,' she wrote to us from New York, 'if I knew there was a corner of England which was for ever me.' Sentimental, loyal, enchanting, provocative Gertie – what compelling force made me go into that meadow one August evening and be quietly standing there when Jeannie came running, calling: 'Gee's dead! . . . a cable from Richard . . .!'

Death can bring anger as well as grief. The old die creeping gently into our sorrow but those with uncompleted lives, promise unfulfilled, gifts unspent, savage the placid sweetness of our memories, thrusting frustrated yearnings into our hands, bruising the tears with cries of what might have been. 'Rage, rage against the dying of the sun!' said Dylan Thomas.

Gertie's life – or Gee or Gertrude – although she herself preferred Gee, belonged to the age when talent of the arts was leisurely matured so that the future was always more enrichening than the past. Time hovered instead of rushing, yielding the opportunity to delve into the secret self, extracting from its recesses the uncorrupted truth. Temptation was not always at the elbow to offer the illusion that sudden fame was permanent success because the arbiters of achievement — the Charlots and the Cochrans — were governed by standards that did not admit false values. Thus Gertie, steered in her youth by their guidance, was able to find as she grew older the gifts deep within her which earned the homage that dipped the lights of Broadway and Shaftesbury Avenue on the August evening that she died.

Gertie had an irrepressible ebullience which enabled the sleek or the humble to rejoice in her company — an audience of 'Private Lives' or that of troops in a concert hall. She had no conceit and beneath the gloss was a perennial wonderment that the little girl who once danced to the barrel organ outside Kensington Oval had become a star in two continents. She preferred to remember her childhood rather than to forget it, and this was the strength of her sympathy for those who were struggling. Danny Kaye made his début on Broadway in 'Lady in the Dark' of which Gertie was the star, and on the first night he brought down the house with a song he sang just before her own big number. Danny, instead of being delighted, was terrified. How would Gertie react? He could not believe that she would be pleased — but of course she was and insisted that he be promoted to star billing. A few years later Danny came to London to repeat his first big triumph at the Palladium, and at the same time Gertie had a great success in Daphne du Maurier's 'September Tide'.

'How's Gee?' he asked Jeannie on the morning of his first night. Jeannie replied that she thought she was rather lonely. 'You see,' Jeannie said to Danny, 'here she is with London at her feet but she is so famous and glamorous that people hesitate to ask her out thinking she would never come anyway, and the result is she often gets left out.' Danny picked up the telephone and asked for Gertie's room. Jeannie heard her tinkling voice reply, then Danny saying: 'Will you be my girl tonight, Gee? The American Ambassador is giving a party after the show.' And there was another day when Danny came rushing into Jeannie's office. 'Do you know what day it is?' 'Yes, of course,' she answered, 'it's Independence Day.' 'No, not that . . . it's Gee's birthday! Here's a card, get someone to send her masses of flowers, and they mustn't cost less than ten pounds.'

I was in San Francisco before the war when Gertie was playing 'Susan and God' at the Curran Theatre, and one evening we decided to make a tour of Chinatown. The Chief of Police offered to be our guide and off we went along the dark alleyways and up rickety staircases, pretending all the time we were risking the dangers that had not existed in years. A British warship happened to be on a courtesy visit to 'Frisco, and towards two in the morning we saw three able seamen swaying slightly in the middle of Grant Avenue. They affected both of us with nostalgia for home, and so we went up to make their acquaintance. By way of introduction, Gertie, in her delightful confident way, with the words going up and down the scale, said: 'I am Gertie Lawrence!' We waited in suspense for their reaction. 'I am Gertie Lawrence,' repeated Gertie, 'you know . . . the actress!' They looked at her a little unsteadily; then one of them mumbled: 'Well . . . if you are . . . sshow ush where we can get shome women!' Gertie pulled three ten dollar bills from her handbag and gave one to each bewildered, weaving seaman. Then she turned to the Chief of Police: 'I think these boys are looking for trouble . . . couldn't you arrange to get them back to the ship . . . gently?' And he did.

Gertie had a passionate love for England and during the war she was the driving force behind a transatlantic parcels service; then later, before and after the Normandy landings, she served in ENSA. One evening, after she had said goodbye at Drury Lane, ENSA headquarters, before returning to America, Jeannie and I were sitting with her in the Grill Bar of the Savoy. 'You know,' she said firmly, 'I have one ambition I am absolutely determined to fulfil.' Gertie was always able to wrap her ambitions in a rich canopy of sentiment, and this was no exception. Her voice changed, a hint of drama.

'That wonderful old theatre,' she went on, 'with all its traditions and glamour and triumphs . . . just think of the emotions it holds within its walls. I was thinking as I walked over here . . . I *must* play there!'

A few years later there was a memorable first night on Broadway at which Gertie triumphed as Anna in Rodgers and Hammerstein's 'The King and I'; and soon afterwards she wrote us a letter in which there was this line: 'Anna's staying two years on Broadway . . . and then THE first night at Drury Lane!' She was not to be there at that first night, for she died a few months after writing to us; but when the night came, Jeannie and I far away at Minack, thought of the gay audience making their way to their seats, the lights going down, the orchestra beginning to lilt the melodies she loved so much, and of the secret wish she never saw fulfilled.

We spent our last New Year's Eve in London with her and her husband Richard Aldrich, and I remember the gusto with which she led the Congo that threaded through the Savoy, boisterously enjoying herself; and I remember the toast she gave us that night after the trumpeters had blared their welcome to the New Year. 'Good luck to you escapists from the rat-race!'

Alas, the Princess of Wales violets in Gee's meadow did not prosper. Our wish to grow the particular variety had been dominated by the whim that we preferred it to any other, and that, of course, is no way to run a commercial flower farm; and the reason we liked it was because, unlike any other commercial variety, the blooms had an exquisite scent. We had been warned it was difficult to grow, that it bloomed sparsely, that the price obtained for the bunches did not recompense these disadvantages – and yet we had obstinately clung to the supreme confidence that in our case the results would be different. The runners bushed into plants and for a few brief weeks we thought our green fingers were going to succeed where others had failed – and then the plants collapsed. We hastily sought advice and the adviser diagnosed the microscopic red spider as the cause of the sickness, but here was a puzzle – red spiders thrive in dry conditions and yet the weather at the time was rain day after day, so wet that it was useless to spray the plants with the concoction which was recommended. Tommy too, was at a loss. 'I've always heard,' he said solemnly, 'that red spiders were bad sailors – yet here they be awash and living.'

Whatever the sickness the plants died and we have never grown Princess of Wales again; but we do now grow a few scented violets of a variety called Ascania. We found it by chance growing wild in a hedgerow, a pale green leaf with a tiny bloom a soft purple in colour and with a scent so sweet and strong that a single small bunch perfumes a room. It is, I believe, the original Cornish violet which was discarded by growers long ago when the hybrid commercial varieties were introduced. It is still useless for sale on its own, but when we have time we add a bloom or two to the bunches we are sending to market and imagine the delight of those who receive them.

While Jeannie worked at her book, I picked the Governor Herrick in the big field. We have now at Minack certain jobs we call lady's jobs and others called gentleman's jobs; and of these, violet picking and bunching are clearly a lady's job. They are fiddling tasks requiring the deft fingers of a seamstress rather than the clumsy hand of a man; and whereas I plod along picking perhaps three dozen bunches an hour, Jeannie picks twice that number. A market bunch consists usually of twenty blooms and two leaves, so when we are picking we count the blooms until we have sixty odd, then collect the six leaves and slip a rubber band over the stalks of the lot; this in violet jargon is a field bunch, a bunch which is not too big to hold and a bunch that, at the end of the day's picking, enables you to know exactly the number of market bunches available.

The stalks are brittle and can easily be snapped off too short; and the blooms, if the plants are big ones, hide among the foliage so that unless you are painstakingly careful you can easily leave a bloom or two behind. You have to examine every bloom to see if it is marked – for there is nothing so irritating to a buncher as having to pick and choose between good and bad blooms; and the secret of speedy bunching is to be free of the responsibility of bloom choice. Normally the marked blooms you have to watch for are those whose petals have been nipped by tiny slugs and snails, insignificant holes but enough to spoil the whole bunch. But there are also the occasions when wind or frost or hail sweep through the plants leaving no bloom undamaged; and then you have the nightmare task of picking not for market, but just to have the useless blooms off the plant.

Leaves are equally liable to damage and there is also a period during the season when they are often in short supply, and then we use ivy leaves in their place. This shortage, except when frost has done its harm, is due to a natural pause in the life of the plant, and it will occur once, or perhaps twice, during the October to April flowering season; the leaves go small like buttons, and yellow, and the crown of the plant is bared to the sky and for a week or two it seems as if the plant is dead; and then miraculously, little green shoots thrust upwards followed by the pin points of the buds, and soon the plants are in bloom again.

In the beginning I used to help Jeannie with the bunching but my laborious efforts, my groans as I fumbled with the stalks which swivelled this way and that in my fingers, became a handicap to her enthusiasm. She was so fast and I was so slow that I was like a runner who is lapped several times in a race; and her bunches were so much better than mine. I have seen professional violet bunchers who work at great speed show no regard as to the final look of the bunches; they gather the required number of blooms, add the leaves, slip on the rubber bands, and that, as far as they are concerned, is another bunch ready for market. Jeannie works as fast but she arranges every bloom to face the same way, so that when you hold up the bunch all the violets are looking at you, wide open like miniature pansies.

There is an art, too, in packing them in the flower boxes. First, however, after being bunched, their heads are dipped in water and the bunches are left overnight in jars filled to the brim with water; violets revel in wet and, as they drink through their petals, they will survive for days if they are dipped regularly. The bunches are packed tightly in the boxes but the number depends on whether they have short or long stalks, which in turn depends on whether it is cold or mild weather; when they are short Jeannie packs forty-two bunches, when long, thirty bunches; and she lays them on white tissue paper, the ends of which are folded over to cover the blooms before putting on the top. Then off the boxes go in the Land Rover to Penzance station and from there on the flower train to whichever market we have decided on; and in two or three days the price returns arrive through the post and we open the envelope in excitement. 'Sixpence!' I shout with delight. Or gloomily I murmur: 'Only threepence.'

It is a depressing experience, an experience which sets the mood for the day, when a box of flowers we have admired, which has caused Jeannie to shout from the flower house: 'You *must* come and see these before I put the top on . . . they're so beautiful!' – when such a box fetches a poor price. We feel cheated and angry, and we curse the salesman, and I scribble a note of complaint. Or we say stoutly: 'We won't send to *that* market again.' Just like the potatoes, just like anything else a market gardener grows . . . once a product is away from the packing shed it becomes a ticket in a lottery. Yet, as there is no alternative, as it is far too complicated a business to sell direct to retailers, one has to learn, like growing old, to accept the situation. We now accept it by sending our flowers regularly to the same salesman season after season. We send to Clifford Cowling at Leeds, the Dan Wuille Group, a firm in Birmingham and to Carlo Naef, the Italian born doyen of Covent Garden salesmen. They receive between them the whole range of our present day output – violets, anemones, daffodils, freesias, wallflowers, forget-me-nots, calendulas, polyanthus, Christmas flowering stocks; and if sometimes their price returns disappoint, enraging us, we have to admit to ourselves that they too are at the mercy of the same flighty mistress; the mysterious, intangible, elusive 'supply and demand.'

The first winter I cared not a rap for such economic

factors because my imagination did not wish to grasp the prospect that they would ever beset me. I was doped by the sheer pleasure of being a peasant; by the plodding work that did not require mental activity; by day-end exhaustion that did not repay with worried, sleepless nights; by the pleasure of achievement after I had defeated the wind and the rain, and the baskets were filled with violets.

Physical effort is so much more gentle than that of the mind and, being new to it, I found it more rewarding. Mine was the pleasure of the mountaineer, the Channel swimmer or the marathon runner – enthusiasm allied with determination that brought victory which is sweet to the senses and provided tangible conquest in a personal battle. I was blessed at the time by the simple belief that flower growing was determined by obeying certain well defined rules, and success was automatic for him who did so; manure the ground, for instance, see there is enough lime, stick the plants in at the right time, and so on. I had, of course, to work hard and be ready to accept advice from experienced growers whenever I was in doubt, and pick their brains whenever I had the chance. I had, in fact, to behave like any intelligent man with initiative, and my reward would be flowers in abundance. I had not the slightest conception of the savage surprises ahead of me, nor of the bewildering contradictions that growing provides. Quite early on, during that first winter, however, my education was to begin.

The Princess of Wales had already disappeared and now the Governor Herrick started to look anaemic; and instead of lush green plants cascading violet blooms like those of my neighbours, they resembled row upon row of pale faced schoolboys in need of a holiday. The stalks were short, the length of my thumb; the blooms were like pin-points and the petals unwilling to open; and the leaves were grey-green and crinkly.

I am giving the wrong impression. They never at any time looked bursting with life, but a philosophy of wishful thinking convinced me they were certain to improve; and only the departure of autumn forced me to admit that something was radically wrong. My best week's picking had been twenty-four dozen bunches; and in view of the number of plants we had it should have been three times that number. 'What's wrong with the violets?' I said at last to Tommy. I was often to be amazed how Tommy, who was so intelligent on many subjects, was so ignorant on matters that directly concerned his profession; or perhaps his profession was to make use of his strength, leaving questions of skill to his bosses. 'They look sick,' was all the answer he could give me.

I had, I now realize, a child-like faith in the wisdom of those who lived close to the soil; and it never seemed possible to me that nature often defeated them. However, it never occurred to me, until experience proved it, that growers, like all experts, frequently offered advice that was diametrically opposite in its content. There was another occasion in another year when our violet runners failed from the beginning to take a grip with their roots; and I travelled the district, samples of dead runners in my hand, seeking an answer to the mystery.

Surely, I said to myself, these people who have been growing violets all their lives will be able to give me the answer; and yet each advanced a different theory none of which, as I learnt later, was the right one. I found out on my own that the damage had been inflicted by myself; in an effort to provide special food for each runner, I had dropped a handful of blood and bone mixture in each hole as I planted them, and this had burnt and killed the fibre roots.

As for the Governor Herrick, one man said the runners

must have come from stock which had become exhausted, another that I could not have put any manure in the ground (I had put plenty of fish manure), and another that the wind had stunted the plants. Jeannie and I came to the conclusion that the latter explanation was the most likely one and we decided, after much discussion, to invest £30 in coconut netting and posts. The gesture, however, had a feeble result. It was too late. If a winter flowering plant of any kind has not become firmly established by early autumn, there is nothing you can do afterwards to bring it to life.

I have learnt now – and how costly the lessons have been – that you must anticipate trouble if you are to be a successful grower; you must be an optimist in the long term, a pessimist in the short, and you must be perpetually on guard against sudden attack by the elements, insects and diseases which are always in waiting to catch you off your guard.

Along the bank above the Governor Herrick we had planted an assortment of daffodils which had come from Gordon Gibson, a famous grower in the Scilly Islands who was an old friend of Jeannie's family. It was not an ideal position for they faced the full blast of a Lizard wind, but we were short of space and the prize position in the wood had been given to 5 cwt. of King Alfred and 2 cwt. of Soleil d'Or. Nor for that matter were they fashionable daffodils; for daffodils like everything else can outlive popularity. We were, however, only too pleased to have them because we could not afford a stock of up-to-date bulbs, and any bulbs were better than none.

Each variety had arrived in the autumn with meticulous explanations from Gibson as to how they would look when the time came to bloom; Hospodar, for instance, coloured best when grown slowly in an open cool situation and would then have a deep orange red centre, in a warm season the colour would be poor; Campernelle, according to Gibson, was a dainty yellow scented jonquil, a lot of which could be packed in a box; Bernardino was white with a heavily frilled cup edged with apricot; Croesus was a mid-season variety with an orange red cup; Coverack Glory was a strong growing scented daffodil with a yellow trumpet. We were bewitched by these descriptions. We forgave the failure of the Governor Herrick in anticipation of this harvest of daffodils.

The first to bloom were the Soleil d'Or in the wood, and the first Sol in any year is a breath-taking moment that lifts the soul on a pinnacle, leaving it there high in the air to contemplate in exultation the wonder of the coming spring. This particular Sol appeared on a late January day, after a harassing morning during which, in our ignorance, we thought we had lost both the Soleil d'Or and all the King Alfred. During the night there had been a hard frost and when we went into the wood after breakfast we found the leaves and the stems quite flat – as if a roller had been driven over the meadow. It was a bitter moment. 'Well,' I said, 'that looks like the end of our daffodil crop.' But I was wrong and it took only a few hours for me to know it; for as the day brightened so did the leaves and stems recover, and then suddenly we saw among the beds of the Soleil d'Or that solitary bloom; a button of yellow too beautiful to pick, its delicate scent touching the cold air like a feather.

Sols, like the early scented Scilly Whites, do not bloom uniformly, so unless you grow a large quantity you can never at one time send away in great numbers; their season protracts over weeks. King Alfreds, on the other hand, once a few blooms have heralded the way, rush in together crowding the meadow with buds. That first year they took us by surprise.

One day at the end of February we had picked a handful, the next I was lugging two baskets back to the cottage. 'Heavens,' I said to Jeannie, 'look at all these . . . and we haven't done a bunch in our lives!'

The remedy was to fetch our old friend Tom Bailey from Lamorna; here was a man who would not laugh at our enthusiasm nor our innocence. 'Tom,' I said, 'we've grown the flowers and now we haven't the slightest idea how to send them away!' I had found him bunching his own daffodils but he showed no irritation at the interruption. 'We'll soon put that right,' he grinned, 'come on, take me up to Minack and I'll show you.'

He was a good teacher because he had a high standard. There are many daffodil growers who seem to have no standards at all, no pride in a beautifully packed box; who bunch blooms however badly marked, jamming them into old cardboard boxes and wrapping them in newspapers if paper at all; farmers, for instance, who during the war and afterwards cashed in on the shortage of daffodils, growing them as if they were a field of turnips.

I once called on a farmer who showed me an outhouse filled with a white variety of daffodil standing in jars on the shelves with the petals stained the colour of autumn leaves. 'Caught the wind,' I said sympathetically, knowing that if they were mine they would all be thrown away. 'Damn nuisance,' he replied, adding blandly, 'I'm afraid it may affect the price.'

The reward for maintaining a high standard comes usually when the markets are glutted with daffodils; and then buyers will ignore the rag and bobtail senders and stick to those whose standards are known. Our own aim is to send every box away from Minack as if it were going to an exhibition; and it is an aim that can only be achieved by having, at times, to dump large quantities of daffodils on the compost heap.

We ran into no trouble with those first King Alfreds, the weather was brisk but there were no strong winds to break the barrage of the wood and hurt them: and we picked when the buds had dipped at right angles to the stems and had begun to open, the yellow just showing. We brought them into the spare bedroom which Jeannie and her typewriter now vacated, and stood them in galvanized flower pails, perhaps for two days, until the bud had formed its full beauty. Then we bunched them in twelves, finding the long firm stems easy to hold and arrange, boxed them in a bed of white paper a dozen bunches at a time, and then sent them off to Honor Bannerman, the head florist at the Savoy, who paid us a price far above anything we would have received in an ordinary market.

This, we said to each other, was a fine way of earning a living; and we had the further satisfaction of hearing of a man who so admired a bunch he bought at the stand in the Savoy's front hall, that he enquired where they came from, then ordered ten dozen to be sent to his friends. Pride, therefore, was mingled with the pleasure of profit; for we had found that in a fortnight's hectic activity we had earned enough to cover the capital outlay of the bulbs, and the bulbs were still there for many seasons to come. 'Just think,' I said to Jeannie with the gambler's aptitude to tot up prospective wins, 'we have taken £56 from 5 cwt. of bulbs . . . seven tons fill an acre, so if we could raise the capital to have that amount, we could earn over £1,500 a year!'

There was the beauty of the work as well. Tiredness, as known in other spheres, had no chance to conquer when the senses were being constantly refreshed by the tangible evidence of spring. Each morning we would enter the wood, then stop and marvel before we began to pick. Overnight buds had dropped, opened and were peering

their golden yellow over the green foliage, each with a
destiny to provide delight. It was like a ballroom of child
dancers, innocent and exquisite, brimmed with an ethereal
happiness, laughing, loving, blind to passing time; and yet,
almost unnoticed, day by day the flowers were leaving,
then gathering speed, until suddenly there was only a floor
of green, flecked here and there by a bloom that had stayed
behind. The dance was over.

Along the bank in the field the Campernelle were flowering and beside them the Hospodar were thick with buds.
Campernelle, Hospodar, Coverack Glory, Bernardino, Croesus . . . they would flower in that order, the poor relations
of the King Alfred. We would not dare to despatch them
to the Savoy, and we would take the luck of the markets;
and yet we still had the advantage of being so far west that
each variety would flower early, earlier than Lamorna,
earlier than Coverack, earlier than Falmouth.

We were well satisfied with the shilling a bunch the
Campernelle were fetching as thirty-six bunches were
packed in a box; and then followed the Hospodar, first an
odd bloom or two and suddenly a rush, stems clawing the
air with nodding buds, a concourse of faces crowding the
bank; and no sooner had these appeared than the Coverack
Glory a little further down the field nearer the sea began
drooping their yellow heads, demanding the attention we
were giving to the others.

Up to then – it was the second week of March – the
weather had been soft and warm, so gentle the wind one
could not believe the gales of winter had ever existed, or
could ever come again. Our only concern was to pick,
bunch and send away. We had no time to anticipate
trouble. We listened to the weather forecast but day after
day it was so monotonously the same that there came an
evening when we did not bother to turn on the wireless.

The sky was clear, the sea still, and there was a pleasant security in the quietness, lulling us early to bed and quickly to sleep.

Suddenly I was wakened by a crash, and in the dimness I saw the curtains billowing before the open window like a sail torn from the mast. I fumbled for my torch and at the same time Jeannie cried out: 'My face cream! That was my new bottle of Dorothy Gray I left by the window!'

I had time neither to sympathize, laugh nor investigate the damage. It was the Lizard wind hissing through the trees, tearing into the daffodils that were scheduled to be picked in the morning.

'Hurry,' I said, 'we must get down to the field . . .' and we pulled on our clothes and in a few minutes were fighting, heads down, against a gale that was to roar across Mount's Bay without pause for thirty-six hours. Our task was absurd, but ignorance at first made it appear feasible, the comfortable optimism at the beginning of a battle, the sheer stupidity of believing we could conquer the elements.

We had one torch which Jeannie held as I grabbed at the waving stems, and unable to stand in the screaming wind

we crawled on our hands and knees up and down the paths between the beds. For ten minutes we fought with the Hospodar and then, only a handful picked, I yelled at Jeannie: 'It's hopeless here ... let's try the Coverack Glory!' Down we staggered to the lower part of the field and the beam of the torch shone on a sight which resembled a herd of terrified miniature animals tethered to the ground. Spray was now sticking to our faces and our hands, and a sense of doom was enveloping our hearts. We could not win. Nothing we could do would save our harvest.

Chapter Nine

FISHERMEN CALL the Lizard wind the starving wind, for the fish hide from it on the bed of the sea and the boats return empty to port. Landsmen solemnly call it the gizzard wind as it bites into the body and leaves you tired when the day is still young. It is a hateful wind, no good to anybody, drying the soil into powdery dust, blackening the grass like a film of oil, punching the daffodils with the blows of a bully. It is seldom a savage wind as it was on the night it destroyed the Hospodar and Coverack Glory; if it were, if it spat its venom then recoiled into quiet, you could cry over the damage and forget. Instead it simmers its fury like a man with a grudge, moaning its grievance on and on, day after day, remorselessly wearying its victims into defeat.

The wasted stems of the Hospodar and the Coverack Glory were piled high on the compost heap and now the Bernardino and Croesus hastened to join them. Nothing dramatic in their destruction, no sudden obliteration to grieve over; the wind bit at each bud as it unfurled from the calex, flapping the edge of a petal until it turned brown; or it maliciously made the stems dance to its tune so that they swayed together hither and thither, the buds rubbing and chafing, bruising each other to an inevitable end.

We watched and did nothing. As strangers to the wind
we bargained that any hour, any moment it might shift to
another quarter – hence we refused to buy coconut netting.
We considered moving that which surrounded the Governor Herrick, but perversely the plants were now hinting at
signs of growth; and, having waited so long, surely it
would be foolish to remove the protection that might at
last ensure us a reward? Thus we dithered, and hoped, and
grew edgy. Our income was blowing away before our eyes,
and a little of our confidence too; and when at last the
wind moved round to the south it was too late. The
Bernardino and the Croesus had enriched the compost
heap while the violets, having demanded our loyalty,
proved in due course their promised growth was a mirage.

The flowers were behind us and the potatoes ahead, and
spring comes to Minack when people begin to ask: 'Are
the taties covering the rows?' Lobstermen were dropping
their pots and I had excitedly told Jeannie I had seen the
first swallow skimming the coast line from its landfall near
Land's End. The green woodpeckers were laughing again
in the wood at hilarious jokes of their own and I would lie
abed in the morning listening to the tap-tap-tap of one
carving a hole in an elm. Sea pinks plumed from fat green
cushions. A bat fluttered briefly as dusk fell. Robins
pounced on worms and hurried off to an early brood.
Foxes were bold, appearing casually in daylight in places
where winter saw only a shadow. Wrens flighted with
feathers bigger than themselves. A male mistlethrush
wooed his lady by absurdly building a nest ten yards from
our door. Monty looked gorgeous, his fur a glistening
titian, as he stalked through the lush green grass. Bluebells
abounded. Primroses lit the banks with their soft yellow
beckoning you to bury your face in their fragrance. These
were the regular signs repeated year after year, bringing

centuries together and denying the passage of time, shining security in a brittle present, taunting the desperation of beehive cities. If a man could not be at peace among them his shadow must be the enemy.

John again was the first to draw his potatoes and as the cart lumbered up from his cliff, I saw the glint in Tommy's eye. 'Better try ours tomorrow,' he grunted. The same old envy ricocheting down the coast – Tregiffian, Boscawen, St Loy, Penberth; all the way shovels were poised, eyes watching neighbours, silver tongued salesmen angling for custom, neat little meadows falling down the cliffs grinning at the sea and green with hope.

'Started drawing yet?' . . . 'Samples any good?' . . . 'Joe's digging two hundredweight a lace' . . . 'Where are you sending?' . . . 'Manchester is strong, Birmingham is weak' . . . 'A shower won't do any harm' . . . 'Farmers will be early this year.'

John's meadows were round a shoulder of the cliff, facing due south and gaining an hour of sun over our meadows which fell into shadow in the late afternoon. That hour's sun meant a week in earliness, and nothing Tommy could do would alter the fact. Thus the ceremony of trying out stems was doomed to failure.

'We'll wait a few days,' I said to Tommy, 'no use murdering them.'

I was not, however, as calm as I appeared, for I too was gripped again with potato fever. It was a deliciously buoyant sensation. Here we were on the edge of retrieving our misfortunes of the flower season. The precious prospect of hitting the jackpot lay ahead, and if I did not wish to appear anxious to Tommy, it certainly did not matter how I appeared to Jeannie. 'Come on,' I said after Tommy had gone home, 'let's go and explore on our own.' It was a gesture of curiosity, not of expectation and we completed the formality without disappointment. 'Another week,' I said, 'at least another week.' And in that week Jeannie, Monty and I gained a companion who, when I started to dig, followed me up and down the row wagging his tail. His name was Gold Bounty.

Gold Bounty was a friendly black greyhound, and his arrival at Minack occurred in this way. A few years before, the White City had offered Jeannie a greyhound to run in her name, and invited us down to the kennels at Barnet to meet it. We were introduced to Gold Bounty who greeted us with such affection, so trustingly muzzled his face in Jeannie's hand, that she wanted to take him back to Mortlake immediately. We were limited, however, to occasional visits to the kennels, but there came a time when he knew us so well that he began to whimper and yelp in excitement as soon as he heard our voices in the corridor.

One day the manager said to us laughingly: 'Well, I can see that Bounty's going to have a good home when he retires.' We, too, laughed in reply. It was a long time off before such a thing would happen. Horizons away, and in the meantime he had races to win. This public side of his life began in sensational fashion; sensational at any rate, and delightful, for Jeannie and myself. When Gold Bounty made his début, we were having dinner in the glass-fronted terrace of the stadium with Don Iddon, the outspoken columnist of the *Daily Mail*, and A. P. Herbert, whose devotion to greyhound racing and football pools has brought him much frustration; and Jeannie was relaxing in the glow of being an owner whose dog was about to race, a situation which has its hazards, as she was later to find out.

For instance, the most unlikely people would sidle up to her: 'See Bounty's running tonight. What's his chances?' The craving for inside knowledge nurtured the delusion that the owner possessed that knowledge. Thus if Jeannie appeared in a mood of optimism, that mood would be responsible for a flow of whispers: 'Bounty's going to win tonight.' If she shrugged her shoulders and said she did not know, the converse was concluded. Unfortunately, she never possessed any secret information, and thus she deserved neither the smiles nor the black looks which followed her imaginary tips.

Indeed as Gold Bounty pursued his career he became a source of embarrassment to ourselves, for loyalty demanded we should back him but circumstances often made us forget; and the times we forgot were those when it seemed he most often won. But there was one awful occasion when he and another greyhound which had been presented to Jeannie called Corporal Mackay, both won on the same night, at combined odds of one hundred and fifty to one. We had not a penny on either. The trainer had told us before racing began that neither had the ghost of a chance.

Gold Bounty's first appearance resulted in a win by a short head after a photo finish. He came up round the last bend from fourth place in the red jacket of Trap Number One, and pipped the favourites on the post. We were hysterical. Alan Herbert shouted like a busker, Don Iddon filled our glasses with champagne, Jeannie stood on a chair yelling: 'Bounty! Bounty! Well done Bounty!' and I shook the hands of everyone at the next table, all of whom were strangers. The custom is for the greyhounds filling the first three places to be walked round the arena after each race; and Jeannie and I ran down to the rails to see Gold Bounty as he passed. He was a beautiful looking greyhound, not very big, and he walked as if on springs. 'Well done, Bounty!' we called. For a moment he looked in our direction, then barked. 'Oh what a good dog am I,' he seemed to be saying. He raced at the White City for four years;

always genuine and intelligent, he was loved by the crowd, and many a night I have heard the arena filled with the roar: 'Bounty! Bounty! Come on Bounty!'

Then came the letter from the manager of one of the kennels saying it was time for Bounty to retire. Would we have him? Otherwise he would have to be put to sleep since he was not of high enough class to be of use at stud. Of course we agreed immediately to do so. At the same time we realized we were heading for trouble. Track greyhounds, being trained all their lives to chase the electric hare, had also the habit of chasing any other small animal on four legs. How could we keep Bounty and Monty apart?

We shut our minds to this problem in the excitement of his impending arrival, and when one late afternoon he was led from the guard's van of the Cornish Riviera we were waiting on the Penzance platform to give him a hero's welcome. He greeted us as old friends, barking excitedly and leaping up on his hindlegs. He was home. We had not let him down. He was going to have a wonderful time!

But as soon as we returned to the cottage we were faced with the reality of the problem with which we had landed ourselves. Monty, whom we had left shut up indoors, met us with an enraged glare from the window; Bounty saw him and started to bark furiously.

'Look,' I said to Jeannie, 'I'll take Bounty for a walk while you try and make peace with Monty.'

Monty never took any notice of a dog if it passed by him when he was on his own; but if we were about his back would arch, his fur rise, and then wham! . . . he would attack. In his own mind I suppose he was protecting us, but his ferocious behaviour was certainly startling to his victims. Jeannie's cousin once called unexpectedly and arrived at the door holding a terrier in her arms. In an instant Monty was at it, and five minutes later the wretched girl herself was having first-aid in the bathroom. The same kind of episode happened time and time again, and the odd thing was this ... whenever we rushed out to warn any visitor with a dog, we were always greeted with the same lofty remark: 'Our dog never goes for cats ... you don't have to worry.'

We, therefore, knew from the beginning that Bounty would never be able to stay with us, although in the moment of welcome we had conveniently forgotten the fact. Our idea was to keep him at Minack for a few days and then to find him a permanent home; sensible but unwise, because every minute he spent with us our hearts became more emotionally involved. He was my shadow. He trotted trustingly at my heels when I took him for long walks, and when I started to shovel out the potatoes he followed me up the meadow, foot by foot, as if he thought his presence was essential. I would return to the cottage with him gambolling beside me, there to find poor old Monty sitting as usual in the window with fire in his eyes.

The nights were chaotic. Our intention had been for Bounty to use the potato hut as a kennel while Monty continued his custom of sleeping on the bed. But Bounty tore at the door and the walls and howled like a hyena until we were driven to silencing him by despatching Monty into the sitting-room, and bringing Bounty into the bedroom. A sliding door divided the enemies and rather than risk one of them slipping through when we opened it, we hopped in and out of the windows. Such a strain could hardly last and its end was sudden.

Jeannie had gone up to the farm to fetch the milk and had taken Bounty with her, and I had stayed behind to weed the garden. Suddenly I saw her running towards me up the lane. She was alone. 'It's happened!' she cried out as she reached me. 'What's happened?' I said, and saw her anguish.

'Bounty's killed a cat and he let out that awful howl as they do when they catch the hare!'

It's a blood curdling sound, a siren of the jungle. 'He must go! He must go!' It was an old cat, a dying one at that, and the farmer who owned it eased our minds by saying he would have had to kill it in any case. But we could not keep Bounty any longer. The honeymoon of his retirement was over.

That afternoon we put him in the back of the Land Rover and set off to find him a home. He thought it great fun. He put his paws on the back of my seat and pushed a wet nose in my neck; and he barked out of the sheer joy of barking. As for ourselves, we were remembering the roars of the White City crowds: 'Bounty! Bounty! Come on Bounty!' – and comparing this memory with the incongruous present; and as happens when one deceives an animal we felt humiliated.

Yet we knew we could find him a good home in St Buryan parish, for it has an ancient tradition of coursing and of breeding greyhound champions of the show ring. And we did. Trethewey looked at Gold Bounty with a grin on his face, and scratched his head in wonderment that such a beautiful dog was being given to him. He had three other greyhounds on his farm, and five minutes was enough to see that he was gentle with them; so we said goodbye to old Bounty feeling assured that he had many years of happiness before him. And it seemed we were right when, a few weeks later, we called and found Bounty curled up in the best armchair by the fire.

The next time I saw Trethewey was three months later when he knocked at the door of the cottage. 'Hello, Mr Trethewey,' I said cheerfully, 'how's Bounty?' He looked at me quietly for a moment. 'He's dead,' he said, 'he died last night of a heart attack.'

We ached our way once again through the potato harvest, and when it was all over and we had counted our takings, we were pleased by the immediate present, but disturbed by the future. We had had a good crop and fair prices, but viewed with dispassion we had to admit the outgoings were proving greater than income. The bliss of the first excursion was being tempered by the knowledge that we had embroiled ourselves in a business that had a considerable appetite. The element of wage paying demanded capital expenditure in order to provide it; thus experience at Minack was beginning to teach us the truth of Parkinson's Law.

If, for instance, you have an acre of land, you may be able to crop it yourself but the work is so exacting and returns so limited that you are certain to decide that you must increase your turnover by cropping more land; and this means you must have labour to help you. More land means more fertilisers, seeds, equipment and general overhead expenses all of which, added to the wage you now have to pay, cancel out the value of the increased turnover. An itch thereupon gets in your mind which worries you into believing that yet more capital expenditure is the answer. If you buy a motor hoe and so lessen the use of the hand hoe, if you buy a motor scythe and dispense with the old-fashioned hand one, if you buy a rotovator and give up digging the ground, if you buy . . . all these purchases, you say, will increase efficiency, spare labour for extra work, and thus bring nearer the elusive margin of profit.

You find the magic result does not materialize, yet the nagging thought develops that you have not been bold enough. What about a greenhouse? And if one greenhouse does not earn what you expect, what about two? Perhaps on the other hand you ought to increase your stock of bulbs, or have a new packing shed, or would it be better to invest in cloches? The ideas for expenditure roll out of your mind as if on a conveyor belt, and you lie awake at night and pace your room in the morning, tussling as to which idea to put into practice.

Funds meanwhile are falling low and instalment commitments increasing. A compelling force drives you to give up your intention of having a new suit in favour of the fertilisers the advisory officer urges you to spread over the bulb ground. Fertilizers, you argue, will increase next year's turnover while a new suit will rest most of the time in the cupboard. You realize by now that you are the victim of your own enthusiasm. So much money has been spent, so much energy expended, that retreat means disaster, and you are drawn by a magnet into a future which is grey with doubt. If the daffodils bloom in profusion, if they do not coincide with a glut, if the violets or anemones are not killed by frost, if it is not a bumper year for everyone else's tomatoes, if the potato plants are not blackened by gales, if their harvest does not have to compete with shiploads of foreign imports . . . then you may expect the year's endeavour to earn you a living.

Market garden efficiency cannot be classified in the same way as a factory. For one thing there is no roof to protect you from the weather; for another you cannot put your goods in a stockroom until there is a demand for their sale because your goods begin to die after they are gathered; and you cannot possibly draw up an accurate budget as you have little idea of what your output may be, and not the faintest notion what price your goods will fetch. Placid looking market gardeners, therefore, are inveterate gamblers and their life is not, as it appears, a plodding one. It dwells in high excitement, and the charm of it is that the grey doubts of the future are invariably quelled by titillating prospects of a new season.

Meanwhile we devised means to live cheaply, and in such efforts the countryman has the advantage over the townsman. Appearances, unless you leave the compound, do not matter and thus old clothes which, in a city, would have been pushed into retirement, continue in rough service for year after year. Rents are a fraction in comparison and nagging bills such as those for warming the house in winter can be tempered by taking a walk and collecting your own logs. You can have your own fresh eggs and by growing vegetables you can spend the townsman's contribution to the greengrocer on something else.

Jeannie and I now began to wonder whether we could catch our own fish in some manner which would not necessitate my dangling a rod for hour after hour when I should be doing something else. I considered the merits of the kite which is used by off-shore lighthouse keepers. This kite with baited hook attached is set off before the wind until it is far enough away to be pulled down into the sea, and then is reeled into the rocks beneath the lighthouse. Such a kite is independent of which way the wind is blowing but obviously, if I were to use a kite, I would only be able to launch it when the wind was blowing off the land.

I then had the idea of a toy clockwork motor-boat sailing out to sea from our rocks attached to a line which I would hold, and towing a short second line with a swivel hook attached. This swivel hook would provide the same effect as one being pulled by a fishing boat, luring perhaps mackerel which are rarely caught within casting distance of the rocks – pollock being the normal catch. I found, however, that clockwork did not have the power to face the sea, and any other model was far too expensive. I thereupon settled for a lobster pot.

But a lobster pot still did not provide the answer. We had an ideal spot to drop it, a rock which jutted out into the small bay then fell sheer to the water so that even at low tide it was thirty feet deep. Our method of operation was to weight the pot with stones, bait it with gurnet which we collected from Newlyn fish market, and throw it with a splash into the sea, watching it gurgle its way to the depths. The connecting rope was fastened to a ring we had cemented in a hole in the rocks – one of several holes each a few inches wide which obviously had been man-made for some mysterious reason in the distant past.

Then we left the pot for twenty-four hours in hopeful expectation that lobsters and crabs would crawl to their doom. We had good reason for hopefulness because the lobstermen themselves dropped their pots out in the cove within a stone's throw of our rocks; and so what was likely to go into their pots had only to travel a few yards to go into our particular one. They did not bother to do so. Our total catch in eight weeks consisted of several useless spider crabs, one lobster, and a three-foot conger eel whose fang-like teeth gave me the fright of my life as I fought for half an hour to extract it from the pot. I was proud of this conger eel and I carried it up the cliff to the cottage as if I were Monty boasting the catch of a mouse. 'Look!' I said to Jeannie, 'look what I've caught!' The dead eyes leered at her, the grey elongated body was slimy in my hands. Quickly I realized my pride was misplaced. 'It's horrible,' she said, 'take it away out of my sight!'

Then one evening in the Mousehole pub we met a fisherman called Ned who described a trammel net to us; and he made it sound so alluring that we concluded we would be able to catch enough fish to supply not only ourselves but our neighbours as well. The technicalities were these.

The trammel net was fifty yards long, six feet deep and had a two-inch mesh. Weights were fastened at intervals along one length of the net and corks along the other, specially balanced so that the net floated six feet deep from the surface of the sea. Normally the net was used by either end being attached to two boats, so that they swept the fishing ground like a minesweeper; but Ned's proposal was that we should adjust this principle to our particular conditions which demanded, of course, that we should 'shoot' the net from the rocks and use a buoy anchored in the cove with a pulley attached. The net had long ropes at either end and one of these was threaded through the pulley, then brought back to the rocks; so that when we 'shot' the net we would haul one rope to send it out to sea, and haul the other when we brought it ashore, both ropes of course being at other times securely tied to the rings we had cemented in the holes in the rocks.

One morning, therefore, when the sea in the cove appeared as quiet and innocent as a cow musing in a meadow, Ned nosed in his boat and dropped overboard a 56 lb. weight with the buoy attached about sixty yards out from where Jeannie and I were standing on the rocks. He had with him the net and the ropes, one of which he threaded through the pulley; then, feeding the net over the side of the boat into the sea, he edged his way towards us until he was near enough to throw the rope-ends which we promptly fastened to the rings. Thus the trap was set and we could see the shadow of the net stretching half-way across the cove; all we had to do was to go away and think of the fish swimming into it.

For a couple of weeks they obliged to such an extent that we had fish for breakfast, lunch and dinner while

Monty stuffed himself with plateful after plateful. The snag was, however, that it was always the same fish – pollock – and we grew sick of the sight of it. True we also caught the bony, many coloured, uneatable rass, but these were thrown back into the sea; there was never a sign of the fish of the fishmonger's slab, the mullet, bass and mackerel. The hope they would come remained. Every day at low tide we went down to the rocks and pulled in the net, picked out the fish, then 'shot' the net once again. The weather was fine and the task was simple except for one aspect; and this was to prove our undoing. There was no clear run between the buoy and where I stood pulling in the net. I had to stand in such a position that the net had to be dragged on a jagged channel of rocks close to the water line, and where in fact we picked out the fish. Inevitably I stood the risk of tearing the net but, heavy and cumbersome as it was to control, there was little danger of doing this while the weather was calm; and if it were rough Ned had already warned us to untie it from the ropes and hoist it far out of danger on to the upper part of the rocks – for if the net was out in the cove when a gale blew up, it would certainly be lost.

The first gale caught us prepared, or so we thought. We heard the warning on the six o'clock shipping forecast, and raced down the cliff, pulled in the net and carried it high and dry above the rocks. As I have said, the net was heavy and when just out of the water, felt like a ten ton weight; so it took time to get it to safety, and the effort brought a sense of satisfaction.

Around midnight I was wakened by such a convulsion of wind roaring round the cottage that I began to worry whether we had taken the net high enough up the rocks. The old nagging worry of the wind which chased us always at Minack; lying cosily in bed with a sound outside like tube trains rushing; as if the cottage had angered a madman who was jabbing at it with a madman's venom. Hate in the wind. Merciless with a bully's power. Wedging a stick of conscience as I lie in bed and listen and fear. Was I careful enough? Or did I only pay court to care? Was I lazy because the day was still, my imagination dull? The seasons lie behind me and the wreckage of the wind cuts into my memory like a general remembering the dying in a lost battle.

At one a.m. Jeannie and I got up and dressed and lit a hurricane lamp, and with heads down against the wind, the light spangling the dancing grasses at our feet, we struggled down the cliff. The seas were enormous. Spray wetted our faces like a sponge and the white crests of the waves ribboned the rocks; and it did not take an instant for us to realize that the net had been dragged from its safety.

'It's my fault,' I shouted, 'I should have taken it further up!' So easy to self-blame when the exception had occurred; such admission softens, too, the disappointment. And yet that night the waves were lunging at rocks, high above the water line we had never seen wet before; where wayward seeds had fertilized, like meadow sweet and sea pinks and wild alyssum, in crevices of wind-blown soil. We staggered forward oblivious of the danger, enraged that care in our fashion had been rewarded by the cheat of the sea. Then, as we stood amid the shower of the waves with the lamp swinging in my hand, I suddenly saw the net stretched like a straddled whale along the rocks; for one instant in black relief in the lamp-light, the next lost in the mouth-wash of the sea.

I gave Jeannie the lamp and she held it above her head, the light shining on her salt-wet face, feebly acting as sentinel, eyeing the gush of water as it recoiled from the rocks, reflecting the quiet pause, flickering a warning as a white mass gathered momentum then crashed in a thousand fragments splintering the night with spray. At each pause I dashed forward and tugged at the net. I loosened it first from one crevice, then another, and above the thunderous noise Jeannie would shout: 'Quick! Come back! Another one coming!' I struggled as if with an octopus, bit by bit, further and further from the water line until the waves no longer grasped with hands but clawed with fingers instead, becoming weaker, strength in spasms, until impotent and defeated they could only stretch at the net as if to caress.

The next morning we looked at the damage, and it was not as bad as we had expected. We laboured up the cliff and took the net to the fisherman's store in Newlyn where we had bought it. It remained there for three weeks during which time an old salt patiently repaired it. By now the net had cost us over £20, and the fish it had so far produced had been highly expensive; but the summer was still young and the lesson to take greater care well learnt. We listened to the forecasts and whenever there was a suggestion of wind we pulled in the net and piled it high up on the rocks. Such methodical caution was admirable provided the forecasts were correct, but one Sunday evening when the net was stretched across the cove, the sea as still as a saucer of milk, the sky clear, the forecast promised the same quiet weather would continue for the next twenty-four hours – yet within twelve the sea was a cauldron.

As dawn broke behind the hills on the other side of Mount's Bay, I was straining with all my might to bring in the net, but just as part of it reached the channel of rocks where it lay when we picked out the fish, the pulley jammed on the buoy that was bobbing like a cork out in the cove. I was in any case in danger and Jeannie was yelling to me to retreat. I watched for a moment the net swirling in the waters and wrapping itself round the jagged points of the rocks like a black serpent. This was goodbye to our fish. No chance would arise now to carry the net like a wounded animal to Newlyn. The sea had exacted its revenge.

Chapter Ten

ONE SUMMER the violets were in the meadow below the cottage which had been a bog when we first arrived, and where Tommy and I had sunk yards of earthenware drain pipes. I was weeding the plants one afternoon when Jeannie, who had gone for a walk over the cliffs, returned highly excited. The delight of her character was the way in which her zest relished our adventure in a manner so natural, so persuasive in its truth, that never at any time did she fail to enthuse even when I, crowding my mind with materialistic fears, blocked her enthusiasm with doubts.

I doubted, for instance, on this occasion when she bubbled the news that the farmer whose land bordered John's to the west, five minutes' walk from Minack, was prepared to rent us two acres. These particular acres together with a cascade of small meadows which fell to the sea below them and which the farmer was to retain for himself, had a reputation in the district of being a potato gold mine. It was a reputation which stemmed from the war when new potatoes fetched ten shillings a pound and daffodils of the most common variety five shillings a bunch. It was early land facing south with the Wolf Rock a finger in the distance, so early that the farmer concerned had never failed to keep his record of sending the first mainland potatoes to market. Thus Pentewan, as the land was called, seemed to provide the chance we were seeking. We were cramped at Minack, but now we could launch out as big growers.

'I wonder why he's giving it up?' I said to Jeannie. My hesitancy was a poor reward for her enthusiasm and she told me so bluntly, nor was my caution to be relied upon. It was a mood which might well be concerned with my dissatisfaction over the growth of the plants I was hoeing, a trivial moment of gloom unfitted to greet a challenge. It certainly was unfair to Jeannie.

'He says there'll be room for four tons of potatoes,' she went on as if she were trying to put a match to my woodiness, 'so that with four tons over here we'll have eight tons of seed next year and at three and a half to one that means twenty-eight tons of potatoes. We could take at least a thousand pounds, and with luck much more!'

If her reasoning sounded optimistic, it also made sense. We had cropped eleven tons of potatoes from three tons of seed during the past season and had averaged £45 a ton; thus Pentewan together with the land we were continuing to reclaim at Minack would put us firmly in sight of establishing ourselves. We would have elbow room, space for more bulbs, be able to grow a greater variety of crops and each on a substantial scale if we so wished. It would counter the disadvantage of Minack where, in view of the endless reclaiming that had to be done, we resembled two people living in a house that was in the process of being built. At Pentewan the meadows awaited us, old hands which knew what was expected of them, a century of sun-drenched labour within their boundaries. I had become as excited as Jeannie.

Meanwhile Jeannie's *Meet Me At The Savoy* for which Danny Kaye had written the foreword had sold as a serial to *John Bull*, and we had invested the proceeds in making the cottage our own particular palace. We installed a petrol-driven pump at the top of the well and became reacquainted with the comfort of a bath and indoor lavatory, having added a wood-built annexe at the far end of the one-time chicken house. This development – hot water came from a calor gas heater – gave us as much pleasure as that of a millionaire sailing a maiden voyage in his yacht. We revelled in our independence of the weather, and the gush of a tap gave us the same sharp wonderment as that of natives being introduced to the plumbing civilization for the first time. We still could not afford a sink with running water from a day and night burning stove, nor a hole through the end wall of the cottage with a connecting lobby to the spare room and bathroom; and it was two years before we could do so. Thus, in order to reach the bathroom, we had to go through the front door, a task which was inconvenient but not disastrous; and as far as the washing up was concerned we had to continue to use a basin, then empty the contents over a neighbouring hedge.

I sometimes wonder whether the ghosts of the cottage cast a spell over us, enabling us to accept this abuse of twentieth-century comfort in the way we did. Inconvenience had pervaded the cottage for over five hundred years, so was it inevitable that we should act as if it were natural? The twentieth century decorates life like a Christmas cake, but it still cannot do anything about the basic ingredients; and there seemed to be a starkness in our companionship which enabled us to find a fulfilment without the aid of man-made devices; as if the canvas of each day was so vast that mirror-smooth techniques of living, coma entertainment like television, would only make it unmanageable. We are still without electricity and we remain thankful we have no telephone; yet it would be a pose to pretend that self denial did not seek its compensations.

We have revelled in occasional brisk returns to the life we used to know, being flattered because we were new faces in an old circle or rejoicing in the stimulation of reunions. It was fun being at the first night of A. P. Herbert's musical play 'The Water Gypsies' which he wrote at Minack, to stay at the Dorchester because Richard Aldrich wanted us to be present when his book *Gertrude Lawrence as Mrs A* was launched. All this was the sugar that titivates a day but does not provide its bread; and the basic fact remained that we could not build Minack by playing as if it were an accessory to our life instead of its foundation.

These sorties to an existence which used to be our daily round confirmed the wisdom of our escape, but, at the time, we were doped by the paraphernalia of sophistication. We delighted in the silliness, the laughter in cocktail bars, relaxing late in the afternoon over lunch, parties at night. No one could have called us peasants. But when we returned to Minack we looked back on those gilded shadows and were thankful they had passed over us so briefly. We felt pity instead of envy for our contemporaries whose company had regained for us so much pleasure. Success in this age breeds only a rackety happiness, providing little time for its own enjoyment. The bite of competition is too sharp for leisure, so success is either pimped by others to further their own ends or creates its own demoralization and betrays the truth from which it sprang. There is no freedom in twentieth-century achievement for the individual is controlled not by his own deep thinking processes but by the plankton of shibboleths which are currently in fleeting fashion; and by his own desperate need to maintain financial survival in the glittering world he has found himself. Jeannie and I have also to fight for survival, but it is an easy battle compared to that in a city. At least the countryman still possesses the luxury of being able to live at the same leisurely pace of another age.

We took over Pentewan meadows and briskly decided to cultivate them by modern methods. They were, for the most part, large sloping meadows which from time immemorial had been shovel-turned in the autumn, shovel-planted with potatoes in early spring, shovel-cropped in the summer. They had never seen a machine, and even the laborious task of hacking the ground into suitable condition before planting had always been done by hand. Obviously my new landlord had found an extra man would be needed on the farm if the meadows were to be worked, and unless the wage was that of a coolie profits would be small; and in any case he could not be bothered with the trouble that labour in such circumstances often involves.

I, on the other hand, untrammelled by tradition, was convinced that the answer to the problem was mechanization; and that once I had gathered around me the correct assortment of machines I would forge ahead with the same relentless success as a gang on a motorway. I was not thinking in terms of the normal sized tractors but of the hand-controlled variety, one of which I had already tried out at Minack; and I thought that if I had a motor-hoe and a motor-driven hedge cutter, tedious time absorbing tasks would be cut to the minimum.

I bought the Minack tractor second-hand, a monstrous looking thing with a plough, and an engine that kicked like a mule every time I started it. Tommy, who could handle any horse, had nothing in common with this example of progress, and he behaved to it always as if he were a fox sniffing danger; and when one day I suddenly saw Tommy careering down the big field towards the cliff, hanging on to the handlebars with the tractor quite out of his control, I decided it was time to get rid of it.

It was exchanged for a second-hand rotovator and this was the machine with which we first went into the attack on the Pentewan meadows. It was a dual purpose machine for if I exchanged the normal small wheels for large ones, removed the rotovator from the engine and substituted a specially designed shaft I could use it with a plough; and a plough can sometimes do work for which a rotovator is useless. For instance some experts will say that a rotovator used often on the same ground will pommel it into uselessness; and that ground should be spared the rotovator and ploughed instead at least once every two years. This probably applies where blades are used but in this instance I had claw-like tines fitted to the machine which churned the soil as if they were forks being used at maniacal speed. The theory was right but the execution wrong, because every time a tine hit a rock hidden beneath the soil it would snap; and as there were many such rocks this method became ridiculously expensive.

I soon found, too, that the machine did not like me; for time and again when I set out to rotovate, the engine obstinately refused to start. Usually, of course, on such occasions the fault can be quickly corrected by a mechanic, and the mechanic if you possess the most elementary knowledge should be yourself. Check plug, clean carburettor, make sure the ignition is all right ... I used to perform these tasks, secure no result, then storm back to Jeannie. 'The bloody thing won't work,' I would shout, 'and I'll have to get them to come and see it.'

'Them' were the Helston people from whom I had bought it, and in due course a kindly mechanic would arrive, tinker an hour or two with the engine, gain no response, then remark: 'I've never known an engine like this before.' My years at Pentewan – and other rotovators behaved in the same way as this first one – are filled with

memories of mechanics in various meadows where the
rotovator of the moment had broken down, unscrewing
things, screwing things up, with me beside them hopefully
staring, waiting for them to arrive, or thanking them for
coming. 'I can't help thinking,' said one, grimly trying to
be cheerful, 'if the firm wouldn't be wise to pitch a tent
here.'

Yet this first rotovator had the advantage of being the
spearhead of our hopes; and the tantrums were forgiven
because we were, in our own minds, revolutionizing the
cultivation of cliff meadows. Others might think their
commercial value was dying out but we were proving that
a new outlook, a dashing grasp of experts' advice, would
lead them to prosperity. Our landlord had a man called Joe
who looked after the cascade of meadows below our own,
vineyards of meadows where no machine of any kind could
reach, falling to the sea amid hedges of escallonia, apple
trees, and banks thick in winter with the fragrance of wild
violets; and Joe would leave a meadow which he had been
laboriously turning with a shovel, and come to watch me
at work; to stare at my method of rotovating or perhaps
just to help me with advice on how to get the engine
started.

Joe belonged to the cliffs in the same way that a cliff fox
or a cliff badger belongs; and he disapproved of change in
the same way that anyone disapproves of action that
changes something directly concerning his own heart. He
distrusted the rotovator. He would stand at the bottom of
the meadow where I was working, an old felt hat on his
head, a pipe in his mouth, eyes that were set wide apart,
young middle age, looking at me bringing the rotovator
down the hill then reversing upwards, my foot on the
metal cover to keep it from lurching the handlebars high
from my grasp. He would watch and say nothing, chewing

the stem of his pipe; and then weeks later I would be in some pub, and I would be told: 'I hear that that there rotovator brings all the soil down bottom of meadow.' I do not agree that this view was right; but it made me aware that Joe as he meandered from his own particular world so near the sea, was watching and judging me as I bent the ways of the clinical present to better the integrity of the past; and so I, too, watched and listened.

Joe used to bicycle to the cliffs from his home with Bish his bull terrier trotting at the wheel; and when Bish grew old Joe carried him on the handlebars. Like all his breed Bish was a fierce protector of his owner and of his owner's belongings and as we shared the same hut there were often occasions when Bish would not allow us to enter. The hut was known as the Pink Hut because it was built of corrugated-iron once painted a red which had faded to pink over the years; and as its main function was for the 'shooting' of potatoes it was so designed inside that layer upon layer of boards could be fixed, each layer rising above another which had received its quota of potato seed. Joe had one half of the hut with its boards, we had the other; and there were times when we wanted to use our half when only Bish was resident in the other. Then Bish, so friendly when nothing of his owner's was threatened, would bare his teeth, snarl, bellow, and frighten us into cupping hands to mouth and shouting downwards towards the seat: 'Joe! Joe! Come up will you? Bish won't let us in!' There would be an answering cry like the hoot of an owl, and in a few minutes Joe would slowly arrive, and Bish would wag his tail and grin at us and apologize.

Joe accepted wild life, not as some countrymen do with the object to kill, but as a means of sharing enjoyment. He hated trapping and when on one occasion he was instructed to do so, he found the next morning in one of the traps a badger. A badger is notoriously, and for obvious reasons, a deadly dangerous animal to release from a trap; and a trapper, if for no other reason except his personal safety, will make certain he has killed it before there is any question of touching it. Not so Joe. He was grievously upset when he found the badger struggling to escape as he walked along the field towards it; and he decided the only thing he could do was momentarily to stun it, then quickly release the foot from the trap. He picked up a stick and hit it, and the badger lay still. Ten minutes later it was still lying there, breathing but without any other signs of life; and so Joe picked it up in his arms, a heavy full grown badger, and carried it gently to the Pink Hut.

I came to the hut later in the morning when Joe was having his tea break, and found the badger lying on a bed of sacks, with another sack so folded that it acted as a pillow. Bish was quiet in another corner, Joe puffing his pipe. 'I hit it too hard,' he said to me sadly after he had told me what had happened, 'that's what I did. I hit it too hard.'

Jeannie and I were, at the time, 'shooting' potatoes and this tedious task kept us for hour upon hour in the hut. This gave us the advantage of keeping an eye on the patient as it lay there. It was early in the afternoon over twenty-four hours later that it stirred, an eye opened, and it whimpered. A badger is beautiful to look at in its true setting, a wild path of its own treading, the moon lighting the white streaks of its head, dark shadows its armour; but lying there in the hut, impotent without our help, a heavy immovable body, its appeal was not in its mobility but the common denominator of suffering. I went outside and down the mountain-like track to where Joe was digging. 'It's coming round,' I said. The smile was one of relief rather than pleasure. 'It is?' and he jabbed his shovel into the ground and came back with me to the hut.

The badger was a patient for six weeks, and every day Joe fed him with bread and milk, then when he got stronger shared his sandwiches. Bish was quite unconcerned and showed no jealousy, and the badger in his turn seemed to accept Bish; and then came the time when the badger, gaining confidence, remembering freedom, began to show restlessness. 'To my way of thinking,' said Joe, 'it won't be long before he's ready to go.' In this he was correct but he did not foresee the manner of his going.

At week-ends, while Joe remained at home, Jeannie and I used to take over as nurses, and one Sunday evening we fed him as usual, saw that he was comfortable, and shut up the hut. I was first back there in the morning and when I had opened the door, a glance was enough to show the badger had gone. The floorboards had been ripped from the centre of the hut as if a man had been at work with a pickaxe, and as there was only soil underneath, it was then easy for the badger to rejoin the wild where he belonged.

Joe used to refer to each meadow as a garden. 'That garden by the quarry is frosty,' he would say. Or: 'I've dug three hundredweight from this garden before May month . . . handsome samples.'

I was in this particular garden one November afternoon during this first year we rented Pentewan, grimly pursuing my task of rotovating the ground. Machines, when seen in a catalogue, appear to perform their duties magically on their own; and if there is a picture of the operator, a broad grin on his face suggests his presence is only a formality. Perhaps it is when the ground is level, but at both Minack and Pentewan the meadows are steep and contracted; and an hour with the rotovator leaves the body pommelled and aching as if it had been stretched on the rack.

The rotovator works the ground downhill and in order

to keep the tines deep in the soil, it is necessary to weight the body on the handlebars, at the same time being prepared to lift it if you get warning of an under-the-soil rock. When you return to the top of the meadow you disengage the rotovator, then put the engine in reverse; but in order to control the machine, to prevent the handlebars shooting skywards, you have to do this job by pressing one foot on the cover of the rotovator while hopping backwards on the other; and at all times your arms are also having to force the handlebars downwards. The job is a punishment, a self-inflicted torture which awaits its compensation only when all the land is rotovated, and you rustle the sweet knowledge in your mind that you have achieved in a week what a labourer with a shovel would have done in eight. The pain was repeated twice a year, first in the autumn and then when the potatoes were being planted, the second occasion, of course, enabling the shoveller to dig through the soil at great speed; but it is a November afternoon that I am remembering in a garden that Joe once prized as one of his best. As I performed my routine, the engine roaring, my limbs craving for rest, I saw John in the distance with a pair of horses ploughing the field that edged Pentewan and his own.

At the time, he and I were not on speaking terms, and although he had to come Minack way almost every day to collect his horses or pass on down to his cliffs, he never spoke; and when sometimes in a flush of trying to be friends again I wished him good day, my wish was left to hang alone in the air. On this occasion I observed that when he and his horses reached the end of the field and were ready to turn, he would wait a moment or two, and stare across in my direction. His action irritated me, little realizing how fortunate, in a few minutes, it would prove to be.

But I was irritated because I had an uncomfortable feeling that he was not wishing me well; he resented our presence at Minack because he did not consider that we belonged there, and he smouldered with vexation that the roughness of the life had not driven us away. Now we had the Pentewan meadows we had become entrenched. He himself would like to have had them. What right had we to move in and collect such a prize?

Physical effort that demands great strain, I have found, creates a pattern of twisted thoughts, the mind is a daytime nightmare, and while the body is being pounded with exhaustion the brain races with a kaleidoscopic jungle of ideas. Such was the course of my thinking as I grimly continued my labour and when, suddenly, while I was reversing, a wheel hit a rock and the machine lurched sideways.

At the same time the catch which disengaged the rotovator slipped out of position and the tines began circulating with great speed. The handlebars shot up skywards and in this instant of my loss of control, my left foot which had been weighting the rotovator cover was twisted under the cover and met the full force of the tines. The next thing I knew was that the machine had turned on its side, the engine had spluttered to a stop, and the tines ceased circulating because my foot and part of my leg was wrapped round the shaft under the cover.

Tommy, I knew, was in a meadow within shouting distance alongside the Pink Hut. I yelled and there was no answer. 'Tommy!' I shouted again. 'Tommy! Tommy! Tommy!' Heavens knows what he was doing, perhaps drowning my cries with some of his own. I lay there immovable, the weight of the tractor on my leg while my foot, I began to realize, was oozing wet in my rubber Wellington boot.

The shock of the accident was now replaced by panic. There was every reason to suppose that no one would hear me; Joe, I knew, was in one of his gardens close to the sea while Tommy, if in one of his moods, might well have his mind and ears in another world. I was beginning to have pain. 'Tommy! Tommy! *Tommy*!' I was reaching that hazy, never-never land which heralds a faint when suddenly I heard the beat of running footsteps to the left of me. I twisted my head around and through the grass which brushed my face I saw John.

'All right, mate . . . lie still, I'll get the tractor off you.' He had the strength of a bull and he heaved up the tractor as if it had the weight of a wooden chair . . . but, as the tractor became upright, so it became clear that my foot was hooked on a tine like a joint on a butcher's hook; the point had gone through one side of my foot and out of the other.

'If you could find Tommy,' I said, 'he could go over and fetch Mrs Tangye and get bandages.' John gave me a cigarette, then disappeared; and a few minutes later returned with a scared Tommy who went off across the fields to Minack. I soon found that I could not begin to free my foot until the boot was cut away, and this John proceeded to do, sawing away with a blunt pen-knife at the rubber. It was several minutes before he was successful and by that time my principal anxiety was that Jeannie might arrive while I was still trapped. Unfortunately when the machine turned over and the engine stopped, the rotovator was stalled in gear; and because of the position of the tine that held my foot, my foot could not possibly be freed until the rotovator shaft had been turned several inches. It would not budge.

'You'll have to rock the machine, John,' I said, 'there's nothing else for it.'

At any moment Jeannie would be appearing over the hedge, and I could not bear the thought of her seeing me.

'Rock it to and fro,' I said, 'I often do it when it stalls after getting a stone jammed in the tines.'

He rocked it gently, my leg moving in rhythm, and suddenly the shaft was free. John's cap was pushed on the back of his head, his face was red, the Woodbine dangled out of the corner of his mouth.

'Now be careful, mate,' he said, 'take yer time with the foot.'

It was an occasion when you do not pause to think, for thinking would bring inaction. I noted the shape of the hook, the way it was pointing, the direction I would have to thrust my leg. It was easy. My foot freed itself at the very instant that a startled Jeannie arrived with water, basin, bandages and iodine.

'John here,' I said, looking at Jeannie and aware that he would not want me to show gratitude, 'John got me out of this mess.'

Chapter Eleven

I WAS IN BED for a fortnight and on crutches or hobbling with a stick for a further six weeks.

Perhaps I should have taken the accident as an omen. What does a shipowner say to himself if a mishap occurs to a new vessel at the moment of launching? I was brought up on the comforting philosophy that single mindedness, a dogged determination to succeed at some specific task inevitably led to conquest; and hence, I remember, I spent hour after hour, week after week, bowling by myself at the nets when I was at Harrow under the misapprehension that it was the road to the Eleven.

That I was laughed at was part of the test, and that I ignored this was part of the philosophy. It is a useful philosophy in the armoury of schoolmasters because boys without talent believe they can gain the same rewards as those who have, and those who have talent are lured to make the most use of it. As far as I am concerned the philosophy has lingered in its influence; and the result has been that, although I have often failed to gain the objectives which from the beginning I had no chance of gaining, my efforts have often brought unexpected but pleasurable rewards. Thus, although I am superstitious enough to be wary of Friday the thirteenth and of walking under ladders, and always feel happier if a black cat crosses my path, I consider omens as incidents to forget however moodily I may greet them. Had I shied from Pentewan as a consequence of my accident Jeannie and I would have been spared countless laborious hours and, for that matter, considerable expense; but we would never have tasted the subleties of the reward for staying.

Obstinacy is, of course, both a virtue and a fault, and the art lies in identifying the dividing line; and in this tussle of identification you can be called courageous one moment, a fool the next, and brilliant the one after that – if your objective has been achieved.

Our particular obstinacy at Pentewan was to heave our energy and enthusiasm against the weather, and every time it knocked us out, to bob up again, roll up our shirt-sleeves and defy it once more. You cannot treat the weather that way. It always wins. It obliterates a thousand hours of effort in a night, with the same abandoned power of a finger smudging a mosquito on a window-pane.

Should we have packed up after the first wail of defeat? We met a little barrel of an old man in a pub shortly after we had taken over the meadows who for many years had worked the selfsame meadows himself. 'Expect,' he said, in a piping voice, 'a bumper harvest once in every four years.' He did not intend to be gloomy. He was giving the glad news that we would make so much money in one year that it would not matter what happened in the other three. Old men of the countryside appear to novices as oracles; as if the lines on their faces, the horizon look in their eyes, the slow motion of their movements harken a confidence within you that echoes your belief in the Prophets. Thus each time the weather struck we revived ourselves with the words of high promise: 'Expect a bumper harvest in every four years . . .'

We needed, however, that good harvest the first year;

and our optimism excited us to expect it. It was indeed vital that it should be a good one. The hazy honeymoon with escapism was being replaced by the conventional necessities of day to day existence, our commitments were increasing, our reserves dwindling. We took on Pentewan knowing it would vastly increase our expenses, but saying to ourselves that if we planned with vision, courage and care, all we would then require would be to have luck on our side; for endeavour, however painstakingly pursued, can rarely receive its accolade unless a magic bestows it.

Yet we were aware that there was something else at stake besides material victory; there was the continuing challenge to prove that we were not flirting with the tedium of manual labour, that our enthusiasm had not been checked by reverses or by the roughness of the life, that we possessed staying power which could earn respect. It was a simple ambition and some would call it a valueless one, but within it there was the prospect of peace of mind born of permanence. There is no permanence in the conventional ambitions that hasten you up the pyramid of power, each step killing one ambition and creating another, leading you by a noose to a pinnacle where, too late, you look back on the trampled path and find the yearning within you is the same as when you were young.

We knew, therefore, that we could not impose ourselves on the countryside but had to be absorbed by it, creating by our efforts an intangible strength that became an element of the beauty, of the wildness, and of the peace around us; and we would then begin to feel and to see the gossamer secrets that are for ever hidden from the casual passer-by. I was about twelve when my father took me to see an old man who lived in a cottage in the woods near Bodmin; why we went or who he was I do not remember; but I remember the untamed setting and how, when we went inside, what seemed to be a cluster of birds flew out of the window. I was disappointed because I had never known birds in a house before, and I wanted to see them flying around.

'Will they come back?' I asked. 'Not till you have gone, I'm afraid,' said the old man, 'you see I've been here a long time and I am accepted like that old fir tree out there.' The incident has always been to me a lesson in living.

My foot had recovered when the time came for planting the potatoes . . . eight tons of them. It had been a mammoth task in the first place, when they arrived at the end of October, to put them away ends up; partly in the Pink Hut and partly at Minack, and as I for most of the time was out of action, the tedious job was shared between Jeannie and Tommy. They were an incongruous couple to be together and I awaited expectantly at home her report on their latest conversation.

'Tommy is in one of his silent moods,' she would say, 'hasn't said a word all morning.' Or: 'Tommy's bought a camera and he's spent the afternoon telling me how he's going to take pictures through his telescope.' Or: 'Tommy's in a terrible state. The police called on him yesterday evening. The camera he bought was a stolen one!' Or: 'Tommy wants us to get a portable tent which he can take along with him as he goes on working in the rain!'

Tommy was undismayed by the quantity of potatoes we were planting, and on one occasion as he was silently putting them away he suddenly roared with laughter.

'What's funny?' asked Jeannie. 'Just you think,' he answered, 'what they are going to say when they see all these going off to the station!' He was foreseeing the harvest, and 'they' were John and any of his previous bosses. 'They won't like it,' he added, 'won't like it at all!'

Tommy was sensitive to the cost of the venture as I had

warned him that we would have to take at least £500 before we showed any profit, and that the profit would have to be large enough to pay for our keep and his, for another six months in any case. As a result he became very concerned with the rats which penetrated through the floorboards of the Pink Hut and of the mice which entered the Minack potato hut. 'Every potato they damage,' he said earnestly, 'means a half-crown thrown away next summer . . . we must have poison down all the time.'

Sometimes, mild as the climate may generally be, we have bitter cold snaps which catch us unawares and the frost bites inside the potato huts; as a result some of the potatoes are either squashed into uselessness or are 'chilled,' which means they will never grow a full crop. One night Jeannie and I had gone to bed when we heard a knock at the door, followed by Tommy's stentorian voice. 'I've come to tell you it's freezing!' He had walked a mile from his caravan to warn us, and to help us carry the paraffin heaters to the potato huts.

It was, however, a comparatively mild winter and we were able to start planting early in January and carry on, except when it was wet, for day after day until all eight tons were in the ground by the first week in March. We had prepared the soil according to advice from the experts; heavily liming the Pentewan soil in the autumn because the analysis showed it had not been given any lime in years; and dressing each meadow as we came to plant it with a compound chemical fertilizer. Our allotted tasks were for Jeannie to cut the potatoes and fill the baskets, Tommy to shovel them in, while I rotovated a piece of ground ahead of Tommy, carried the baskets from the hut to the meadow concerned, and dropped the potatoes in the drill Tommy had opened up.

These tasks may seem straightforward, but they caused

arguments. We were so anxious now that we had suddenly become big potato growers to perform the planting according to the best advice available that we confused ourselves with a plethora of advisers. We were soon told, for instance, that we should be using fish manure and not the compound fertilizer of which we had bought two tons.

'You want body in this ground, not chemicals,' said one esteemed farmer of the neighbourhood. This worry, however, had come too late to concern us; and we consoled ourselves with remembering the opposite view of the agricultural adviser who told us that chemicals were the only fertilizer for the early crop as they acted so much more quickly. Next came the pros and cons about cutting the potatoes. Then the question of space intervals in planting, and how much soil should cover the potatoes. As in other more important matters, the experts contradicted each other. Cut each potato in as many pieces as there are shoots, was the advice of one old farmer who had grown potatoes in the district for thirty years. His neighbour, on the other hand, asserted with equal confidence that potatoes should not on any account be cut, unless the planting was in March. Plant them seven inches apart and fifteen inches between the rows said one; plant them twelve inches apart and eighteen inches between the rows said another. Cover them with plenty of soil, cover them so there is only a shallow layer above the shoots. The opposites briskly met each other and left us bewildered referees.

It is easy to understand that the more you cut the potatoes, the more plants you will have as a result; and thus greed encouraged us to cut them. But the anti-cutters maintained that a cut potato produced a vulnerable plant, a plant that had no reserve to fall back on if it were pulverized by a frost or lambasted by a gale . . . and Pentewan, its meadows lying facing the threatening sweep of the sea, suffered constantly the prospect of obliteration.

'Ah,' said an old pro-cutter appearing to be wise, 'it all depends on weather.'

This wisdom also applied to the advantages and disadvantages of shallow planting. A potato likes to be near the surface of the ground to bask in the warmth of an early spring sun and, in times of dry weather to drink the benefits of dews and light showers.

'But,' said a saturnine farmer, 'I've known all shallow planted potatoes be rotted because of a freeze-up.'

Thus, it seemed, the gods had to be on your side if you engaged in cutting or shallow planting, and Jeannie and I were not prepared to trust them. We would play for safety. We would cut only the biggest of potatoes, and we would cover them liberally with soil; but there was still the question of space intervals in planting.

We were, in any case, concerned as to whether we had enough cultivated land for our eight tons; and so the variation between the theories of space intervals in planting were important to us. The difference, for instance, between a seven inch space interval and a twelve inch, would mean that the latter would require nearly twice as much land; and then there was still the difference of fifteen or eighteen inches between rows to worry about. Such closeness of planting is a joke to the normal potato grower who expects to have two feet between the rows and perhaps eighteen inches between each potato; but on the cliff it is different. The pundits declare that the more closely the potatoes are planted, the more likely they are to protect each other because the green tops sway in a solid phalanx in a gale, instead of each green top being whipped on its own; and that in a period of drought, the shadow of the leaves hides the sun from the moisture which is in the soil.

Jeannie and I listened to the profusion of advice like foreign students at an English lecture; we made notes, held discussions, but in the end felt lost because experience could be the only interpreter. Nobody seemed to know what were the best methods. There was no standard law. Each season had different growing conditions. Every section of the cliff had a special character of its own; and even the meadows had individual personalities.

'It takes a bit of time to get to know them,' said Joe glumly to me one day, 'and half a meadow is sometimes different to the other half.'

Thus, it appeared, old meadows were as temperamental as human beings; and ours at Pentewan, time seemed to prove, were like overworked clerks in need of a holiday. They were exhausted. After a hundred years of hard labour in producing potatoes, they chose to rebel when Jeannie and I arrived as their masters. The soil was sick of potatoes and wanted a rest; but we in our innocence believed they were the mirror of our future prosperity, and when I dropped the last potato of the eight tons behind Tommy's shovel I celebrated. I was now a big grower, probably the largest grower of cliff potatoes west of Penzance, and I mused happily over my succulent objective – the Cornish new potatoes which would surprise the townsmen like the advent of fresh garden peas, bringing us the cash which would ensure security.

Jeannie holds the view that the pleasantest part of the growing season is when the land has just been ploughed, or a crop just planted. Then there is nothing to worry about, the soil looks clean and rich and the mind is full of comfortable calculations of the prosperity to come. It was in this mood that we surveyed our handywork of the past two months and each day, wresting time from daffodil bunching, we toured the meadows with Monty trotting

along with us. Gradually we began to notice the green
buttons bursting out of the soil, and we started to use the
language of potato growers: 'The meadow below the gate
is in rows' or 'The meadow above the Pink Hut looks
backward.'

The Minack meadows had been the first to be planted
and thus the first to be peppered with green but the
Pentewan meadows, aided by the extra hour of the sun
they received as they stared south towards the Wolf Rock,
were quick to catch up. Soon, in the ideal mild weather,
the plants were growing so fast that the pundits were
talking of the earliest potato season on record; and Jeannie
and I rejoiced that it seemed we were scheduled for beginner's luck. John was happy enough to smile and volunteer
good mornings, and Joe's boss – the farmer who rented us
Pentewan – forgot his quiet self and made jokes. There
was a pleasant camaraderie on the cliffs, and confidence
that all would share unenviously in the prosperity ahead.

One afternoon, it was Thursday March 27th, we heard a
chiff-chaff making its monotonous call, the first of the
year, the wonder of its African journey transferred to
Minack woods; and it gave us the cool pleasure of confidence in ourselves and our surroundings. The cry followed us: 'Chiff Chaff! Chiff Chaff!' – and the sound of its
limited note, amid trees pinking with buds, moss brighten-
ing with growth on old rocks, primroses a secret ecstasy
unless unexpectedly discovered, pools of ragged robin and
bluebells ... the sound of its limited note derided the
tyranny of the automaton age and the warped values that
advance the putrid aims of the dodgers of truth, the cynical
commentators of the passing scene, the purveyors of mass
inertia. The dull two notes of the tiny bird trumpeted
defiance of the fake and the slick, bringing to the shadows
in the woods the expanse of its own achievement; until the
sound

gently entered the evening, and as night fell, hid among the trees.

It was suddenly cold, and as I came back from shutting up the chickens a sudden breeze hit the branches above my head, a sharp thrust from the east. Indoors Jeannie was stirring soup on the stove while Monty was behaving as if scissors were after his tail and dinosaurs awaiting his pounce.

'What on earth's wrong with Monty tonight?' And I bent down and tried to pick him up. He darted to the door and when I moved to open it, rushed to the sofa, forking his claws in the side raking the material, and earning a 'Shut up, Monty!' from Jeannie. There was a sound outside as if a car was driving up to the cottage. 'Listen,' I said, and we paused, tense. 'It's a plane,' said Jeannie, relieved. There it was again, a rushing, moaning sound. 'It isn't,' I answered knowledgeably, 'it's the wind.'

It was the sound of the scouts, the fingers of the wind, stretching ahead probing the hills and woods, the rocks and hedges, the old cottages, the lonely trees acting as sentinels of the land. They probe and jab, searching for

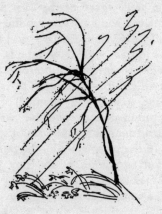

flying leaves, decaying branches ready to fall, for flowers youthfully in bloom, for the green swath of the potato tops; and finding, they rush on searching for more, magnificently confident that the majesty of the gale which follows will crush and pound and obliterate. And when they have gone there is an instant of stillness to remind you of a quiet evening, the passing assurance of a safe world, and you wait; you wait and wonder if you were wrong and the wind is innocent; you listen, your mind peeling across the green meadows whose defences are impotent; then suddenly the slap of the face and the braying hounds of hell and the heaving mountain of maniacal power.

Chapter Twelve

THE GALE ROARED without pause till the afternoon of March 29th, vicious, friendless and with frost in its scream; here was man as helpless as the foam on the rocks, centuries of rising conceit contemptuously humbled, the joke of the tempest. Action was masochistic. We struggled heads down as if fighting a way through invisible jungle grass, buffeted, pushed back, soundless in our shouting, kneeling to the ground to gape at a meadow in its progress towards obliteration, then hustled home as if our coats were kites, running without effort, feathers in air.

We sat and waited. The vapid wait, droning the hours away with our fears, calculating losses, listening to the ships' waveband as vessels neared Land's End ('I don't fancy going round the corner'), unknown voices sharing our company, leaping to the window when the noise for a second abated, hearing the sea hissing like a coastline of cobras, sleeping with demons in our dreams. Waiting, waiting, waiting. And when it was over, when our ears were still humming with the beating drums of fury and the sea still heaved in mud-grey valleys, we went out into an afternoon that had suddenly become as caressing as a summer's day; as if a lost temper had been replaced by shame and the cost of havoc was being guiltily assessed.

The Minack meadows were a pattern of black stumps; in

pocket-size havens the wind had entered like a tornado, and there were gaps where not even stumps were to be seen. At Pentewan the army of green, the plants the size of cabbages had become a foot-high petrified forest drooping in the sunshine like melting black candles. Black also was the grass on the banks, filmed as if with tar, and the stinging nettles which once taunted us to scythe them down; and here and there wild daffodils stared forlornly with petals shredded into tea-stained strips; or with necks broken, their heads drooped against the stems like victims of the gallows. The desolation looked up at the blue sky and the fleck of a lark singing. A magpie flew by coarsely chattering, and for a second I saw a fox silhouetted on a rock above the quarry. A boat chugged by outward bound to the fishing grounds beyond the Isles of Scilly, and we looked down at the men on deck as if we were on a hill and they in a valley. Normality was returning even if the thrash of the whip was still in our ears; ideas began to form, the warm challenge born of disaster quickened our minds, the sense of comradeship which frays in tedious defeat but sharpens in sudden defeat, became exhilarated, and I greeted Joe as if victory was our companion.

He was standing gloomily by the Pink Hut at the head of the path that corkscrewed steeply downwards to the sea, wearing his mildewed green trilby, an unlit pipe in his mouth and incongruously an old telescope slung from his shoulder. Bish was at his feet and she wagged white body and tail as I approached, whimpering a greeting.

'Does a gale like this often happen?' I asked with mock humour. Joe, after all, had been part of this cliff for seventeen years and he would have the answer to the permutation of emergencies.

'I've known nothing like it,' he said glumly, then grinned as if this might be a shield against the consequences, and went on: 'Coming so late with taties up like that they'll never recover . . . I don't think so, not in time at any rate.'

The tone in which he spoke sent a chill through me. Up to then my instincts had been charging me to get to grips with retrieving the disaster by discovering what wise old farmers would do and by energetically putting their proposals into effect. As simple as that. It was a setback not a finality, and means were available, if I could learn about them, which would put things right. But Joe had talked about time, and time had not entered into my calculations.

Now I suddenly saw that time was the vital factor in any recovery. The cliff no longer held the advantage over the inland potato growers stretching up the country to the great potato areas of Lincolnshire. The cliff potatoes would have to pause, summon strength to send out new shoots, push out into a second cluster of leaves . . . and all this before there could be any question of making actual potatoes. Instead of being ahead they would be behind in the race. The inland potatoes would be still underground or just breaking through, and thus they would continue to grow with the speed which comes of normality; and the avalanche of their harvest would crush the markets while the cliff was still being jabbed with shovels. The prospect scared me.

During the following days inland farmers roamed the cliff in the same way some people like to visit and stare at the scene of an accident. They were solicitous, but one suspected their sudden appearance was connected with assessing how our misfortune might result in their good fortune. They got on Tommy's nerves. 'Serve 'em right,' he snorted, 'if they have hard frost after Buryan feast.'

Feast Day was the second Sunday in May and it was traditional that frost could be expected up to that date but not afterwards; and so Tommy was wishing them ill at a time when their potatoes would be at the same advanced stage as ours had been. But Tommy's personal chip of revenge was no reply to the predicament with which we were faced. We had gambled so heavily on the prospect of a harvest with handsome returns that failure inevitably would drain the last of our capital reserves. We would either have to return to London or Tommy would have to go, and leave us to carry on with the work on our own. It was the kind of situation which lies naggingly at the back of your mind but which you refuse to accept seriously while an element of hope still exists; and both Jeannie and I could not believe that such total defeat was possible. Our armour was our enthusiasm and, just as useful, our ignorance. We were, therefore, both determined to attack the next few weeks as if energy provided the certainty of victory.

But there was little we could do. Convalescence cannot be successful overnight, nor can plants grow with the speed of those in a nature film; and the only action we could take was to dose the meadows with nitro-chalk. Among potato growers nitro-chalk is considered a menace by some and a blessing by others. Its purpose is that of a pep pill and given convenient conditions such as warm and damp weather, the effect begins to show within a fortnight by veining the leaves with dark green; thus strength enters the leaves which, on reaching maturity, return it to the developing potatoes. This description sounds like the alluring advertisement of a quack medicine, and it possesses in degree the same deception; for the success of nitro-chalk depends on conditions over which you have little control at the time of sowing. Moreover, and this is the chief objection against it, nitro-chalk though increasing the size of the crop does so at the expense of making it later. Thus if a spell of dry weather follows the time of sowing before rain comes to wash it in, the crop will be later than ever.

'I wouldn't use it if I were you,' said one. 'I'd certainly sow nitre,' said another. My final decision was based on the fact the plants looked so battered and terrible that I felt compelled to take some kind of action to help them; and, as it happened, that was the only satisfaction I had. The nitro-chalk on this occasion provided no sudden elixir of potato life; and to prove it there were two meadows side by side one of which had received its quota of nitro-chalk, while the other had been spared it. Six weeks later the tops of both were still the size of mushrooms, and by this time the grim fact had emerged that the harvest would resemble that of peas rather than potatoes. The plants had been unable to recover, not even our caution in leaving the seed uncut had been able to save them.

We had, however, an ace up our sleeves. It is an obvious calculation that the sum total of man hours required to dig potatoes is the same if there is one man at work or four. Thus one man would take four hours to perform a task which would take four men an hour; and so the pursuit of this idea inevitably led us to the tempting prospect that if we were able to engage two men to help us, the harvest would be cleared in half the time it would take Tommy and myself; and that more extra men would further reduce the time in proportion. Thus, according to this theory, we still had a chance to save the situation by disposing of our miserable harvest when the price was still high; and it could mean, we argued cheerfully to ourselves, that we could take just as much money as with a crop twice the size but half the price.

Our neighbours, however, did not agree with these views. They never had spent any money on extra labour and they were not going to do so now. It was an attitude that pleased us. It gave us an understandable source of contentment that we had a chance to show our teachers that we had the intelligence to cope with a crisis. The problem was, however, where to find the men to help us.

It was now that we had a stroke of luck. We remembered the miners from St Just, Jack and Maurice, who had dug us the well, and off we went to see them.

St Just is a solid town which revolves around the Geevor tin mines and spreads a spider's web of grey cottages with the square as its centre, the sea on one side, and the wild hilly moorland on the others. It is unique for a town of its size in that it is five miles from the nearest railway station, Penzance, and this fact, along with the Atlantic fogs which sweep through the streets in winter, seems to exude a sturdy self-sufficiency among its inhabitants. They are tough, reliable, kind, and aim to see a good day's work performed before they add up the money which rewards it.

Jack and Maurice promptly agreed to help but they would only be able to do so between shifts at Geevor. They therefore proposed they should organize a succession of miners, and that by running a shuttle service in the Land Rover we would collect and return them at times to dovetail with each shift. Thus we could if we so wished collect one group at eight in the morning after the night shift, another at three in the afternoon after the early morning shift, and another at six in the evening after the day shift, the latter working on till dusk. We were also able to engage a retired miner called Willie and a postman, Eddie, both of whom were ready to come full time – the latter taking his annual holiday specially to do so. This galaxy of manpower so excited Jeannie and myself that we marvelled with gratitude that the fates should so generously come to our rescue.

Within a week we had cleared the Minack cliff, sent away five tons and had grossed £250. We were up to schedule both on time and price. But the tight little meadows restricted the use of our full labour force, and only Willie, Eddie, Jack and Maurice provided the extra help. It was a scouting force compared to the army to come, and which proceeded to descend on the larger, sloping meadows of Pentewan.

I now had what I thought was an excellent idea. The method of gathering potatoes in a field is for a tractor to drive its length while the pickers-up are each given a station of perhaps twenty yards for which they are responsible. I decided to adjust this method to the meadow. I fixed the plough and the large wheels on my hand-controlled tractor, gave each miner a station, then grimly drove the machine in such a way that the plough tipped each row to one side where hands seized the tops, shook them, and picked up the potatoes.

It was a method suitable for a flat field, but I had chosen meadows that were square, oblong, round, steep in one direction then in another, with rocks as obstacles, requiring strength and ingenuity even to get the tractor with its large wheels to enter them. Obstinately I stuck to my task, stripped to the waist, my hands ripped with blisters, my body aching with fatigue, dazedly going on and on in the belief that I was the instrument of speed.

It was a delusion. The tractor broke down and when, in its place, shovels were used, the primitive once again proved its superiority over the modern. Two shovellers each took a row, and racing each other up the meadow, they tossed the plants to one side, leaving the rest of us to scramble our hands through the soil bruising our fingers against the stones, chaffing each other with mock accusations.

'Hey, Eddie, have you gone home?' meaning that he had been slower to pick up than the rest of us. Or if a shoveller had sliced a few potatoes as he thrust up the meadow, 'We've got the chips, Willie, so now you'd better catch the fish.' The forced jokes which come with monotonous tasks, remarks which are contrived to bolster minds and bodies which are tiring. 'Dick's in love . . . that's why he's leaving them all behind.' 'Them' being potatoes and Dick being a hunk of a miner who had just got engaged. Long silences, then inconsequent comments on sport. 'Good boy Peter May . . . he's a good boy Peter.'

Periodically Jeannie would appear with tea, cakes and sandwiches, heavy loads which she carried over from Minack, balancing them as if they were jewels while she clambered over the hedges; then a break for everyone, and afterwards Jeannie would join the pickers-up, in shorts, with delicate hands and quicker than any of them. A group had to go back to Geevor and another collected. 'Don't you ever need sleep?' I'd say. 'Well we can last till Saturday.' Tough, cheerful, unsparing in their willingness to help, I felt a tiring sadness that the rarity of their unstinting capacity of giving was tainted by the inevitability of failure.

The price had begun to drop. 'What is it today?' one of them would ask. 'Gone down to thirty-five,' I would answer, and there would be silence; and although they would be getting their pay at the end of the day, such was their rugged, honest independence that they did not feel at peace that they should gain and we should lose.

Jeannie and I became unaware of days and nights, we blazed with the fanatic's zeal to remove every potato from Pentewan in time . . . we were up at dawn to weigh and address the bags, then one of us would collect the first group from St Just, then load up the Land Rover two or three times until yesterday's digging had been driven to the place where Carbis, the St Buryan carrier, would load them on his lorry and take them to the station. Waiting for the post and prices, tea and sandwiches, drive a group back to St Just and collect another, more tea and sandwiches, another drive to St Just, then in the evening rough cider with the sandwiches and jokes afterwards: 'Maurice is seeing so many double taties that he can't pick up one.' Then back to St Just with the last group, and because we were both very tired we would go together.

We were aware soon after beginning Pentewan that we were doomed. Minack meadows had survived in some degree because they were new, the soil was fresh to production and had reserves to face the wound from the slash of a knife, but those at Pentewan were like tired old men who saw no virtue in fighting nor possessed the capacity for doing so. The crop almost uniformly was the size of marbles; and when the shovellers had disposed of a meadow and I looked up in my record book to compare the seed potatoes we had planted and the harvest we had gathered, I found it more comforting to keep the information to myself.

Yet speed might still save us. Jeannie and I clung to the belief that time was our ally, that our town-inspired briskly intelligent ideas would outweigh the true facts. We maintained the illusion until one night, after returning the last of our friends to St Just, we called in on the way home at a pub whose outward fame is its name, The First and Last (pub in Britain), but whose inward fame was provided by the Lancashire brothers who had kept it for twenty-five years. 'You've heard the news?' said Jesse Fox, one of the brothers, as I raised my glass, 'taties have hit the floor. They're £6 a ton at Bristol.'

Next morning I looked at Tommy when he arrived, the old shabby clothes, the faded Panama hat, and I said to myself: 'Why does he look so distinguished? It would be so much easier if he looked sour and bad tempered.' He performed the motions of his job seemingly unaware that his time with us was at an end. I delayed. When it was all over and Eddie and Willie, Maurice, Jack and our passing friends like Tommy May, nightwatchman at Geevor and collector of sea debris by day, and Dick and all the others . . . when I had said goodbye to all these, I was faced with the vacuum of telling Tommy Williams that his time with us was over.

I had braved myself to do so when, as I was leaving the cottage, a man arrived whom I had casually met a few days before. He was a brisk, efficient young man possessed with the certainty that his current opinions would secure his advancement. He was like hail on a summer's day, and as I watched him, uninvited, undo his knapsack, then heard him say: 'It's quite all right, don't worry about me, I've got my own sandwiches' . . . I felt only too ready to brain him.

But, and this was the irritation of the occasion, there was a security about his behaviour which mocked the unreasonableness of our own. He represented sense and an arid existence, while Jeannie and I had nothing to show him or anyone else except an intangible happiness. Thus, unknowingly, he provided me with an angry brashness, a reaction to his own normality, when at last I saw Tommy and said I could not pay him any more. 'I knew that was coming,' he said, and his eyes were looking far out over Mount's Bay; 'I'll go back to Birmingham where I was for a time during the war. I'll get a good job there in Birmingham Parks.'

He was down the bottom of the cliff when I told him, and I had a long way up to walk with the knowledge that an unpleasant task had been achieved. I did not feel despair but anger, as if the zest which had led us to the kind of life we had chosen had been stung into fury by conformism pirouetting in self-justification. Ah, you fool, I heard voices mocking, you should have stayed with the herd, the herd breathes safely in the expanse of the plains, its thoughts locked in convention, moving through time sheltered in the security of dullness. The herd does not look for trouble as you have done. The herd is content, it is not greedy like you.

I climbed slowly up the cliff path and found Jeannie waiting for me at the top. 'He took it very well,' I said, 'he's going to sell his caravan and go north. He says he's certain to get a job with what he calls Birmingham Parks.' I spoke with assurance as if I were certain that Tommy was thankful his mind had been made up for him. 'It's funny,' I added, 'but I've always had an idea he hankered after Birmingham Parks and he's only stayed with us because of a queer notion it meant scoring a revenge over the farmers he detested.'

Jeannie did not reply and we began to walk arm in arm up the field towards the cottage. The silence hurt both of us. We had been consumed by the mission I had just fulfilled, and now we were left with thoughts that frightened us. We had not only lost our gamble, but were faced with retrieving its cost without anyone to help us. We had

not bargained for failure when we left London, and its arrival, the sudden barefacedness of its arrival, brought unbearable depression.

And then, just as we gloomily reached the old stone stable and the slope which led up to the cottage, Jeannie suddenly said in a voice that sounded as if our problems had been solved: 'Look! There's a gull on the roof!'

Chapter Thirteen

THE GULL ON the roof is called Hubert. He joined Monty as a witness of our endeavour and the pleasure that has come with it. He watched us fight back at Minack working for a year on our own. He saw us beginning to succeed then rushed by the elements into retreat, then forward again. He is old now, his feathers have lost their sheen, and when he gathers himself to fly away he is like a rheumaticky old man shuffling to rise from an armchair.

He was old when he arrived, or so we thought. 'They come to man when they're ailing,' Joe had told us, 'you won't see him for long.' But the years have passed and he is still with us, and it is only on days when a gale is raging that he fails to spread his wings over the cottage and alight on the roof. Then when I see him again I will say, 'The gale is over. Hubert's back.'

A. P. Herbert came to stay a few days after his first appearance, and A.P.H. was the instrument which gave him his name. We were in the main street of Penzance one morning when first one person then another asked A.P.H. for his autograph. A little crowd gathered among whom was a young girl who, we noticed, was pushed forward by a friend. 'Can I have your autograph?' she asked, holding out notebook and pencil. A.P.H. bowed ceremoniously, then asked kindly, 'And whose autograph are you expecting?' The girl looked at him doubtfully, 'Sir Hubert ... or something.' And for that slight reason Hubert became Hubert.

A.P.H. has always remained Hubert's admirer and on this occasion he bought a gaily painted toy bucket with the idea of filling it with limpets for Hubert's benefit. He would clamber down the cliffs to the rocks, spend an hour or two unclamping the limpets, then return to the cottage where he would spend another hour cleaning them from the shells ... so that Hubert could gobble them in a few seconds.

One evening we were listening to a broadcast performance of Cesar Franck's Symphony in D Minor conducted by Sir Malcolm Sargent when Hubert began to cry like a baby screaming for attention. A.P.H. went to the door and looked up to the roof. 'Shush, Hubert,' he said, 'or I'll tell Sir Malcolm.' Hubert miraculously remained silent for the remainder of the performance, and the following morning A.P.H. wrote to Malcolm Sargent to inform him of the incident. A few days later there came a solemn reply. 'I'm delighted to hear of my new and unusual fan. Tell him I hope he enjoys Tchaikovsky's Fifth next Monday.'

Hubert provided us not only with the jest of his companionship but also, in this period of defeat, he showed us the prize of our way of life. This attention from the untamed was an antidote to loss of confidence. It revealed that eyes in the sky watched our comings and goings and now accepted our presence as shadows on the landscape. We were no longer strangers. We had nudged our way into a kingdom that had the passage of time as its passport; no easy short cuts, no synthetic substitutes, no man-made device can breed the trust of the wild. You have to wait.

Others followed Hubert. He remained king of the roof and he would savagely attack any usurper, but during the hours he was absent strangers began to call until they too became friends. They came singly, wary of rivals, plummeting down on the ridge of the roof, then peering into the garden to see if we had noticed their approach. They flew out of the anonymity of the sky, from the vast gatherings on the rocks along the coast, and became in their own way rebels against conformism. We know them now as one knows animals on a farm; and if we are a field or two away and a gull is winging towards the cottage we can often name it by the manner of its flight; or if we are on the other side of the valley and we see a silhouette below the chimney the size of a fist we are quite likely to be right when one of us says: 'Knocker's waiting for us.'

Knocker, Peter, Philip, Squeaker, Gregory, these join Hubert as our regular visitors and, although sometimes they are away for a month or two, they return and are easily recognized. Knocker announces his arrival by rapping on the roof with his beak, so loudly and briskly that time and again we are deceived into thinking someone is at the door. He has an uncanny sense of knowing when we are in, or perhaps it is that after alighting on the roof he waits to hear our voices before he begins to knock; for we have watched him arrive from afar off and he perches, head erect, waiting; but when we return and go indoors, a minute later the knocking begins.

Peter is shy, he stretches his neck this way and that eyeing us nervously, as if he felt guilty of trespassing. Philip has a confident, lazy, 'no harm can come to me' kind of attitude, and when he is in the mood he will follow us on our walks. Squeaker is a silly bird who has never grown up. He still makes the same piping, wheedling noise that he made when he first began visiting us as a first year bird in mottled grey plumage. He sits on the roof endlessly squeaking, bending his head up and down in the same manner as a nestling demands food from its parents. We throw up a piece of bread, hope for silence, then when the whine continues I am driven to shout: 'Shut up! Shut up!' And afterwards, when he has flown away, I am sorry I have been so abrupt.

Gregory has one leg, the other presumably lost long ago in a trap; and because the source of his strength is unbalanced he has become barrel chested like a plump duck. He is the easiest to recognize when in flight because his chest seems to protrude like the front cone of an aircraft. He is a lonely gull. I have often seen him attacked by others and driven twisting and turning across the moorland to the sea; and there was one occasion when he was caught unawares on the roof and bullied screaming off it so that he fell in the garden. Hubert was the villain and I rushed out and stood by, until Gregory had recovered sufficiently to hop away to the path and take flight. Usually he calls about an hour before dusk but if someone else is still on the roof I see him waiting and watching in a field across the valley, a white speck against the soil. Then, when the roof is bare, he is with us.

I am wondering now whether I should not have written about Gregory in the past tense. We have not seen him for months. He has been absent before now for several weeks on end, usually in the summer, and we have mocked him on his return. 'You've been cadging from the visitors,' we have accused him, 'you've been hopping on the beach luring them to say "we must feed that poor bird with one leg."' But he has never been away for so long and we are worried. Has a fox caught him as he hopped in a field? Or has his own kind swooped and battered him into the sea?

I wonder, too, whether Hubert is nearing the end of his reign as king of the roof; age becomes driftwood wherever it may be. Once he had only to bellow a screeching warning for any gull on the roof to flee at his approach. But the other day I watched him being himself attacked, pounced upon by a newcomer as he was warming himself on the chimney; and the newcomer, a brash, bossy gull who, without being friendly, greedily demands his food, unbalanced poor Hubert in such a manner that he fell like an untidy parachute to the grass below.

Hubert is fussy. He dislikes shop bread, tosses it in disgust in the air if he is given it, and insists instead on Jeannie's home-made variety. He loves cheese, but his favourite dish is bacon rinds. 'Let me know when Hubert arrives,' Jeannie will say, 'I've got bacon rinds for him today.' In wintry weather his visits are brief, long enough to have a meal, then he flies majestically away towards the sea, sloping his flight down the valley to the rocks below the cliffs which are his home. In normal weather he may stay with us for most of the day announcing his arrival with a squeak; then he will squat on the wide rugged stones of the chimney as if on a nest, or he will stand looking bored and disconsolate on the ridge of the roof, or walk to and fro along it like a sentry on a parapet. He observes us. We are always aware of his scrutiny.

In the beginning Monty was irritated rather than jealous of him. Monty would doze in the garden, look up when Hubert started to cry, then curl his upper lip in a soundless snarl. Or if we were having breakfast on the white seat below the cottage and Hubert was strutting within throwing distance of a piece of toast, Monty would lie and stare; then, as if he thought some gesture of defiance was required on his part, he would gently growl like a dog. In time they became friendly enough to ignore each other.

Monty was indifferent to birds and we were never made anxious by the sight of him stalking. He once caught a wren but it was hardly his fault. He was lying somnolent on the grass by the apple tree while a covey of baby wrens flew around him, teasing him as if they were flies and he a tired old horse. I saw him flick his tail in impatience, then pounce, and a wren was in his mouth; but his actions were so gentle that when I rushed to the rescue, shouting at him, he let it go and it flew away unharmed.

He had other temptations but there was a placid quality in his nature that helped him to ignore them. We had, for instance, the usual company of tom-tits, blue-tits, dunnocks, buntings and sparrows flitting about the garden in expectation of crumbs, and he took no notice of any of them; but in particular we had Charlie the chaffinch and Tim the robin.

Charlie attached himself to us soon after the arrival of Hubert, and like Tim he is still with us. He is a bird with a dual character; that of the spring and summer when he is resplendent in plumage of slate-blue, pink, chestnut, black and white wings and tail, is boastful and demanding; that of the winter when his feathers have the drabness of faded curtains, is apologetic, as if surprised he was worthy of any attention. In spring and summer his call is as loud as a trumpet, in winter it is that of a squeak. He has an endearing personality. We may be anywhere in the environment of Minack and suddenly find him hopping about beside us or flitting in the trees as we walk through the wood. We seldom see him any distance from the cottage though once I found him on the edge of the Pentewan meadows. I said: 'Hello Charlie, what are you doing here?' in the tone of voice that might have greeted a friend I thought was in London. Then, when I started back to the cottage, he came with me.

There was one winter, however, when he disappeared for four or five months and we sadly concluded he was dead. But one March morning when Jeannie was in the chicken run which we had moved to a clearing in the wood, she suddenly heard 'cheep, cheep' from a branch above her head. It was Charlie; and she rushed back to the cottage to tell me. 'Charlie's back!' she said excitedly, 'I must get him a biscuit!' And by that time Charlie had followed her and was sitting on the bird-table cheeping away like a dog barking a welcome. Where had he been? In the autumn hordes of migrating chaffinches sweep along the coast past Minack on the way to Southern Ireland, so perhaps Charlie went along with a group. It does not seem the trip was a success. He has never gone away for the winter again.

Charlie is a diffident character compared with Tim. Charlie never comes inside the cottage whereas Tim will perch on the back of a chair and sing us a song. Charlie, when we are bunching flowers, will cheep on the doorstep of the flower house while Tim is inside hopping about on the shelves. Charlie shies away if you put out a hand, Tim will stand on my outstretched palm until my arm aches.

One November, Tim, like Charlie, disappeared. Tim's territory consisted of the cottage, about forty yards of the lane beyond Monty's Leap, and a field bordering it. One morning a few days after we had noticed Tim's disappearance we observed another robin, a nervous robin, flying about the same territory. Robins, of course, compete with each other for desirable territories, so we looked at this robin and wondered whether he had driven Tim away or moved into the territory because Tim was dead. We did not look with favour; for whatever had happened was distressing.

It was a fortnight later that we saw Tim again. We were strolling along a cliff path a half mile from the cottage when suddenly, perched on a twig of quickthorn, I saw Tim. There was no mistaking him. He was perched with

his feathers fluffed out, motionless, watching us. 'Tim!'
Jeannie said with delight, 'what are you doing here?' I had
a few crumbs in my pocket which I held out on the palm
of my hand. A second later I felt the touch of his legs, as if
two matchsticks were standing upright.

The following day we returned to the same place. There
was no Tim. We pushed our way through the brush calling
his name, walking in ever widening circles. At Minack he
always used to answer his name. We would stroll a few
steps down the lane calling, 'Tim!' – and a few moments
later he would be with us. But this time there was no sign
of him, nor the next day, nor the day after. 'Well,' I said to
Jeannie, 'I hope that hawk which has been around hasn't
had him.' Jeannie did not like the casual way I spoke. Tim
was as much a friend as any human could be.

You can, of course, always win the attention of birds by
throwing them crumbs, and you reap the pleasant reward
of watching them; but it is when an individual bird enters
the realm of companionship that the soul is surprised by a
gossamer emotion of affection. Tim was not greedy. He
did not call on us just because he was hungry. I have seen
him time and time again flutter at the window of the
flower house, then, when we have let him in, mooch
around for a couple of hours among the jars full of
flowers, warble a little, perch on a bloom with feathers
fluffed out watching us at work.

'Where's Tim?' I would ask Jeannie.

'He was up on the top shelf among the King Alfreds a
moment ago.'

We missed him when February came and daffodils began
filling the flower house again. We would be silently bunching when one of us would break the silence; 'I wonder
what *did* happen to Tim?' We knew we would never see
him again.

But we were wrong. One afternoon in the last week of February we had gone into the cottage for tea and left the door of the flower house open. Twenty minutes later we returned and quietly continued to bunch. You get in a daze doing the job, picking the daffodils out of the jars, building them three at a time into a bunch, stacking the bunches into galvanized pails where they will stay overnight before they are packed. Your hands move automatically. You only pause to count the number you have done. I had turned to pick out three blooms for the first layer of a bunch when I happened to look up at the beam which crossed the house.

'Jeannie!' I said, 'look on the beam!'

Gazing down at us, serenely confident, head on one side and in best spring plumage, was Tim.

Chapter Fourteen

Hubert up there on the roof looks down on green-houses now at Minack. First a small one thirty feet long and twelve feet wide; then another, one hundred feet long and twenty-two feet wide; then two mobiles, dutch light type glasshouses which are pushed on rails covering two sites and two separate crops in a year, each seventy feet long and eighteen feet wide; and two more the same length but twenty feet wide.

We now work some of the land which John used to have, for John has left the district to go to a farm of his own. Walter and Jack have taken his place; and these two, and Bill who has the other farm which pivots from the collection of buildings, are neighbours who are always ready to help.

We have changed our pattern of growing. Our hands no longer grovel after potatoes in the soil, and we have returned Pentewan to its owner. We have learnt to hate potatoes. Once they promised to be the crop of our prosperity, and instead they have absorbed money, patience and countless aching hours of our labour. 'Once in four years you can expect a bumper harvest,' said the old man with the piping voice when we took over Pentewan. We waited and it never came.

The weather was too dry or too cold or too windy. The

weather was always exceptional. 'Never known an April so dry' – and the potatoes instead of swelling would remain the size of golf balls. 'Never known such bad weather in February' – and instead of getting on with our planting we had to wait, knowing the farmers in their fields would catch us up. 'Never known a spring so cold' . . . Every year the old men in the pubs would drag out from their memories their gloomy comparisons. At first it was comforting to know the season was exceptional, then irritating, then a threat to enthusiasm.

As the cost of production has risen so have the prices fallen. Foreign potatoes flood the markets during the period when those of the Cornish cliff used to reign by themselves. Palates are jaded, and size rather than flavour is the arbiter of purchase. The Cornish cliff new potato is no longer a desirable delicacy; the shovels in the tiny meadows beside the sea, the tedious walks up the cliffs with a chip in each hand, the neatly packed chips being loaded at Penzance station . . . these are the actions of another age. Thus along with the remarks about exceptional weather, there are those about exceptional prices. 'Down to £30 already? I've never known anything like it.'

We were the first to break with tradition. Others have followed us, and Joe no longer haunts the cliffs that have known him for seventeen years. It is sad when hopes are slowly battered, and events burrow reality into your mind. It is sad, even, when the cause is the humble potato.

Flowers, tomatoes and lettuces are the crops we grow at Minack. We plant every year an acre of winter flowering wallflowers, one hundred thousand anemone corms, a half acre of calendulas and four thousand violet plants. We have fifteen tons of daffodil bulbs. The greenhouses have forget-me-nots, freesias, iris, polyanthus and stocks during the winter; and three thousand tomato plants during the summer. We aim to sell forty thousand lettuces between April and October.

Such is the blueprint of our annual output. Unfortunately, a market garden for the most part is like a factory with workshops open to the sky. The sky is the ceiling. There are production problems as in a factory, selling problems as in any business; but however clever you may be in overcoming these, it is always the weather which dictates your prosperity. Thus I may pay staff for several months of preparatory labour – preparing land, planting, weeding – but lose everything in a hard frost, a few gales, or as in the case of some crops, a period of wet muggy weather.

Or it may be a hot spell at the wrong time which has hit us. An excessively warm March defeated our Wedgewood iris gamble. The thirty-six thousand which we had planted in one of the greenhouses were scheduled to be marketed before the outside Wedgewood in the Channel Islands came into bloom. But a March resembling mid-summer brought both indoor and outdoor iris into the markets together, deluging the salesmen and bringing despair to the growers. 'Well,' I said to Jeannie, 'we'll never grow iris again.' But we did. The best course a grower can take is to follow one year's bad market with the same crop the next.

Frost, gales, muggy weather, unseasonable heat-waves . . . sometimes Jeannie and I wonder whether we should ever expect normality. Of these frost is the least of our worries, for it is very seldom indeed that there is a persistent hard frost in West Cornwall. Gales, however, will chase us to the end of our days though sometimes they seem to take a rest and leave us in comparative peace. They blow but lack viciousness, or they launch an attack at a time when there are no crops to harm. Such a period lulls us into forgetfulness, and we deceive ourselves into thinking that optimism is a substitute for realism; and so we plant a crop in a meadow which is doomed as soon as a frenzied gale blows again.

The first time we grew anemones in any great number was following a winter that was as gentle as a continuous spring, when our flowers had bloomed in steady profusion and we were happy in the confidence born of success. So confident indeed that we proceeded to act as if gales were no longer an enemy.

We decided that the Dairyman's Meadow at Pentewan would be ideal for the anemone crop, and that another meadow over there would be suitable for the cloches we had recently bought. The Dairyman's meadow, so called because the use of it was once the perk of the man who looked after the cows on the farm, sloped south, dipping downwards from a high bank to the crest of the cliff. The other meadow, known as the thirty lace meadow because of its size, was more exposed but being flat it was exactly what we required for the cloches. We were going to use them as a cover for winter-growing lettuces.

By October the anemones were in full bloom, long stems and brilliant colours; and we congratulated ourselves on our good fortune. 'There you are,' I said to Jeannie, 'it just proves we *do* sometimes know more than the old hands.' For the old hands, in the person of Joe, had warned us that nobody had ever succeeded in growing anemones on the cliff.

That year we had advertised a private box service, sending flowers direct to the home; and the anemones proved such a success that time and again they were specially asked for in repeat orders. We were particularly delighted when one lady ordered twenty dozen ... to decorate a house for a wedding reception; and she carefully instructed us to be certain they arrived the day before, December the first.

We never sent them, nor did we send any more anemones away that season. The gales had returned, blasting away the illusions that we could grow anemones on the cliff. A monster had roared in from the sea during the night of November the twenty-ninth, and when we reached the meadow in the morning it was as if a khaki coloured carpet had been spread across it. Not an anemone, not a green leaf was to be seen. The meadow was a desert.

It was another monster, three months later, that sent the cloches skidding across the thirty lace meadow. Never before or since have I known a gale which blew so hard as on that March morning, so hard that I had to crawl on my hands and knees in order to make any progress against it. Glass seemed to be flying like swallows skimming the cliff, and there was nothing for me to do except watch and curse and wait.

And as I waited, sheltered a little by a hedge, I suddenly saw Jeannie fighting her way towards me. It was her birthday and I was miserable that it should have begun so disastrously. There was no reason why she should have joined me. I had not asked her nor expected her. She was joining me because it was in her nature that trouble should be shared.

'Here,' she said as she reached me, 'I've brought you a flask of tea ... I thought you might need it.' I most certainly did. 'And I've put Glucose in it to help you keep warm.' I poured out a cup, spilling some of it in the wind, then took a gulp. It was awful. It tasted like quince. 'You've poisoned me, Jeannie!' I shouted jokingly into the gale, 'what on earth did you put in it?'

When we returned to the cottage we found the lid was firmly pressed down on the Glucose tin; that of the Epsom salts lay loose on the table.

Gales, then, will always be our enemy but they are an enemy which attacks without guile; and it is easier to deal with a man who boasts his hate rather than with one who hides it. Muggy weather, warm wet sticky sea fog which covers the fields like a dirty stream, achieves its destruction by stealth.

It creeps into the greenhouses sponging the tomato plants with botrytis and mildew, or blearing the freesias with tiny brown smudges making them useless for sale. Outside, it browns the tips of the anemone blooms, and sometimes it does this so slyly that the damage is revealed only after the flowers have been picked and have remained in their jars overnight.

But it is at daffodil time that muggy weather can gain its great victories. A gale can beat at a wall but on the other side you can rest in its shelter. Muggy weather gives no chance of such rest. It envelops the daffodils in a damp cocoon and brushes the petals, either in bud or in bloom, with the smear of its evil. There is no defence. You have to put up your hands in surrender.

There was one year when we lost eighty per cent of our daffodils in this way, and the compost heaps were piled high with their stems. The previous year had been a bumper one. We had bought ten tons of bulbs and in two months had earned their capital outlay. Thus our expectations were high when the new season began; but instead, basket after basket brought in from the meadows had blooms which were unworthy of being despatched to market.

This dismal experience had a curious feature, a feature which only affected those daffodils within a half mile or so of the sea. First there was a brown mark on the petal, the next day it had turned green, and the third day there was a tiny hole in the same place as if it had been burnt by a red-hot pin. The experts were evasive. They could give us no exact explanation. 'Looks like daffodil flu,' was all they murmured.

Nor could they explain the unhappy events that followed. For two years the affected bulbs were sterile, scarcely a bloom was to be found among them; and those of us who lived on the coast, as well as the Scilly Islanders, disconsolately stared at our meadows of green foliage while growers inland were rushing their blooms to market.

Jeannie had her own interpretation of what happened. Shortly before the daffodils were attacked, canisters of atomic waste were dumped off Land's End; and one of the canisters, it was reported, burst during the dumping. Jeannie blames our misfortunes on its contents being blown back on to the coast mingled in spray. It is as good an explanation as any provided by the experts.

Few people pass Minack at any time of the year, and even at the height of the summer when conventional places are awash with humanity, a figure on the landscape cries out for our comment. 'Somebody's on the Carn!' I'll call to Jeannie . . . Or we will shout the absurd alarm of Alan Herbert: 'White men! White men!'

The occasional hikers plod by, some delighting in the untamed nature of their walk, some indignant that a highway through the undergrowth along the coast is not maintained for their benefit; some stimulated by the need for initiative, some at a loss. 'I've never had my legs so scratched in all my years of walking,' said one furious lady . . . then, as if it were my fault, flinging the threat at me, 'I'm going to write to *The Times*!'

Sometimes we have seen strangers who have had a menacing air about them, as if belonging to the mechanism of progress from which we sought to remain free. Men who have come to survey the district, men walking by who were too well dressed to be hikers, two or three who have spent their days hammering holes in the rocks; and there was one threatening week when an aeroplane flew up and down each section of the coast towing a box-like contraption behind it. On such occasions we bristled with suspicion. Others in beautiful, lonely places have watched such activities, waited and wondered, then found themselves faced with the roar of a motorway, or on the site of some other monument to progress.

One day a man called at the cottage and said he was studying rock conditions in our area on behalf of a certain Ministry. He asked for permission to study those on our land.

'Of course you can,' I said, then added suspiciously, remembering the other activities, 'if you're looking for uranium I hope you won't find it.'

The man stared at me. 'But my dear sir,' he said loftily, 'if I found uranium just think how rich you would be!'

Jeannie was with me at the time and it was she who answered him. 'Had we the choice,' she said, 'between a uranium mine and Minack, I can assure you we would choose Minack.' The man retreated to his duties and Jeannie and I set off to weed the anemones.

We know now there is no possibility of any part of this area being exploited. Buildings and caravans are forbidden, there is no place for a motorway to go, it is too inaccessible even to fear the prospect of an atomic power station; and the scientists have announced the region is bare of uranium. Perhaps I am being over-confident. Such remoteness will always tempt someone to plot its destruction.

But today we can go out of the cottage and shout to the heavens and no one will hear; or lie on the rocks with only cormorants, oyster catchers and gulls as companions; or stroll in the wood with Charlie hopping from branch to branch above our heads, or pause to talk to Tim, or say to each other: 'The gannets are passing along the coast early this year' . . . 'I saw the first whitethroat this morning' . . . 'If you look to the left of those quickthorns you will see a fox sunning itself in the bracken' . . . 'The Seven Stone lightship was towed past this morning' . . . 'We'll have lunch on the rocks and watch the seal in the bay' . . .

These belong to the pleasures which have pleased since the beginning of time. They await in remoteness, hiding their secret in solitude, unhurt by man-made glitter and away from his intrigue, seemingly insignificant moments which enrich the soul. They live with us at Minack so that whatever material disappointments we may have, however hard may be the consequences of a failed harvest, they take us forward again. It is a way of life which belongs to the ages instead of ourselves.

Monty was fifteen years old when he began to ail. There was nothing sudden about his illness, and as the weeks went by there were times when we made ourselves believe that we were worrying unnecessarily. Sometimes he was his old jaunty self, following us in our walks round Minack, then sitting purring on my knees in the evening. We made the customary remarks that are made by those who watch the sick. 'I think the medicine has done him a lot of good' . . . 'He really enjoyed his walk this morning.' And then quite suddenly the sickness within him began to hurry.

He died on a May morning, a morning that was soft and warm and full of sweet scents, the sort of morning Jeannie would have said to me: 'Let's take Monty a walk before breakfast.' As I was dressing he had begun to cry, and I knew instinctively there was nothing more that we could do. I went away to telephone the vet and when I returned I found Jeannie had carried him out into the sun. He was lying, breathing gently, stretched out on the grass; and, strangely, Charlie was on the ground within a yard of him, Tim was perched on a rosebush two feet from his head, and Hubert was up there on the roof. All were silent.

Monty was the only cat I had ever known and my loyalty was to him and not to his breed. One day during his illness I was telling him that I would never have another to replace him. I was in fact thinking of those sympathetic meaning people who hasten to replace an old friend with a substitute. 'The only exception,' I said, and this I wrote down in my diary, 'is if a black cat whose home could never be traced cried outside the door in a storm.'

At the beginning of March the following year, Jeannie and I became aware of a black cat running wild on our land. We scarcely took notice of it except to observe, after a time, that it was always on our land and never on that of our neighbours. But it was so wild that it was only a black dash in the distance.

One evening, at the beginning of April, Jeannie was sitting after dinner talking of Monty. A gale was blowing and rain lashed the cottage. Suddenly I said: 'Did you hear a cry?' And without waiting for Jeannie to answer I went and opened the door.

In came the black cat. She is beside me now as I end this story.

A Cat in the Window

To Jeannie's mother

I HATED CATS. I was brought up to consider them vermin. I had been brought up in a dog family, and I loved the dogs of my life . . . Bruce of my childhood, Lance of my boyhood, an old English sheepdog, Mary a Maltese terrier, Pickles another Maltese terrier, Roy, also an old English sheepdog who was my companion in a cottage near Truro where I began to write *Time Was Mine*. All this before I met Jeannie.

Jeannie's mother advised her not to marry me because of my attitude towards cats. 'You can't be happy with such a man,' she had said, knowing Jeannie's adoration of cats. When, however, she realized that marriage was inevitable, she formed a plan; and the plan materialized into fact two months after we had married. She acquired a ginger kitten, the colour of autumn bracken, from a girl assistant at her hairdresser's in St Albans . . . and brought it to Jeannie's office, Room 205, at the Savoy Hotel.

It was there that I first saw Monty, the hero of this book; and in this book I describe Monty's conquest of me, and my realization that cats were not vermin, as my family background had led me to believe. And I was to learn, as the years went by, that a cat is capable of loving in the same way that a dog can love.

Chapter One

THE OPENING paragraph of my book, *A Gull on the Roof*, which told how we came to live in Cornwall, was about our cat Monty of whom I said: 'He was, for both Jeannie and myself, the repository of our secret thoughts.' I am writing the story of Monty in *A Cat in the Window*.

I first met Monty in Room 205 of the Savoy Hotel. He was six weeks old, and when I came into the room was tumbling, chasing, biting, an old typewriter ribbon dragged temptingly across the carpet by Lois, Jeannie's secretary. He was the size and colour of a handful of crushed autumn bracken. At the time I did not notice the distinguishing marks I was later to know so well – the silky white shirt front, the smudge of orange on the left paw, the soft maize colour of the fur on his tummy. I did not notice his whiskers, nor his tail with its dark rings against cream, the rings graduating in size to the tip which, in his lifetime, was to flick this way and that, a thousand, thousand times. I saw only a pretty kitten with great big innocent eyes gambolling in the incongruous setting of Jeannie's office, and I wondered why.

'What's this?' I said to Lois, looking down at the two of them, 'what on earth is this kitten doing here?' I had seen Ambassadors, film stars, famous journalists, politicians of all parties, in Jeannie's office, but I had never before met a cat. It made me suspicious.

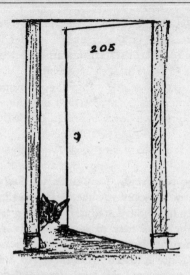

'Come on,' I said, 'come on, Lois, tell me what it's all about?' But Lois, the perfect secretary, went on playing as if she hadn't heard me. 'Lois, you're hiding something from me. Where's Jeannie? What's she been up to? Both of you know I dislike cats and if . . .'

'She'll be back soon.' Lois was smiling and refusing to be drawn. 'She had to go over to Claridge's. General Montgomery has just arrived and nobody is allowed to know. She won't be long.' As Public Relations Officer of the Savoy Group it was part of Jeannie's job to keep certain news from the Press, just as much as it was on other occasions to get other news widely publicized.

But on this occasion, on this particular warm, summer afternoon as I awaited her return with Lois and the chocolate box cover of a kitten, her task was specially important.

Monty had arrived to make a progress report to Churchill on the Battle of the Desert.

I came from a dog family. In the walled garden of my rambling Cornish home was a row of wooden crosses with painted cries of Victorian sentiment. 'Alas, poor Rosa,' 'Sweet, gentle Cara,' 'Farewell Little Gyp.' And in my own childhood I remember the crosses going up again. My parents had no desire to disclose their emotions so, in their day, only the birth and death and name of the dog appeared on the cross. Rex, Bulger, Bruce, Mary, Lance, Roy, Pickles. These sparse tributes to devotion were sometimes countered in my mind by unexpectedly finding my father standing opposite a cross quietly puffing his pipe. Young as I was, it touched me to feel the memories that were passing through him.

My personal friends were first Bruce and then Lance; or Sir Lancelot by which, until I found the name too much of a mouthful, I first called him. Bruce was a mongrel of indescribable parentage while Lance, an Old English Sheepdog, brought with him from the kennels where he was born a list of relations bearing the names of sheepdog royalty. Bruce was in our family before I was born and by the time I was seven I thought he was immortal. He was to me a brother of my own age, and for hours on end I would tease him or wrestle or play hide and seek with him among the gorse and tamarisk covered land around our home. Bruce was the answer to any doubts of my mother as to how I could spend my time.

Then he died and grief being suddenly to me an emotion instead of a word, my father countered by producing Lance. He moved subtly. He knew that what I needed was a dog I could call my own, and he devised a means that would make me, the small boy, feel he was my own. He told me one evening after I had gone to bed that he was driving to London the following morning and that, if I liked, I could go with him to Exeter, then return to

Newquay by myself on the Cornish Riviera. He made me feel grown up and, unsuspectingly, I excitedly accepted. But when we reached Exeter station and the Riviera rolled in I found I was not to be alone on my return journey; for in the guards van curled timidly in a wicker basket was Lance.

I matured with Lance. First the same childish games I had with Bruce, then the tearful partings before school terms, wild barking reunions, and soon the long walks of doubtful youth, Lance at my side in the winding lanes sharing my puzzlement. I was a man when Lance died.

Dogs, then, had been entities in my life. Cats, as if they were wasps with four legs, had been there to shoo away. They did not belong in my life nor in my family's life. All of us were united that whenever we saw a cat the most important thing to do was to see it out of sight.

But as I moved slowly out of the environment of my family, I found naturally enough people and homes who accepted cats as we accepted dogs. Cats were not vulgar, as, in some mysterious way, I had been led to believe. I began to note that cats were able to bestow a subtle accolade upon their apparent owners which made these owners rapturous with delight.

I resented this. Dogs, and by this I mean well mannered, full of character, devoted dogs who did not snarl or bark unnecessarily, were to me the true tenants of a home. Cats were vagrants. They did not merit affection.

I sensed, of course, that my attitude in a home where there was a cat or cats was unsatisfactory; so I developed a pose that after a while I made myself believe was genuine. I was allergic to cats. The proximity of one produced asthma. I felt dizzy. I behaved so strangely that any owner of a cat who was entertaining me was convinced that if I were not to prove a sickly embarrassment the cat had to be removed. I know there are some people who genuinely feel like this, but I was not one.

It was in this mood that I paid my first call on Jeannie's parents in their handsome house on the hill of St Albans. I sat down in the sitting-room and promptly Tim, Jeannie's cat, a huge blue Persian, jumped on my lap. Unthinkingly I played my customary part. I gave Tim a violent push and, in so doing, knocked over a small table upon which was my untouched cup of tea. From that moment I began to realize it was dangerous to appear to dislike cats.

For Jeannie is a cat lover, not only the slave of an individual, but an all-embracing cat lover. If she sees a cat on the other side of the street she will want to cross over to talk to it. Any pretty little thing, any handsome Tom, will receive her caressing and cooing. She fawns on the breed. Little wonder her mother after my visit had ended cast a humorous doubt on a successful marriage. Could a cat lover live happily with a cat hater?

My future dealings with Tim were, therefore, cautious. I was careful not to cause offence by throwing any make-believe tantrums, yet I was equally careful not to appear affected by the lofty gaze he sometimes cast on me. I was polite but distant. I was determined to hold fast to my traditional dislike of the species. I was not going to be hypnotized by gentle purrs, soft kneading of paws, an elegant walk across the room and a demand to jump on my knees. I disliked cats. I most certainly would not have one in our home after we had married.

This was my mood as I waited for Jeannie to return from Claridge's. We had been married three months.

Chapter Two

BUT I MADE no scene except a mock one. It was an inevitable defeat. I could only bluster. I could not enter my married life with an argument about a cat.

Monty chose the moment of Jeannie's return to pounce upon the toe of my shoe; then disappear up my trousers, except for a tail. He tickled my leg until I had to stoop and, for the first time, touch him. Jeannie and Lois watched hopefully the effect this would have on me. He was very soft, and the wriggle with which he tried to escape me was feeble, like the strength of my little finger. I felt the teeth nibble my hand, and a tiny claw trace a tickle on my skin; and when I picked him up and held him firmly in front of me, the big eyes stared childishly at me with impotent resentment. I had never held a cat in my hands before.

'This is diabolical,' I said in pretence fury, addressing Jeannie and Lois, 'and don't think I haven't a card up my sleeve . . . I'm going to chuck this thing over Hammersmith Bridge on the way home.' I spoke so vehemently that Lois seemed half to believe me. 'Yes I am,' I said, rubbing it in, 'I'll stop the car and fling the cat over the parapet.'

'Kitten,' murmured Lois.

'Monty,' said Jeannie.

There is no defence against women who sense your heart has already surrendered. The head, however astute in

presenting its arguments, appears hollow. If Jeannie wanted
Monty she had to have him. How could I deny her? The
best I could do was to learn to tolerate his existence; and
make an attempt to impose conditions.

'All right, I won't do *that*,' I said, and was immediately
irked by the gleam of victory in their eyes, 'But I'll tell you
what I *will* do . . .' I looked defiantly at both of them. 'I'll
make quite certain he is a *kitchen* cat. There'll be no
question of him wandering about the house as if he owns
it.'

This display of authority eased me into seeing the situation in a more comforting perspective. Jeannie would be
happy, Monty out of sight, and I could continue my
aloofness towards the species as before.

'But if he doesn't behave himself,' I added, looking at
the little ball of fur in my hand, 'he'll have to be found
another home.'

The weakness in my attack was my responsibility for
Monty's arrival. It was indirect, but a fact. We had mice in
our cottage at Mortlake; and when, at Jeannie's request, I
set traps and caught the mice, I was so sickened by the task
of releasing the dead mouse from the trap that I preferred
to throw both the mouse and the trap into the river.

The cottage, with a roof the shape of a dunce's cap, was
within a few yards of the finishing post of the Boat Race,
and only the towpath separated the front steps and the
river. On the ground floor was the dining-room, the
kitchen and the spare bedroom; on the first, two bedrooms,
one overlooking the river, and the other the garden; and
on the top floor were the bathroom and the sitting-room
which stretched the breadth of the cottage. Across this
room at door level stretched two massive old oak beams
and from them, dove-tailed by wooden pegs, were two
spans ancient as the beams, triangular, supporting the

inside of the dunce's cap which was the ceiling. In one corner was the fireplace and opposite, along the length of the room, were the windows from which we watched the Thames flowing to the curve at Barnes Bridge; and beyond, the silhouette of London.

The cottage was once upon a time an inn, and one of the innkeepers was a waterman who married a Shakespeare player. I used to dig up broken old clay pipes in the garden, sometimes part of a stem, sometimes a bowl, and when I sent a sample to the British Museum they confirmed they were Elizabethan. From then on I used to hand pieces to visitors, telling them the story of the cottage. 'You had better keep this,' I would say, 'Shakespeare may have used it.'

It was a small walled garden the length of a cricket pitch and the width of half a tennis court. At the top end was the concrete shelter in which we crouched during bad air raids . . . except the night we were celebrating our first wedding anniversary with a party in the cottage; and the roof was blown off.

On the other side of one wall was the garden of the Ship, the pub next door; on the other side of the opposite one was a passage-way from the river to Mortlake village; and within a hundred yards of both were Sandy Lane and West Road with the Brewery towering in the background. Along the river bank were three or four houses and beyond them, three minutes from the cottage, was Chiswick Bridge. In time, in the early morning, Monty used to walk with us to the Bridge but he would go no farther. He would sit down when we reached the archway and, however much we coaxed him, would not budge. He was never, in fact, to be a wanderer while he lived at Mortlake. His world, for seven years, was to be the small walled garden; except after the bombing when he came with us to Jeannie's old home at St Albans. And it was from St Albans in the first place that he came.

I complained once again one morning to Jeannie about my trap task. In retrospect I know, of course, I was being ridiculous, but at the time, when I had to perform the task, I felt disgusted.

'Now if we had a cat,' replied Jeannie, and she gave no sign that she was trying to influence me unduly, 'you wouldn't have to worry about traps at all . . . you see, the very smell of a cat keeps mice away.'

In due course I was to find this statement to be untrue, but at the time, in the frame of mind I was in on that particular morning, it interested me.

'You mean to say that a mouse never comes into a house where there's a cat, and all that catching and squealing takes place outside?'

'Oh, yes,' said Jeannie blandly, 'mice are very intelligent and they know they haven't a chance if a cat finds them in a house.'

'And what about birds?' Jeannie, I knew, once had a

favourite cat called Tubby who spent much of her time in the spring climbing up trees to catch nestlings for her kittens. Jeannie, when she could, would gently take the little bird from Tubby's mouth when she reached her kittens and return it to the nest.

'Well,' she said, making the answer sound very simple, 'all you have to do is to have the cat doctored. Cats only catch birds for their families.'

Here again the ardour to convert me misled her sense of accuracy. True, Monty was seen to catch only one bird in his life, and that was a wren which annoyed him and which he promptly let go when we advanced on him; but he, I think was an exception. Most cats, if they don't catch for their families, will catch for the fun of it, or because they are bored. You can't blame them. They are no worse than the man who takes out his gun for an hour or two of rough shooting.

'Anyhow,' I said, by way of ending the conversation, 'I still don't like them.'

On reflection, I believe my dislike was based on their independence. A dog, any dog, will come to you wagging its tail with friendliness if you click your fingers or call to it. There is no armed neutrality between the dog world and the human race. If a human is in need of affection and there is a dog about, he is sure to receive it, however frail affection from a stranger may be. Dogs are prepared to love; cats, I believed were not.

I had observed too, that cat owners (but who, I wondered, would call himself the owner of a cat?) were apt to fall into two types. Either they ignored the cat, put it out at night whatever the weather, left it to fend for itself when they went away on holidays, and treated it, in fact, as a kind of better class vermin; or else they worshipped the animal like a god. The first category appeared callous, the second devoid of sense.

I had seen, for instance, a person sit rigid and uncomfortable in a chair because a cat had chosen his lap as the whim of its own particular comfort. I had noticed, and been vexed by her, the hostess who hastens away at the end of a meal with titbits for the cat which has stared balefully at her guests during the course of it. Cats, it seemed to me, aloofly hinted the power of hypnotism; and as if in an attempt to ward off this uncanniness, their owners pandered to them, anxiously trying to win approval for themselves by flattery, obedience, and a curious vocabulary of nonsensical phrases and noises. A cat lover, I had found, was at the mercy of the cat.

I was now to learn for myself whether this was true. My education was about to begin. My morning conversation with Jeannie had made her believe there might be a gap in my armour; and by the time I had forgotten the conversation, she had already rung up her mother to disclose her hopes. 'I think he's weakening,' she said, 'we must seize the chance.'

And so no time was lost. Her mother had an appointment at the hairdressers and she promised that immediately afterwards she would go to the pet shop to see what kittens were available. The visit never took place. At the hairdressers she confided her mission to the girl who attended her. 'But I've got a kitten that nobody wants,' the girl said, 'it's a ginger, the last of a litter, and if we don't find a home by tomorrow he'll have to be put away.'

I would not have agreed if my advice had been sought. One less kitten in the world would not have seemed very important to me. But my advice wasn't sought and Monty was saved.

For the price of my mother-in-law's weekly chocolate ration, he entered our lives.

Chapter Three

As soon as I picked him out of the wicker basket in which we had brought him home, I explained to our housekeeper that Monty was to be a kitchen cat. 'I don't want to see him at all,' I said, 'he's here to catch mice and although he may be small for that yet, I've been told the very smell of a cat will keep them away.'

I looked at Jeannie. She was busily unwrapping a small paper parcel. 'Isn't that true? Didn't you say that?'

'Oh yes . . . yes.'

An object had now appeared from the paper. A small *sole bonne femme*. It was freshly cooked and succulent.

'Good heavens, Jeannie,' I said, 'where did you get that?'

'Latry gave it to me,' she said. Latry was the famous maître chef of the Savoy. 'He's cooked it specially as a celebration present for Monty.' I looked at the fish and then at Monty. Only a few hours before, the girl in the hairdressers was frightened he would be put away on the morrow.

'Really, Jeannie,' I said crossly, 'you can't go cadging food for the cat.'

'I wasn't cadging. Latry *gave* it to me, I tell you. He loves cats and felt honoured to cook Monty's first meal.'

'Honoured,' I murmured to myself, and shuddered.

Jeannie mashed the fish up in a saucer, put it on the floor and began cooing at Monty who, never having seen a fish before, tottered off in the opposite direction.

'There you are,' I said, as if I had achieved a minor triumph, 'he doesn't like fish.'

Of course he was soon to do so; and during the course of his life he was to eat vast quantities of it, although sole was not his favourite. It was whiting. The cottage, and also in due course our cottage in Cornwall, was often to reek with the stink of it when the water in which it was cooked boiled over from the pan on to the stove.

But on the first morning of his life with us, the morning on which I awoke to a disquieting awareness that the pattern of my life was about to be re-adjusted, the sole from the Savoy kitchens awaited him. 'I wonder whether he has eaten it,' pondered Jeannie aloud as she dressed.

Oddly enough I found myself wondering too. It was as if time being momentarily dull I was awaiting the BBC News to hear if the announcer had anything to say to stir the pulse. 'I'll go down and see,' I said, and was off through the door in my dressing gown.

The stairs were narrow and steep, of polished wood and slippery; and on the third step from the bottom, too frightened to go up or down, was Monty. 'How have you got there?' I said; and my voice was as firm as could be allowed when a child gets caught in a predicament. 'Your place is in the kitchen. It's no use you trying to learn to climb stairs.' The tiny miaows did not protest against my firmness, they appealed for my help; and so I picked him up in one hand and took him to the saucer of the night before where it had been placed under the kitchen table. It was empty.

Jeannie was encouraged by my apparent gentleness on this occasion; and I observed, during the days that followed, how she cunningly began to use Monty to help pierce my utilitarian attitude towards him. The process continued from days into weeks until one afternoon an incident took place which, she considered, set the seal on her triumphant tactics.

The first of these tactics was her good sense in realizing it was unwise to make too much fuss of Monty in my presence. She made up for this apparent coolness in my absence, but this I was not to know; and I was not to know, for instance, that Latry, the Chef, continued to supply her with delicacies which she fed to Monty surreptitiously while I was in the pub next door.

Nor when, as he grew older, he began successfully to climb the stairs, did she encourage him to do so; and on the evening he was found for the first time in a tight ball on the bed, she impressed me with her scolding. Indeed I felt a twinge of sympathy for Monty as I carried him, on Jeannie's instructions, back to the kitchen. I found myself wondering against my will whether it was fair he should be banished when it was so obvious he was prepared to give both of us his affection.

Monty played his own part very well because from the beginning he made it plain he liked me. It was a dangerous moment of flattery when I realized this and I believe, had it not been for my entrenched posture of dislike for the species, I would have fallen for it without more ado. There was, however, a thick enough layer of prejudice inside me for me to hold out.

He would seek to play with me. I would be sitting at dinner and feel a soft cushion gently knocking my foot, and when I put down a hand to stop it my fingers were enclosed by small teeth. In the garden he would perform his most bewitching tricks in front of me, the clumsy chase of a butterfly, the pounce on an imaginary demon leaving a spreadeagled posterior to face me. And when at the end of the day we returned to the cottage, unlatched the door and went inside, it was strange how often he came to me instead of paying court to Jeannie. Did I perhaps impose an intuition upon him that my prejudice, once defeated, would leave a vacuum that he alone could fill? My prejudice has long ago disappeared, but I am still a one cat man. I have never developed a taste for a household of cats, each with a colourful name, each having to share the affection accorded to them all, each leading a life so independent that one of them can disappear for a few days without causing undue worry. It is a taste in cat worship I will never share. I am incapable of spreading my affection so widely. Monty needed only to vanish for a few hours and we both would fill ourselves with imaginary fears.

But the talk of these cat lovers among Jeannie's friends was part of my education. She enlisted their aid. I listened to the language they used, both spoken and unspoken, and became aware there was a streak of connoisseurship in this world of cats. It was the snobbery of an exclusive club; and if the flavour of conversation was an acquired taste, it was no more so than learning to like jazz or Bach. They perused Monty and unanimously pronounced he would grow into a beautiful member of the fraternity; and fraternity henceforth replaced for me the words of species or breed. They admired his head and foretold, quite correctly, it would become like that of a miniature tiger, not snouty and elongated like some ginger cats. They assessed his mother as a tortoiseshell and his father as a tabby. They liked his whiskers which at that age were wisps of white. They forecast, as he had been doctored, that he would become a huge cat. They discussed him, men and women of distinction in various walks of life, in the tone one associates with relations probing the future of an infant of noble heritage. Would his appearance measure up to his responsibilities? Young as he was, did he show signs of a strong character? Would his movements prove elegant? How thick would become his coat? Monty was fussed over and cooed at as if to win his favour was an ambition far out-weighing in importance any achievement in the daily task. I watched amused, comforting myself with the know-ledge that Jeannie's friends were not as serious as they appeared. Monty was only a diversion. He was a toy for temporary enjoyment. A cat could never possess a personal-ity which could be remembered except by those with whom he lived.

In any case, during the initial period of this homage bestowed on him, Monty did not appear very attractive. He would not wash. His body was dull and dusty, the white on his left paw a dirty cuff, the crescent of white on his little chest a grey, soiled shirt. 'He looks like an alley cat,' I taunted Jeannie.

My coolness towards him, my inclination to niggle at any of his failings, naturally increased the sense of protec-tion she had for him; and during this phase of unwash she was afraid I might have the excuse to get rid of him. Yet, to my surprise, I did not feel that way at all. I too, felt a sense of protection; and the evening, Jeannie having gone home before me, I returned to find Monty on a chair in the kitchen his fur shining bright, I was as delighted as Jeannie. I did not know she had damped him all over with plain water; and he had licked himself dry.

It was another homecoming a few weeks later, an unex-pected one, which finally witnessed my capitulation. I had spent the day in the cottage and was not thinking of Jeannie's return till the evening. I was in the top room alone when there was a noise at the door as if it were being kicked by a soft boot. I opened it and Monty came scampering in. He rushed to the sofa, jumped up, climbed on the back walking along it tail up, then down again to the floor and across to where I was standing, arching his back, rubbing his head against my leg and purring. All this in less than a minute, and performed with such élan that it made me wonder whether he was telling me in his particular fashion that I had been making an ass of myself. I bent down and stroked him, and he thereupon carried out a manoeuvre which he was often to do when he aimed to be especially endearing. He twisted his head as if he were going to fold up in a ball, collapsed on the floor and turned over, and lay with his back on the green carpet, paws in the air, displaying his silky maize underparts while a pair of bright yellow eyes hopefully awaited the pleasure the sight would give me. The reward he expected was a gentle stroke until he decided he had had one too many when there would be a savage mock attempt to bite my fingers.

But on this first occasion I was holding a pipe cleaner in my hand and I tickled him with that, which led to a game, which led half an hour later to his sitting on my desk, a

large kidney shaped Regency desk with a top like a table, performing ridiculous antics with a pencil.

I was sitting there roaring with laughter when the door opened. In walked Jeannie.

Chapter Four

My capitulation was complete, and within a few weeks there was no pretence that Monty was a kitchen cat. Every room in the cottage was his kingdom; and at night, if his fancy was to sleep on the bed, I would lie with legs stiff so as not to disturb him while he curled in a ball at the bottom. I endlessly wanted to play with him, and felt put in my place when he was not in the mood, stalking away from me tail in the air showing he had something more important to do, like a vigorous if temporary wash of the underparts.

Sometimes my games were gently malicious, as if taking a friendly revenge on the way he had captured me. I used to lift him on to the beam in the sitting-room where he glared down at me, then ran along the beam to find a place from which to leap on to the floor, only to find I had moved along too and was there to stop him. I would put up a hand and receive a slap from a paw.

There was another game with an ulterior purpose or game perhaps is the wrong word for it. Three months had gone by and there was still no evidence that he had caught a mouse; no remains had been found, no victory bellow heard, no sign that there were fewer mice than before. It was disturbing. His presence had brought no fear to the mice and so he seemed as useless as a dog for the purpose required of him. 'Perhaps he left his mother too soon,' said Jeannie, apologizing, 'and she didn't have time to teach him.'

I no longer wished to prise Jeannie's defences and whereas in the beginning I would have ridiculed such a remark, I now said nothing. Monty was growing fast and his appetite was enormous, so the best thing to do, I decided, was to keep him hungry for a while and let his natural cat's instinct develop out of necessity. After twenty-four hours he was prowling around like a tiger, and Jeannie was yearning to yield to his fury. 'You're cruel,' she said, 'to do this to him.' It was often to be like that, Jeannie always ready to surrender to his whims while I, my anti-cat upbringing still somewhere within me, endeavoured to insist on discipline.

But my plan on this occasion was to put him up in the attic, a dark, forbidding world of rafters, cobwebs and, without doubt, mice. Standing on a chair, my arms outstretched above me, I shoved Monty through the trap door, and returned to the sitting-room to await results. After half an hour Jeannie argued it was time to let him out. After an hour I was restraining her from standing on the chair. She was furious. I was anxious less my plan had misfired. Another ten minutes and I admitted I was wrong. I stood on the chair to push upwards the trap door. At that instant there was a wild scramble on the ceiling, followed by squeak, squeak, squeak . . . and a few seconds later peering down from the opening above me was Monty with a mouse like a fat moustache, in his mouth.

As Monty grew larger Jeannie's lap became too small for his comfort, and he transferred to mine. He would approach where I was sitting, arch his back, claw for a brief second at the chair's fabric, leap up and settle down, then turn his head upward to me as if he were saying:

'Thank you very much.' That was not, however, the moment when I required any thanks because I always felt flattered he had chosen me, above all other comfortable spots in the house, to rest on a while. It was later when I deserved the thanks, when my feet had gone to sleep, my legs had got cramp, and I had refrained from doing any job I had intended to do. I never dared move him. I would watch him comfortably dozing, occasionally adjusting his posture while I sat stiff as a ramrod: such a gesture as selecting my lap was an accolade I could not refuse. I was to spend hours, days, weeks of my life like that, while Jeannie sat opposite watching the two of us.

There were times, however, when first he paid me this attention, that circumstances forced me to move him. It was the period of the little blitz, the bitter late winter when Hitler again attacked London. The sirens would wail while we sat upstairs in the sitting room and we would wait, pretending we were not tense, until the guns began firing. 'They're not very busy tonight,' I would sometimes say, which only meant I had not heard any bombs fall in the neighbourhood. But there were other times when a stick would fall uncomfortably close, and then I would tuck Monty under my arm and we would all hasten to the shelter at the top of the garden. We would crouch there, the dark being flashed into brilliance while Jeannie, a hand clutching Monty, would declare she was more afraid of the spiders than she was of the bombs.

On the night a near miss blew the roof off, leaving our sitting-room facing the stars, we were not in the shelter. It was the evening of our first wedding anniversary and a number of friends were celebrating with us when we heard the stick coming . . . one, two, three, four and wham! The Brewery had a direct hit and the fire that followed lit the night into daylight, and we knew that this tempting sight might lead to another attack. None of us was hurt, only covered with plaster, but the room we loved so much was a terrible sight; and Jeannie and I were standing at the door looking at it, thinking how only an hour or two before we had spent such care getting it ready when suddenly she said: 'Where's Monty?'

We ran down the stairs asking as we went whether anyone had seen him. We ran into the kitchen shouting his name, then into the dining-room, then into the spare bedroom that led from the kitchen. No one had seen him. I ran into the garden calling his name, the guns still firing, the flames in the Brewery leaping into the sky; and I remember how even in that moment of distress I found myself marvelling at the silhouette of a fireman's ladder that was already poised high against the fire, a pin-point of a man at the top of it. 'Monty,' I yelled, 'Monty!' No sign of him there so I went back to the house asking everyone to look, then out on to the river bank where I knew Jeannie had gone. I found her, but no Monty; and after searching for a while we felt our task hopeless, nothing to do except go home and wait. 'He'll turn up,' I said, trying to encourage her.

And half an hour later into the kitchen came one of our guests, a burly Australian war correspondent, with Monty held in his arms like a child. His fur was powdered with plaster, as white as if he had spent the night in a bakery house.

'He'd got in his foxhole,' the Australian said with a grin on his face, using the phrase of a soldier. 'I found him upstairs in the airing cupboard!'

He was unharmed except for the temporary mess of his fur; and later, when dawn was breaking and the raiders had gone, he decided to sit on the kitchen table and receive the homage of the firemen for whom Jeannie was pouring

cups of tea. The powdery plaster had been licked away; and he sat, tail gently flicking, eyes blinking, dozing like a miniature tiger in the midday sun, utterly sure of himself amidst the hubbub of chatter. He was calmer than any of the humans around him.

And when, to commemorate this end of our first year of marriage, we asked the firemen to sign their names in the visitors' book, one of them scrawled alongside his signature:

'Monty, the handsomest cat I ever saw.'

Chapter Five

WE LEFT MORTLAKE two days later to become evacuees with Jeannie's father and mother at St Albans; and within an hour of arrival at his temporary home there was an incident which had an effect on Monty for the rest of his life. He had always been suspicious of dogs, but until St Albans, he had never come face to face with one in the same room.

Bryher Lodge stood on the hill facing east towards London; and on nights when duties did not perforce make us stay in the city we would stand on the terrace above the garden which sloped down to the wood at the bottom, and watch the inferno in the distance. First the little blitz, then, a few weeks later and shortly before we returned to the cottage, the beginning of the flying bombs. We would watch for a few minutes this insanity of the human race, then return indoors to the private war between Judy the Scottie in the house, and Monty.

With Judy, when we came, was Tim the Persian. Tim was the placid old cat with blue grey fur so thick that it made him look as if he was wearing a muff, whose unwelcome attention on my first visit resulted in me knocking over the table on which stood my cup of tea. I was friends with him now, of course, and he was so placid that even Monty's sudden appearance could not annoy him. Tim and

Monty tolerated each other from the beginning but Judy, after one look at the evacuee, decided she would not give him a moment's peace. Monty was an interloper, and Judy was never to allow him to forget it.

My own opinion is that Jeannie and her mother were partly to blame because of the method of introduction they chose to arrange. I myself favoured a gradual acclimatization, an interchange of left-over sniffs after one or the other had left the room, a sight of each other in the garden with one of them safely behind a window. I was cautious, I had an instinct of inevitable trouble if suddenly they were placed nose to nose.

I expect trouble was inevitable in any case, but it certainly exploded with the least delay. I unloaded our luggage, lumbered it up to the bedroom and then heard Jeannie cry out: 'Come on downstairs, we're going to introduce Monty to Judy.' Their theory, and I suppose there was some sense in it, was that as Judy and Monty were going to live in the closest proximity, they might as well learn to be friends as quickly as possible; and I arrived in the room just as the introduction was made.

It was over within thirty seconds. Judy leapt at Monty and snapped at his paw. Monty then jumped on a table crashing a vase, remained there for an instant with fur like an upturned brush, then on to the floor dashing between the legs of Jeannie's mother who grabbed him, holding him until he freed himself, whereupon he raced across to the blue velvet curtains, up them like a monkey and remained on the pelmet, snarling like a mad thing at Judy yapping hysterically below.

We ourselves, for a moment, were quite silent. Each of us was thinking how such enmity could possibly be handled during the weeks to come. Jeannie and I, and Monty, despite it being her old home were guests in the house and we could not be expected to be popular if we brought chaos along with us; and Jeannie's mother was saying to herself that at all costs the welcome of our arrival must be brought back to normal. She did so by never disclosing that Monty had gashed her so sharply with his claws that the following day she had four stitches in her arm.

Monty and Judy never came face to face again, yet the atmosphere of their hate remained. If one was allowed free in the house, the other was shut in a room; and the one which was free would be aware of the door behind which was the other. Judy would scratch, Monty would sniff and his fur rise up. It was an unhappy period for both of them, and the immediate effect on Monty was to lessen the affection he had for Jeannie and me. He became remote from us. There were no purrs. It was as if he had lost his personality and was just an animal on four legs which had no thought in its head except to eat and sleep. He would not play. He would not sleep on the bed. His behaviour, in fact, made me lose interest in him. He was a silly, characterless cat.

This zombie attitude continued for four months until, the cottage repaired, we returned home; and within a few minutes of our arrival Monty's old self returned too. He proved it by jumping out of the kitchen window. The window had been his own private entrance, not the main casement window but the small one above it, open and shut by a lever. We had always kept it half open for him, day and night, and he would leap to its frame, pause a moment and disappear outside; or at night we would be in the kitchen and become suddenly aware that Monty had silently appeared from the darkness without and was poised up there, watching us. On this occasion he had not been in the kitchen a minute before he jumped up to this window, then down to the garden; and without waiting he was up again to the window and into the kitchen. We watched him repeat this act, as if it were a celebration dance, four or five times; and as we watched we could sense the dull attitude which had developed disappearing, and the old relationship becoming real again. 'He's actually glad to be home,' I said to Jeannie, as if I were surprised such a feeling could exist within him. 'He really *knows* he's home.'

My simplicity had its reaction later that night when I was lying awake. I found myself thinking that as I had learnt to get on perfectly well without considering Monty while at St Albans, I had better do the same now at home. I was retracing my steps. I was having a midnight revolt against my over indulgence of the cat. I had been hastening to become as cooing as the cat lovers I used to despise, submerging my own personality for Monty's benefit, becoming a slave to his wayward habits; and it was time for me to stop.

St Albans had taught me that one could give a roof to a cat without losing one's own identity; and although Monty had been plainly uncomfortable he did not run away, he remained clean, he had a good appetite. He could, therefore, lead a useful but negative life with us at the cottage, have his meals and his freedom to wander about, but, as at St Albans, there was no need for him to enter the stream of our life.

I would not, for instance, become excited just because he jumped in and out of the kitchen window. I would not consider myself favoured when he sat on my lap; I would push him off if it suited me. Lying there in the dark I realized I had been showing all the faults of the convert, all the undisciplined enthusiasm the novice displays. I had been behaving, before the change at St Albans, like a fawning servant before its master. It was ridiculous and tomorrow I must set out to regain my independence what-

ever tricks Monty might produce. Of course Jeannie was going to be difficult; but if I were cunning, if I did not take any positive action against Monty, if I were polite but distant, she would have no need to suspect that great change that had suddenly taken place inside me.

She was sound asleep, and Monty was also on the bed, down at the bottom alongside my feet. I suddenly thought: why not set the pace of my new attitude towards him immediately? My legs were cramped and had he not been occupying so much room, I could have stretched them and been comfortable, and I might even have fallen asleep. Here goes, I said to myself; and gave him a shove. A second later there was a thud on the floor, then, a few seconds later he was on the bed again. Another shove. Another thud.

And at that moment Jeannie woke up, shouting excitedly as one does when alarmed from a dream: 'What's wrong? What's wrong?'

'Nothing at all,' I said soothingly, 'only Monty fell off.'

Chapter Six

Monty's memory of Judy, had he been human, might have been eradicated on a psychiatrist's couch; but as it was the rage he felt against her simmered inside him, erupting in an explosion at intervals during the rest of his life. He was determined to fight a ceaseless battle of revenge.

His first victory, soon after our return, was over a bulldog pup belonging to a friend who lived close by. Outside our front door was a tiny garden, enclosed by a three foot wall to help keep out the high tides of the Thames; and we went over this wall from the garden to the tow path by a ladder of stone steps. These steps were never a particular favourite of Monty's, indeed he usually avoided the tiny front garden as if he disliked the bustle of the towpath on the other side of the wall; but on occasions he liked to sun himself there, and one pleasant morning he was lying on the top step when along came the bull-dog pup.

The pup was a bandy-legged brindle and he came jauntily down the alleyway from his home with a sniff here and a sniff there, up to the pillarbox and across to the lamp-post. I was standing myself by the open front door and I watched him amusedly; he looked like a schoolboy on holiday without a care in the world.

But Monty was watching as well. He watched until the pup was within five yards of the steps, then crouching as if to spring at a mouse, he waited for it to come another yard nearer ... and pounced. I was so surprised that I just stared; but the pup, thank goodness, had been attracted the same instant by the railings on the other side of the towpath; and he moved away as Monty sprang, so his stumpy stern met the onslaught instead of his back. A yell of fright from the pup and it set off at a gallop for Chiswick Bridge. It was still galloping long after Monty had stopped the chase; for Monty, as if to put fear into a bulldog was victory enough, returned nonchalantly to the steps after a chase of a few yards and unconcernedly began an elaborate wash. He never attacked the pup again, it never came near enough to let him.

Monty did not seek out his battles with dogs, creating a quarrel because he had nothing else to do. I often, for instance, saw him sitting in contemplation while a dog passed by without his ever making a move. It was when we were about that he became enraged. He either considered himself our protector or, more likely, the memory of Judy ground such jealousy in his mind that for a few moments he reverted to the wild cat of the jungle. No dog was safe whatever the size or breed and, for that matter, no human was safe who tried to stop the attack.

The first human to suffer was an elderly lady who arrived at the cottage with a small terrier on a lead. We did not fully appreciate Monty's temper at the time, and we had taken no steps to shut him in a room when the lady and the terrier entered the downstairs hall. Bang! Monty was hurtling out of the kitchen straight at the terrier and in the shambles that followed the poor lady was gashed in the leg. I had to take her to hospital.

This incident, of course, put us on our guard. We had so

to speak to put a notice outside the front door: 'Beware of the Cat.' We had to meet anyone who arrived with a dog and shout: 'Wait out there a minute while we put Monty away.' And if Monty could not be found, the visitor and the dog had to be sneaked in, then rushed upstairs to the sitting-room, and the door firmly shut. Then, when the visit was over, I would act as a scout and see whether Monty was lurking anywhere on the stairs. I had to act like a conspirator, and I used to be thankful when the visitor and his dog were safely waved away.

Yet I never met a dog owner who did not at first believe we were playing a joke. Dog owners inflict their doggy devotion on others more officiously than their cat counterparts, or some of them do. Some dog owners I have found, for instance, are either deaf or peculiarly insensitive. They shut a dog in a house or shed in the garden, and have a sadistic relish in the barks that follow for hour after hour, bringing despair and wild exasperation to the neighbours. It is a form of torture to which I am particularly vulnerable. I lie awake at night and each bark is a hammer blow, and if it comes from a distance, from somewhere unknown to me, I have an uncontrollable desire to get dressed and go searching for the exact source of the hell. The daytime yap, the yap, yap, yap on some afternoon in high summer has seen me seize a stick and march towards the noise, only to halt a few minutes later and go back. For what is the use of action? It is a strange thing about such dog owners, if you complain, if you say you cannot sleep, or get on with your work, or that you are being driven slowly mad, you are seldom met with apologies. You are made to feel it is your fault, certainly not that of the dog or its owner.

Cats, of course, make a hullabaloo on the tiles but only if other cats are there too. Cats on their own are silent while a dog on its own will still bark. Cats may impose their personalities on visitors to their homes but, as they are too independent to go on visits themselves, strange homes are spared them. Dogs bounce out of the car on arrival, go galloping over the flower beds in excitement, ignoring the cries of discipline; or come on a rainy day, shaking their wet coats, mapping the carpet with muddy paws. In our case, however, we had Monty; and so whenever a dog appeared one of us would cry out the alarm: 'Look out, Monty's about!'

The snag lay in the fact that unless the dog owner had visited us before, the reaction was not what we intended. The answer to our alarm was a display of supreme confidence.

'Oh don't worry,' would come the lofty reply, 'our dog *never* chases cats!' We would try to explain how it would be Monty who did the chasing. 'Don't you understand?' we pleaded, 'Monty will chase *your* dog!' Meanwhile the dog would be running around and, in the distance, we would see a menacing Monty approaching.

At Mortlake we had the front door as the barrier, and so a clash was comparatively easy to avert. But when we came to live at remote Minack, our cottage in Cornwall, Monty could be lying in wait anywhere. Hence the attacks at Minack were more frequent. Monty was only making certain he would never again share his life with a dog.

It was also at the time of his return from St Albans that he developed a growl. Most cats growl at some time or other but it is a sound that is a close cousin to a purr. Monty's growl was a deep throated challenge of such resonance that he might have acquired it from one of the larger dogs he hated. Yet it was not a weapon of war, a threat to frighten an opponent.

It was a means of self reassurance, a method of bolstering himself when he found himself in a situation not to his liking. Any odd noise he did not understand would bring forth the growl and, for that matter, any big noise too. He growled at the guns which fired at the flying bombs, and at thunder, and when rockets took the place of flying bombs he growled at them. The first rocket which ever landed in Britain landed within a mile of Mortlake; and it is Monty's growl I remember, not the explosion.

Sometimes the growl made us laugh because he uttered it when caught in a predicament. There was an elm tree close to the cottage at Mortlake and up it he went one day,

leaping from branch to branch, higher and higher, showing no sign he was soon to lose his nerve. I have never understood this particular blind spots of cats, how time and again they will climb to inaccessible places with the greatest of ease, then become transfixed by the height they have reached. I hate heights myself. I have an occasional nightmare which has me racing to the top of Everest; nothing hinders my climb, no hint of fear, until there I am looking out above the world . . . and quite incapable of descending. Monty too was incapable of descending and I had to fetch a ladder, and when the ladder did not reach him I had to climb up to him branch by branch. He was obviously terrified but he was not miaowing. He was growling.

A time came when we had chickens at the top of the garden, a dozen Rhode Island Reds penned in a small compound by wire netting on the side that faced the garden. On the other sides were high walls and on some point on these walls Monty would sit looking down on them while they clucked in troubled excitement. He was fascinated by their antics. Hour after hour he would crouch like a Buddha, eyeing them, trying to make up his mind what could be the purpose of their presence. At last he decided to make a closer investigation and he descended from the wall to the compound. I did not see him make his descent but I was in the garden reading a book when I heard the cacophony that hens make when a fox is among them. It was only Monty, an embarrassed Monty, surrounded by twelve furious ladies whom he was keeping at bay with his growl.

Chapter Seven

My MIDNIGHT revolt, my show of independence when I kicked Monty off the bed, was in retreat by next morning. It takes two to sustain a revolt. You cannot keep up a revolt if the opposition insists on showing affection. Monty ignored my off-hand behaviour, forcing himself on my lap whenever he wished to do so, kneading my knees with his claws, letting me watch his back bulge like bellows with his purrs. For my part I could not refrain from stroking his silky fur, gently massaging his backbone and tracing a finger round his beautiful markings. I would have been of stone if I hadn't. His presence was therapeutic, and he brought a calm to the hectic life we led.

In the years which followed the end of the war we were seldom home in the evenings except at weekends. The nature of our work rushed us from party to party and we used to return home increasingly exhausted as the week developed. One becomes casual in such circumstances. One is so absorbed in fulfilling the basic responsibilities, that one is inclined to be blind to the subtleties that enrich life. Monty was a subtlety, and although we were always sure to give him a rapturous greeting whatever hour of the night we got back, he was, I think, treated by us more as a toy than an animal. It was a period that I look back upon as distressing; and yet it had its value. It helped us in due course to form our decision to pack up our jobs and leave London. It helped us, for instance, to realize it is more important to be true to oneself than to accept unthinkingly the standards of others.

Monty, in this period, was like a toy because the haste in our life only spared us the time to bestow affection on our own terms. He was like a child in a Victorian family who was shoved into the drawing-room by a nurse only at times when the parents were in a mood to see him. He would be used as a receptacle of our emotions, hugged and kissed in times of distress, expected to play games if we demanded them, shown off like an exhibit to appropriate friends. I have seen many cats, and dogs, treated in this way, and have disliked the sight of it. When human beings use their pet animals as agents of their own exhibitionism it means humiliation both for the human being and the animal; except that the human being concerned is too dumb to feel it. Often, of course, there are people who are frightened to show affection, or think it a curious kind of bad form either in themselves or in others; hence they consider pets should be treated as if behind bars in a zoo. These are the people who bury a cat or a dog one day, and buy a substitute the next, preferably of the same colour or breed so that the sequence of outward appearance remains undisturbed. Sometimes of course, this is done not because of callousness but of fear, a fear of being unable to live a while with a memory. Either case provides an attitude which is unfair to the pet; for the first suggests it was no more important than an old kitchen chair while the second proposes that the death of a friendship can be swopped for a physical resemblance. I do not advocate a mourning, but I suggest that as a pet is a giver during its life and a human is usually a taker, a human should not accept an animal in his home unless he is prepared to make sacrifices which deserve affection.

One can also go to the other extreme and behave to an animal like a neurosis-ridden parent to his child; who must not swim because the sea might be dangerous, or own a bicycle, or stay out after dark, or who is fussed over like an invalid. Pampered animals can be observed any day of the week. Yet this other extreme need not be a form of neurosis or, for that matter, of exhibitionism. One can love

an animal overmuch because of its vulnerability, because it makes one feel secure in an insecure world, because as it grows older it reflects the years of one's life. In due course we loved Monty overmuch but at this time, at this brittle period of our life, he was a toy; which had the merits of an anchor in our restless existence.

He would glare at us from inside the dining-room window as we arrived home, the sweep of the headlights shining on his fierce face. 'We're in trouble again,' I would say as I put the key in the door. It was perfectly true that he had the knack of making us feel we had misbehaved, that two o'clock in the morning was a disgraceful hour to return home. We would switch on the light and hurry into the dining-room ready to gush a greeting, only to find he had not moved, that he was still staring out of the window pretending to be unaware of our arrival except for the sharp flicks of his tail.

Jeannie used to come ready to bribe on these occasions and after she had purposely clattered plates in the kitchen and unwrapped some small paper parcel that had been donated by the Savoy restaurant, Monty would enter with the air of a cat who was ready to let bygones be bygones. He would devour the delicacy, lick the pattern off the plate but, unfortunately, would not pay the price expected of him. Jeannie's caresses were spurned and he would struggle free from her arms, jump first on the sink then up through his private entrance above the kitchen window, and disappear into the night. He was an opportunist, not a weak character open to a bribe.

There were other times when there was no doubt he had become unhappy in our absence. I knew the sign when we stood at the front door and heard him come thumping down the bare wood stairs, wakened by the sound of the car as we drew up. 'He's only hungry,' I would say to Jeannie, mocking his greeting. But if he was hungry it was not the hunger which was the result of a bribe. He did not bellicosely clean the plate, then away into the night. He would eat a little then look up at us watching him; and I defy the person who does not believe he was saying thank you. And afterwards he would not refuse to pay the price of his meal. Jeannie was permitted to hug him, as many hugs as she wanted, and carry him upstairs and deposit him on the bed where he lay curled through the night. There was now no fear of my kicking him off.

He was not on his own all the time. We did not leave

him at nine in the morning and let him fend for himself until our return at any old hour. He had his friends. There was our daily, Mrs Hales, who had to queue for his whiting before she arrived at the cottage; whiting the staple diet, with the stink that hung for hours in the cottage. Mrs Hales was ill one day but as she lay in her bed she realized that the whiting, bought and cooked two days before, must have been consumed. 'Oh dear,' she said, explaining the situation to us later, 'oh dear, there I lay thinking of poor Monty. Whatever will he do, I said. All by 'imself and nothing to eat. It mustn't be I said. So I got up and called a neighbour through the window. "Our Monty," I said, "'asn't got 'is whiting. Do me a favour will you?" I said, "go to the fish shop and get three nice whiting. I can manage to cook 'em . . . then I'll send me 'usband up to Monty when 'e comes 'ome from work."'

There were Mr and Mrs Foster who lived next door at the Ship. The Fosters had been landlords since 1912, through the times when the Ship, as the pub at the finishing post of the Boat Race, was a pivot of the great day. Maharajahs, Cabinet Ministers, famous actors and actresses, as Gus and Olivette Foster never ceased telling us, used to be their customers then, shouting the crews to victory between glasses of champagne. There was none of that now; the bars were crowded on the big day, the steps of the pub and the towpath in front were jammed with people, but for the Fosters it was a poor imitation of what they remembered.

A high wall divided our small garden from theirs; and theirs was large enough for Gus Foster, in the distant past, to tether the trotting ponies the racing of which was once his hobby. This wall was Monty's favourite and he would reach it by way of the kitchen window and the flat roof of our spare room which ran along a short way beside it.

Thus Monty, as he patrolled the top of this wall, could be observed not only from our side but also from the back windows of the Ship by anyone, such as the Fosters' son with the nickname of Whiskers, who might be at work in the garden.

Both Whiskers and his sister Doris had a particular interest in Monty, but as Doris worked in London during the day, it was Whiskers, the barman in the pub, who mostly kept a watch on his outside activities. He was in his garden one day digging a patch of ground when he heard a terrific hullabaloo on the other side of the wall as if it came through an open window from inside the house. Quite obviously the noise was of two fighting cats and one of them, presumably, was Monty.

Now the Fosters kept the key of our front door for just this kind of emergency, and Whiskers we always considered as a guardian of Monty in our absence. He was about to rush in for the key when the noise suddenly rose to a crescendo, followed a few seconds later by a huge tabby racing along the top of the wall with Monty at his tail. Whiskers said afterwards he was so delighted to see such a victory that he shouted: 'Well done, Monty!' at the top of his voice. But Monty, left alone on the wall after the tabby had fled over another, was obviously hurt. He lifted up a paw, looked down at Whiskers and miaowed loudly.

So Whiskers fetched the key and went inside our cottage and into the garden, and coaxed Monty down from the wall and into his arms. It was a nasty bite and we had the vet for him that evening; for Whiskers had immediately rung up Jeannie to tell her of the battle.

And what was the battle about? Instead of the stink of fish in the kitchen there was the stink of a tom cat. The tabby had stolen the whiting.

Chapter Eight

NOT ONLY THE Fosters but others along the river bank kept a watch on Monty. He was a talisman to the passers-by as he sat in the dining-room window, hour after hour, waiting for our return. One autumn we spent a month in Paris and when we got back we were looked at reproach-fully by those who had seen him day after day in the window. 'You should have seen him late at night when the street lamp lit up his face,' said a neighbour, 'he looked so mournful.' We hated to hear such remarks because we felt we were in the wrong. Of course he had been well looked after by his guardians but he had been very lonely. And yet what does one do if ever one wishes to go away for a holiday with an easy conscience? Deposit a cat at the vet and you may think it is safe but you cannot possibly persuade yourself that the cat in such strange surroundings does not believe it has been deserted and has been left in a prison. There seems to be no answer except never to take a holiday.

Monty's big day in the dining-room window was Boat Race day. The Boat Race party, as far as we were concerned, came round each year much too quickly. An annual affair which had such raucous results as a Boat Race party, is apt to dissolve in some mysterious way with its predecessors. Time stands still. The guests have never left, or they are always just arriving or saying goodbye. Hence my old friends Mr and Mrs X are greeted by me at the door and I feel I am simultaneously greeting them this year, last year and the year before. Ours used to be a bottle party and as the Boat Race generally took place at some unearthly hour in the morning, guests began to arrive with their bottles at 9 a.m. The trouble with a bottle party is the stress it puts on the host and hostess who are inclined to greet their guests with graduated enthusiasm, according to the importance of the bottle. We had one guest who regularly brought a bottle of milk. I never found out whether this was a joke, for he consumed alcohol like everyone else; but I remember how our greeting became dimmer each year until it would have become extinct had we not departed for Cornwall.

The preparations, of course, began at the crack of dawn and as it was always a marathon day of festivity, large quantities of food were prepared to cope with late breakfasts, lunch, tea and those who still had the stamina to stay for supper. For Monty these preparations were a nuisance and this might be considered surprising because, with so much food about, one might have expected him to be the official taster. But he was never a greedy cat. He ate his requirements and no more, although like all of us he had certain favourite dishes, chopped pigs' liver, for instance, which he gobbled faster than others. He considered these preparations a nuisance, I think, because he wanted to get on with the party. He had a role to play, and it was a role which he enjoyed.

He would keep out of sight, the airing cupboard was the ideal hiding place, until he had the good sense to realize the towpath was waking up; shouts of small boys who without reason for loyalty to either University were violently partisan on behalf of one or other of the crews, odd couples booking places on the railings, then the appearance of hawkers with dark and light blue favours. There was a pleasant atmosphere of impending excitement, and it was now that Monty appeared and expected attention.

Both Jeannie and I were Cambridge supporters and before our first Boat Race party Jeannie had bought Monty a large light blue ribbon which she tied in a bow round his neck. I did not approve. I thought such a gesture was

ostentatious and silly and I anticipated confidently that Monty would wriggle free from the encumbrance as soon as he had the chance. He did not do so. True the ribbon became more and more askew as the day wore on with the bow finishing up under his tummy, but this had nothing to do with any action on his part. It was the attention he received which caused that.

Hence the light blue ribbon became an annual ritual and invariably, after the bow had been tied, he would sit in the dining-room window staring with a lordly air at the crowds; and the crowds looking for a diversion until the race began would call to him and shout to their friends about him. He adored this period of glory. So much on his own but now at last receiving his due. And when our guests arrived, a hundred or more packing the cottage, a cacophony of laughter and talk, cigarette smoke clouding the rooms, people sitting on the floor and the stairs, glasses everywhere, Jeannie and I rushing around with bottles and plates of cold food, Monty was as cool as a cucumber. He would stroll from room to room, pausing beside a guest when the praise was high, even deigning to jump on a lap, ignoring the cat haters, refusing with well-bred disgust any morsel dangled before him by some well-meaning admirer. He was unobtrusively sure of himself; and when the rackety day was over, when Jeannie and I had gone to bed feeling too tired to sleep and we put out a hand and touched him at the bottom of the bed, we both felt safe. Safe, I mean, from the tensions among which we lived.

Sometimes I wonder if we would ever have come to Cornwall had it not been for Monty. Decisions are often based on motives which are not obviously apparent, and cool intellects certainly would not believe that two people could change the mainspring of their life because of a cat. Such intellects, however, are free from turbulent emotions. They are the human version of the computer; to be envied, perhaps, because they are spared the distractions of light and shade. They can barge through life indifferent to the sensibilities of others because they have none themselves. Materialism in their view, is the only virtue.

Monty became a factor in our decision because he reflected, in his own fashion, stability. It did not matter how tired we were when we reached home, how irritated we might be by the day's conflict of personalities, how worried by inflated anxieties, how upset by apparent failures, Monty was solidly there to greet us. His presence, you might say, knocked sense back into us, He thus gave a clue to the kind of reward we might have if we exchanged our existing way of life for one that had a more enduring standard of values. We did not say this self-consciously at the time, too many other factors were involved; but on reflection I realize his example helped us to take the plunge.

The process of changing over from a city to a country life was spread over a year and more. We made several sorties to the cottage near Land's End during that time, and Monty was usually a companion. He appeared to be quite unconcerned by the long car journey except once, and that was my fault. I was naturally on guard against him jumping out of the car in a panic whenever on the route I had to slow down or stop; but there came a time when I exchanged my ordinary car for a Land Rover. A saloon car you could shut tight but a Land Rover with its canvas hood had potential gaps through which a determined cat might escape. I therefore bought him a basket and at the instant of leaving Mortlake I pushed him in it, banged down the lid and tied it, and set off. It was an appalling miscalculation. Instead of appreciating my action as a gesture towards his own safety, he took it as an insult. He was enraged. He clawed and spat and cried and growled. I was half way to Staines when the noise of his temper forced me to stop, and I gingerly lifted the lid up an inch. A pair of eyes of such fury blazed through the slit that I hastily banged down the lid again.

Now Jeannie was with me on this occasion and inevitably this incident developed an argument. She wanted to take him out of the basket. I was too scared that once allowed to be free there would be no holding him. My imagination saw him gashing us with his claws as he fought to escape, then away like a madman into the countryside. She, however, insisted that only the basket angered him and he would be his old gentle self as soon as he was let out. So the argument went on, past Staines, past Camberley, past Basingstoke; it was not until we reached the outskirts of Andover that I gave in. Monty was released and, with a look of disgust in my direction the purrs began.

There was another occasion when he travelled as a stowaway on the night train from Paddington. Jeannie was always very proud of this exploit as she was the architect of its success. She was due to join me for the weekend and was dining at the Savoy before catching her sleeper when she suddenly decided she would like Monty to accompany her. She dashed back to Mortlake, found him, after a five minute desperate search, crouched on the wall at the end of the garden, and arrived at Paddington with three minutes to spare. Monty was an admirable conspirator. He remained perfectly still as she rushed him along the platform wrapped in a rug. Not a miaow. Not a growl. And nobody would ever have known that the night train had carried a cat, had Jeannie been able to curb her vociferous enthusiasm when she arrived at Penzance.

But she behaved as if the Crown Jewels were in her compartment. She was in such a high state of excitement when I met her that she did not notice the car attendant was directly behind me as she slid open the door to disclose her secret.

Monty's aplomb was superb. He stared at the man with regal indifference from the bunk. And as I recovered from my surprise and Jeannie muttered feeble excuses, all the car attendant found himself able to say was: 'Good heavens, what a beautiful cat!'

Five minutes later we were in the car on the road to Minack.

Chapter Nine

MONTY WAS WARY in the beginning at Minack. He did not relax on those initial short visits, seldom put his nose outside the cottage, making even a walk of a few yards in our company a notable occasion. He was seven years old and needed time for readjustment.

Minack is a cottage a few hundred yards from the cliff and cupped in a shallow valley with a wood behind it. The walls grow up from great rocks which some crofter a few centuries ago decided would make the ideal foundation. The stones of the walls are bound together with clay and, when we first came, the floor inside the cottage was of earth layered over by thin boards. There are two rooms; one, which is the length of the cottage is our living-room and kitchen, the other a tiny one, is our bedroom; and there is a third room which we added as an extension along with a bathroom that became known in his lifetime as Monty's room. On one side of the cottage the windows stare out undisturbed, except for the old barn buildings, across moorland to the sea and the distant coastline rimming Mount's Bay; on the other, two small windows on either side of the door face a pocket of a garden. The old crofter, the architect of Minack, wished to defend the cottage against the south westerlies; and so this little garden, and the cottage, were set in the hill that rose away to the west. Thus, if we walk up the hill fifty yards and look back, the eye is level with the massive granite chimney; the chimney which to fishermen sailing back to Mousehole and Newlyn in a stormy sea gives the comfortable feeling they are near home.

There is no house or eyesore in sight; and this freedom amid such untamed country provides a sense of immortality. As if here is a life that belongs to any century, that there is no harsh division in time, that the value of true happiness lies in the enduring qualities of nature. The wind blows as it did when the old crofter lived at Minack, so too the robin's song, and the flight of the curlew, and the woodpecker's knock on an elm. This sense of continuity may be unimportant in a world with the knowledge to reach the stars; but to us it provided the antidote to the life we had led. It was a positive reminder that generations had been able to find contentment without becoming slaves of the machine. Here around us were the ghosts of men and animals, long forgotten storms and hot summer days, gathered harvests and the hopes of spring. They were all one, and our future was part of them.

Our plan was to earn a living by growing flowers and, the speciality of the district, early potatoes in pocket meadows on the cliff. We were, however, more influenced by the beauty of the environment than by its practical value; hence we presented ourselves with difficulties which had to be borne as a sacrifice to our whim. There was, for instance, no lane to the cottage. A lane ran from the main road a half mile to a group of farm buildings at the top of the valley; but once past these buildings it became rougher and rougher until it stuttered to a stop amid brambles and gorse. In due course we cut a way through and made a road, but in the beginning the nearest we could take the car to Minack was the distance of two fields; and across these two fields we used to carry our luggage ... and Monty.

Jeannie on the first visit put butter on his paws. There had been a sad, remarkable case in a newspaper of a cat that had been taken away from his home near Truro to another near Chester from which he had immediately disappeared. Several weeks later he arrived back to his old Truro home but so exhausted and close to starvation that he died a day or two later. I do not pretend to believe this story, documented in detail as it was, but Jeannie did, and she had a vision of Monty dashing from Minack and making for Mortlake. Thus she used the old wives' recipe for keeping a cat at home by buttering his paws; the theory being of course that the cat licks off the butter and says to himself that such a nice taste is worth staying for. A slender theory, I think, though comforting.

But it was soon made clear on that first visit and repeated on succeeding ones that Monty had no intention of running away. It was the opposite that provided us with problems. He never had the slightest wish to leave.

During this period, as I have said, he distrusted the outside around the cottage, made nervous perhaps by the unaccustomed silence and the unknown mysterious scents; and when we urged him to come out with us, he would usually turn tail as soon as we dropped him to the ground and rush back indoors. He was, in fact, sometimes so timid that he annoyed me, and I would pick him up again, deliberately deposit him a hundred yards from the cottage, then, impotently, crossly, watch him race back again.

Why, then, did he always disappear when we were due to start back for Mortlake? The bags would be packed, one load perhaps already lugged across the fields to the car, and there would be no sign of Monty. Obstinately remaining inside the cottage when we wanted him to be out, he

was now out when we wanted him to be in. But where? The first disappearance resulted in a delay of two hours in our departure for we had no clue where to look. He had no haunts to which he might have sneaked, because he had never been long enough out of the cottage on his own to find one; no haunts, that is, that we knew of. Yet apparently on one of his brief excursions he had made a note of the barn, and how at the bottom of the barn door was a hole big enough for him to wriggle through; and that as the barn at the time was not ours and the door was kept locked, and the key kept by a farmer ten minutes away, it was a wonderful place to hide in. It became a ritual for him to hide there at the end of each visit. The key fetched, the key returned, and in between I would have had to climb to a beam near the ceiling where Monty glared balefully down at me. Or was he saying: 'I like it here. Hurry up and make it my home'?

It became his home one April evening when the moon

was high. We had now cleared a way through the brush of the lane and though the surface was too rough for ordinary cars, it was suitable enough for a Land Rover. On this particular evening we bumped our way along it, the canvas hood bulging with our belongings. Monty alert on Jeannie's lap, both of us ecstatically happy that at last the time-wasting preliminaries had been completed. We drew up with a jerk and I switched off the engine. It was a beautiful moment. No sound but that of the surf in the distance. The moon shimmering the cottage as if it were a ghost cottage. Here was journey's end and adventure's beginning. All we had worked for had materialized.

'Good heavens, we're lucky,' I said, then added briskly as if to foreshadow the practical instead of the romantic side of our life to come. 'I'll get the luggage out . . . you go ahead with Monty and light the candles.'

But it was Monty who went ahead. He jumped from Jeannie's lap, paused for a moment to see she was ready to follow, then sedately led the way up the path. A confident cat. A cat who knew he was home. A cat, in fact, who was happy.

Chapter Ten

MONTY'S TRANSITION into a country cat was a gradual affair. An urban gentleman does not become a country gentleman simply by changing his clothes. He must learn to adopt a new code of manners and a new approach to the outdoors; to be less suave and to show more bluster, to accept the countryside as a jungle which has to be mastered by skill and experience. Monty, as an urban cat, had therefore a lot to learn.

He first had to acclimatize himself to having us always around and he showed his delight in various ways. There was, for instance, the in-and-out window game, a game which was designed not only to display his affection but also to confirm his wonderment that we were now always present to obey his orders. Thus he would jump on a window sill and ask to be let out, only, a few minutes later, to be outside another window asking to be let in. This performance would continue for an hour until one of us lost patience, saying crossly: 'For goodness sake, Monty, make up your mind what you want to do.' He would then have the good sense to stop the game, replacing it probably by a short, though vigorous, wash.

There were the unsolicited purrs. A cat has to be in a very bad mood if a human cannot coax him to purr. There is little honour in this achievement, only the satisfaction that a minute or two is being soothed by such a pleasant sound. But the unsolicited purrs belong to quite another category. These are the jewels of the cat fraternity distributed sparingly like high honours in a kingdom. They are brought about by great general contentment. No special incident induces them. No memory of past or prospect of future banquets. Just a whole series of happy thoughts suddenly combine together and whoever is near is lucky enough to hear the result. Thus did Monty from time to time reward us.

My own preference was for the midnight unsolicited purr. For the first years, until we found a fox waiting for Monty to jump out, he had the freedom of the window at night. He used to go in and out and we were never disturbed if he chose to spend the night outside, perhaps in the barn. But when he did choose to remain indoors, and instead of settling on the sofa, preferred a corner of our bed, we felt flattered. It was then that I have relished when sometimes I lay awake, the rich, rolling tones of an unsolicited purr.

In those early days the unsolicited purr was bestowed on us frequently. Later, when country life became to him a continuously happy routine it became rarer; but in the beginning the new pattern of his life was so ebulliently wonderful that he could not restrain himself. There he would be on the carpet in the posture of a Trafalgar lion and suddenly the music would begin. For no reason that we could see. Just his personal ecstasy.

There were other times when his show of affection was awkward. It was then that he posed a question that as a cat hater I used to find easy to answer, but now as a cat lover I found most difficult. How do you summon up courage to dismiss a cat who is paying you the compliment of sitting on your lap?

If you have a train to catch, if your life is governed by rules not of your own making, the excuse for removal is ready made. But in my case time was my own, the work to be done was the product of my own self discipline, I could not blame anyone else if I shoved off Monty who was comfortably enjoying a rest on my lap. I would gingerly start to lift him up, my hands softly encircling his middle, with the intention of placing him gently on the spot I was about to vacate; and he would hiss, growl and very likely bite my hand. True this was a momentary flash of temper with more noise than harm in it; but the prospect of its display, the certainty I was offending him, were enough time and again for me to postpone any action.

My subservience was made to look even more foolish when Jeannie, as she often did, served a meal on a tray. My seat was always the corner one of the sofa and so I used to endeavour to balance the plate-filled tray partly on the sofa arm, partly on Monty's back; trying, of course, to take great care not to put any weight on Monty. If, however, he showed signs of annoyance, if he woke up from his sleep and turned his head crossly round at me, I would edge the tray further over the arm so that it balanced like the plank of a see-saw. I enjoyed many meals this way in the greatest discomfort.

Rational people would not behave like that. I can imagine my own sneers if a few years before I had seen into the future and found I was going to behave in such a fashion. But there it was, I enjoyed it. I was glad to be of some service, and I used to be tinged with jealousy if he chose on occasions to honour Jeannie instead. Such occasions were rare because her lap was not up to his measurements. He overfilled it. He was like a large man on a small stool. She would sit, transfixed into immobility, and if at the time anything was being cooked in the oven it was sure to be burnt. Pleasure is relative to the desire of the individual. I do not know what pleasure Jeannie could have been offered in exchange for such moments with Monty.

These incidents may suggest that, now that the three of us were always together, Monty was spoilt. But is not a cat's nature, any cat, impervious to being spoilt? You can spoil a child and it can become a nuisance. You can spoil a dog and everyone except its owner is certain to suffer. A cat on the other hand, however luscious may be the bribes, remains cool and collected. Indulgence never goes to its head. It observes flattery instead of accepting it. Monty, for instance, did not consider himself an inferior member of the household; a pet, in fact. Thus he loathed it when condescension was shown to him; and many a misguided stranger trying to lure him with snapping fingers and 'pussy talk' has seen his haughty back. He was cotenant of the cottage. He was not to be treated in that imbecile fashion so many people reserve for animals. The compliments he wished for were of the kind we gave him; we set out to implement any decision he made on his own by helping to make the result as successful as possible. We played the role of the ideal servants and we won our reward by watching his enjoyment. And there was another reward which Jeannie called 'paying his rent'.

His rent was making him do what he did not want to do. Hence this was the reward we forced him to give us when we felt in the mood to assert our authority. Jeannie might suddenly pick him up, hold him in her arms and hug him, when it was perfectly obvious that he wished to be left by himself. He would lie in her arms, a pained expression on his face, as she talked sweet nothings to him; and then, the rent paid, he would rush across the room to a window sill and sit there, tail slashing like a scythe, demanding to be let out.

I always maintained that Jeannie demanded more rent than I did. I think she had good reason to do so because she was responsible for his catering; and she was always filling plates or picking up empty ones or asking him to make up his mind what he wanted. 'Oh really, Monty,' she would say in mock fierceness, with Monty looking up at her as she stood by the sink, 'I've just thrown one saucer of milk away, you can't want another!' Or it might be one more morsel of fish required, and out would come the pan and down would go the plate.

His menu, now that we lived near a fishing port, was splendidly varied, and twice a week Jeannie would collect from Newlyn a supply of fresh fish. None of that shop-soiled whiting he used to have but sea-fresh whiting, boned megram sole or a little halibut or, what became his most favourite of all – John Dorey, the fish which fishermen themselves take home for their suppers. He would gobble John Dorey until he bulged, one of the few things which lured him to greed; and to satisfy this greed he would try to show his most endearing self to Jeannie. The spot where his saucers were placed was opposite the front

door on the carpet at the foot of a bookcase which hid one corner of the sink. When he was hungry, a normal hunger not too demanding, he would sit on this spot, upright with front paws neatly together and the tip of his tail gently flicking them. His eyes would be half closed and he would sway imperceptibly to and fro. A meal was due but he was in no hurry.

Yet if John Dorey was on the menu and was simmering in a pan on the stove he could never restrain his impatience. He would walk excitedly up and down the room, roaring with anticipated pleasure, rubbing himself against Jeannie's legs, looking up at her as if he were saying: 'I love you, I love you.' Here was a cat who was no longer retaining his dignity. Nothing could hide the fact that at this particular moment Monty was thinking that Jeannie was the most wonderful cook in the world.

He would then have been ready to promise her, I am sure, all the rent she required.

Chapter Eleven

Monty's hunting at Mortlake had been limited to indoor mice, or indoor mice which happened to be outside. He soon began to find at Minack a variety of potential victims the like of which he had never seen before; and in some cases he was at a loss to the technique of attack required. I found him once, for instance, staring at a patch of ground under which a mole was digging.

My own first experience of a mole digging was the morning after a night out. It upset me. I was walking across a field, my head down, when I was suddenly aware that a patch of soil the size of a hat was moving. I stopped, stared and pinched myself. The soil circled like a slow spinning top, rising upwards, the texture of a seed bed. Monty saw this for the first time and was as startled as I had been. He put out a paw as if he were thinking of touching a red hot coal, then leapt backwards with a growl. 'It's only a mole, old chap,' I said knowledgeably, 'only a mole digging a mole hill,' He was reassured enough to advance again. He touched the soil with his paw, then, meeting with no reaction, in fact finding there was no danger or excitement for him at all, he walked away with nonchalant composure; as cats do when they suspect they have made fools of themselves.

Another puzzle for him was what to do when he found

an adder. A lizard, a slow worm or an ordinary grass snake was an easy excuse for a few minutes play, but an adder he sensed was a danger; and he was certainly right. We have too many of them about. We are always on guard during the summer wearing Wellington boots whenever we walk through the undergrowth; although it is in a warm spring when they are at their most viperish. I have been happily picking Scilly Whites on the cliff when I have suddenly seen the poised head of one within a few inches of my hand, hissing like escaped steam. In the summer they will wriggle away as you advance towards them and will whip up their heads and strike only if you step on them or tease them. In the spring they will attack at the slightest provocation and, as they have been hibernating through the winter, the venom injected into the wounds made by the fangs is a dose built up over the months. I learnt my lesson after the Scilly Whites, but Monty never learnt his lesson not to tease.

I have seen him touching the tail of an adder with his paw as if he were playing a dare game. It might have been even a form of Russian roulette because an adder can kill a cat, though this is very rare. As an adder is thirty inches long, perhaps he was deceived in to thinking that the head was too far away to catch him, or perhaps I was worrying unnecessarily. He certainly never was bitten by an adder, nor for that matter did he ever kill one. He flirted with the danger. It was a game . . . and yet, I wonder. There is a tradition in Cornwall that the capture and killing of an adder is the peak of a cat's hunting career; and when the rare victory is achieved the trophy is ceremoniously dragged whatever distance to the home and deposited on the floor of the kitchen for all to admire. Perhaps this was Monty's secret ambition. Perhaps above all he longed for the plaudits awarded to an adder killer. If so, the fates were against him.

I will not, fortunately, ever know the differences in flavour of mice — indoor mice, harvest mice, long tailed mice, short eared mice and so on. Shrews must be unpleasant because Monty, although he would catch them for fun, never ate them. But it seems obvious to me after watching the attitude of Monty that outdoor mice have a far better flavour then the ordinary household mice. At Mortlake, he became, without being flamboyantly successful, a sound indoor mouse catcher. At Minack he spent so much time outside on the alert that often he lost the desire to fulfil his inside duties; and since the excitement of the chase should be the same both in and out, it occurred to me sometimes that the cause of his extraordinary behaviour may have been a bored palate.

I would be quite wrong to suggest that we were riddled with mice at Minack. For months we would be totally free of any sign of a mouse but at intervals one or two would arrive and cause us annoyance. They would make an unwelcome noise on the boards which provided our ceiling, and on occasions would descend to the sitting-room. Here Monty was often sleeping on the sofa. 'Monty!' I would say sharply, 'there's a mouse in the cupboard.' And Monty would go on sleeping.

The cupboard concerned was the shape of a large wardrobe, shelves climbing two sides while the back was the wall of the cottage. Apart from the china on the shelves with cups on hooks, there was a table in the cupboard on which stood a calor gas refrigerator; and under the table was the gas cylinder, pots and pans, a bread bin and various other household paraphernalia. Thus the cupboard was crowded and a mouse had a wonderful place to hide unless we set about clearing a space by removing the chattels into the sitting-room. We would perform this tedious task, then wake up Monty, carry him to the cupboard, and deposit him there. He was alone, except for the gas cylinder which was too much trouble to move, with the mouse.

Here, then, was a situation that was often repeated. Monty one side of the gas cylinder and the mouse on the other, and Monty had only to race once round the cylinder to catch it. Yet he would not budge. He would sit looking at me as if he were trying to tell me the mouse was his dearest friend. 'Go on, Monty!' my voice rising to a crescendo, 'go on, you ass. Catch it!' The mouse would move its position and I would push Monty towards it so that they met nose to nose. Still not a whisker of interest. Nor any sign of fear from the mouse. I would push and exhort and be angry and in the end give up in despair. Monty had a pact with the mouse and nothing I could do would make him break it.

But why? He was swift as a panther when outside. He would be across the land and into the hedge and back again with his capture inside a few seconds; and when necessary he had infinite patience. I always found it an endearing sight to look through the window and see him in the distance perched on a rock, staring intently at the grass a yard away; then begin to gather himself for the pounce, shifting the stance of his paws, swaying gently forwards and backwards, until he gauged the great moment had come. And when he missed, when by some miscalculation he ended up in the grass with his back legs spread-eagled and a waving tail denoting his failure, I sensed with him his disappointment. His successes, of course, were loudly trumpeted. He consumed his victims not at the place of execution but on a square yard of ground on the edge of the path leading up to the cottage. No matter how distant the capture he would return with it to this spot; and I would see him coming jauntily up the lane, a

mouthful of grass as well as the mouse. A few minutes later when nothing was left he would let out the bellow of victory. 'Well done, Monty,' we would say, 'well done!'

He was a wonderful hunter of rabbits, and he had an earnest idea that these should always be brought into the cottage and left under my desk until I had seen them. This behaviour was prompted by my enthusiasm for the first rabbit he caught. It was a baby one and the incident took place within a month of his arrival at Minack; and because I was so anxious to see him settle down, my enthusiasm and that of Jeannie was far too vociferous.

I was writing a letter and never knew he had entered the room until I heard a soft jungle cry at my feet; and there was Monty, like a retriever, looking up at me with the rabbit beside him. He was inordinately proud of himself. He strode up and down the room as we praised him, with purrs loud enough for three cats, rubbing against us, then scampering back across the room to have another sniff. He never forgot the glory of this moment, and time and again we had to suffer a repeat performance. If we saw him coming we shut the door, and there was always plenty of time to do so. A rabbit was far too big for him to carry in his mouth, and he would pull it along on the ground. 'Poor rabbit,' Jeannie would say, dead though it was.

Monty never touched birds, except one when I saw him

catch a wren which annoyed him. Wrens can be foolish and this one was foolish. They are so small that if they kept themselves to themselves no one need know their whereabouts; instead they proclaim their presence by the cross rattle of warning and, in spring, enjoy baiting any objects they dislike. There was Monty lying somnolent in the garden while a pair of Wrens rattled around him until he lost his temper and snatched one. I dashed forward, caught him, and put a hand to his mouth; and as I did so, he let the wren go and it flew safely away to a bush where it began its rattle again. And Monty went back to doze.

Monty's docile attitude to birds met its response from them. They showed no fear of him. It was I, if anything, who felt fear. I was always waiting for the incident that never happened.

Chapter Twelve

I BECOME VAGUE when I try to isolate the years. I would like to have them arrayed in my mind in neat compartments but I find instead they merge into each other, and incidents connect themselves by haphazard association rather than by dates. Thus the flower seasons here at Minack, each of which has a slow moving yet mounting dramatic entity of its own, become dissolved in my mind into all flower seasons. The hours I have crouched weeding anemones or picking violets, lugging baskets of daffodils to the packing shed, rushing the flower boxes in the morning to Penzance Station, these hours do not belong to one year but to all years. So also appear the storms that have battered Minack, and the lazy pleasure of hot summer days, the first scent of the may, the arrival of the chiff chaffs, the wonder of an angry sea with a fishing boat fighting for home. I have grown older not by passing each incident as if it were a milestone, but by being absorbed by them.

As Monty grew older his contentment was so obvious for all to see that we felt part of it. If something had gone wrong, if we had suffered some defeat which left us despondent, the sight of his magnificent person poised perhaps on some wall with the sun glinting his red bracken coat, his head alertly surveying the scene around him, would be enough to quell our momentary fears. His example was a positive contribution to the life we had chosen for ourselves.

I suppose it was this contentment that produced in him his calm attitude to birds. There was no need for him to kill for the sake of killing because he had so much else to do and, for that matter, so much else to think about. He was a great thinker. We have seen him so many, many times blinking away in the sun, not asleep, not awake, sitting upright with paws bunched, a shining white shirtfront, tail round his haunches, the tip flicking delicately. 'Look at Monty,' Jeannie would say, 'He's having his million and one thought.'

And while he was contemplating, the birds would be hopping around him. We had a bird table in the pocket garden opposite the front door and inevitably the crumbs we put on it used to be blown off on to the ground; neither Monty nor the birds were perturbed as they collected them. Of course if you live in the country you are certain to make friends with individual birds which respond to your approach with more trust than others. In our case we had two particular friends who hopped around Monty collecting the crumbs, whom we called Charlie and Tim.

Charlie was a chaffinch and Tim a robin, and they both treated Monty as if a cat was the most harmless thing in the world. Charlie was a bossy character who, in the spring and summer, used to follow us around cheeping all day. Even a bird's voice can sometimes sound too persistent and we used to chafe Charlie for the monotony of his cry. A gentleman chaffinch, if you look at it closely, is a beautiful bird. There is a touch of the tropics about its plumage of slate-blue, pink, chestnut, black and white wings and tail; only its voice is humdrum. Thus Charlie's voice as he perched on certain favourite places was a high pitched note repeated over and over again, until I marvelled sometimes that Monty was not irritated into action.

He would hop, for instance, at the entrance of the flower house while Monty was dozing on a bench and we were bunching the daffodils, piping away on and on until in exasperation I would say: 'For goodness sake, Charlie, think up another song.' Or he would perch on a certain stunted old apple tree under which in the lush grass Monty used to like to slumber; there would lie Monty curled in a ball while above him, with the monotony of a pneumatic drill, sang Charlie. But it was when we sat out of doors having breakfast or lunch that Monty was put most to the test.

We used to sit on a white seat, the scent of a verbena bush pervading the air, the sea in the distance, Monty at our feet, and Charlie a few yards away on the gravel path determinedly demanding crumbs from our plates. Nor would Charlie be alone, for he would have with him the dim little person who was his wife; and thus Monty had two to look at, to be tempted by, and yet to ignore.

In winter Charlie was a more silent individual, as if the summer had consumed his song. His feathers would lose their sheen, he would crouch rather than perch on a branch as if days were made to be borne instead of enjoyed. Sometimes he would disappear for weeks on end, and there was one winter when he was so long away that we made up our minds that he was dead. We missed his perky presence. We regretted our rudeness about his voice. We yearned to see his busy little nature once again. And we did. In the spring he suddenly appeared one day in the wood while Jeannie was feeding the chickens, the same old song, the same old Charlie, bossy as ever.

Tim was a gentle robin, if you can think of a robin as gentle. At least we ourselves never saw him attacking another or trying to assert his personality at the expense of other birds. Charlie would drive him off the bird table at any time. Tim simply did not fancy a battle. He preferred to wait cunningly until Charlie had had his fill, then he would return and stay there until perhaps a tom tit would harshly tell him to go; Tim, in fact, believed in appeasement. This possibly was the reason why he liked so much to be indoors with us, or in the flower packing shed when we were there. He found life less troublesome, felt safer, if he sat on a corner of my desk, despite the fact Monty might be wandering about the room. It was a remarkable sight seeing Tim on the back of a chair while Monty was on the chair itself. Or looking for crumbs on the carpet while Monty lay stretched by the stove. Or just flying around the room while Monty appeared not to take the slightest notice. Of course, Monty knew he was there. He observed Tim out of the corner of his eye, but it was an eye that never had the suspicion of a glint.

Yet Tim at times became so over-confident that he seemed to be going out of his way to court attack from Monty. I remember him once in the flower packing shed standing delicately on one leg on the cup of a daffodil that rose from a galvanized pail. The pail was with others on the floor and there was Monty threading his way between them until he reached the spot where Tim was on the daffodil looking down on him, while a paw stretch away he was looking up at Tim; but neither bothered to show any interest.

The height of Tim's foolishness was when he urged his lady of the year to build a nest at ground level among a bed of polyanthus. Heaven knows what caused him to choose such a place because it was in an area fifty yards from the cottage which Monty had found a particularly fruitful hunting ground. Perhaps Tim had done so because it was so near to the packing shed, which meant he could have an idle time indoors without being too far from his mate. Anyhow I found the nest while I was picking the polyanthus, flushing the mate away as I did so.

At that moment, I saw Monty coming towards me, walking earnestly between two rows of plants, tail erect, a benign expression on his face which suggested that for some reason I was particularly popular. This was a moment to enjoy not to spurn, but I hastened towards him, swept him up in my arms and carried him, now cross, away to the cottage. Then I returned with bamboo sticks and a coil of wire netting and proceeded to encircle the nest in a cage. It looked safe when I had finished, but my activities had upset even Tim. The nest was never used again.

A third friend was Hubert the gull. He was far too superior, of course, ever to use the bird table, and he would stand on the rim of the roof waiting for us to throw food to him. Quite often Charlie would be there too, hoping to pinch a bite from under Hubert's beak; and Charlie would look ridiculous, so tiny beside Hubert yet so importantly awaiting us, that I used to call out: 'Charlie seagull is up on the roof!'

Our postman saw them up there together one day, and he told us the story of a seagull at Mousehole who paraded every day on a certain balustrade. A sparrow used to like it there too for visitors passed frequently by, and thus the sparrow and the seagull were regularly fed. One day, however, after the end of the season and the visitors had gone and food was no longer thrown to them, the gull suddenly eyed the sparrow, waddled quickly towards it, snapped it up and swallowed it whole. For a while after hearing that story we kept a watch on Hubert when Charlie was up there alongside him . . . just in case.

Hubert behaved towards Monty in his large way as Charlie and Tim did in their small way. Monty himself, at first was not sure of him. Hubert would sweep down from the roof, land on the path and advance towards Monty who retreated nervously looking round every few seconds and curling his mouth in a soundless snarl. I feel sure Hubert had no intention of attack. He was curious perhaps. He succeeded, however, in those first weeks after his arrival at Minack in establishing a moral superiority for a while over Monty.

Yet if a cat and a gull can like each other these two did, or at least they learnt to tolerate each other. I have seen them both on the flat rock that stretches out from one side of the cottage like a sacrificial stone, Monty at one end, Hubert at the other, and neither of them appeared to be perturbed.

Hubert never behaved so calmly when another gull arrived on the roof. The roof was his personal kingdom and if a gull swooped down and settled at one end, Hubert exploded in fury, half ran, half flew towards it, lunged out with his beak, then sailed into the sky in a storm of squawks chasing the offender this way and that until both disappeared over the fields towards the sea. A few minutes later he would return, fluff out his feathers and be at peace again as king of the roof.

There were times when Monty was certainly jealous of him. During those meals outside when Charlie and his squeak were ignored Monty would watch Hubert suspiciously as he stood with the presence of an eagle a little way off; and as soon as he began to come too close, Monty would advance timidly but surely until Hubert decided it was wise to retreat. But it was when Hubert accompanied us on our walks that Monty became most annoyed for he liked to have us to himself on these occasions and Hubert spoilt his pleasure.

Hubert would leave the roof as we set off down the lane, come swooping low over our heads, then up again into the sky, wheeling with the grace of a swallow; and when he came low again, his wings hissing the air with their speed, Monty would crouch and look up and glare. At other times we would be wandering around our meadows and fields with Monty trotting along with us when Hubert would dive from the sky, land on the ground twenty yards away, then strut on a parellel course; or if we had paused he would remain stationary, looking at us as if he were saying to himself, 'I wonder what they are up to?' These moments particularly infuriated Monty. He would begin to creep along the ground, stalking Hubert as he would a mouse, getting nearer and nearer, making a weird noise which was neither a growl nor a miaow. It was a comical sight. Both knew there would be no attack. Both knew the parts they had to play. It was a question of split second timing. As soon as Monty had arrived within a few feet, Hubert, to save him the embarrassment of coming any nearer, flew off.

In spring, Monty's thick coat began to moult and we used to give him a daily combing. He would lie on my lap as I traced the comb up and down his back, on his sides

and up around the jowls of his neck. He loved it. He purred happily until I turned him over and began the same task on his underparts. There would now be silence except for a series of little grunts. He found it awkward to purr on his back.

And when it was all over I would collect the silky fur in my hand, go outside and throw it into the wind. It floated into the air soaring and billowing, eddying in the end to some thorn bush or tussock of grass or entangling itself in the sea pinks on the wall. It did not stay in any of these places for long. The fur was much sought after. Most nests around Minack were lined with it.

Chapter Thirteen

As the years went by we became increasingly sensitive to the hazards that faced Monty. In the beginning we were so content with our new way of life that we foresaw the possibility of trouble neither for ourselves nor for him. Then, as the nature of our struggle became clear, we realized that we were going to have anxiety as well as contentment. The defeats and shocks we suffered, the lost harvest of daffodils, a field of beautiful anemones destroyed in a night by a southerly gale, a drought at a time when moisture for cliff potatoes was vital, brought home to us the extent of the battle in which we were engaged. Hence there were times when nervousness was substituted for calm and the foolish mood of anticipating trouble created unnecessary fears.

This foolish mood developed one evening at dusk when I saw an owl chasing Monty, diving at his upturned startled face as if it were aiming to peck out his eyes. I rushed forward shooing it away, only for it to come back ten minutes later, and again the following evening, and the evening after that. I treated it as Monty's enemy, obsessed with the idea that it might blind him. 'That damn' owl is there again,' I would say, and hasten to frighten it away.

Jeannie's attitude towards it was quite different. She viewed my actions as utterly stupid and whenever I hurried to perform them she would crossly say: 'Leave it alone. It's perfectly harmless ... It's *fond* of Monty.' This streak of romanticism had its origin in her childhood when she first came upon the rhymes of Edward Lear. A famous one had caught her fancy and she now saw the opportunity of watching its particular theme come to life.

> The owl and the pussy cat went to sea
> In a beautiful pea green boat.
> They took some honey and plenty of money
> Wrapped up in a five pound note.
> The owl looked up to the stars above
> And sang to a small guitar:
> 'Oh lovely pussy, oh pussy my love,
> What a beautiful pussy you are, you are,
> What a beautiful pussy you are.'

Nothing would shake her conviction that the owl pursued Monty out of a curious kind of affection; and I had to admit when several weeks had passed and no unpleasant incident had occurred that my fears were probably groundless. I refused to accept, however, that the owl *liked* Monty; and yet there were certain features of the relationship which were a puzzle. The tawny owls at Minack, and this was a magnificent tawny owl, nest at the top of the elms which surround a meadow close to the cottage. Very few cats could climb the specially favourite elm, and Monty was certainly not one of them. But the annual nest in this elm, just a cleft in the tree trunk, was a very foolish one and, usually, one or other of the nestlings would fall out. I would find one on the ground, a bundle of white feathers and two large unhappy eyes, and then laboriously climb up the tree and replace it beside its fellow. During this particular spring, however, I found no bewildered baby owl and as, later in the summer, I frequently saw the two sitting together like identical twins on various trees in the wood, it was clear no casualties had occurred. Hence Monty, against his nature and in a fit of madness, could not have climbed the elm and attacked the nest or killed a fallen nestling. He had, in fact, done nothing to incur the ire of the parent.

Yet there it was, the owl haunted him. It pursued him like a large dog with wings, swooping up and down as he walked innocently down the lane, cracking the evening air with its harsh cries of *kewick, kewick*. Nor would it leave him alone if he were happily curled on a chair indoors. It wanted Monty to be out with it. It would demand his presence by perching on the wall outside the front door harshly repeating again and again *kewick, kewick*. 'Didn't I tell you?' Jeannie would smile and say. And I would reply abruptly: 'For goodness sake don't be so whimsy.'

In the end I learnt to take the relationship for granted. It went on throughout the summer and as I never saw the owl make a direct attack on Monty I lost my concern that it might do him harm. But there was one incident which surprised me. I was coming up the path from the cliff one evening when there was still another hour or two of daylight, when on turning the corner close to the cottage I saw the owl perched on the back of the white seat. It stared unblinkingly back at me, incongruous in such a daylight setting as if it belonged to another world. But what surprised me was that Monty was only a few feet away, lying comfortably like a Trafalgar lion in front of the seat. He saw me coming, got up and stretched, and walked slowly forward; while the owl heaved itself into the air and flapped off into the wood. I felt as if I had disturbed two people having a gossip.

I had other fears for Monty which were to prove more

tangible. He was too like a fox, for instance. I did not appreciate this until a farmer one day came hurrying up the lane to warn me he had seen a fox in the field close to where we kept the chickens. It was Monty, of course, a Monty with a burnished bracken coloured coat which, I thereafter realized, certainly did make him look like a fox. The same mistake was made at another time by a man with a gun whom I saw stalking beside the hedge which ran up from the wood. I charged across the field shouting at the top of my voice and when I reached the fellow, flustered and out of breath, he looked at me with disdain. He was about to shoot a fox. Up there in the corner where the winter gorse was in bloom. Can't you see it? Look it's moving . . . and Monty, alert at seeing me, came quickly through the grass towards us. These alarms put us on guard about the Hunt. The hounds might mistake Monty for their quarry and so when the Meet was at St Buryan or

Lamorna Turn or anywhere else nearby, we used to keep him in all day.

But the hounds only once rushed through Minack and Monty was curled up on the bed at the time; and the reason we have been so lucky is that it is obviously dangerous for the hounds when they run for the cliff. Thus when a fox makes for our area the hounds are called off and the fox, sidling along the hedges of our fields to the impenetrable brambles and thorn trees which slope steeply to the sea, is safe. My instinct is always to be on the side of the fox. I suppose I have found that when one lives as we live, our daily existence posted like that of the ancient grey rocks which heave out of the untamed countryside every-where around us, one is incapable of killing for sport. We share our life with the wild. We are part of it. Hence I will kill should an animal become an enemy, but never for fun.

Yet a fox, as everyone knows, can become an enemy; and one summer when Monty was growing old, a fox's earth was found by a neighbour outside of which were the skeletons of four cats. The discovery thus explained why cats over a period of time had been disappearing from the homes of our neighbours, disappearances which hitherto had been blamed hopefully on the wandering instincts of farm cats. Then, two or three weeks later, a friend of mine saw a fox catch a cat. He saw the cat three fields away from where he was standing, intently looking at a point in the hedge, then poising himself for a jump, so full of concentration that it was deaf to the fox that was stalking through the grass behind it. My friend yelled at the top of his voice but the sound disappeared in the wind. He could do nothing but watch the fox pounce, then hurry away.

I do not believe that all foxes are cat-killers. You get a rogue which develops the taste for them, just as you get a rogue badger which brings calumny on his race by developing a taste for chickens; but whatever the case, whether one fox or two were guilty, a cat-killer was at large around Minack and Monty was in danger. We kept watch on him within the limit of ever being able to keep watch on the peregrinations of a cat; and although he did not usually wander far, he obstinately chose this period to do so. 'Have you seen Monty?' I would ask Jeannie, and when the answer was no we would forget the importance of what we were doing, and set out to search. We used to hasten around his known hide-outs, a dozen or so of which found favour in rotation, and when he was in none of these we were inclined to develop a panic.

On one such occasion I ran one way towards the sea and Jeannie another up the field towards the farm buildings at the top of the hill. When I rejoined her she had Monty in her arms, holding him tight and telling him what a fool he'd been. This is what had happened. She had reached the entrance to the field that faced our lane and was looking across the field to the far side when to her horror she saw a red object chasing another red object. She instantly guessed a fox was chasing Monty, and she began to run across the field calling his name; and she had run only a few yards when the second red object stopped and looked back at her. It was Monty. He was chasing a cub. Of course he did not know that it was running back to the earth where the cats were killed.

Soon after this we realized the killer was after Monty. We had proof of this one evening when we heard a fox barking as if on the doorstep followed by Monty flying in through the window. He plummeted at my feet and then turned glaring at the open window, growling. I ran to the door and out to the corner of the cottage which looks down the lane. I saw nothing and all I could do was to make a noise, the human version of an angry animal, which I thought would frighten the fox away. But Jeannie and I were now to behave extraordinarily foolishly.

We accepted the fact we had been stupid enough to allow him out at night without keeping him company, and so we decided from then onwards he would be kept indoors after dusk. Monty was furious. He had lived at Minack for six years and was over thirteen, and for the first time in his life he was forbidden the freedom of the night. He made such a hullaballoo, woke us up so often with his miaowing demands to be let out that three days later – and this was our foolishness – we gave in. 'All right, you go out,' I said, 'I'm not going to be kept awake by your fuss. I'm tired. I want to sleep. But you look out for that killer. He was after you last week. He'll be after you again.'

Our bed lay alongside the window so that if Monty was lying on it, then decided he wished to investigate what adventure awaited him outside, he had only to creep from the bedclothes to the sill and jump down on to the flower bed below. There he was tucked in on the bed when on the very next night after his freedom had been foolishly granted, he woke me up with the noisiest growl I have ever heard. I put out my hand and felt him creeping for the window. And then, from the daze of my sleep, I suddenly sensed there was danger. I grabbed Monty with one hand, and with the other found my torch. It was a torch with a new battery; and when I shone it out of the window I saw a magnificent sight.

A fox, the size of an Alsatian. At first directly beneath the window sill. Then gliding away down the lane, so silently, so superbly a thoroughbred that for a moment I forgot he was a killer and I called out to Jeannie:

'Quick! Wake up! You'll never see such a beautiful fox!'

And up to now, I have never done so again.

Chapter Fourteen

THERE WERE OTHER hazards beside foxes; and there are two episodes in Monty's life at Minack that I would like to forget, but which remain painfully in my mind. Yet, and this is the paradox, I like also to remember them because of the happiness which followed, that magical sense of happiness when someone you love is reprieved.

The first took place the year before myxomatosis swept the rabbits away from our area, and when the gin trap was still the method used for their elimination. Such was our isolation at Minack that the fields where the traps were set were in a ring around us; and we were so far from other habitations that we alone suffered the hell of the traps' successes. We heard the momentary screams and the silence which followed. We lay in bed awaiting the next anguished cry, as we awaited once the next stick of bombs. A long way away those who were responsible for setting the traps would be pursuing their evening enjoyment while Jeannie and I, as if in the midst of a battle, listened.

A chill went through us whenever we heard the signal of traps being laid, the metallic sound of the trapper's hammer; and if Jeannie heard it first she would run looking for me, and we would both then go looking for Monty. I admit that rabbits had in some way to be controlled but it was the manner in which gin traps were used which was so barbarous. It was seldom that any steps were taken to cut short the pain of the trapped. The traps, set perhaps an hour before dusk, reaped most of their harvest in the first half of the night as the rabbits came out of their burrows. The screams then followed each other as if they were an endless series of echoes and we would have little time to remain tense, waiting for the next; but after midnight we had to wait, ten minutes, half an hour, or suddenly two or three, one after the other, then silence. It was not often that anyone considered it humane to come at midnight and kill those caught during the evening flush. We had to lie there thinking of them.

It was late one lovely May afternoon that Monty got caught in a trap. We knew that traps had been laid in the field adjoining the cottage but traps were not supposed to be actually set until dusk; and thus Monty should still have had an hour or two in which he could have wandered around in safety. Nevertheless we were nervous for him. We were in the mood to anticipate trouble and I said to Jeannie: 'I don't think we ought to let Monty out of our sight for an instant this evening.' There seemed to be no reason why we should. Our day's work was ended and we were both pottering about the garden and the cottage while Monty was in one of his benign moods. He was lying half-hidden among the wall-flowers outside the front door, blinking sleepily, as if he were relaxing after a large meal. He was the epitome of content-ment, a much loved, magnificent ginger cat who was at peace with his private world; and heaven knows what prompted him suddenly to go somewhere he had never been before.

Unseen by us, he left his nest under the wall-flowers, entered the field where the traps were laid and walked the length of it, miraculously threading his way through the traps until he was caught by one at the far end, close to a gap in the field which led down to the cliff.

I do not think five minutes had elapsed before I noticed his absence from the garden; and instinctively I knew what had happened. I shouted to Jeannie to follow me, then ran the few yards to a bank which rose above the field. I stood on it for an instant while my eyes peeled along the base of the hedge where the traps were set. I saw nothing but young green corn; until suddenly in the far distance I saw an object at ground level languidly flopping up and down. It was Monty's tail.

The next twenty minutes are a jumble in my memory. We raced across the field, enraged that our care for him had cheated us; and when we reached him and saw his yellow eyes looking trustingly up at us while his little front paw with the white smudge on it was squeezed in the gin, we broke out with curses against those responsible for setting it.

'I'm going to throw it away!' Jeannie cried, 'right away in the sea.' But this outburst did not help us release Monty.

He began to struggle so I put my hands firmly round his body while Jeannie tried to open the gin; and as only a few weeks before she had released a trapped dog she could not understand why, on this occasion, the fangs had stuck fast. Poor Monty; sweat began to moisten his fur and his mouth frothed, and then panic seized him and for an instant he freed himself from my hold.

'Look out!' I shouted. He lashed out with his three free legs, claws like spikes, too quick for Jeannie to move away in time and I saw a line of blood on her arm. A second later he was quiet again, lying panting on his side, tongue lolling, uttering little cries, and his paw still trapped.

I do not wish to remember again the ten minutes which followed. A hideous time against the background of a sea-scented evening, larks exultant in the sky, early swallows skimming in from the south, the pilchard fleet chugging out into Mount's Bay. I do not wish to remember the anguish of those ten minutes; only the sweet relief we had when at last we had him safe. He lay exhausted for a while on the sofa while Jeannie tried to tempt him with warm, sugared milk and we angrily discussed what we should do.

The trap would go into the sea. I would make a complaint. We both, in fact, blistered with fury; and yet, maddeningly enough, there was nothing we could righteously be furious about. We did not possess the field concerned, and so Monty, in the legal sense of the word, was trespassing. Thus the whole incident revolved around the question of standards. The countryman had grown up to expect a layer of cruelty in his life. We had not. Thus when Jeannie threw the trap away and I made my angry complaint, it was inevitable that a feud should begin. We did not mind of course. We at least had proclaimed our indignation against cruelty. And in any case the vet had seen Monty. No permanent harm had come to his paw.

The other episode took place when he was fourteen years old. We now had a splendid greenhouse a hundred feet long and twenty feet wide, and during this particular winter we were growing sweet peas for early spring flowering. We spent hours of our time pinching them out and layering them and it was only natural that Monty should be with us during these sessions. He amused us while we pursued the monotonous task. For no reason at all he would race up and down the rows or ridiculously treat a sweet pea tendril as an enemy, or interrupt the flow of our work by turning upside down at our feet requesting his tummy to be tickled. There were no signs that he was an old cat. He looked in magnificent condition and when one day we put him in a basket which hung on the potato scales, he weighed eighteen and a half pounds net.

Yet there were a couple of incidents during the daffodil season – it begins with us late in January and ends according to the warmth of the spring in the latter part of March – that made us puzzle about him. On each occasion he appeared momentarily to stagger and yet so briefly that it could have been an accidental lack of balance and not a signpost to coming illness. In between times he was completely normal, the usual large appetite and as agile as ever.

Then one day at the end of March we went out and did not return till after dark; and as so often happened, the headlights as we came up the lane to the cottage lit up his fierce face as he glared at us from the bedroom window. He had the gift of making us feel we had neglected him. It was an echo of those late Mortlake nights. 'Where have you been?' he seemed to be crossly saying.

On this occasion we performed the inevitable rites of apology, picking him up and hugging him, and hastening to bribe him to return our affection by the obvious method of filling his plate with fish. Jeannie had turned to the sink to collect the fish pan when I suddenly saw Monty begin to stagger and half stumble across the carpet to a spot under my desk, where he collapsed.

'Look at Monty!' I shouted, and rushed over and knelt beside him, stroking him; and because I met with no response, his eyes seemed to be glazed and unseeing, I picked him up and carried him to our bedroom. He was desperately ill.

'You stay here,' I said to Jeannie, not certain whether I was asking her to carry out the best or the worst of the two tasks, 'while I race up to the farm and telephone the vet. If he's in he'll be here within half an hour.' And miraculously he was in and, within half an hour he was at Minack. We both looked at his face as he carried out his examination, seeking to read the signs we hoped to see. 'Is it a heart attack or a stroke?' I murmured, fearing his answer.

He was a quiet Scot with the comforting assurance of his race; and goodness knows why but I always prefer it when advice comes in a Scot's accent. 'I don't think so,' he said slowly, 'you see his eyes are rolling, and look how he's struggling.' He paused for a moment. 'You haven't been putting any poison down, have you?' I hadn't, but I suddenly remembered the sweet peas and the dust we had been using on them to check disease, and I rushed out into the night to find the tin. I brought it back and the vet slowly read the instructions and list of chemical ingredients.

'That's the trouble all right,' he said, 'he's been poisoned though there's no mention here the dust is dangerous. The fact is he's absorbed the dust in his fur and body over the months and now he's got enough inside to hit him.'

He was in a coma for two days and nights. He lay on the pink bedspread in the spare bedroom while one of us sat always with him. The treatment was bicarbonate of soda every four hours and as it required both of us to pour the dose down his throat the one who was on night duty woke up the other when the fourth hour came round. About six o'clock on the second morning we had carried out our duty and we were standing together watching him . . . and suddenly there was a purr.

'Oh Monty Monty!' cried Jeannie, 'you're safe. You're safe!'

For us the remaining year of his life had the delicate pleasure of borrowed time.

Chapter Fifteen

IN PREVIOUS YEARS we had occasionally to go away, never for more than three or four days, and elaborate arrangements of course were made for Monty's welfare. A travelling fish salesman supplied fish from his van, and whoever it was we had helping us at Minack at the time would cook it, and keep a saucer filled with milk from the farm. Monty was allowed to wander about as he liked during the day but in the evening he would be locked indoors; and when we were going to bed three hundred miles away in London, there was comfort in the thought he was safely ensconced within the cottage. We hated leaving him and he in his turn thoroughly disapproved of our absence; and on one occasion he nearly made us miss our train.

We were going by night, and while in the afternoon Jeannie was packing, he sniffed around the suitcases in that apprehensive fashion that both dogs and cats are apt to show when travel is scheduled. He then quite suddenly began to limp. I had never seen him limp before but there he was hobbling about as if he had only three legs. This continued for an hour; and so theatrical were his gestures that Jeannie declared she would not catch the train unless he was seen by the vet. The vet was fetched and he pronounced Monty a malingerer. There was nothing wrong with him at all; and Monty, admitting his bluff had been called, promptly began walking normally again.

Our returns usually had a chilly reception. He liked at first to pretend that he could get on perfectly well without us and it was immaterial whether we lived at Minack or not. The pretence lasted until we went out for a stroll to see how things had been growing while we had been away; and as we walked we would suddenly hear a bellow of a miaow, then see Monty running towards us. We would continue our stroll with him at our heels, while at intervals the bellow was repeated. It was a touching experience for in the sound was the agony of loneliness. We knew then how much he had missed us.

But in the last year of his life there was no need to go away, and although sometimes we were absent during the day we were always with him at night. He recovered splendidly from the dust poison, and by the early summer he was his usual beautiful self. 'Oh, what a beautiful cat!' some caller would say as he passed through Minack seeing Monty perched aloofly on a stone. 'How old is he?'

No one believed he was nearly fifteen. Nor did I for that matter. Time deceives in its pace, luring years into yesterdays, garlanding memories without intervals, seeping the knowledge of age into one's mind. I did not want to say how old he was. I did not want to remember that for so long he had been the recipient of our secret thoughts. Each of us had talked to him in that mood of abandon which is safe within friendship. Maybe it was only a cat's friendship, but secure never to be tarnished, easing problems because the aftermath of confession did not breed the fears of disclosure.

He was an integral part of our failures and successes at Minack, and a hulky miner from St Just whom we once had helping us called him the foreman. 'Look out, the foreman's coming,' he would shout as he lunged away with his shovel in a potato meadow, 'we'll get our cards if we don't do our job properly.' Monty would appear and walk leisurely down the row where he had been digging, sniffing the discarded potato tops which spreadeagled on the side as if he were checking that all the potatoes had been collected from the plants. It was always a solemn inspection. There were no games. And when he had completed it, and had left the meadow, disappearing out of sight, the hulky miner would stab his shovel into the ground, rub his hands together and call out: 'All clear boys. We can have a smoke now.'

He was sometimes an inconvenience when we were picking flowers. At daffodil time the pace of picking has to be so fast that there is no time for distractions; and yet Monty would often insist on accompanying us, walking ahead between the daffodil beds at a very slow pace of his own choosing so that our feet tumbled over him. 'Hurry up, Monty,' I would say, but at the same time I did not want to sound too brusque. I was glad that he wished to be with us; and so I would stop the rhythm of my picking and bend down and stroke him. Then, if he did not move, I would step over him.

He had a passion for violet plants and, in his time, we used to grow three or four thousand every year. The variety was called Bournemouth Gem and each plant bushed dark green leaves that perfumed the meadow in which they were grown even before the violets themselves appeared. Monty liked rolling among them. The rich orange of his fur against the dark green was a pretty sight and although you would have expected him to do damage, little damage was done; the plants were such fat cushions that the few broken leaves had plenty waiting to replace them. So we let him roll and only became alarmed when he jumped on a plant, gathered as much of it as he could with his four paws, turned on his side, and proceeded furiously to disembowel it. The fact is he liked the smell of violets. I have often seen him walking on his own down a row, his tail pointing like a periscope above the leaves, smelling the plants on either side of him. 'Monty's picking violets,' I would say to Jeannie as a joke.

He enjoyed sitting on the bench in the packing shed hemmed in by galvanized tins of wall-flowers or jars of violets or anemones. He would sandwich himself in a space and if you looked in from the outside you would see through the window a splendid array of early spring flowers and in the midst of it all the dozing face of Monty. I remember a flower salesman coming to see us one day who was so amazed by what he saw in the packing shed that he nearly forgot to discuss his business; for there was Monty among the daffodils, and Tim the robin up on a shelf warbling a song from a jar of anemones, while Charlie the chaffinch was looking up at us calling his monotonous

note from the floor. These three had three flower seasons together and this particular occasion was the last. First Monty, then Tim eighteen months later, and Charlie six months after that. And all the while up there on the roof was Hubert, observing everything, majestic, so compelling a character that neither of us would dare to let him remain hungry if he were demanding a meal, however busy we might be. 'Jeannie!' I would call out as I was stacking flower boxes in the Land Rover ready for Penzance Station, 'Hubert's hungry. Have you got anything?'

Monty was always tempted by boxes. If a parcel arrived and Monty was in the room and we unpacked it, he was certain to fill the vacant space. Perhaps he was born in one. Perhaps a psychiatrist would be right in saying that parcels and cardboard boxes recalled exquisite incidents of kitten-hood. He certainly loved flower boxes and the tissue paper we put in them; and many a time we used to relieve the intensity of our work by pretending Monty, lying in a flower box, was indeed a flower. 'Shall we send him to Covent Garden?' one of us would say absurdly. 'They'd certainly call him a prize bloom,' the other would reply equally absurdly. When we were working at great pressure, it was a relish to have Monty to distract us, in so kind and pleasant and trivial a way.

Chapter Sixteen

ONE OF MONTY'S lovable characteristics was the way he enjoyed going for walks with us, trotting along like a dog at our heels. Sometimes when we wanted to go on a proper walk, a walk far longer than he could manage, we would sneak down the path planning to get out of sight without him realizing we had gone; but from some hide-out in which he was spying upon us, he would suddenly appear, all smiles as if he were saying: 'Going for a walk? Good idea, I'll come too.' Then, of course, we had to cancel our plans and go on a limited walk instead.

He played games on these walks, some of which were vexing, some charming. He had the usual whim of a cat to tear up trees as if the wind were in his tail, but as many of the trees were elders he never climbed high. It was at night that these climbs were annoying.

We would be taking a late night stroll and wishing to return to go to bed when he would race up the elder which is opposite the old barn and obstinately stay there. My voice would at first sound coaxing, then commanding, and then frankly I would lose my temper. 'Come on, Monty, come down!' I would shout at him. He would not budge so in the end, with Jeannie standing beside me holding the torch, I would climb the tree towards the pair of phosphorescent eyes which stared down from above. I would be up there among the branches trying to grab him, while Jeannie was laughing at both of us in the darkness below.

He had an endearing game he played when he thought a walk required livening up; or perhaps because he decided we were not giving him enough attention. He would wait until we had gone several yards ahead of him, crouching meanwhile on the path and shifting his paws as if he were about to spring . . . and then race at terrific speed up to and past us, coming to a full stop a couple of yards away. Thereupon we inevitably bent down and made a fuss of him. Then we would go on, and soon the game would be repeated.

The longest walk he used to take was to the Carn we can see from our windows at Minack and which stands above a cascade of rocks that fall to the sea below. It is a rough walk most of the way, a track through gorse and brambles and bracken while on either side of a long stretch of it there is a whole series of badger sets. In spring time the land around is sprayed with bluebells while may trees plume white from among them; and ahead is the Carn and the panorama of Mount's Bay.

We used to make it an early morning walk when the dew was still wet on the grass, and a peaceful one if Monty was in a docile mood; but there were times when we would pass the badger sets thinking he was behind us, and suddenly find he had disappeared down one of the cavernous holes. It would take us a few minutes before we found which hole he had chosen, then we would see him looking up from the dark, just out of reach. I found myself thinking on these occasions he was taking a mischievous revenge on the only time I ever had power over him . . . when he wanted me to open a door or a window; for there he would be holding up the walk, and nothing we could do except await his decision to rejoin us.

His favourite walk, or stroll I should call it, was fifty yards down the lane to the stream; a stream which rushed water from November to June, then dried up and became a dip in the roadway. It was a stroll that now has a significance for Jeannie and myself because it represents in our memories the joy of his first stroll and the sadness of the last.

The first night on which we came to live at Minack the moon was high, and after I had transported our luggage to the cottage, we celebrated the freedom we had captured by taking this stroll. The moon was shining, except for the murmur of the sea and the hoot of owls, on silence.

Monty, who in the first week or two was going to be shy in daylight, came with us, nosing his way down the lane which to him was full of imaginary dangers, sniffing, hesitating, taking no action except to advance steadily towards the sparkling water that ribboned ahead of him. And when at last he reached it and put out a paw in puzzlement I felt this was an occasion when I must not allow him to have any further apprehension; and so I bent down to pick him up and carry him over. He was quick to expose my foolishness. He slipped from my hold, and with the grace of a gazelle he leapt the stream. From that moment, this miniature valley across the lane has been called Monty's Leap.

It was in daffodil time that his illness began to threaten the normality of his days. Nothing sudden, no pain, just a gradual ebbing of strength; so that first the bluebell walk to the Carn had to be abandoned, then the one we used to take along the top of the cliff, and then even the strolls to the Leap became less frequent. I would watch him from the corner of the cottage wending his way down the lane, and my heart would yearn to see a spring in his movements I knew I would never see again. He would reach the stream, drink a little, then turn and come slowly back. This stroll was the yardstick of our hopes, and sometimes Jeannie would come running to me: 'He's been twice to the Leap this morning!' . . . and her voice would have the tone that the inevitable was going to be defeated.

But I knew sooner than Jeannie that there was nothing we could do, nothing that her loving care and nursing ever could achieve. Each time I saw him set off for the Leap I was on guard; and there was one evening, the last evening, when on seeing him, from our window, start down the lane we ran to follow him only to find that after a few yards he had lain down. Then on a few yards and down again; and yet he was such an old warrior that when I picked him up he tried weakly to struggle free . . . as if he were saying: 'Let me be, I can make it!' I gently gave him to Jeannie to take home to the cottage, and as I watched er I realized that she too now knew that our life with him as over.

He died on a lovely May morning in his sixteenth year. I ad hurried to fetch the vet and on my return I found eannie had taken him out into the warm sun and he was reathing gently on a bed of lush green grass. Up above on he roof was Hubert, quite still, his feathers bunched, as if e were waiting for something; and within a yard or two f Monty were his friends, Charlie and Tim. No sound rom either of them. Tim on a rosebush, Charlie on a grey ock. They were strange mourners for a cat.

The next day, soon after the sun had risen above the izard far away across Mount's Bay, we carried him down he lane to the stream and buried him beside it. Between is paws we placed a card:

Here lies our beloved friend Monty who, beside the stream that crosses the lane and is known as Monty's Leap, is for ever the guardian of Minack.

Warner Books now offers an exciting range of quality titles by both established and new authors. All of the books in this series are available from:

Little, Brown and Company (UK),
P.O. Box 11,
Falmouth,
Cornwall TR10 9EN.

Fax No: 01326 317444.
Telephone No: 01326 317200
E-mail: books@barni.avel.co.uk

Payments can be made as follows: cheque, postal order (payable to Little, Brown and Company) or by credit cards, Visa/Access. Do not send cash or currency. UK customers and B.F.P.O. please allow £1.00 for postage and packing for the first book, plus 50p for the second book, plus 30p for each additional book up to a maximum charge of £3.00 (7 books plus).

Overseas customers including Ireland, please allow £2.00 for the first book plus £1.00 for the second book, plus 50p for each additional book.

NAME (Block Letters) ....

....

ADDRESS ....

....

....

☐ I enclose my remittance for ....

☐ I wish to pay by Access/Visa Card

Number ☐☐☐☐☐☐☐☐☐☐☐☐☐☐☐☐

Card Expiry Date ☐☐☐☐